Managed Care Essentials: A Book of Readings

Managed Care Essentials: A Book of Readings

Health Administration Press | Chicago, Illinois

04 03 02 01 00 5 4 3 2 1

Library of Congress Cataloging-in-Publication Data

Managed care essentials : a book of readings
p. cm.
Includes bibliographical references
ISBN 1-56793-112-X (alk. paper)
1. Managed care plans (Medical care)—United States. I. Health Administration Press
RA413.5.U5M3612 1999
362.1'04258'0973—dc21

99-43249
CIP

The paper used in this publication meets the minimum requirements of American National Standard for Information Sciences—Permanence of Paper for Printed Library Materials, ANSI Z39.48-1984.™

Health Administration Press
A division of the Foundation
of the American College of
Healthcare Executives
One North Franklin Street, Suite 1700
Chicago, IL 60606-3491
312/424-2800

Contents

Foreword
John A. Russell, FACHE vii

Part I Managed Care/Health System Overview

Introduction 1

1 Working Toward an Ideal System
Stephen M. Shortell, Robin R. Gillies, David A. Anderson, Karen Morgan Erickson, John B. Mitchell 3

2 The Health Services Delivery System: Managed Care
Phoebe Lindsey Barton 25

3 Managed Care Mythology: Supply-Side Dreams Die Hard
Jeff C. Goldsmith and Michael Goran 55

4 Managing Risks in Managed Care
Kyle L. Grazier 65

Part II Operations

Introduction 85

5 How HMOs Structure Primary Care Delivery
Suzanne Felt-Lisk 87

6 Taking the Step Toward Capitation Payment in Managed Care Contracts
Douglas Conrad, Robert Bonney, Michael Sachs, and Robert Smith 103

7 Developing Structures for Effective Managed Care Contracting
Douglas Conrad, Robert Bonney, Michael Sachs, and Robert Smith 121

8 Information Systems: Managed Care Applications
Brian T. Malec 143

9 Marketing and Managed Care
Arthur C. Sturm, Jr. 161

10 Using Consumer Satisfaction Surveys to Assess Quality of Care: Current Practices and Issues
Marsha Gold and Judith Wooldridge 169

11 Can Ethical Management and Managed Care Coexist?
Leonard H. Friedman and Grant T. Savage 195

Part III Effects

Introduction 207

12 Understanding the Managed Care Backlash
Robert J. Blendon, Mollyann Brodie, John M. Benson, Drew E. Altman, Larry Levitt, Tina Hoff, and Larry Hugick 209

13 Assessing the Effect of Increased Managed Care on Hospitals
Charles A. Mowll 225

14 Shifting the Paradigm: Monitoring Access in Medicare Managed Care
Elizabeth R. Docteur, David C. Colby, and Marsha Gold 237

Part IV Future Models

Introduction 259

15 The Sixth Stage of Managed Care: New Models for the Post-Reform Era
Russell C. Coile, Jr. 261

16 Managed Care: The Next Generation
Michael Sachs 281

17 The Future of Managed Care Organization
James C. Robinson 303

Foreword

Managed care has emerged as the most powerful force shaping healthcare reform initiatives in the United States. Advocates claim that managed care would contain or reduce healthcare expenditures, shift the focus of the delivery system from acute care to disease prevention, reduce physician practice variations, ensure better outcomes of care, and rationalize the use of scarce resources. The primary focus at this time is to contain costs and restructure the system. This timely anthology has been compiled to assist healthcare providers and academics to clarify what is happening and prepare for a rapidly changing future. The book should be of particular interest to healthcare trustees, government officials, health plan administrators, and students preparing for health careers.

Managed care came to the United States after many legislative and regulatory attempts to reform the healthcare system failed. The most ambitious effort to change the healthcare system was led by the Clinton administration between 1993 and 1995. This massive campaign to contain healthcare costs and improve access to care was soundly defeated and was a major factor in helping the Republicans gain majority control of the House of Representatives and the Senate in 1994.

By 1995 it was apparent that the problems demanding healthcare reform, especially upwardly spiraling healthcare costs, would not be solved by government, and private forces stepped into the power vacuum to promote managed care initiatives. These initiatives were led by the health insurance industry, employers, and government officials who were responsible for the Medicare and Medicaid programs. Their solution was to aggressively promote the creation of and enrollment in managed care health plans. A primary goal of these emerging managed care organizations was to integrate the financing and delivery of health services by an entity that has a fiduciary interest in the interactions between them.

Managed care has become the mainstream delivery system for health services in a relatively short time, and it has created many problems for physicians, hospitals, and other providers. The primary problem is that managed care changes the way healthcare is provided and delivered. Providers were trying to operate in a fee-for-service system at the same time they were trying to make the necessary changes required by the new system. The most pressing challenge for all successful healthcare organizations is to craft a successful working relationship with physicians.

Hospitals responded aggressively to the new environment by focusing on their financial viability, organizing integrated delivery systems, creating risk-assuming organizations, launching new ambulatory centers, and creating new community outreach activities. Since hospitals have become the treatment place of last resort in a managed care environment, most hospitals have reduced their number of acute-care beds and have attempted to convert the bed space to new revenue-producing initiatives. The transition from autonomous hospitals and physicians to integrated delivery systems has created complex corporate structures rivaling those of industry in size and dollar volume. The dominant attitude among healthcare executives is that size matters to survive in the new healthcare system. Hospital mergers have produced some very successful integrated delivery systems and some financial disasters, such as the Allegheny Health Education and Research Foundation (AHERF) bankruptcy in Pennsylvania.

Physicians require a different practice style under managed care. The physicians' autonomy of practice is affected by the managed care plans in the use of specialty services, physician referrals, drugs and services, and other technologies. Physicians' incomes may be reduced. Managed care rewards primary care physicians, strongly encourages group practice, employs many physicians, and can drive practicing physicians crazy with reporting requirements.

The role of government in healthcare reform has shifted dramatically with the arrival of managed care, from a healthcare system dominated by government rules, regulations, legislation, and payment practices to a system dominated by market forces. Government continues to operate the Medicare and Medicaid programs that have a major impact on the system, but the strategy for both programs is to enroll their beneficiaries in managed care plans. The primary role for government currently is to intervene when market forces are not working properly and to set standards to which all health plans must comply.

Managed care is a work in progress with much to be done if it is to achieve its advocates' stated goals. The missing links are a shared vision for the kind of healthcare system that should be established in this country and a leadership plan to get there. The most pressing problem is to find a solution for providing health insurance to all of our citizens. Finally, if we are truly going to manage healthcare, we must begin building healthier communities and start solving many of our social problems to keep them from ending up in hospital emergency rooms.

I commend the authors for producing this book. I plan to use it in my classes with graduate students in health administration as the definitive book on this timely subject.

John A. Russell, FACHE

John A. Russell, FACHE, is former president and CEO of the Institute for Healthy Communities in Harrisburg, Pennsylvania. He won the American College of Healthcare Executives Gold Medal Award in 1994; this award recognizes exceptional individuals who exemplify the highest standards and values of the profession.

PART

I

Managed Care/ Health System Overview

INTRODUCTION

Although the term "managed care" is omnipresent in healthcare today, a clear sense of its definition, shape, and effect is hard to come by. A glance at the alphabet soup of organizational structures related to managed care (PPO, POS, PSO, EPO, SHMO, etc.) indicates the difficulty in pinning down how managed care is carried out. Likewise, the goals of managed care are characterized as everything from increasing profits to increasing access. The effects of managed care are even more difficult to determine, with anecdotes about undertreatment competing for attention with claims of enhanced efficiency and quality.

To launch effective strategies in an environment dominated by managed care, healthcare managers must have a solid grasp of just what this phenomenon is and how it fits into the structure, delivery, financing, and quality of healthcare in the United States.

To that end, Part I systematically examines the following:

- the forces that have given rise to managed care, including those related to economics, quality, and accountability;
- the various models of managed care and how they operate;
- the actual and potential strengths and weaknesses of managed care;
- managed care's market presence in various regions of the United States; and
- current and future policy issues surrounding managed care.

Included in this part of the book is a chapter that includes six executive summaries of some of the most salient issues related to healthcare delivery in a managed care environment: measuring and managing risk, measuring and improving clinical outcomes, managing behavioral health under managed care, managing chronic illness under managed care, establishing risk-sharing contracts with physicians, and collaborating among managed care plans to improve quality.

This section is the foundation on which subsequent sections of this book will build with more detailed information about managed care's operations, effects, and future directions.

CHAPTER

1

Working Toward an Ideal System

Stephen M. Shortell, Robin M. Gillies, David A. Anderson, Karen Morgan Erickson, and John B. Mitchell

Some time ago, one of the authors overheard the following conversation in the waiting room of an ambulatory care clinic. Speaking to the receptionist, a patient made the following comment (expressed in a tone of slight exasperation):

> You know, I have a pretty simple wish. I want to stay healthy and productive. When I become sick I want to get well as quickly as possible. But I know that costs are also important. So I want to know what's done to me is really needed and is done as efficiently as possible. Do you think that's too much to ask for?

We can ask for anything, but it doesn't mean we are going to get it. This patient was a well-educated, reasonable sophisticated and motivated consumer of health services. But not everyone is. For example, while few individuals desire to be sick, many are unwilling to make the necessary investment to remain well. The health care system deals with a tremendous variety in patients' genetic stock as well as their ability to and willingness to enhance, maintain, and restore their health. This diversity presents challenging organizational problems.

"*I want to know what is done to me is really needed . . . .*" But medicine is both an art and a science. Physicians and other members of the health care team often don't know what is really needed. It has been estimated

Reprinted with permission from *Remaking Health Care in America*. San Francisco: Jossey-Bass, 1996.

that as much as 70 percent of medical treatment is provided without a firm scientific basis (Williamson, 1991) even though the best medical judgment and clinical experience are being used.

"*And is done as efficiently as possible.*" There are currently great pressures to contain costs, improve productivity, and increase efficiency. The challenge lies in achieving efficiency not just for an individual at a single point in time but across a group of patients over time. What may not seem efficient for an individual patient may be efficient on average for a group of patients—for example, block scheduling of patient appointments. The challenge is one of *mass customization* (Davis, 1987; Kotha, 1995), that is, establishing procedures and processes that apply to most patients while building in flexibility to adapt to the idiosyncratic needs of each individual.

THE IDEAL HEALTH SYSTEM: THE PATIENT'S PERSPECTIVE

So what might an ideal health system look like to a patient? The following two scenarios, one real and one fictitious, introduce us to some of the elements of an ideal system.

Scenario I

On August 13, 1994, Robert Morris, CEO of Laurel Health System in Wellsboro, Pennsylvania, was involved in a serious motorcycle accident that left him with multiple fractures, a collapsed lung, and related injuries. We pick up Mr. Morris' story shortly after surgery:

> As Morris began showing signs of improvement . . . the demand for trauma beds required his transfer to a general intensive care unit (ICU). What Egan [trauma nurse Liz Egan] did in response deeply impressed the 44-year-old Morris, who knows about the workings of hospitals through his experience as a hospital CEO.
>
> Egan not only accompanied Morris to the ICU but stayed there to brief the staff on the nuances of his condition. She even returned several times to check up on him. As Morris traveled the inpatient continuum from the ICU to a trauma transition unit leading up to his discharge four days after the accident, Egan visited him twice more.
>
> "My condition was apparently more precarious than I was aware of, and Liz wanted to make sure that nothing fell through the cracks with me," says Morris. "I was impressed by what she did, either by the hospital's design or on her own to maintain continuity of care. Surrounded by all of that wonder whiz-bang technology and clinical ability, her concern for me made the difference."

You see Liz Egan–style behavior all the time in health care. It's what Morris calls an "other centered" approach that he's attempted to foster across the many sites and services that make up Laurel Health System. It's the smooth hand off from one care giver to the next, the connections between services, the communication that ensures a smooth transition: seamless care.

Many hospitals do this well within their own walls, as patients traverse from one unit to the next, and many segments that make up the continuum do so individually—from ambulatory clinics to physicians' offices to home health to hospice. But as integrated health systems evolve and push into their communities to provide total care for defined populations, the passing of the baton from one care setting to the next becomes more important—and much easier said than done.

It is the smooth functioning of the continuum of care that separates real health systems from loose alliances of providers. A well coordinated continuum adds value to a system's performance. [Lumsdon, 1994, p. 28]

Scenario II

Mr. Dwight Taylor is a fictitious patient featured in the *Henry Ford Health System 1994 System Report*. His story is told below:

> I remembered telling my friend Fred at lunch that I had awakened with a terrible headache. I had ended up rushing to work and still missed a conference call. Then Fred started laughing and said, "Dwight, you are losing it, you are drooling."
>
> I reached for a napkin to wipe my mouth, but I couldn't get it to my mouth. Something was wrong. My hand couldn't grab the napkin, and it felt heavy. I was feeling very strange. Fred looked blurred, out of focus. My left arm was tingling, and my speech was slurred. I thought, "I am having a heart attack." After that, I remember that Fred was yelling for someone to call 911. . . . I ended up in an ambulance then a hospital emergency room. Later, I found it was Henry Ford Hospital in Detroit. . . .
>
> When I [next] woke up, standing over me was a man in a white coat who introduced himself as Dr. Steven Levine, a neurologist at Henry Ford. I remembered him from the emergency room. He said the stroke I had was a moderate one. He tried to reassure me but said he still needed to do some more tests to figure out why I had a stroke.
>
> Dr. Levine said that because I was a Henry Ford patient, he had been able to call up my medical history on the computer in the emergency room the night before. He had also talked with my family physician, Dr. Dickenson, about my condition. Dr. Levine noted that I'd been a heavy smoker for some 25 years. . . .
>
> Dr. Levine told me that I needed speech and occupational therapy. He talked with Dr. Dickenson again who Dr. Levine said would oversee the

> rest of my care. He arranged for me to have my rehab at Henry Ford's Cottage Hospital in Grosse Pointe Farms, which is across the road from Dr. Dickenson's office and not far from my house.
>
> Rehab took several months, but after only about six weeks, I was able to go back to work part time. That made me feel better knowing I could still support my family and do my job. (p. 8)

As an accompanying note to Dwight Taylor's saga, Henry Ford's brochure notes that "the Taylors have ready access to the full range of services that 'an integrated' health care system provides—coordination of referrals, a life long medical history and continuum of care, a common patient log and ready access to primary care, specialty and support services at a network of convenient locations. . . . The system also offers the advantages of test results being shared, not repeated. And care provided at one site can be reviewed electronically at another site, upon the patient's transfer or referral" (Henry Ford Health System, 1994, p. 6).

These two scenarios illustrate the importance of *caring, communication,* and *information* in providing coordinated continuous patient care. In Mr. Morris' case, the caring, communication, and information transfer appeared to depend primarily on the commitment and competence of Liz Egan. What might have happened if there had been no Liz Egan? In Mr. Taylor's situation, the caring, communication, and information seem to be more institutionalized or "integrated" within the Henry Ford Health System's practices, policies, and procedures. And yet one knows that how things are described in a glossy annual report are not always how they appear in practice for each individual patient. The hallmark of an excellent health system is its ability to *consistently* provide well-coordinated, continuous care that produces desired outcomes for each and every patient day in and day out.

THE IDEAL HEALTH SYSTEM: THE HEALTH CARE EXECUTIVE'S PERSPECTIVE

The daydream of an ideal system—and the harsh reality—are illustrated below by Mr. John Smythe, CEO of the fictitious General Health System (Voluntary Health Systems of America, 1994).

The Daydream

> The board meeting ended 15 minutes early, and John decided to spend a few quiet minutes in the solitude of his office before going home. As he walked to his office, he thought about how unusually harmonious his day had been. No, it was just that this day was unusual—the whole situation seemed too perfect to be real. "I used to only be concerned with the operations of my hospital" he marveled.

Now John ran a large regional delivery system with myriad highly evolved characteristics:

- Focused on meeting the needs of a specific population
- Offering facilities and service capacity exactly matched to the needs of the population
- Managed not by controls or incentives, but rather, through a strong, positive culture
- Allowing physicians to practice collegiality without worrying about the business side of their practices. Clinicians collectively determined the most appropriate clinical pathways to follow for each disease and/or condition
- Accessible and responsive to the purchasers of care in the community for delivering quality of service, value, and cost-effectiveness
- Supported by integrated information technology linking various clinicians and distant locations, supplying information for reviewing clinical approaches, monitoring outcomes of procedures and patterns of care, and placing the most recent and advanced clinical knowledge in the hands of the clinician at the point of care
- Endowed with sufficient capital to meet investment needs and allocate resources in a system-wide (not entity-specific) manner
- Consistently managing care across the care continuum with a long-term focus
- Positioned where financial incentives are aligned through the entire delivery system to meet the needs of purchasers

The Harsh Reality

As John opened the door to his now dark office, he was jolted by a loud pounding. Were the decorators still at work at this late hour? . . .

"This meeting will come back to order." John Smythe, CEO of the City General Hospital, shuddered, quickly shook his head and realized that he had been dreaming. . . . The hospital's Medical Executive Committee was being called back to order after a short break. It was time to continue discussing how the hospital and physicians could work together to meet the challenge of new managed care plans. The local HMO wanted to begin capitating primary care physicians and put the hospital at risk for length of stay.

John looked around the room and realized how far from reality his short daydream into a future fantasy world had taken him. The advanced concepts needed for advanced provider integration seemed irrelevant to his organization in its current state. His head was swimming:

- Managed care? We haven't begun to learn to live with the small amounts of insurance risk involved in our holdbacks for the local HMO.
- Collegial medical practice? The physicians are in 300 separate small groups, each claiming to practice the highest quality medicine pos-

sible. There is no discussion among physicians about appropriateness of anything they do in their own individual offices.

- Align incentives? Each physician is thinking about his or her own practice economics—and each physician/hospital/HMO issue is always framed in a defined-sum manner.
- Balanced capacity? My people are trying to figure out how to fill more beds!
- Work in a capitated framework? We're still arguing about the appropriate discount from charges the surgical specialists need to give the PHO.
- Advanced information systems? We can't even supply encounter data to understand from a transactional standpoint what our overall utilization experience has been.
- Improved health status? We haven't even measured the current health indicators in our community, let alone our impact on the community's health.

Suddenly John realized the enormity of the task in front of him. None of the current paradigms, working relationships, organizational and management structures, payment mechanisms, etc. were sufficient to even begin working within the new health care environment and its challenges—managed care, accountability for cost and quality, and the need for integration.

His daydream needed to become a reality. He knew where he needed to go but not how to begin. "How do I get there from here?" he cried.

These scenarios introduce almost all of the elements of an ideal health care system, which are summarized in the list below and are similar to the four key characteristics of community care networks that have been put

Key Elements of an Ideal Health Care System

- Focuses on meeting the population's health needs
- Matches service capacity to meet the population's needs
- Coordinates and integrates care across the continuum
- Has information systems to link patients, providers, and payers across the continuum of care
- Is able to provide information on cost, quality outcomes, and patient satisfaction to multiple stakeholders—patients, employees, staff, payers and purchasers, community groups, and external review bodies
- Uses financial incentives and organizational structure to align governance, management, physicians, and other caregivers in support of achieving shared objectives
- Is able to continuously improve the care that it provides
- Is willing and able to work with others to ensure that the community's health objectives are met

forth by the American Hospital Association (AHA), namely, having a community health focus, providing a seamless continuum of care, managing within fixed resources, and being accountable to the community (American Hospital Association, 1993b).

What we as patients want from a health care system are:

- Providers knowledgeable about our health history—allergies, family/genetic predisposition to illness, life-style, history, and so on
- Up-to-date information on health maintenance and improvement, disease prevention, and cost-effective treatment innovations *before* we might need them
- Convenient access when we do need care
- Excellent treatment from people who work well together
- Polite, courteous attention, and having our questions answered
- Appropriate and coordinated follow-up care
- Smooth handoffs from one provider to another and one treatment setting to another as appropriate. We don't want to have to repeat the same answers or provide the same information
- To be informed of changes in the organization and its providers *ahead of time*
- An organization that can learn from its mistakes. Errors and mistakes are inevitable (Leape, 1994), but providers and organizations should not make the same mistake twice. They should continuously get better over time

This is a tall order, but if we expect no less from organizations that make our television sets, digital pagers, cellular phones, and automobiles, why should we expect less from those that provide our health and medical services?

The primary challenge is to overcome fragmentation. The culprits include imperfect information, incomplete communication, conflicting incentives, and organizational and professional biases (Institute for the Future, 1993a). In order to counteract these influences, an integrated system needs to create a team-oriented culture, develop flexible organizational structures, invest in information systems, and offer relevant incentives. But the question remains: how do we get there from here?

THE COMMUNITY HEALTH CARE MANAGEMENT SYSTEM

Based on four years of research involving eleven organized delivery systems across the United States, we believe a starting point is to develop a *community health care management system*, as shown in Figure 1.1.

The system begins with knowing its current and future "customers" and the communities in which they reside. We refer to this as *community/popu-*

Figure 1.1 The Community Health Care Management System

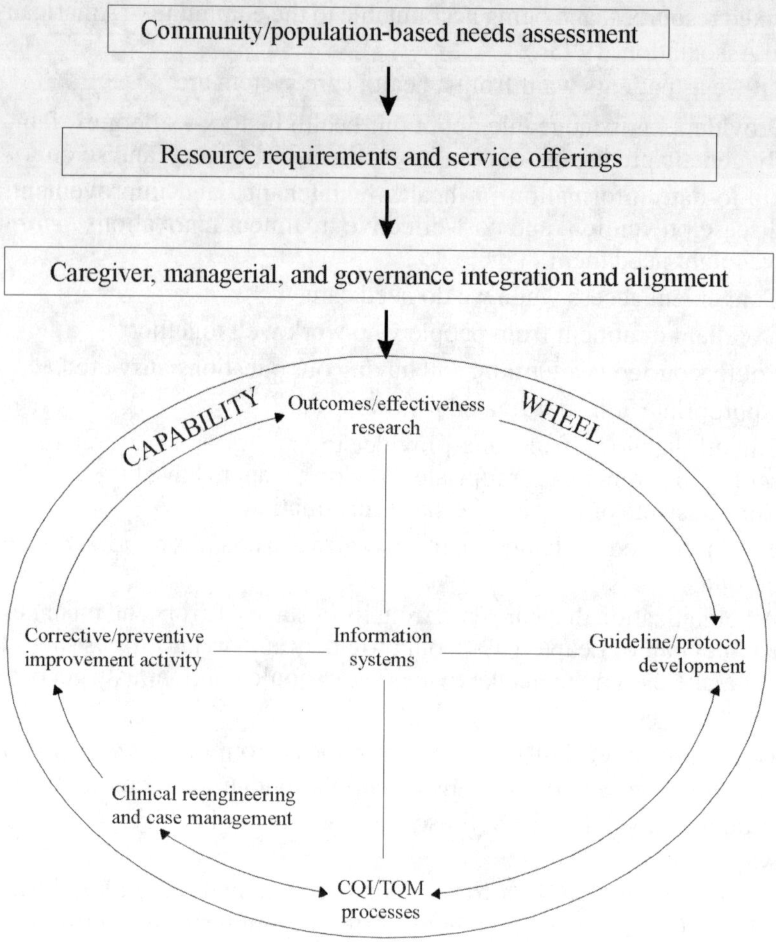

Source: Shortell, Gillies, and Devers, 1995, p. 151. This figure first appeared in *The Milbank Quarterly.*

lation-based health needs assessment. This involves defining the specific segments of the population and the geographic area that the system wishes to serve. This will be determined by the system's mission and values and by the configuration of other health providers, systems, and resources in the community relative to the populations of interest. It will also be influenced by the system's perceived capabilities relative to those of others. These populations are likely to include individuals both with and without health insurance coverage. Those with insurance can be broken out by whether they are an "enrolled life" in either the system's own managed care product or a contracted managed care product. Those without insurance coverage and special populations (for example, children on Medicaid) can be broken out by geography, education, income, and ethnic characteristics, among others. What is important is to project the needs of the different groups and convert these into likely utilization of health care services and resources. To the extent that capitated payment or prepayment of some form continues to grow throughout the country, health systems have an incentive to take a more assertive and activist stance toward maintaining and promoting the health of the population they serve. This incentive will also require a system to take a *broader* perspective of what contributes to good health and, therefore, become more involved in issues that influence community health such as crime, alcohol and substance abuse, and domestic violence.

This requires systems to go beyond traditional data collection and analysis. For example, the Hospital Association of Pennsylvania has developed a five-phase model of assessment: (1) developing a county health profile that "blends" data from multiple sources, including small-area variation analysis of clinical practice patterns; (2) collecting original data on personal health behaviors combined with a community health resource inventory profile and a health care economic impact statement; (3) sharing information from the preceding two phases with a series of focus groups comprising individuals likely to be affected by the decisions made; (4) developing a community action plan based on all of the above input; and (5) monitoring the implementation and evaluating the impact as actions unfold (Hospital Association of Pennsylvania, 1993). The Crozer-Keystone Health System in Media, Pennsylvania, has used many components of this model and, in the process, has directly linked top management compensation to achievement of selected community health objectives, such as immunization rates and provision of prenatal care in the first trimester (Gardner, 1994). Allina, an evolving insurer-provider integrated systems based in Minneapolis–St. Paul has used health status needs assessment to develop such explicit objectives as (1) to increase from 75 percent to 95 percent the number of children in the system who are fully immunized for childhood diseases by age 2; (2) to reduce by 50 percent the incidence of breast cancer that reaches an advanced stage before being detected; and (3) to increase early detection of adult-onset diabetes by screening 90 percent of high-risk members (Voluntary Hospitals of America, 1994). Such objectives are targeted only to Allina's enrolled population and membership, and, thus, ignore the larger Minneapolis–St. Paul community. Allina's plans, objectives, and data need to be coordinated with those of other organized delivery systems in the area in order to achieve maximum community-wide impact.

Based on community/population-based health needs assessment, systems can determine the resources and services to offer. The system must be "right sized" to met the selected population's anticipated needs. This involves determining the number and location of primary care providers, specialists, acute care beds, rehabilitation beds, long-term care beds, home health services, hospice services, and the like. The system must make decisions involving the breadth and depth of services it will offer (Shortell, Gillies, and others, 1993). *Breadth* refers to the number of different services provided across the continuum of care to serve the populations of interest. For example, a system that provides thirty-five different services ranging from primary care to acute care to rehabilitative care has more breadth than one that offers only twenty-five services that may be more narrowly focused on acute care. *Depth* refers to the extent to which a given service is provided at multiple locations or operating units within a system. For example, a system that offers psychiatric care at five of its operating units has more depth (in that service line) than a similarly sized system that offers it at only three locations. As systems across the country examine the breadth and depth of services needed by the community, many find that they have up to 50 percent more specialists, approximately 25 percent less primary care capacity, and up to 50 percent more acute care beds than needed. This is understandable given that the "dominant logic" (Prahalad and Bettis, 1986; Bettis and Prahalad, 1995) of U.S. health care has until recently been the provision of acute illness–oriented inpatient care. But a new dominant logic based on disease prevention, health promotion, and primary care is emerging, resulting in a significant amount of restructuring activity. Just as IBM, the "big three" American automobile companies, and the airlines have had to relearn their business and construct new "dominant logics," so it is that U.S. health care organizations must do the same.

As shown in Figure 1.1, once the resource requirements and service offerings are determined as a function of the community/population-based health status assessment, the system faces the challenge of aligning its caregiver, management, and governance structures. *Alignment* means that those who actually deliver health and medical services (caregivers), those who manage them (managers), and those who oversee the process and are accountable to the community (governing boards) are working together rather that at cross-purposes with each other. For example, given the pressures for more cost-effective care, physicians, nurses, and other caregivers are having to reorganize themselves into multidisciplinary teams and service lines using treatment protocols, guidelines, pathways, and outcome data to coordinate care across the care continuum. In like fashion, management and governance structures must change to support the new forms of delivering health and medical services. The multidisciplinary provision of care across the continuum will not work if attempted within outmoded management and governance structures. Management structures must be changed to reflect continuum of care and service line responsibilities. Similarly, governance structures must be changed to reflect area-wide responsibilities for the health of defined populations, with greater attention given to achieving systemwide objectives in addition to individual operating-unit objectives.

Once the population's needs are defined, the system is "right sized," and the clinical, managerial, and governance functions are aligned, the system is ready to "perform." This is represented in Figure 1.1 as a *capability wheel* comprising interrelated processes: outcomes and effectiveness research, guideline and protocol development, CQI/TQM processes, clinical reengineering, case management, taking corrective and preventive action, and measuring the outcome of these actions. All of these activities are anchored by the information systems depicted in the middle of the wheel.

The underlying logic of the capability wheel is as follows. One first begins with obtaining benchmark data and information on state-of-the-art outcomes and effectiveness for a given condition, procedure, or state of health. This serves as a base for developing the system's own guidelines, protocols, and pathways for managing the health of defined populations. These guidelines, protocols, and pathways both serve as inputs to quality improvement opportunities and solutions and are influenced by the system's CQI/TQM processes. Hence, the double-headed arrow between the two in Figure 1.1. In turn, a system's CQI/TQM processes influence its efforts at clinical reengineering, which is defined as the elimination and/or significant reorganization of fundamental clinical functions. Clinical reengineering and case management also has a reciprocal effect on the system's CQI/TQM processes. Ultimately, corrective and preventive improvement activities are undertaken that in turn result in assessment of the outcomes: what worked, what didn't work, and why. This "local" information and experience feeds back into new developments nationally in an iterative fashion as the wheel turns, continuously measuring and improving the defined populations' (the communities') ability to prevent disease and to maintain and improve its health.

Three points about the community health care management system should be emphasized. The first is that the capability wheel applies to disease prevention, health maintenance, and health promotion activities, as well as to acute and chronic care treatment. In fact, it can be argued that outcomes research, protocol development, CQI/TQM processes, and related activities that are focused more on disease prevention and health maintenance and promotion will have a larger impact and payoff than much of the current focus on acute and chronic care (Rundall and Schauffler, 1995). For example, avoiding one low-birthweight infant can save between $14,000 and $30,000 in health care costs (Office of Technology Assessment, 1991), and investments in improved prenatal care have been shown to result in cost savings of direct medical care of $3.38 for every $1.00 spent (Institute of Medicine, 1988).

The second point is that, at least in metropolitan areas, no single organized delivery system can develop all components of a community health care management system nor does it have to own all of the components that make up the system. The community health care management system will be composed of *virtual organizations*, networks of organized delivery systems and community agencies willing to share risk, costs, rewards, knowledge, and skills. Most of the study systems have developed significant strategic alliances with other providers and insurers as well as with public health departments and social and community service organizations.

The third point is to emphasize the important integrative role played by information systems. In some respects, this is the least-developed aspect of the community health care management system concept. Because of its central role, this underdevelopment slows down achievement of the other components of the system. Study participants are spending tens of millions of dollars to expand and upgrade their information systems so that they can link patients and providers across the continuum of care. But beyond that is the need to incorporate community and public health data and to link one organized delivery system's data with another's. The Community Health Information Networks (CHINS) represent a potentially promising approach to the issue.

The community health care management system concept is consistent with the American Hospital Association's community care network concept (1993), the Hospital Research and Educational Trust's work (1994) on creating community action learning laboratories, the Institute for Health Care Improvement's community collaborative work (1994) involving the application of CQI/TQM principles and processes to community-wide health care problems, and the Healthcare Forum's work (1994) on building healthier communities. The renewed interest in community health care has its historical roots in the landmark report of the Committee on the Cost of Medical Care (1932; Sigmond, 1995). Although there is growing recognition that building healthier communities must extend beyond the efforts of individual organized health care delivery systems, such systems are essential building blocks. To achieve their mission and their potential for community collaboration, these organizations must be infused with the principles of *holography*.

THE HOLOGRAPHIC ORGANIZATION

A *hologram* is a photographic plate containing all of the information necessary to produce a complete image in each of its parts. When you switch the picture from one part to another, you still see the whole image. The elements required for the whole image are contained within the parts.

The hologram is a powerful metaphor for organizations (Morgan, 1986), systems, and community development. Holographic properties exist at the organizational level to the extent that the organization is represented in each of its constituent parts—divisions, departments, task forces, committees, and individuals. The organization is not merely the sum of its parts but *exists* in each part. This is quite easy to understand in the case of the one-person entrepreneurial firm. In this case, the individual *is* the organization, performing essentially all of the functions associated with product or service development, sales, marketing, accounting, and so on. But as organizations grow large and more complex, they begin to lose their holographic properties: layers of hierarchy, bureaucracy, and specialization emerge. The challenge for large, complex organizations is to regain some of the holographic properties of their youthful beginnings. One way to do this is to become small again by creating smaller organizations within the larger organization. For example, 3M has no division greater than four hundred employees, and Microsoft organizes itself into units of no more that two hundred people each. These companies believe that beyond a certain size, a division or unit will have difficulty sustaining close face-to-face interaction, coordinating activities, and stimulating creative, innovative ideas. Other companies such as Federal Express, Johnson & Johnson, and Xerox attempt to achieve holography by developing a strong culture that unites people across divisions, departments, lines of business, and geography. Organizations also become more holographic when they engage in such activities as training people to perform multiple functions, making greater use of multidisciplinary teams, blurring line and staff responsibilities, providing people with matrix management skills, and developing information systems that facilitate communication among people throughout the organization, thus increasing the opportunities for learning. From the perspective of a patient, as much of the entire health care organization as possible should be embedded or "hard wired" into each person, group, or team that the patient encounters in the process of receiving care.

From an organized delivery system perspective, each operating unit involved in the continuum of care—prevention, primary care, acute care, rehabilitative care, and maintenance care—should have "the system" embedded within it. As discussed in subsequent chapters, this is achieved through functional integration, physician-system integration, and clinical integration. This leads to what we have elsewhere called a sense of "systemness" (Shortell, 1988), in which each unit of the system understands the strategic role it plays within the overall system. In such systems, strategy and structure are viewed as being embedded within the other like an intertwined rope. For example, a system's vertical integration efforts, its strategic alliances, and its decentralization and empowerment efforts should each be seen as both strategy and structure.

A community health care management system can have holographic properties when the community's overall health and well-being are embedded or contained within each organized delivery system operating in the community. In this way, the organized delivery system's goals and objectives would reflect community-wide goals, and a sense of interdependence would foster collaboration rather than unnecessary competition.

Holographic organizations and systems increase the probability of providing more holistic, coordinated, and continuous cost-effective care to patients and health enhancement services to populations. Holography is the antidote to runaway fragmentation and specialization. At the social and organizational level, *learning* is the key mechanism by which holography operates. Learning is also one of the keys to community-building. Holographic properties rapidly increase the speed of learning throughout an organization or system, and is the means by which the whole is embedded with each part.

Generating holographic properties is a daunting task because the dysfunctions of fragmentation, needless competition, and reactivity are deeply embedded in our society and culture. Kofman and Senge (1994) suggest that these maladies need to be replaced by what they call "regaining the memory of the whole," recognizing the community nature of the self, and by using language as a creative act (p. 6). They term this transition the Galilean Shift—moving from an emphasis on fragmented parts, individual competition, and reacting to problems, to an emphasis on the whole, on the community, and on creativity (p. 6). Among their suggestions for making this shift is to create experimental and managerial "practice fields" where people can experiment with new approaches for working together, applying skills, and, in our terms, developing holographic properties (p. 22).

To do this, organized delivery systems constituted as holograms will engage continuously in "double loop" learning: questioning the underlying assumptions and dominant logic upon which current practices and policies are based (Argyris, 1982; Senge, 1990). For example, most health systems have assumed that strategic plans should be built around the hospitals within the system, given that hospitals have been the primary generators of capital and the entities with which most physicians were associated through the medical staff organization structure. But some systems are now questioning this underlying assumption as hospitals become less central to the provision of health care services and as physicians join groups and form their own organized entities separate from the hospital. Increasingly, system strategic plans are built around physician groups and primary care networks.

Organized delivery systems with strong holographic properties create more options for themselves—they are no longer psychic prisoners of old paradigms. Such organizations are "clever organizations" (Handy, 1989, p. 15): sharing and pooling resources and knowledge through task forces, creating and executing strategies with the involvement of those closest to the issues, making ongoing use of differentiated structures; they are information based, with great emphasis on continuous learning.

THE ROLE OF INTEGRATION

Integration is defined as the process by which activities are formed, coordinated, or blended into a functioning or unified whole (Webster's, 1990). Integration is an essential process to building a holographic organization because before the whole can be embedded in each part, it must first exist as a "whole"—that is, something must be brought together from different elements. For example, in order for a hypertensive diabetic patient to receive the same quality care from multispecialty Clinic A within a given system as the patient would from multispecialty Clinic B (that is, for the "whole" to be in each part), the nature of what constitutes high-quality "holistic" hypertensive diabetic care needs to be defined and implemented. This might be done, for example, through the development of guidelines and protocols that stipulate how a variety of steps are to be executed and in what order. Overall case or care management systems would play a similar role. The result is a "whole" that can then be implanted in each part of the system. Thus, integration is both a cause and an effect of a holographic organization. It is a cause in that certain elements, processes, and activities must be coordinated with each other to create "wholes." But integration is also an effect, because as the whole is reflected in each part, the parts give rise to greater integration potential with other parts of the system. A well-integrated part has greater "carrying capacity" to link up and energize other parts of the system and thereby create greater value.

We believe that functional integration, physician-system integration, and clinical integration (Gillies and others, 1993) are the key elements in creating the holographic properties that must exist within an organized delivery system. *Functional integration* is defined as the extent to which key support functions such as financial management, human resources, information systems, strategic planning, and total quality management are coordinated across the operating units of a given system so as to add the greatest overall value to the system. *Physician-system integration* is defined as the extent to which physicians are economically linked to the system, use it facilities and services, and are active participants in its planning, management, and governance. *Clinical integration* is defined as the extent to which patient care services are coordinated across people, functions, activities, processes, and operating units so as to maximize the value of services delivered. Clinical integration includes both horizontal integration (the coordination of activities at the same stage of delivery of care) as well as vertical integration (the coordination of services at different stages)—for example, between acute care and post acute care (Conrad and Dowling, 1990; Fox, 1989).

"STAGING" THE IDEAL SYSTEM

Building a community health care management system cannot be achieved overnight. Certain key stages or steps must take place before other changes can occur. There needs to be a certain degree of functional integration to assist physician-system integration efforts. In turn, both functional integration and physician-system integration are essential to achieving clinical integration. While putting these steps or building blocks in place can be accelerated (indeed, we argue that they must be accelerated), trying to skip over them altogether results in failure.

The pace and type of integration called for is largely driven by market and external forces. These include the degree of overall managed care penetration in the marketplace, the specific degree of capitated payment that exists, the degree of competition among systems and networks, the activities of major employers and business coalitions, and state health reform legislative initiatives. There exist several classifications of health care market profile stages or phases (American Practice Management, 1993; Coile, 1994; Advisory Board Company, 1993; Voluntary Hospitals of America, 1994). Table 1.1 provides an overview of some of the more important characteristics of each stage; Table 1.2 suggests several delivery system integration activities appropriate to each stage.

As one moves from left to right through the four stages of "market maturity," the components of delivery system integration build on each other. This starts with acquiring the "pieces" of a delivery system and functionally integrating them in the unstructured "access" market stage, and culminates in the need for a high level of clinical integration, associated outcomes reporting, and taking on responsibility for community health status in the "value" market stage.

What Tables 1.1 and 1.2 do not show may be the most important factor in managing the pace of change. This is the amount of *time* before a given market moves from one stage to another. The challenge for those who lead organized delivery systems is to position their systems so that they are only somewhat or "loosely" fit for their current environment while preparing for

Table 1.1 Market Stages and Delivery System Organization

Stage 1 **Unstructured "access" market**	**Stage 2** **"Loose cost" market**	**Stage 3** **Consolidated "advanced cost" market**	**Stage 4** **Strict managed care "value" market**
• Independent hospitals/providers	• Hospitals/providers begin to merge and forge alliances	• Critical mass of systems/networks emerge	• 3–5 systems/networks dominate metropolitan markets
• Independent payers	• Largely independent payers	• Payers consolidate	• Highly consolidated payer base
• Few HMOs/PPOs	• HMOs/PPOs grow	• Local HMOs/PPOs consolidate and achieve critical mass	• Purchaser-provider linkages
• Little managed care penetration— < 20 percent	• Managed care penetration grows—20–40 percent • Excess inpatient bed capacity develops	• Managed care penetration—40–60 percent • Significant inpatient bed reduction	• Managed care penetration—>60 percent • Capitation payment emerges as a force
• < 25 percent physicians in groups	• 25–49 percent physicians in groups	• 50–74 percent physicians in groups	• 75 percent or more physicians in groups
Example markets Atlanta Little Rock Pittsburgh Savannah	*Example markets* Chicago Detroit	*Example markets* Los Angeles Portland Seattle San Francisco	*Example markets* Albuquerque Minneapolis–St. Paul San Diego

Sources: American Practice Management, 1993; Coile, 1994; Advisory Board Company, 1993; Voluntary Hospitals of America, 1994

Table 1.2 Suggested Level of Delivery System Integration Activity by Market Stage

Stage 1 Unstructured "access" market	Stage 2 "Loose cost" market	Stage 3 Consolidated "advanced cost" market	Stage 4 Strict managed care "value" market
• Acquire the pieces • Build functional integration • Reduce costs	• Expand functional integration efforts • Accelerate cost-reduction efforts • Accelerate bed-reduction efforts	• Expand physician-system integration efforts • Expand risk-based contracting • Explore relationships with insurance partners	• Expand clinical integration efforts • Consolidate relationships with insurance partners • Use outcomes data for external accountability and internal quality improvement
• Question the decentralization of capital to operating units • Look for physician and other partners	• Develop primary care physician network capacity • Develop other parts of the continuum of care, e.g., home care	• Initiate clinical integration efforts • Emphasize disease prevention and health promotion	• Expand population-based planning efforts • Forge stronger partnerships with public health, community and social service agencies
• Question acute inpatient focus	• Begin physician-system integration efforts • Begin to consolidate capital development	• Establish new management and governance structures	• Take greater responsibility for community health status and well being

the newly emerging environment. This is tricky business. The danger in making changes before one has to or in making too large a change is that the market (in other words, the payers) will not yet reward you for it. In the process you may also alienate key groups, particularly physicians. The danger of waiting until the market has sufficiently "evolved" is that others may have beaten you to the punch, leaving you with a long, uphill struggle. The secret of success lies in developing what we might call the "Gretzsky Response." When interviewed regarding his phenomenal success as a hockey player, Wayne Gretzsky responded to the effect that other players skate to where the puck is and that he tries to skate to where the puck is going to be. From an organized delivery system's perspective, this requires three skills: (1) the ability to properly assess where the environment is going to be; (2) the ability to assess *how long it will take to get there*; and (3) the ability of the organization to get there slightly before or at least at the same time that the changes in the environment materialize relative to the competition. In other words, direction, speed, and timing are of the essence.

We believe that most, if not all, communities throughout the United States are moving out of Stage 1 to Stages 2 and 3 with a few advancing to Stage 4 markets. For example, it is estimated that whereas in 1994 36 percent of the United States' population lived in Stage 1 markets, 38 percent in Stage 2 markets, and 24 percent in combined Stage 3 and 4 markets; in 1998 only 6 percent will live in Stage 1 markets, 31 percent in Stage 2 markets, 29 percent in Stage 3 markets, and 34 percent in Stage 4 markets (Johnson & Johnson, 1994).

It is more difficult to assess the speed of change occurring in different communities throughout the country. Based on our experience, however, we believe that the *slowest* part of the transition is going from Stage 1 to Stage 2, due to the considerable inertia exhibited by individual hospitals, fee-for-service payment, and fragmented payers in Stage 1 communities. Once managed care activity is in the neighborhood of 35 to 40 percent penetration (characteristic of Stage 2), the movement to Stage 3 is extremely rapid. Once in Stage 3, the movement to Stage 4 may be somewhat slower that in going from Stage 2 to Stage 3 but not as slow as that from Stage 1 to Stage 2. In Stage 3, the organized delivery system is essentially in a position to accept greater amounts of capitated payments, but the extent to which payers/purchasers are interested in full capitation varies largely as a function of experience in assessing risk. Thus, we envision that Stage 4 markets will exist with various modes and degrees of capitated payments, which in turn will send somewhat mixed signals to organized delivery systems regarding the speed with which they need to continue structuring themselves to care for enrolled populations. As a result, the transition to a Stage 4 delivery system may be somewhat slower. This transition would, of course, be greatly accelerated if national health care reform legislation were passed guaranteeing a set of benefits to all Americans within a range of given premiums that reflect geographic, health status–related, and other adjustments.

What does all of this have to do with creating the ideal health care system as might be reflected in a community health care management system? It is a realistic reminder that creating such a system is a *journey*. It is a reminder of individual and organizational vulnerabilities and limitations in building community (McNerney, 1995). Organizations need time to develop the necessary depth of leadership to be able to learn from each other. The rewards for all must come from achieving milestones along the way. But there will also be accidents and mistakes.

REFERENCES

Advisory Board Company. *The Grand Alliance: Vertical Integration Strategies for Physicians and Health Systems*. Washington, D.C.: Advisory Board Company, 1993.

American Hospital Association. *Transforming Health Care Delivery: Toward Community Care Networks*. Chicago: American Hospital Association, 1993b.

American Practice Management (APM). *Health System Market Profile Characteristics*. New York: APM, 1993.

Argyris, C. *Reasoning, Learning, and Action: Individual and Organizational*. San Francisco: Jossey-Bass, 1982.

Bettis, R.A., and Prahalad, C.K. "The Dominant Logic: Retrospective and Extension." *Strategic Management Journal*, 1995, *16*, 5–14.

Coile, R.C. "The Five Stages of Managed Care: Organizing for Capitation and Health Reform." *Hospital Strategy Report*, Sept. 1994, 6, 1–8.

Committee on the Costs of Medical Care. *Medical Care for the American People: The Final Report of the Committee on the Costs of Medical Care*. Publication no. 18. Chicago: University of Chicago Press and the Commission on Medical Education, 1932.

Conrad, D.A., and Dowling, W.L. "Vertical Integration in Health Services: Theory and Managerial Implication." *Health Care Management Review*, 1990, *15*, 9–22.

Davis, S.M. *Future Perfect*. Reading, Mass: Addison-Wesley, 1987.

Fox, W. "Vertical Integration Strategies: More Promising Than Diversification." *Health Care Management Review*, Summer 1989, *14*, 49–56.

Gardner, K. "A System That 'Walks the Talk.'" Interview with John C. McMeekin and Richard W. Billings. *Trustee*, Apr. 1994, pp. 6–9.

Gillies, R.R., and others. "Conceptualizing and Measuring Integration: Findings from the Health Systems Integration Study." *Hospital & Health Services Administration*, 1993, *38*(4), 467–489.

Handy, C. *The Age of Unreason*. Boston: Harvard Business School Press, 1989.

Healthcare Forum. *What Creates Health? Individuals in Communities Respond*. A national study conducted by Dyg, Inc., for the Healthcare Forum. San Francisco: Healthcare Forum, 1993.

Henry Ford Health System. *Henry Ford Health System 1994 System Report.* Detroit, Mich.: Henry Ford Health System, 1994, pp. 6, 8.

Hospital Association of Pennsylvania. *A Guide for Assessing and Improving Health Status.* Harrisburg, Penn.: Policy Research Department, Hospital Association of Pennsylvania, 1993.

Hospital Research and Educational Trust (HRET). *Community Action Learning Laboratories.* Chicago: American Hospital Association, 1994.

Institute for Health Care Quality Improvement. Community Healthcare Collaborative, Boston, Mass., 1994.

Institute for the Future. *Health Care Outcomes, Year Seven: First Theme Report.* Menlo Park, Calif.: Institute for the Future, 1993a, p. 28.

Institute of Medicine. *Prenatal Care: Reaching Mothers, Reaching Infants.* Washington, D.C.: National Academy Press, 1988, p. 232.

Kofman, F., and Senge, P.M. "Communities of Commitment: The Heart of Learning Organizations." *Organizational Dynamics*, 1993, *22*(2), 5–23.

Kotha, S. "Mass Customization: Implementing the Emerging Paradigm for Competitive Advantage." *Strategic Management Journal*, Summer 1995, *16*, 21–42.

Leape, L.L. "Error in Medication." *Journal of the American Medical Association*, Dec. 23, 1994, *274*, 1851.

Lumsdon, K. "Crash Course: Piecing Together the Continuum of Care." *Hospitals & Health Networks*, Nov. 20, 1994, pp. 26–28.

McNerney, W.J. "Community Health Initiatives Are Widespread, Challenging Our Sense of Civic Obligation." *Frontiers of Health Services Management*, Summer 1995, pp. 39–44.

Morgan, G. *Images of Organization.* Beverly Hills, Calif.: Sage Library of Social Research, 1986.

Office of Technology Assessment, U.S. Congress. *Identifying Health Technologies That Work: Searching for Evidence.* OTA-H-608. Washington, D.C.: U.S. Government Printing Office, 1991.

Prahalad, C.K., and Bettis, R.A. "The Dominant Logic: A New Linkage Between Diversity and Performance." *Strategic Management Journal*, 1986, *7*, 485–501.

Senge, P. *The Fifth Discipline.* New York: Doubleday/Currency, 1990.

Shortell, S.M. "The Evolution of Hospital Systems: Unfulfilled Promises and Self-Fulfilling Prophecies." *Medical Care Review*, 1988, *45*(2), 177–214.

Shortell, S.M., Gillies, R.R., and others. "Creating Organized Delivery Systems: The Barriers and Facilitators." *Hospital & Health Services Administration*, 1993, 38(4), 447–466.

Sigmond, R. "Back to the Future: Partnerships and Coordination for Community Health Benefit." *Frontiers of Health Services Management*, Summer 1995, pp. 5–36.

Voluntary Hospitals of America. *Integration: Market Forces and Critical Success Factors*, Irving, Tex.: Voluntary Hospitals of America, 1994, pp. 1–6.

Webster's Ninth New Collegiate Dictionary. Springfield, Mass.: Merriam-Webster, 1990.

Williamson, J. "Medical Quality Management Systems in Perspective." In J.B. Couch (ed.), *Health Care Quality Management for the 21st Century.* Tampa, Fla.: American College of Physician Executives, 1991, pp. 23–72.

CHAPTER

2

The Health Services Delivery System: Managed Care

Phoebe Lindsey Barton

INTRODUCTION

This chapter considers characteristics of the health services delivery system, linking discussions of health system organization and financing, resource production, and economic support. The recent and ongoing shift from a fee-for-service system reimbursed through indemnity insurance to a system of managed care, in which the financing and delivery of services are integrated, is the central theme of this chapter.

This chapter opens with a review of the many definitions for the term "managed care." Following a review of the reasons for the shift in the focus of the delivery system and the expectations of many for managed care, this chapter includes sections on models of managed care, the strengths and weaknesses of managed care, and the market for managed care. It concludes with a review of the policy issues related to this shift from fee-for-service to managed care.

DEFINITIONS OF MANAGED CARE

David Mechanic (1994) captured a general frustration with the term "managed care" when he commented that "managed care is used so promiscuously as to have no meaning at all." It can also be said that the term has as many referents as it has users, each holding a somewhat different notion of

From Barton, P. L. 1999. *Understanding the U.S. Health Services System.* Chicago: Health Administration Press.

what the term means. "Managed care" as a term suffers from some of the same amorphousness as does the term "quality of care." Most would agree that at least one concept is central to the meaning of managed care: it is an integration, at some level, of the financing and delivery of health services.

In managed care, both patient utilization and provider practices are managed by an entity that has a fiduciary interest in the interactions between them. Thus, the term managed care serves as an umbrella for a range of organizational and reimbursement mechanisms in the U.S. delivery system. Entities that provide managed care are sometimes referred to as managed care organizations (MCOs). Change is occurring so rapidly, with new organizational forms emerging and mutating, that defining this moving target more precisely may contribute only to the lexicon of obsolete definitions.

THE SHIFT FROM FEE-FOR-SERVICE TO MANAGED CARE IN THE U.S. DELIVERY SYSTEM

As does any dynamic organism, the U.S. delivery system has grown rapidly and incurred changes, particularly since the mid-1960s, when access to care increased for some populations and technologic advances continued to expand the capacity to save lives and extend life spans. Despite the growth and changes, the delivery system through the 1980s could generally be described as a public-private system in which people with social or private health insurance could autonomously seek care from the provider(s) of their choice. Providers would be reimbursed for their care of individual patients on a fee-for-service basis. Other systems of care, such as prepaid care provided through certain types of HMOs, were labeled "alternative delivery systems," part of the overall diversity of the U.S. society but relegated to the role of a minor player.

Within less than a decade, the preceding general description of the U.S. delivery system has become outmoded and inaccurate. What was once considered an alternative delivery system—care in which the financing and delivery were integrated at a certain level—has become part of the mainstream delivery system, which we have loosely termed "managed care." What constitutes the essence of this shift, and why is it occurring?

The Nature of the Delivery System Shift

To oversimplify the nature of the shift in the delivery system is tempting; oversimplification tends to classify the systems according to extremes such as:

- fee-for-service care focuses on individual patients, whereas managed care focuses on the health of a population;

- fee-for-service care centers around acute care, whereas managed care emphasizes disease prevention and health maintenance;
- fee-for-service care provides incentives for overservice, whereas managed care provides incentives for underservice;
- fee-for-service care is largely patient-initiated, with few access barriers other than financial ones, whereas managed care controls and restricts patient access to providers.

Although these extremes harbor elements of truth, they are too polarized to serve as effective distinctions.

A better description of the essence of the shift may be that the focus of the delivery system is moving from the level of interactions between an individual patient and an individual provider to a focus on the comprehensive needs and care of individual patients and of a population of patients who obtain their care from the same providers. The focus thus shifts from episodic care of the individual patient, in which each episode is separately reimbursed, to holistic care of individuals and groups of individuals. Reimbursement in the latter instance may be based on episodes of care, on a fixed fee for all covered care regardless of how much is utilized, or on another basis.

Reasons for the Shift in the Delivery System

The U.S. health services delivery system is reputed to be one of the most advanced in the world but it is an imperfect system. Its imperfections include its lack of universal coverage, its cost-and-expenditure upward spirals, the increasing amount of the gross domestic product (GDP) it absorbs, and its potential for becoming the black hole of U.S. domestic economy and policy. National-level initiatives to rationalize the system, the most recent of which was the 1993 Health Security Act, failed in part because the price tag appeared too formidable (Ellwood and Lundberg 1996) to a partisan Congress wrestling with budget and trade deficits.

Despite the failure of national-level health system reform, system changes, driven by a range of market forces, are occurring at a pace and to an extent that few prognosticators would have dared predict even ten short years ago. What could not be accomplished using regulations over several decades, such as a reduction in excess capacity in the system, is rapidly occurring through facility mergers, acquisitions, and closures as providers, payors, and others joust for market share and survival. Books will continue to be written about the forces prompting this shift; this chapter is limited to listing some of the forces that are stimulating change and to the reminder that future change is likely to occur, even in areas where we are not currently anticipating it.

Forces for change

A number of forces are influencing changes in the delivery system. Among those discussed in the following sections are:

- the raised level of consciousness that employers and payors are experiencing about the costs of providing employee health insurance;
- the perverse incentives that fee-for-service care establishes;
- the effects on utilization of self-referral, doctor shopping, and open access to specialists;
- the need of both private and public payors to better predict total health expenditures;
- the need for accountability of health expenditures within a society;
- the belief that optimal rather than maximal use of limited resources is appropriate; and
- the need to increase efficiency in the system, including the appropriate use of inpatient and outpatient services and the reduction of overcapacity.

All these forces reflect utilization of the current system; none adequately takes account of the significant proportion of the population that has no assured access to health services.

Increased Cost of Providing Employee Health Benefits

The costs of providing employee health benefits have risen sharply in recent years, as evidenced by substantial annual premium increases through 1993, the prediction by economists and actuaries that after 1997 premiums will again increase (Ginzberg and Ostow 1997), and the growing proportion of employer expenditures for health as a share of total business revenues. Additionally, employers are paying an increasing share of the total health bill. They paid 29 percent in 1990, almost double the 16 percent total in 1965 (Drake 1997). As employers recognized the financial consequences of the types of employee health benefits they were providing, they began to:

- organize business coalitions to increase their bargaining power with insurers;
- become self-insured rather than negotiate contracts with insurers;
- negotiate discounts with providers;
- negotiate the provision of services directly with providers, eliminating the insurance function altogether; and
- adopt a range of other cost-reducing strategies.

From a passive to an aggressively active role, employers are exerting a noticeable influence on how care is delivered in the United States.

Fee-for-Service Incentives

The fee-for-service reimbursement system, which pays separately for each care event (i.e., each physician visit, laboratory service, prescription drug, hospitalization, or other service) creates a perverse incentive to regularly provide a wide range of services, not all of which may be appropriate or needed. Ordering duplicative sets of tests, for example, each of which would be reimbursed under a fee-for-service system, may have increased each provider's flexibility but underscores the inefficiency and misuse of resources in the system. Assuming the patient is insured, the provider stands at little or no financial risk for this practice and may stand to gain financially. Some types of managed care reduce the potential for unneeded or duplicative services and thus reduce the expenditures for health services.

Effects on Utilization of Unconstrained Access to Care

Prior to the recent changes in the delivery system, an insured person or one who had other resources had relatively open access to health services, depending on the availability of providers. As one analyst described the previous system, health insurance provided an individual with a "hunting license" to hunt for the care he or she needed (Feldman et al. 1989). The insured individual thus initiated care in many instances, could directly seek care from a specialist rather than await a referral from a primary care provider (i.e., self-referral), and could "doctor-shop," switching providers to the extent that providers were available and willing to see additional patients.

Consumer choice, one of the hallmarks of the U.S. system, remains a strong consumer preference, but it can also create misuse or overuse of health services. As utilization of services increases, the costs of and expenditures for services also increase, contributing to the upward spiral of health expenditures.

The Need for Predictability and Accountability of Expenditures

The open-ended nature of health benefits under the fee-for-service delivery system, especially evident in entitlement programs such as Medicare and Medicaid, permitted individuals to seek—and providers to provide—essentially unlimited health services, resulting in the potential for unlimited expenditures.

Although various cost-containment efforts were attempted, their success in curbing expenditures varied. Some efforts that did curb expenditures, such as patient cost-sharing, also had adverse effects on patients' health.

Open-ended systems may also compromise the ability to adequately account for utilization and expenditures in a system. Employers and public payors are among those who are seeking ways to eliminate open-ended systems and thereby increase the predictability and the accountability of their health expenditures.

Optimal versus Maximal Use of Resources

In a technologically advanced health services system where providers are trained to use every intervention to save and prolong lives, the maximal versus the optimal use of resources may occur. Society has a difficult time acknowledging that some resources may be limited and addressing the explicit rationing of resources. Whether it is acknowledged as such, medical care is already rationed by the availability and scope of health insurance, and by market place mechanisms (Mechanic 1994). Resource use at either end of the utilization spectrum continues to be a debated issue as the delivery system undergoes transition.

Need for Increased Efficiency in the Delivery System

The open-ended, fee-for-service system that has been a U.S. standard for decades incorporates many inefficiencies that have not resolved the problem of those without access to care and have contributed to rapidly increasing expenditures for care to those who have financial access. Among the most apparent inefficiencies is system overcapacity, including excess hospital beds, a disproportionate number of physician specialists, and duplicative and underutilized technologies.

Until recently, the laws of supply and demand that govern many other markets appeared to have little effect in achieving a balance in capacity: Hospital overcapacity led only to higher hospital charges (Drake 1997), and a disproportionate supply of physician specialists did not suppress physician incomes. Attempts to regulate capacity through initiatives such as the certificate-of-need program had a limited and generally short-term effect on capacity.

After years of convincing evidence that market principles did not effectively apply to much of the health services system, the market is now aggressively dealing with overcapacity in the system. Among the possible explanations for this change is that providers, anticipating an adverse regulatory environment in various system reform proposals, determined to control the system by merging and consolidating resources to reduce overcapacity. Led by Medicare, payors weighed in by constraining the ability of providers, particularly of hospitals, to cross-subsidize the care of unprofitable clients by charging higher prices to paying patients. The supply of physicians, fueled by generous policies on the training of international medical graduates (IMGs), became large enough that payors could divide and conquer, negotiating prices and working conditions in a previously unheard of manner. The growing influence of proprietary providers at both the hospital and HMO levels is also affecting the shape of the delivery system.

A Range of Expectations for Change in the Delivery System

The imperfections in the U.S. delivery system identified in the preceding sections generate a wide range of possible solutions and a wide range of expectations of patients, payors, providers, and others about these solutions. Many of the solutions have been identified as managed care solutions, and the term has been vested with more promise than it is likely to deliver. Among the range of expectations of managed care is that it will:

- rationalize the use of resources, avoiding overuse or underuse;
- provide greater accountability at all levels;
- enable a more accurate prediction of health expenditures;
- contain and/or reduce health expenditures;
- shift the focus of the delivery system from acute care and crisis intervention to disease prevention and health maintenance;
- reduce physician practice variations; and
- ensure better outcomes of care.

Several models of managed care and their likelihood in meeting some of the preceding expectations are examined in the following sections.

MODELS OF MANAGED CARE

Many kinds of organizations fit under the umbrella of managed care. This section describes some better-known models and introduces some of the more recent developments. New models or variations of models are emerging; some will flourish and others will adapt to changing circumstances, while still others will not survive. The appearance of models of managed care seems much like using a kaleidoscope: the elements, or participants, may remain constant, but a slight turn of the glass will introduce a new pattern or model.

Table 2.1 provides a summary of some of these models including information on provider payment mechanisms, provider incentives, enrollee incentives, cost-saving mechanisms, and risk assumption.

Prepaid Group Practices

Prepaid group practices (PGPs) were recommended as the most effective care delivery system as early as 1932 in the report of the Committee on the

Table 2.1 Managed Care Models

Model	Description	Provider Payment Mechanisms	Provider Incentives	Enrollee Incentives	Cost-Saving Mechanisms	Risk Assumptions	Comments
HMO (Staff Model)	• Medical care delivery through salaried employee physicians who provide a specific set of services to a defined population	• Salary; physicians are employees of the HMO	• Defined patient population • No claims processing • Low/no start-up costs for new physicians	• Comprehensive range of services for a fixed price • Coverage of primary care and preventive services • Community rate-based premiums	• Utilization review • Provider bonuses based on productivity and meeting utilization targets • Education of providers and patients • Gatekeeping	• HMO	• Concerns voiced about incentives to underutilize in a capitated system
HMO (Group Model)	• Medical care delivery through a medical group practice contracted to provide a specific set of services to a defined population	• Capitation for group; salary or FFS reimbursement for participating physicians	• Defined patient population • No/few claims processing • Low/no start-up costs for new physicians	• Comprehensive range of services for a fixed price • Coverage of primary care and preventive services • Community rate-based premiums	• Utilization review • Provider bonuses • Prior approval • Financial incentives through withholding accounts • Education • Gatekeeping	• HMO and group	• Concerns voiced about incentives to underutilize in a capitated system

HMO (IPA/ Network Model)	• Medical care delivery through a panel of contracted providers for the provision of a specific set of services to a defined population	• FFS reimbursement • Capitation	• Can accept patients from multiple plans and/or retain indemnity patients • Rapid claims turnaround • Increased pool of patients • Some flexibility in referral	• Comprehensive range of services for a fixed price • Coverage of primary care and preventive services • Community rate-based premiums • Greater likelihood of maintaining patient/provider relationship	• Utilization review • Prior approval • Financial incentives through withholding accounts • Gatekeeping	• Purchasers	• Until the advent of POS options, IPAs were the fastest-growing HMO model. • The primary-care-to-specialist ratio can affect cost savings (i.e., greater ratio of specialists reduces cost savings) • Capitated forms are found to be more effective in reducing costs
PPO	• Contractual arrangement between a panel of providers and purchasers of health services for the provision of a specific set of services to enrollees	• Discounted FFS reimbursement	• Patients form multiple plans • Increased pool of patients • Rapid claims turnaround • Low financial investment	• Reduced cost sharing for within-plan use • Expanded benefits • Partial coverage for out-of-plan use • Reduced premiums	• Utilization review • Prior approval • Selective contracting of cost-efficient providers • Discounted reimbursements • Movement toward gatekeeping	• Purchasers	• Potential for monopsony if purchaser becomes very large

Table 2.1 Managed Care Models (*continued*)

Model	Description	Provider Payment Mechanisms	Provider Incentives	Enrollee Incentives	Cost-Saving Mechanisms	Risk Assumptions	Comments
EPO	• Contractual arrangement between a panel of providers and purchasers of health services for the provision of a specific set of services to enrollees	• Discounted FFS	• Increased pool of patients • Rapid claims turnaround • Low financial investment	• Low/no cost-sharing • Expanded benefits • Reduced premiums	• No out-of-plan reimbursements • Utilization review • Prior approval • Selective contracting of cost-efficient providers • Discounted reimbursements	• Purchasers	• Most states' insurance regulations prohibit restrictions on access to providers as it constitutes "restraint" of trade
POS Model	• Subscriber chooses provider at the point of service rather than upon enrollment into the plan	• Varied	• Potential to attract a broader range of subscribers	• Flexibility to choose provider			
PSO	• Joint ventures between physicians, hospitals, and other providers	• Capitation	• Guaranteed panel of patients		• May reduce or eliminate insurance or other costs	• Provider	

SHMO	• Medicare demonstration combines social and health services for frail elderly	• Capitation	• Ability to provide more comprehensive and continuous services, both social and health	• Availability of additional services • Potential avoidance of institutionalization	• Deferred institutionalization • Reduced rates of hospitalization	• Provider
Integrated Delivery System/ Network	• Network of services to a defined population	• Varied	• Maintain panel of patients	• Broader choice of provider	• Depends on payment mechanism(s)	• Provider

Costs of Medical Care (CCMC). The PGP is an early model of managed care. Insurers, employers, or other parties contract with either a single specialty physician group or more usually a multispecialty physician group to provide a predetermined range of benefits or services to a specific population for a fixed price. Early PGPs include Ross-Loos, established in Los Angeles in the 1920s, and Kaiser Permanente, established on the West Coast in the 1930s. Providers may have been at risk for providing care (i.e., the full extent of covered benefits had to be provided), regardless of whether the cost of those benefits to the provider exceeded the preestablished payment rate.

Health Maintenance Organizations

PGPs were the precursor for health maintenance organizations (HMOs) which began to appear in the early 1970s. The HMO was an outgrowth of Congressional frustration with the uncontrolled utilization and expenditures of the Medicare program (Ellwood and Lundberg 1996), and was proposed to officials in the Nixon Administration as a way to address both issues. The result was the 1973 Health Maintenance Organization Act, which established federal standards for HMOs and required employers of a certain size to offer at least one HMO to their employees. Large corporations that purchased employee health benefits from HMOs were a major influence in shaping the present marketplace (Ellwood and Lundberg 1996).

Several different HMO models exist including: the group model, the staff model, the independent (sometimes referred to as individual) practice association, and the network model. All are distinguished by the following characteristics:

- To varying degrees, each model combines the delivery of care with its financing.
- An HMO assumes a contractual responsibility to provide or assure the delivery of a stated range of health services, including at least ambulatory and inpatient care.
- An HMO serves a population defined by enrollment in a plan.
- Subscriber enrollment is generally voluntary but may be mandated by the payor.
- The subscriber and/or the payor pays a fixed monthly or annual premium that is independent of the utilization of services.
- The HMO assumes at least part of the financial risk in the provision of services.

The following characteristics of each model may help to distinguish them. What is important to remember, however, is that a process of hybridization is occurring among these and other models of managed care that blurs their once-sharp distinctions.

Group model HMO

A group model HMO is a type of HMO where a single large multispecialty group practice is either the sole or a major source of care for the HMO enrollees. The group may have existed before the corporately distinct HMO entity formed, but it has an exclusive contract only with the one HMO. Some groups also see fee-for-service or preferred provider organization (PPO) patients; others are not permitted to do so. Because of the similarity with the staff model HMO, the term "staff/group model HMO" is often used to denote these large HMOs (Weiner and de Lissovoy 1993).

Staff model HMO

A staff model HMO is a type of HMO in which the majority of enrollees is cared for by physicians who are on the HMO staff. Although these physicians may be involved in risk-sharing arrangements, a majority of their income usually is derived from a fixed salary. The group-cooperative, consumer-controlled HMOs are usually staff model plans. Because the physicians in this type of HMO are also organized into groups, the term "group/staff model" is used to encompass both this and the group model HMO (Weiner and de Lissovoy 1993).

Independent practice association

The independent practice association (IPA), sometimes referred to as the individual practice association, is an open-panel type of HMO in which individual physicians or small group practices contract to provide care to enrolled members. The primary care physicians may be paid by capitation or fee-for-service with a "withhold" risk-sharing arrangement.

An IPA entity may be legally distinct from the HMO entity with which the member enrolls. Physicians participating in IPAs retain their right to treat non-HMO patients on a fee-for-service basis (Weiner and de Lissovoy 1993).

Network model HMO

A network model HMO is a type of HMO in which a network of two or more existing group practices has contracted to care for the majority of patients enrolled in an HMO plan. A network model HMO may also contract with individual providers in a fashion similar to an IPA. Providers contracting with a network model HMO are usually free to serve fee-for-service patients as well as those enrolled in other HMOs and PPOs (Weiner and de Lissovoy 1993).

Social health maintenance organization

The Social Health Maintenance Organization (SHMO) is a Medicare demonstration project to determine the feasibility of combining social, health, and medical services under one capitation payment.

Preferred provider organization and exclusive provider organization

Until the early 1980s, the models described in the preceding sections constituted the realm of managed care. Discontent with the imperfections of the delivery system led to the introduction of another model, the preferred provider organization (PPO), and to a variant, the exclusive provider organization (EPO).

The PPO is a type of integrated delivery system in which the PPO entity acts as a broker between the purchaser of care and the provider. In a PPO, consumers have the option to either use or not use the preferred providers available within the plan. Consumers are channeled toward in-plan providers through the use of lower cost sharing and greater benefit coverage. In return for patient referrals, providers agree that their care will be managed. Providers are usually paid a discounted fee-for-service payment and they do not participate in financial risk sharing.

EPOs are a type of PPO in which the patient must exclusively use the providers within the PPO, although he or she may pay out-of-pocket to see out-of-plan providers (Weiner and de Lissovoy 1993).

Although a PPO affords the consumer greater choice than the staff model HMO, for example, its ability to control expenditures is limited by the level of discount that can be negotiated with providers. This limitation helped to give rise to another variant, the point-of-service (POS) model.

Point-of-service model

The point-of-service (POS) model is a hybridized managed care plan that offers consumers a choice of options at the time they seek services rather than at the time they choose to enroll in a health plan (Weiner and de Lissovoy 1993). The POS model is one of the fastest-growing models of managed care (Drake 1997), principally because it offers the subscriber flexibility in choice of providers. Choice is considered a key to promoting quality (Stauffer 1997). Consumers who choose POS plans are likely to have higher cost-sharing in the form of deductibles, coinsurance, and copayments, but may elect this coverage because it ensures freedom of choice of provider. A number of state legislatures are deliberating over whether to require MCOs to provide POS plans. Before the 1997 legislative session, only Georgia, Maryland, Minnesota, New York, and Oregon had enacted POS laws; by

October of 1997, 30 states had introduced measures requiring MCOs to offer a POS option. Most of these proposed measures address, to some extent, three key issues related to POS plans: the market to which the option applies, the type of care that must be offered through the option, and the level of cost-sharing imposed on consumers to use the option (Stauffer 1997).

Although HMOs introduced the POS model within the last decade as a way to maintain their competitiveness, the POS is not the ultimate organism in this evolutionary process. Recent steps in the process include integrated delivery networks, and provider sponsored organizations (PSOs).

Integrated delivery networks

Integrated delivery networks (IDNs), sometimes called organized delivery systems, integrate a variety of organizations to deliver a broad array of health services across the continuum of care in a cost-effective manner. Shortell et al. (1993) define an organized delivery system as "a network of organizations that provides or arranges to provide a coordinated continuum of services to a defined population and is willing to be held clinically and fiscally accountable for the outcomes and the health status of the population served."

The integration of health organizations may be vertical or virtual (Robinson and Casalino 1996). Vertical integration combines hospitals, medical groups, and other delivery system elements under one umbrella with a unity of purpose and control. Vertical integration creates substantial pressure for capital funds for acquisition purposes. Two weaknesses are inherent in the vertical integration approach to developing integrated delivery networks: the incentive system becomes lessened or weakened by the organizational hierarchy that is established, and influence costs—the effects of internal struggles over the control of resources—increase greatly.

Virtual integration achieves coordination on a contractual basis. This type of integrated delivery network has more autonomy to adapt to changing environmental circumstances because it is unencumbered by a large-salaried work force and the need to maintain hierarchies or the bureaucratic structures that seem inevitable in a vertically integrated organization.

The apparent trend in this evolutionary development is greater integration of the provision and delivery of care with its financing. A recent development includes efforts by large corporations to bypass the insurance industry altogether by negotiating directly with hospitals, medical groups, and other providers to deliver health services to a defined population. The Buyer's Health Care Action Group in the Minneapolis–St. Paul area is an example of this approach to changing the delivery system.

Provider-sponsored organizations

Provider-sponsored organizations (PSOs) are a variant of an integrated network. The PSO label appears to be eclipsing that of the integrated network; the concepts are so similar that it is difficult to differentiate between them.

PSOs, sometimes called provider service networks (PSNs), are provider affiliations organized to offer both health insurance and health services to local or regional populations to counter-balance the growing market power of national and regional health plans and insurers (National Health Policy Forum 1996).

Organizationally, PSOs may range from loose affiliations of physicians to highly integrated networks of physicians and hospitals. They sell services to a variety of purchasers including individuals, other PSOs, HMOs, traditional insurance companies, employer health plans, and governmental agencies, accepting a range of payment mechanisms, from fee-for-service to full capitation (National Health Policy Forum 1997).

Depending on how they are structured, PSOs bear some financial risk for the services they contractually provide. Although PSOs may contract with health plans and insurers, they are seen by many as end runs around the traditional delivery and financing arrangements, bypassing plans and insurers to contract directly with private and public health services purchasers for the care of specific populations (National Health Policy Forum 1996).

A type of PSO organized to provide care to Medicare beneficiaries (except those with end-stage renal disease) is described in the 1997 Balanced Budget Act (PL 105-33) as a public or private entity that:

- is established or organized and operated by a health services provider or group of affiliated health services providers;
- provides a substantial proportion of contractually specified care items and services directly through the provider or affiliated providers; and
- with respect to the affiliated partners, shares directly or indirectly in substantial financial risk in the provision of such items and services and has at least a majority financial interest in the entity.

The Balanced Budget Act envisions the PSO as a primary mechanism for hospitals and physicians to offer health insurance or health benefits coverage to Medicare beneficiaries as a Medicare+Choice health plan. Under this act's provisions, PSOs would be licensed by states and certified by the Health Care Financing Administration (HCFA) as eligible to provide care to Medicare beneficiaries as an alternative to fee-for-service care.

Another type of PSO, the physician-hospital organization (PHO), was in the policy spotlight in the early 1990s. PHOs are joint ventures between a hospital(s) and its medical staff to contract with HMOs or self-insuring employers to provide services to an enrolled population. PHOs typically assume risks for services they provide under a capitation arrangement. In the mid-1990s, many large hospitals created or planned to create such entities, but interest in this type of organization appears to be waning.

STRENGTHS AND WEAKNESSES OF MANAGED CARE

Managed care offers both strengths and weaknesses as the mainstream system of health services delivery in the United States. Strengths or accomplishments attributed to managed care include:

- slowing of health expenditures in the early 1990s (Ginzberg and Ostow 1997);
- lower hospital admission rates, shorter hospital lengths of stay (LOS), less use of expensive procedures and tests, mixed results on outcomes, somewhat lower consumer satisfaction with services but higher satisfaction with costs (Miller and Luft 1994);
- creation of new organizations to allocate money and talent in a rational way (Ellwood and Lundberg 1996);
- reliable and pervasive tools for measuring health outcomes (Ellwood and Lundberg 1996);
- growing consensus on the importance of preventive services (Ellwood and Lundberg 1996);
- the best clinical practices incorporated into guidelines (Ellwood and Lundberg 1996);
- initial public reporting mechanisms regarding quality of care (Ellwood and Lundberg 1996);
- information systems that support, monitor, and provide feedback on the effects of health services (Ellwood and Lundberg 1996);
- potential, if responsible, administrative safeguards are applied to function as a more reasonable way of determining appropriate treatment than market mechanisms (Mechanic 1994);
- the attempt to eliminate waste and redundancy in the system (Kassirer 1997); and
- greater attention to management of chronic diseases (Kassirer 1997).

Weaknesses or failures of managed care noted by analysts include:

- a reduction of the power of physicians and hospitals to protect their professional and economic interests and to act independently in the interests of their patients (Ginzberg and Ostow 1997);
- lack of principles of accountability to the public for health quality (Ellwood and Lundberg 1996);
- inability to reduce national health expenditures despite some ability to reduce costs and offer value for money (Enthoven 1993b);

- unevenness of utilization review that is performed by review firms as a carve-out function; such firms may not review practices that could improve agency accountability, may underutilize methods to educate providers, and may not effectively use appeals mechanisms (Schlesinger et al. 1997);
- forced choices physicians must make between the best interests of their patients and their own economic survival (Kassirer 1997);
- lack of regulations to protect the delivery of care, leaving the "amoral and impersonal mechanisms of the market" to determine how care is delivered (Kassirer 1997);
- potential for underservice exemplified by such practices as "drive-through deliveries," short inpatient hospital stays for childbirth mandated by some managed care organizations (Drake 1997; Ginzberg and Ostow 1997); and
- lack of information systems, which makes evaluating the contents of care difficult (Ellwood and Lundberg 1996).

Each list will lengthen as greater experience with managed care is achieved. Several important caveats must be noted about these lists:

- What some see as strengths, others see as weaknesses (e.g., the status of information systems).
- Many of these same statements could be applied to a fee-for-service delivery system.
- The observation may reference some but not all forms of managed care, given the considerable variation in models of managed care shown above.
- Much of the research on managed care focuses on the staff model HMO with salaried physicians, most of which are organized as not-for-profit organizations (Woolhandler and Himmelstein 1995; Mechanic 1994); such research findings may be applied in error to other forms of managed care.

Regardless of the various models' strengths and weakness, what is clear is that managed care in all its various forms is the mainstream delivery system.

MANAGED COMPETITION

Managed care is still a "work in progress," according to many (Ellwood and Lundberg 1996). Managed competition, a refinement of the managed care concept, was proposed in the late 1980s by the Jackson Hole Group, analysts and policy leaders including: economist Alain Enthoven; Paul Ellwood, a pioneer in the HMO concept; and others. Managed competition is a purchasing strategy to obtain maximum value for both consumers and employers. Central to the managed competition concept is the role of the sponsor, a Health Insurance Purchasing Cooperative (HIPC), which purchases coverage for a large group of subscribers, and, in so doing structures and adjusts the market to overcome attempts by insurers to avoid price competition (Enthoven 1993a). Thus, managed competition incorporates elements of price competition and market regulation.

Competition occurs among large health plans. Regulation is instituted to prevent efforts to avoid price competition. The 1993 Health Security Act relied heavily on the concepts of managed competition. Despite Congress' failure to pass this act, principles and adaptations of the managed care concept are evident in many health services markets today (Schlesinger 1997; Luft 1996; Zwanziger and Melnick 1996).

MANAGED CARE MARKET SHARE

Managed care has become the mainstream delivery system in the United States. Seventy-five percent of U.S. workers with health insurance receive their health services through a form of managed care, whether it is an HMO, a PPO, or a POS model (Jensen et al. 1997). As of June 1996, 11 million Medicaid enrollees—about 30 percent of total enrollees—received their care in a form of managed care (USGAO 1997). Most states are aggressively seeking to enroll a larger proportion of their Medicaid populations into a form of managed care.

Enrollment of Medicare beneficiaries into managed care has been slower-paced. An estimated 11 percent of Medicare beneficiaries are enrolled in the Medicare risk program, but the rate of enrollment has accelerated, increasing nearly 50 percent between the end of 1994 and the beginning of 1997 (HCFA 1994 and 1997, as cited in Nelson et al. 1997).

The growth of managed care is not yet evenly distributed but rather concentrated in certain areas. The Minneapolis–St. Paul area and the entire state of Minnesota have a high concentration of managed care organizations and a broad portion ofof Minnesota's population is covered under a MCO. In California, managed care clearly dominates the delivery system. Half those with private health insurance are in HMOs and the other half are in PPOs; about one-third of Medicare beneficiaries are in HMOs and more than half the Medicaid enrollees are in HMOs (Robinson and Casalino 1996). Other high concentrations occur where sufficient populations of consumers or subscribers and an adequate-to-excessive supply of providers and facilities exist.

The growth of managed care is not evenly distributed across all models. Enrollment in staff and group model HMOs has slowed, influenced in part by the domination of self-insured organizations, which account for 45 percent of the coverage to employees with health insurance (Cunningham 1997). The growth rate for IPAs, in recent years the fastest growing among the various models of managed care (Kane et al. 1996), may soon be eclipsed by that of POS models (Jensen et al. 1997; Drake 1997).

Each of these types of managed care appeals to subscribers because of a greater range of provider choices. Figure 2.1 shows the growth rate of workers in various managed care models for two recent years, 1993 and 1995, and Figure 2.2 shows the growth rates for Medicaid enrollees in managed care in recent years.

The number of HMOs peaked in 1986 (Feldman et al. 1996) and has since declined, but HMO enrollment continues to rise. The same phenomenon occurring in the hospital industry is occurring among HMOs: Acquisitions, mergers, and consolidations are reducing the number of players, resulting in fewer but larger and more-powerful organizations. Many of these organizations are regional or national in scope. Eleven national managed care organizations now account for half of all HMO enrollees (The Commonwealth Fund 1996). The large size of these organizations raises con-

Figure 2.1 Change in Percentage of Workers of Various Types of Health Plans (1993–1994)

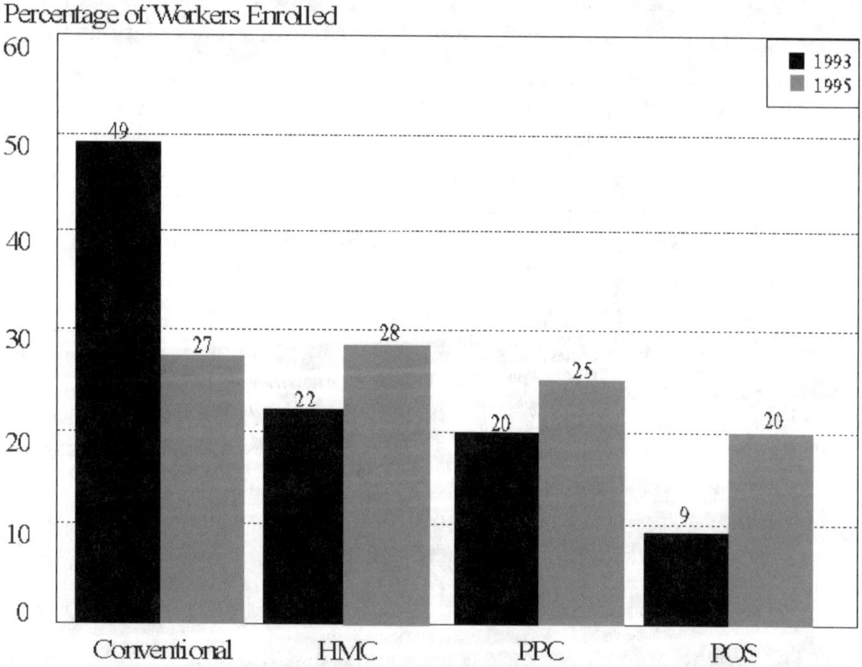

Sources: KPMG Peat Marwick/Wayne State University surveys, Copyright 1997 The People-to-People Health Foundation, Inc. All Rights Reserved. Adapted with permission. "New Dominance of Managed Care." Morrisey et al. 1997. "Percentage of Persons Unable to Obtain Care." *Health Affairs* 16 (1): 126.

Figure 2.2 Managed Care Enrollment (1991–1994)

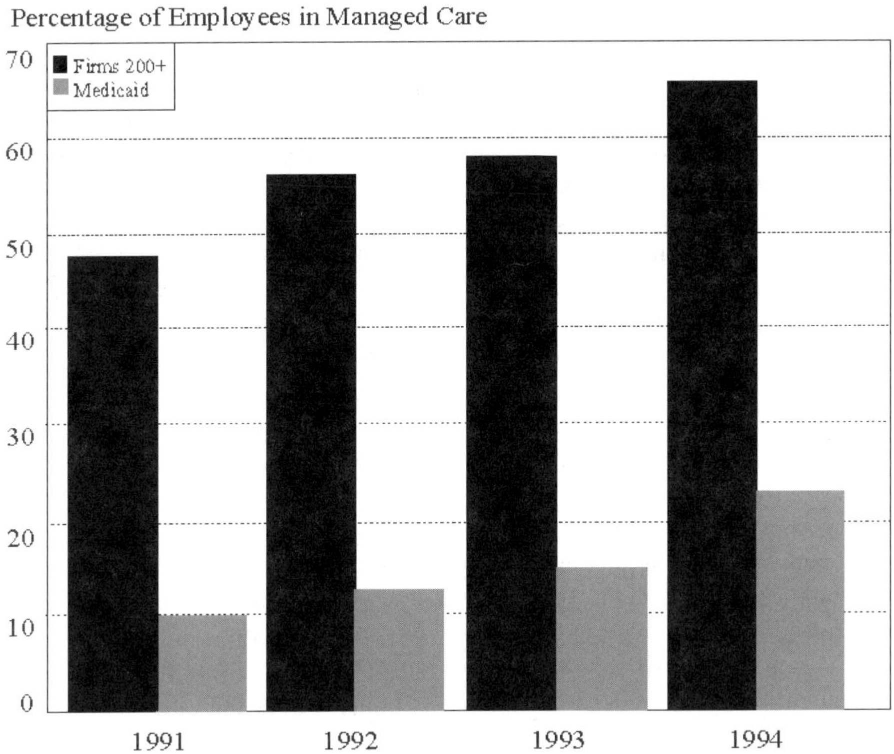

Note: Employee managed care enrollment includes HMO, PPO, and POS. Medicaid enrollment includes HMO, PPO, and primary care case management.

Source: The Commonwealth Fund. 1995. *Patient Experiences with Managed Care: A Survey*. July 19, 1995.

cerns among some, who fear that "merger mania" may create organizations that are too big to fail (i.e., organizations that enroll such a significant part of the population that governments may have to bail them out if they get over-extended to protect the health and welfare of the population [Fuchs 1997].)[1]

The growth of managed care organizations and the market share they represent also are not evenly distributed between proprietary and not-for-profit organizations. Although many of the first-established HMOs were created as not-for-profit organizations, the growth in recent years has been among proprietary HMOs. As of 1995, investor-owned HMOs had 60 percent of all enrolled HMO members (Cunningham 1996). Whether this growth in the proprietary sector serves the delivery system well is still being debated. Concerns have been raised about the willingness of such organizations to support the production of such public goods as health professional education, research, and care of indigent populations (Lawrence et al. 1997; Ginzberg and Ostow 1997).

Medicare and Medicaid Managed Care

Medicare and Medicaid managed care constitute a special part of the managed care market and generate issues particular to the care of vulnerable populations. The Medicare program has permitted managed care options from the outset and introduced a risk-sharing contract option in 1972.[2] Currently, 325 managed care plans participate in the HCFA risk contract program (Reichard 1997), receiving a capitation payment equivalent to 95 percent of the average adjusted per capita cost (AAPCC). Although only about 11 percent of Medicare beneficiaries are currently enrolled in HMOs, enrollment grew 27 percent in 1995 and 36 percent in 1996. HCFA hopes to have 25 percent of Medicare beneficiaries enrolled in managed care by the year 2000 (Reichard 1997). HCFA proposes to reduce the AAPCC from 95 percent to 90 percent by the year 2000 (Cunningham 1997), a move sure to be opposed by providers.

Enrollment in Medicaid managed care programs has traditionally occurred primarily through Medicaid 1915 and 1115 waivers that permit managed care. The 1997 Balanced Budget Act, however, gives states more flexibility in developing managed care programs. Mandatory managed care may be implemented by amending the state's Medicaid State Plan, which generally requires action by a state's legislature, rather than by seeking a waiver, which requires HCFA approval and must be periodically renewed.

By 1995, all states but Alaska had implemented some kind of Medicaid managed care. Nearly one-third of Medicaid enrollees now gets care through some type of managed care plan. Medicaid managed care enrollment nearly doubled in 1994 and increased 51 percent in 1995 (Grogan 1997). Future enrollment growth will depend on the ability of Medicaid to identify managed care programs that can appropriately care for vulnerable populations that have significant physical and mental disabilities.

POLICY ISSUES SURROUNDING MANAGED CARE

Because managed care is a work in progress, the list of policy issues surrounding it is a dynamic one. This chapter cannot begin to do justice to the universe of issues, but rather briefly discusses those related to physician practice, enrolled populations, quality of care, regulation, and effects of managed care on cost containment.

Physician Practice

The pervasiveness of managed care suggests that few physicians have the luxury of avoiding participation. In fact, the majority of physicians have entered into at least one contractual arrangement with managed care entities. In 1995, more than 80 percent of physicians worked with at least one managed care contract (Peterson 1997).

Gag rules

Managed care requires a different practice style and orientation than that in which many of today's physicians were trained. The physician has traditionally been trained to function as the patient's advocate, helping the patient to navigate the complex delivery system to obtain appropriate care. Most believe that maintaining the advocacy role is essential (Mechanic 1994; Ginzberg and Ostow 1997), but the physician's advocacy for a patient may put him or her on a collision course with a managed care organization's practice guidelines. As a result, some managed care organizations have issued—either as a part of their contract with a physician or as a separate policy statement—what have come to be referred to as gag rules. A gag rule is defined as:

- a contractual provision between a plan and providers that limits information, advice, and counsel that a provider may give a patient;
- anti-criticism provisions in contracts that prohibit a provider from making any communication that may adversely affect confidence in the health plan; and
- any health plan practice that inhibits open communication between a physician and a patient (Etheredge and Jones 1997).

Congress came close to passing a prohibition against gag rules in 1996, and several states have passed or are considering passing such laws.

Physician autonomy

The physician's autonomy of practice in the use of specialty services, physician referrals, drugs and devices, and other technologies may be affected by the type of managed care system in which he or she practices. To contain expenditures, physicians have to control utilization of services. What constitutes appropriate utilization is still widely debated.

While a delivery system based on fee-for-service reimbursement is conducive to the overutilization of services, the specter that haunts many who are apprehensive of managed care is the potential for underutilization of needed services as a way to contain expenditures. Physicians fear being "squeezed between their patients and their employers" regarding a patient's needs and the managed care plan's guidelines on utilization (Kassirer 1997).

Physician satisfaction with managed care

Given the significant changes in practice that may be required of a physician who practices in a managed care environment, how satisfied are physicians with this type of delivery system? Based on a mailed survey, a recent study of physician experiences with managed care (Collins et al. 1997) reported substantial physician concerns about their practice environment, clinical autonomy, the continuity of care they were providing, and their ability to refer patients and ensure patient access to specialty services. The physicians surveyed practiced predominantly (i.e., 75 percent or more of their practice) within a group or staff HMO; physicians practicing in other types of MCOs may have responded differently. Whether these concerns will diminish as the delivery system matures remains to be seen.

Enrolled Populations

Managed care changes the ways in which patients seek and obtain care. Among these changes are the narrowing of consumer choice of provider; the predisposition of consumers to select plans that best match their self-assessed health status (selection bias); the often involuntary turnover in plans, which affects continuity of care; and the satisfaction levels that consumers express about managed care.

Consumer choice

Managed care organizations, particularly those that developed from the prepaid group practice (PGP) model, have made some consumers wary because their choice of provider is limited to those on the managed care organization's provider panel. Aged people, or people with chronic conditions or severe physical or mental disabilities may avoid managed care enrollment if their preferred caregivers are not empanelled (Hellinger 1995). The demand for choice, a central tenet of this society, led to the development of PPOs and POS plans to address this demand.

Selection bias

Adverse selection occurs when people with the greatest anticipated health services needs flock to the managed care organization that offers the richest benefit package, thus ensuring higher service utilization and expenditures for this plan. Robinson and Gardner (1995) studied adverse selection among multiple competing HMOs and found that utilization was based not solely on epidemiologic factors, but also on certain organizational and economic factors in particular health plans. Their findings contradict the popular belief that HMOs attract only the younger, healthier enrollees.

Hellinger (1995), who looked at selection bias in HMOs and PPOs, found that all plans that restrict the enrollee's choice of provider (i.e., group practice HMO, staff HMO, IPA HMO, and EPO) enjoy favorable selection among the non-elderly and the elderly, in part because individuals who want to retain provider choice do not enroll in these plans.

One way to reduce selection bias is to seriously consider the development of specialized HMOs for people with disabilities; such HMOs would be staffed appropriate to specific needs and would include a payment rate reflecting an enriched benefit package (Mechanic 1994). Such a development may be the only way to secure additional Medicaid enrollment, because a majority of the healthiest enrollees are already in a managed care system.

Turnover

Subscriber turnover in managed care plans is a significant issue, affecting the continuity of care provided and received, and potentially influencing the organization's incentives to maintain a long-term perspective on individual and population health status. According to a recent study of managed care (The Commonwealth Foundation 1995), working Americans change health plans frequently, and most of this change is involuntary because the employer drops one or more plans, replacing them with new plans that offer the employer a better deal.

Surveyed physicians who practiced in group or staff HMOs reported that at least 9 percent of their patients had left their practices in 1995 because of changes in their health plan coverage (Collins et al. 1997). Fifty-three percent of the people enrolled in managed care plans as an employee benefit have been in that plan for fewer than three years, whereas only 37 percent of employees enrolled in fee-for-service plans have been in that plan for fewer than three years. The turnover of Medicaid enrollees in managed care plans can be even greater, approaching 100 percent in a year, due to inconstant eligibility and other factors (Buchanan et al. 1992).

Consumer satisfaction

Although the proportion of the population receiving health services from a managed care system is growing, patient satisfaction with managed care varies. A recent study of the patient's perspective on managed care compared satisfaction of managed care enrollees with that of those who received care in a fee-for-service system (The Commonwealth Fund 1995). Managed care enrollees reported lower satisfaction levels than their fee-for-service counterparts along the following dimensions: plan attributes, overall plan, quality of services, ease of changing physicians, choice of physicians, access to specialty and emergency care, and waiting time for appointments.

Those enrolled in managed care plans who were not afforded a choice of health plan had higher dissatisfaction levels than people enrolled in managed care who had been able to choose among health plans. The type of managed care plan in which the respondent was enrolled also affected his or her satisfaction level.

In the sample population surveyed, enrollees rated group and staff HMOs similarly overall to ratings by enrollees in fee-for-service plans. Independent practice associations (IPAs) were associated with slightly higher dissatisfaction levels; network/mixed-model HMOs and PPO plans received the highest dissatisfaction ratings. Ratings for overall quality of service varied widely across the models of managed care, as well. In at least one area, out-of-pocket costs, consumers indicated higher satisfaction with managed care plans as a group than did people in fee-for-service care (Davis et al. 1996).

Quality of Care

Does the quality of care rendered under managed care differ from that of fee-for-service care? Fearful of managed care's incentives for underservice, dire predictions have been proffered about the inferiority of care received under managed care systems. The inappropriateness of lumping together many different kinds of organizations and the care they provide under the umbrella of managed care is clearly apparent where quality of care is concerned. As was noted above, many of the findings about quality of care in managed care systems pertain to long-established PGP-type organizations; some of the more recent managed care models have not been established long enough for definitive conclusions about quality to be drawn. Fuchs (1997) notes that the pursuit of quality has had little role in the spread of managed care. Many analysts are maintaining a watchful wait, conceding that there is as yet little or no evidence to suggest that the quality of managed care is inferior to that of fee-for-service care (Ellwood and Lundberg 1996; Kassirer 1995) and emphasizing that monitoring health outcome performance must be a crucial element of any health services delivery system (Miller and Luft 1994).

Regulation

Although the market influence over the delivery of health services has clearly grown in recent years, is the delivery of health services to be regulated entirely by market forces as is any other commodity? Views on this issue vary, but many long-established health services researchers and analysts believe that some regulation of the delivery system is necessary. Even the managed competition concept, which emphasizes price competition, also incorporates regulatory mechanisms to control entities that would attempt to avoid price competition.

Kassirer (1995) identifies the fundamental question of managed care as whether health services should be subjected to the values of the marketplace. Fuchs (1997) points out that the social control of medicine requires professional norms, market competition, and governmental regulation.

Mechanic (1994) calls for both state and federal regulation of managed care. Ginzberg and Ostow (1997) call for regulatory control in managed care to protect patients. Zwanziger and Melnick (1996) cite the need for a governmental role to ensure competition in health services markets but also to ensure that access to and quality of care are not adversely affected in managed care plans.

Cost Containment Under Managed Care

A primary motivation in the development of managed care was to contain costs of and expenditures for health services. What does the evidence show? The following list summarizes the findings, but many of the findings are specific to a particular type of managed care organization, principally the PGP-type:

- In a study of managed care in California, Robinson (1996) found that hospital expenditures grew 44 percent less rapidly in markets with high HMO penetration between 1983 and 1993.
- During the period 1985–1993, hospitals in areas with high rates of HMO penetration and growth had a slower rate of growth in expenses than hospitals in low-penetration areas (Gaskin and Hadley 1997).
- Zwanziger and Melnick's (1996) study of managed care in California and Minnesota concluded that managed care appeared to have controlled costs.
- Managed care has reduced spending by reducing services to patients, providing services more efficiently, and squeezing incomes of physicians and other providers (Fuchs 1997).
- HMOs in areas with more competitors have lower premiums than HMOs established in less competitive areas (Feldman et al. 1996).
- Managed care growth in the 1980s led to a slowing of expenditures in the early 1990s, but whether this slowing is a one-time event or the beginning of a trend is not clear (Ginzberg and Oster 1997).
- Selective contracting with providers (i.e., permitting only those who meet certain standards to provide care to defined populations) is an effective cost-containing strategy (Drake 1997).
- A study of managed care plan performance found that compared with indemnity plans, HMOs had somewhat lower hospital admission rates and shorter lengths of stay and used fewer expensive procedures and tests (Miller and Luft 1994).

The effects of managed care on costs and expenditures will continue to be examined as one of the most significant questions about the U.S. health services delivery system.

SUMMARY

The shift from a fee-for-service to a managed care delivery system continues to substantially affect all participants. Physicians and other providers are required to practice in new ways and some are experiencing declining incomes; their satisfaction levels with these changes remain mixed. Hospitals and other facilities are experiencing changes as downsizing and other reductions in capacity occur. Payors for health services are exerting greater influence on how the delivery system is shaped. Consumers are also accommodating to changes in the traditional ways in which they have sought and obtained care. The extent of change indicates that the system has not yet reached equilibrium.

NOTES

1. The concern about organizations too big to fail is not without foundation. In the early 1970s in California, a number of managed care organizations were created—at least on paper—to serve the Medi-Cal (Medicaid) population. When these organizations were unable to meet their service commitments, state government had to step in to ensure care for this population. This debate stimulated federal governmental regulations as part of the 1976 HMO amendments that prohibited any HMO's enrollment of Medicaid enrollees or Medicare beneficiaries to exceed 50 percent of total enrollment. This proportion was revised upward to 75 percent by the provisions of the 1981 OBRA.
2. Under Medicare's initial authority for paying HMOs for care to Medicare beneficiaries, HMOs could choose a risk option, which limited their profit potential and made them fully responsible for losses, or a cost-based option. The risk option had little appeal to providers, and the cost-based option lacked strong financial incentives to reduce unnecessary care and to deliver care efficiently. Consequently, a 1982 legislative change, which established a fixed monthly payment—the AAPCC rate—made Medicare risk contracts more attractive to providers (USGAO, 1997).

REFERENCES

Buchanan, J., P. A. Lindsey, A. Leibowitz, et al. 1992. "HMOs for Medicaid: The Road to Financial Independence Is Often Poorly Paved." *Journal of Health Politics, Policy and Law* 17 (1): 71–96.

Collins, K. S., C. Schoen, and D. R. Sandman. 1997. *The Commonwealth Fund Survey of Physicians' Experiences with Managed Care*. New York: The Commonwealth Fund.

The Commonwealth Fund. 1996. *Health Care Coverage and Access Program*. New York: The Commonwealth Fund.

———.1995. *Managed Care: The Patient's Perspective*. New York: The Commonwealth Fund.

Cunningham, R. 1997a. "Clinton Cuts a Threat to Growth of Medicare HMOs?" *Medicine and Health* 51 (4).

———1997b. "Hybrids Take Center Stage as New Phase in Cost War Looms." *Medicine and Health* 51 (14).

———1996. "Will For-Profit Trend Hold up as HMO Mergers Decline?" *Medicine and Health* 50 (46).

Davis K., C. Schoen, and D. R. Sandman. 1996. "The Culture of Managed Care: Implications for Patients." *Bulletin of the New York Academy of Medicine* 73 (1): 173–83.

Drake, D. F. 1997. "Managed Care: A Product of Market Dynamics." *Journal of the American Medical Association*. 227 (7): 560–3.

Ellwood, P. M., and G. D. Lundberg. 1996. "Managed Care: A Work in Progress." *Journal of the American Medical Association* 276 (13): 1083–6.

Enthoven, A. C. 1993a. "The History and Principles of Managed Competition." *Health Affairs* 12 (Supplement): 24–48.

———1993b. "Why Managed Care Has Failed to Contain Health Costs." *Health Affairs* 12 (3): 27–43.

Etheredge, L., and S. B. Jones. 1997. "Consumers, Gag Rules, and Health Plans: Strategies for a Patient-Focused Market." *Research Agenda Brief.* Washington, DC: The George Washington University.

Feldman R., D. Wholey, and J. Christianson. 1996. "Economic and Organizational Determinants of HMO Mergers and Failures." *Inquiry* 33 (2): 118–32.

Feldman, R., J. Kralewski, and B. Dowd. 1989. "Health Maintenance Organizations: The Beginning or the End?" *Health Services Research* 24 (2): 191–211.

Fuchs, V. R. 1997. "Managed Care and Merger Mania." *Journal of the American Medical Association*. 277 (11): 920–1.

Gaskin, D. J., and J. Hadley. 1997. "The Impact of HMO Penetration on Hospital Cost Inflation, 1985-1993." *Inquiry* 34 (3): 205–16.

Ginzberg, E. and M. Ostow. 1997. "Managed Care—A Look Back and a Look Ahead." *New England Journal of Medicine* 336 (14): 1018–20.

Grogan, C. M. 1997. "The Medicaid Managed Care Policy Consensus for Welfare Recipients: A Reflection of Traditional Welfare Concerns." *Journal of Health Politics, Policy and Law* 23 (3): 815–38.

Health Care Financing Administration. 1997. *Medicare Prepaid Health Plans Monthly Report.* Baltimore, MD: HCFA.

Health Care Financing Administration.1994. *Medicare Prepaid Health Plans Monthly Report.* Baltimore, MD: HCFA.

Hellinger, F. J. 1995. "Selection Bias in HMOs and PPOs: A Review of the Evidence." *Inquiry* 32 (2): 135–42.

Jensen G. A., M. A. Morrisey, S. Gaffney, et al. 1997. "New Dominance of Managed Care: Insurance Trends in the 1990s." *Health Affairs* 16 (1): 125–36.

Kane N. M., N. C. Turnbull, and C. Schoen. 1996. *Markets and Plan Performance: Summary Reports on Case Studies of IPA and Network HMOs.* New York: The Commonwealth Fund.

Kassirer, J. P. 1997. "Is Managed Care Here to Stay?" *New England Journal of Medicine* 336 (14): 1013–14.

Kassirer, J. P. 1995. "Managed Care and the Morality of the Marketplace." *New England Journal of Medicine* 333 (1): 50–52.

Lawrence, D. M., P. H. Mattingly, and J. M. Ludden. 1997. "Trusting in the Future: The Distinct Advantage of Nonprofit HMOs." *Milbank Quarterly* 75 (1): 5–10.

Mechanic, D. 1994. "Managed Care: Rhetoric and Realities." *Inquiry* 31 (2):124–8.

Miller, R. H., and H. S. Luft. 1994. "Managed Care Plan Performance Since 1980." *Journal of the American Medical Association* 271 (19): 1512–19.

National Health Policy Forum. 1997. *The Medicare Risk Contract Game: What Rules Should PSOs Play By?* Issue Brief No. 702. Washington, DC: The George Washington University..

———1996. *Trends in Health Network Development: Community and Provider Incentives in a Managed Care Environment.* Issue Brief No. 690. Washington, DC: The George Washington University.

Nelson, R., R. Brown, M. Gold, et al. 1997. "Access to Care in Medicare HMOs, 1996." *Health Affairs* 16 (2): 148–56.

Peterson, M. A. 1997. "Introduction: Health Care into the Next Century." *Journal of Health Politics, Policy, and Law* 22 (2): 29–34.

Reichard, J. (Ed.) 1997. "Briefly This Week." *Medicine and Health* 50 (37): 4.

Robinson, J. C. 1996. "Decline in Hospital Utilization and Cost Inflation under Managed Care in California." *Journal of the American Medical Association*. 276 (13) 1060–4.

Robinson, J. C., and L. P. Casalino. 1996. "Vertical Integration and Organizational Networks in Health Care." *Health Affairs* 15 (1): 7–22.

Robinson, J. C., and L. B. Gardner. 1995. "Adverse Selection among Multiple Competing Health Maintenance Organizations." *Medical Care* 33 (12): 1161–75.

Schlesinger, M. 1997. "Countervailing Agency: A Strategy of Principled Regulation under Managed Competition." *Milbank Quarterly* 75 (1): 35–87.

Schlesinger, M. J., B. H. Gray, and K. M. Perreira. 1997. "Medical Professionalism under Managed Care: The Pros and Cons of Utilization Review." *Health Affairs* 16 (1): 106–24.

Shortell, S. M., R. R. Gillies, et al. 1993. "Creating Organized Delivery Systems: The Barriers and the Facilitators." *Hospital & Health Services Administration* 38 (4): 447–466.

Stauffer, M. 1997. *Point of Service.* Washington, DC: National Conference of State Legislatures, Policy Training Service.

U.S. General Accounting Office. 1997 *Medicare HMO Enrollment: Area Differences Affected by Other Than Payment Rates.* Washington, DC: USGAO. GAO/HEHS-97-37.

———. 1996. *Medicaid Managed Care: Challenge of Holding Plans Accountable Requires Greater State Effort.* Washington, DC: USGAO. GAO/HEHS-97-86.

Weiner, J. P., and G. De Lissovoy. 1993. "Razing a Tower of Babel: A Taxonomy for Managed Care and Health Insurance Plans." *Journal of Health Politics, Policy, and Law* 18 (1): 75–103.

Woolhandler, S., and D. U. Himmelstein. 1995. "Extreme Risk—The New Corporate Proposition for Physicians." *New England Journal of Medicine* 333 (25): 1706–8.

Zwanziger, J., and G. A. Melnick. 1996. "Can Managed Care Plans Control Health Care Costs?" *Health Affairs* 15 (2): 185–99.

CHAPTER

3

Managed Care Mythology: Supply-Side Dreams Die Hard

Jeff C. Goldsmith and Michael J. Goran

As managed care gains increasing influence over the American health financing system, economic pressures and emerging market realities have created a fertile climate for wishful thinking on the part of hospital executives and physicians. Rather than accept the inevitability of reducing excess capacity and incomes, providers cling to self-serving myths about managed care's strategic direction. Here are five of these myths along with their contrasting market realities.

MYTH 1. INTEGRATED DELIVERY SYSTEMS WILL DOMINATE THE MANAGED CARE MARKETPLACE.

There is a remarkable unanimity of opinion, particularly among multihospital system executives, that future regional healthcare markets will be controlled by a handful of integrated delivery systems that offer a broad-spectrum, closed-panel menu of physician, hospital, and community-based health services for a fixed price. Indeed, this was the Ellwood/Enthoven vision of the end state of managed competition: multiple closed-panel integrated health enterprises competing for enrollment.

This belief has led to an unprecedented volume of mergers, consolidations, and physician practice acquisitions as systems position themselves to emulate the classic, closed-panel entities like Kaiser or the Group Health Cooperatives.

Reprinted with permission from *Health Forum,* (Nov/Dec) 1996: 42–47.

The reality is that employers and consumers are asking the healthcare system for something very different: a seemingly incongruous mixture of broad choice and economic discipline. Employers and consumers are profoundly reluctant to disrupt long-standing relationships with physicians and hospitals that have met their needs in the past.

The over-supply of hospital beds and specialty services, and the resultant provider panic at the bargaining table, has enabled IPA and network style plans—and even PPOs in many cases—to offer the amenities of fee-for-service medicine at HMO prices. As a result, the growth in health plan enrollment has bypassed the closed-panel plans.

Consumers and health plans simply do not gain economic or qualitative advantage by selecting provider-packaged services from a closed panel. Many traditional group- and staff-model health plans find themselves in the anomalous position of being three down to their broader-based competitors: They are (1) more costly, (2) less convenient, and (3) offer poorer service. As a result, enrollment in closed-panel plans peaked in 1989, and has since fallen significantly (see Figure 3.1).

The pressure toward broad, inclusive networks has been so intense as to force the historically closed systems like Kaiser and Group Health to build point-of-service network relationships with the private practicing cohort of the physician community (against which they have competed for three generations!). These "partnerships" have stimulated bitter dissension among

Figure 3.1 Total Staff- and Group-Model HMO Enrollment

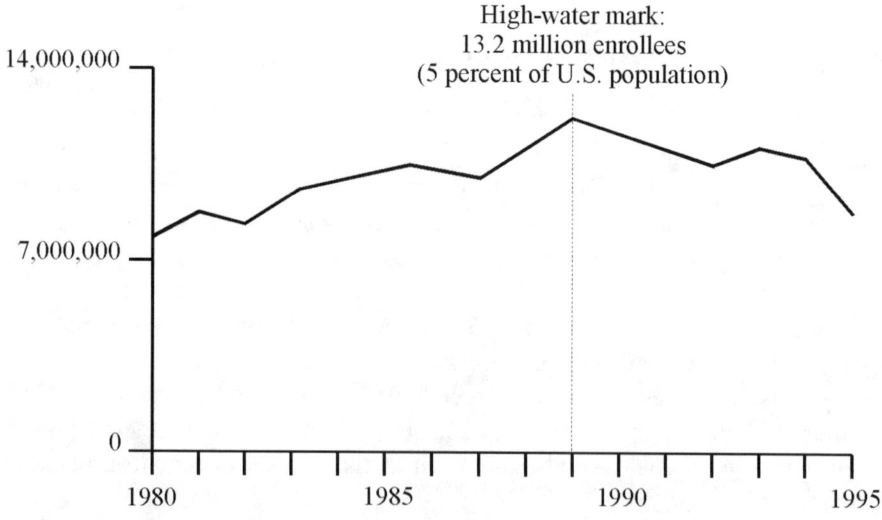

Published with permission from The InterStudy Edge.

the traditional group- and staff-model physicians, who viewed participating in the managed care movement as a "just cause."

The imperative to attack the physician cost and productivity problem has led traditionally closed-panel plans to make dramatic departures from their historical strategies. FHP and CIGNA, both mixed-model health plans, recently spun off their staff-model physician clinic systems in the West (and, in FHP's case, their owned hospitals, as well), citing unacceptably high fixed costs and poor productivity. For the traditional "prepaid group practice" plans like Kaiser and Group Health, improving physician productivity and responsiveness has become the central management challenge.

On the hospital side, the marginal cost of an inpatient day has fallen to the point where having "captive" hospitals within a health plan no longer makes economic sense. Kaiser has decided to close its Bess Kaiser Hospital in Portland, Oregon rather than replace it, and to contract with rival systems, the Sisters of Providence and the Legacy Health System, to hospitalize its north Portland patients. Kaiser has also decided to close, rather than replace, several of its San Francisco area hospitals and to contract with community hospitals for inpatient care.

For many years, the conventional wisdom in the managed care world has been that closed-panel group- or staff-model health plans were the "end state" in the evolution of health systems. The economic realities of the Nineties have led to a different conclusion: Closed-panel "integrated" plans may be dinosaurs incapable of competing in an increasingly cost- and access-conscious healthcare marketplace. The decline in market share and profitability of closed-panel plans is not temporary; rather, it reflects fundamental defects in the strategy.

An important implication of this market reality is that most of the tremendous expenditure of funds or energy by providers in creating new closed-panel entities—through mergers, practice acquisitions, and physician-hospital organization development—seems likely to be wasted. Those systems burdened with high acquisition costs or increased debt will find themselves struggling to operate profitably in a tightening healthcare market.

Major re-engineering of clinical and management systems will be required to salvage the positions of the long-established "integrated" organizations. Evaluating the economics of the "make or buy" tradeoff for each component of a system's product will be a management imperative for the vertically integrated system. Selective "disintegration" through outsourcing and creation of internal competition between provider panels within broad networks will be the ultimate management response to the disabilities of asset- and employment-based systems.

MYTH 2. HEALTH PLANS FEAR DIRECT CONTRACTING BY PROVIDERS AS A COMPETITIVE THREAT TO THEIR BUSINESS.

Providers believe that employers are eager to bypass health insurers and contract directly with providers. Hospitals and physicians look hungrily at the difference between premiums and medical expense as either pure profit or waste, and believe that by cutting out the middlemen, they could pay themselves more generously that current market rates and reduce irritating oversight of their activities. In this comforting vision, health plans simply melt away, and provider systems and business groups contract directly with one another on an at-risk basis.

The reality is less comforting: Most employers continue to view health plans as effective counterweights to provider economic interests and as market consolidators and simplifiers. It is difficult for employers who blamed hospitals and doctors for the massive run-up in their health costs during the Eighties to believe that providers have had a "religious" experience and are now wholeheartedly in the cost-containment business.

The lack of provider credibility in this arena has had visible market consequences: the nearly universal lack of success of physician-hospital organizations in direct contracting with employers (or even with health plans, for that matter). As long as event-driven (e.g., per admission or per procedure) payment for health services remains the principal payment methodology (see Myth 4), provider incentives remain linked to generating more volume and cost, and employers will continue to view health plans as bulwarks against future health cost inflation. While some health plans may explore "administrative services only" relationships with a few well-organized provider systems, the likelihood is that employers will continue to rely upon health plans to organize and discipline the medical market. Direct contracting may succeed in a few places, but for most providers, it will remain only a tantalizing mirage that distracts them from the less glamorous but necessary task of putting their own houses in order, and learning how to be profitable, high-quality vendors of health services.

MYTH 3. MANAGED CARE IS A HIGHLY PROFITABLE, LOW-RISK BUSINESS.

Many providers characterize insurers as simply packagers of providers' services, laying vitually all the risk of future cost increases off onto providers through capitation, and then pocketing the huge differences between premium and cost. While this may describe some health plan strategies, many health plans decline to share risk with providers, relying instead on their bargaining power and external utilization controls to contain cost (please see Myth 4).

Health plan executives also have long memories; they remember that underwriting medical risk is a brutally cyclical business. During the last "bottoming" of the underwriting cycle in 1986–87, health insurers—HMOs included—lost billions of dollars. Despite record profits during the early Nineties, the next three years will see narrowing or vanishing profits in health insurance, and serious cash-flow problems for overextended plans. Providers need to remember that bearing risk has a downside, and that it is possible to drown in a river that is on the average only a foot deep.

Historically, HMO operating margins have averaged around 5 percent across the underwriting cycle (though there remains great dispersion around this average depending on plan underwriting and enrollment strategies).

The rest of the difference between premium and medical expense consists of working capital, the cost of reinsurance, broker commissions, customer service/claims management, and marketing. The latter functions are not only a bloody nuisance and poorly automated, but areas where providers have been, if anything, even more inept than most insurers. How many hospitals can yet generate an intelligible bill, or "interface" with customers on medical claims without infuriating them?

Yet, the lure of "owning the premium" has attracted an increasing number of provider groups, even Columbia/HCA, to enter the health insurance business. It would be difficult to think of a worse time to enter the health insurance market than today: when health insurance is on the downcurve of the underwriting cycle.

Health insurers cannot raise rates even to cover modest cost inflation for most of their group insurance customers. In many health insurance markets, rampant price cutting is the order of the day. And most health plan managers understand that the systems they have in place will not adequately protect them against the next, inevitable upsurge in medical expense. Finally, health plans are politically vulnerable if they run very low medical loss ratios for a sustained period, because the loss ratio is an alluring regulatory target.

Middlemen exist in markets for a reason: to matrix with a highly fragmented customer base and to cushion the variability in product expense. Neither the fragmentation nor the variability seems likely to disappear in the foreseeable future.

MYTH 4. CAPITATION WILL BE THE DOMINANT OR EXCLUSIVE FORM OF PROVIDER PAYMENT IN THE FUTURE.

This is a major current topic for debate in the managed care community. The nature and amount of risk sharing in health plan contracting varies significantly from region to region around the country. For much of the

South and East, managed care payment is still event-driven (for example, fee-for-service with withholds for physicians and per diem or per case for hospitals).

Many health plans see little reason ever to share risk and premium with hospitals or hospital systems, since physicians control hospital use decisions. There is profound philosophical division among health plan managers over whether and how to share risk even with physicians. Some plan managers anticipate moving to a protocol-driven framework for managing cost, while continuing to pay physicians on a fee basis. Other plan managers, particularly those with long-term successful relationships with IPAs or medical groups, are more willing to share risk with physicians.

Now, however, with increasing numbers of high-risk patients from the Medicaid and Medicare programs entering health plans, there are the beginnings of a backlash against capitating the primary-care physician (see Myth 5), instead keeping the risk as the group level. Increasing questions are raised about how much control primary-care physicians can or should exert over specialty use decisions.

Capitating specialists appears to provide health plans more leverage for controlling procedure volume and hospitalization rates, particularly in broad-based plans that can rely on competition between panels of specialists for primary-care referrals or patient-directed choice. By carving out capitated niches along specialty lines, however, health plans run the risk of unacceptable fragmentation of patient experience. The whole patient seems likely to be far greater than the sum of the carved out parts, and coordination and communication problems may ultimately doom this approach.

The reality is that no one has yet devised a method for paying physicians that will optimize clinical effectiveness. Capitating the individual physician and capitating the hospital will probably not be the mechanisms of choice for paying providers in the future. In the final analysis, risk will probably devolve from health plans to broad-based physician entities, and then be suballocated to physician/nonphysician teams based on acuity of illness or patient demography. Hospitals will have to learn to make money and deliver effective care on a per diem or per case basis.

MYTH 5. PRIMARY-CARE PHYSICIANS WILL FUNCTION AS INCENTED GATEKEEPERS FOR THE HEALTH SYSTEM.

Many health plans presently require their subscribers to select a primary-care physician who will function as a "gatekeeper" for their use of health services. The health plan then creates incentives from the primary-care physician to minimize healthcare use, particularly hospitalization and consultation with medical and surgical subspecialists.

The current view is that having your own network of primary-care physicians to function as gatekeepers for enrolled populations is the key variable in determining the success of the health plan.

Yet consider the following situations and ask yourself how helpful the gatekeeper model is likely to be in producing a good outcome.

- A 32-year-old female who has recently experienced debilitating episodes of fatigue and depression. She eats only irregularly and has lost weight. She lacks the energy to maintain her professional career, take care of her two young children, and keep her marriage together.
- An 18-year-old male who is comatose in a hospital ICU as the result of a motorcycle accident.
- A 45-year-old male at the pinnacle of his professional career who has a father with Alzheimer's disease in a nursing home, is divorced, and maintains joint custody of his two teenage children. He is stressed out, unhappy with his job, and unable to manage financially the transition to a new job or career. He is drinking too much, is overweight, and at a recent physical exam was found to have hypertension, an irregular heartbeat, and an abnormal stress test.
- A 24-year-old female who has debilitating rheumatoid arthritis, frequent attacks of asthma, and appears to be diabetic.
- A 74-year-old female who has chronic depression, low blood pressure leading to fainting spells, periodic recurring upper respiratory infections, and osteoporosis. During the past six months, she has been hospitalized for pneumonia, a hip fracture, and a possible stroke. She calls her primary-care physician's office at least twice a day seeking help or advice on her problems, both medical and non-medical.

Conceivably, several of these situations could be handled by a competent general internist, but the economic pressure to minimize specialty consultation would probably result in suboptimal care for the patients with multiple symptoms. Results would probably be better in several of these instances if the appropriate subspecialist assumed the role of "attending physician." In other instances, the need for a less expensive point of contact between the patient or family than a physician is obvious.

It is ironic that America has spent many billions of dollars creating the knowledge framework of subspecialty competence, and now is spending billions more to prevent physicians from using their knowledge. What is missing is an appropriate and agreed-upon division of labor between primary care and specialty care for given medical problems.

Arriving at a consensus on this issue has been complicated by the politization of relations between these important and interdependent branches of medicine. Huge income inequality between primary-care and specialty physicians has lent a "class warfare" quality to physician relationships, which health plans have exploited.

The central issue in managing care should be making sure that the fit between patient problems and clinical resources is both optimal and dynamic, and that communication among physicians and others with differing clinical competencies and knowledge is improved. Polarizing relationships between primary-care physicians and specialists via gatekeeper systems will not achieve either goal.

This issue will become more important as more poor and elderly patients enter the managed care risk pool. Effective care for the multi-functionally impaired, chronically ill elderly should be team-based. The team leader may not even be a physician, but a professional care manager. With the Medicaid population, one-third of whom are now enrolled in managed care plans, there is a similar need for a seamless blending of medical and social/human services.

Finally, in life-threatening crises, the primary-care gatekeeper is simply an administrative headache for the critical-care team charged with saving the patient's life.

As managed care plans better understand the constellation of health risk in their pools, they will develop a more sophisticated method of matching clinical needs to appropriate health resources than a single, predetermined primary-care physician.

Even for the largely well or worried well populations, a system that relies solely upon a physician as the principal contact point may not be either the cost-effective or patient-friendly solution. Multiple patient pathways and staffing approaches will be required depending on the acuity of patient needs. Dr. Sidney Garfield, the visionary founder of the Kaiser Health Plans, anticipated such a multi-path approach in a remarkable article that appeared in *Scientific American* in 1970 (see Figure 3.2).

Health plans that base their clinical architecture on a primary-care gatekeeper, or for that matter on an all-physician clinical system, may find that the rigidity of this approach will cost them both dollars and lost subscribers.

In this problem may lie the seeds of comparative advantage for physician systems with strong enough governance to managed the increased use of nonphysician caregivers and care managers. This will be a very difficult transition for network-style health plans and hospital systems with large numbers of private practicing physicians. The fragmentation of private medical practice will provide a window of market opportunities for health plan or care systems that can re-engineer the patient's pathway through the system, and create systems that manage clinical risk before illness strikes.

Figure 3.2 Multiple Patient Pathways for Optimal Outcomes

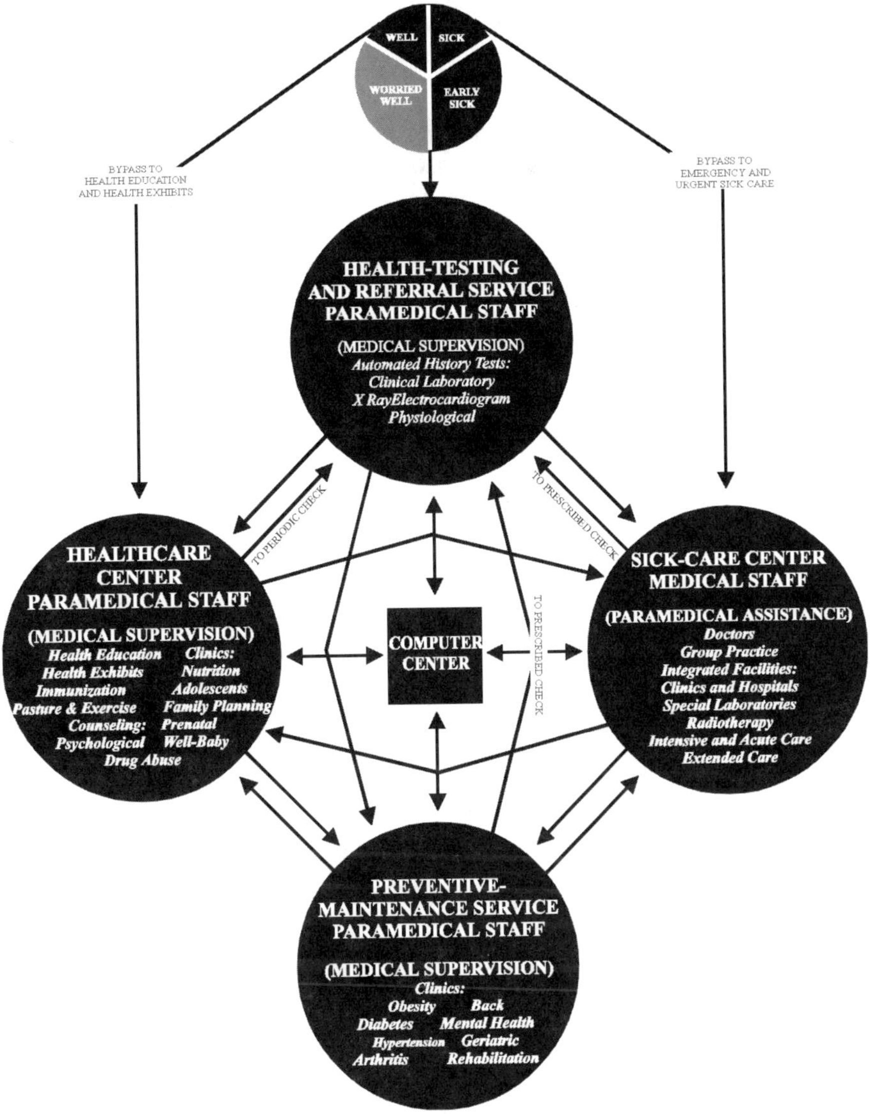

Printed with permission from "The Delivery of Medical Care," by Sidney R. Garfield. Copyright © April 1970 by Scientific American, Inc. All rights reserved.

Careful examination of the reality behind each of these five myths casts doubt on the vision of a future medical marketplace as a zero-sum contest between closed-panel enterprises. The emerging market appears to be a more complex melding of collaborating and competing enterprises and exciting, more responsive models of care. Provider organizations will learn painfully that understanding and leveraging their core competencies is a more reliable strategy over the long term that seeking to aggrandize control over patients.

We continue to believe that physician-directed enterprises capable of bearing and managing risk have a very bright future. Acquiring these competencies and developing strategic partnerships among hospitals, health plans, and accountable physician entities will be essential as managed care continues to grow.

CHAPTER

4

Managed Care at a Glance

Kyle L. Grazier

The issues involved in managing care are so diverse and complex that even a seasoned healthcare professional can easily get overwhelmed. Confronted with the breadth of factors involved—from underwriting to medical management—a healthcare manager looking for knowledge about managed care might be unsure where to turn first. Having chosen an area to study, a manager might easily get drawn into a highly nuanced study at the expense of learning about other equally important areas.

This chapter of *Managed Care Essentials* is designed to give readers ready insight into the most salient issues related to healthcare delivery in a managed care environment. Each section offers a concise look at the given issue. In the aggregate this chapter should help a reader to be conversant in most of the key challenges that a provider or payer would face associated with managed care.

The sections that follow, which are drawn from columns published in the *Journal of Healthcare Management*, cover risk management, provider profiling, behavioral health and managed care, the chronically ill and managed care, physician contracting, and collaboration for improved quality.—The Editors

Reprinted from *Journal of Healthcare Management*, vols 43 and 44.
Chicago: Health Administration Press.

MANAGING RISKS IN MANAGED CARE

Being a manager in a healthcare organization is probably not listed on the underwriters' list of riskiest jobs. But given the risks that healthcare managers face on a daily basis, maybe it should be. There is business risk, financial risk, investment risk, interest-rate risk—not to mention the potential nosocomial infections arising from working in a health services facility. Managed care is premised on the belief that the assumption of some forms of risk results in efficiency and social benefit. Capitation for all care, in combination with utilization management, should encourage the on-budget, appropriate use of beneficial services by the right type of provider for the right type of patient. But understanding the population and predicting future medical expenses are, of course, major challenges. In addition, assuming risk for behaviors outside a plan's control may not be efficient, wise, or result in better health.

The decision to bear the financial risk associated with health services delivery should be informed by a knowledge of the health status and health behaviors of a population, as well as by an understanding of how providers deliver healthcare and respond to payment. How can a healthcare organization that provides capitated services, or contracts with entities that do so, be so all knowing, and if they cannot, how can they hedge their bets? How can they be paid more for the care provided to individuals likely to consume more resources? How can they reduce the likelihood of adverse selection, improve access, and encourage development and marketing of specialty services?

Current payment systems incorporate little information on the characteristics of potential enrollees and the expected expenses, which leads plans to fear adverse selection and individuals to fear exclusion. Current methods also discourage the development, or at least the advertisement, of some forms of costly or well-recognized specialty care for fear of attracting high-risk and high-cost users to the plan.

Extensive research and demonstration efforts are under way to improve the way in which these types of risks are defined and quantified. Risk adjustment is an attempt to define characteristics of a population and/or its use in such a way as to categorize use and users into homogeneous resource-based groups. These groups differentiate and discriminate among levels of expected costs. The categories can be thought of as risk pools in an actuarial sense, and they can be used as the basis for capitation rates or premiums, to develop new programs, or to profile providers.

Risk adjustment should help in understanding an organization, a community, the users of services, provider behavior, and expected expenses. If done properly, risk adjustment can increase access to services, reduce selection biases, minimize underutilization and overutilization, and help determine reinsurance levels.

Risk assessment and adjustment methodologies most commonly include traditional demographic variables, such as age, gender, and geographic location of the enrollee. Medicare's adjusted average per capita cost (AAPCC), the Health Insurance Plan of California, and some state experiments rely in part on these types of variables to set reimbursement rates for at-risk plans. These features capture the variation in expected use between a 20-year-old male in the city versus a 50-year-old female in an isolated rural area. These demographic descriptors explain some of the variation in expected costs, but not nearly enough. The 50-year-old female with diabetes could easily incur substantially more expenses than another 50-year-old female with no chronic disease. Methodologies that limit risk adjustment to the measurement of demographic variables may miss the real reason behind the resource use.

As a result, several researchers propose that some indicators of disease and/or severity of illness be included in the risk adjustment measure. In addition, they recommend that treatment intensity, due to the type of provider or the method of payment, also be captured. Leading methods base risk adjustment on diagnoses, diagnostic markers, and/or treatment patterns commonly recorded in inpatient and/or outpatient records. These provide additional information beyond the demographics of enrollees to predict the spending in populations.

While they are an improvement, these methodologies, like the current AAPCC, still require compromise. Data are historical, and plans must make assumptions about probabilities of continued use. The data also reflect the source of payment; services received under capitation may differ from those under fee for service both in quantity and type. In calculating expected expenses for a new population, analysts must recognize the benefit features of the plan under which the data on past care and health status were generated—particularly in a new or changing managed care market.

When used as a management tool, risk adjustment must also address issues of administrative simplicity, incentives to "game" the methodology, and the potential volatility of underlying measures. Information systems maintained by employers, providers, and some communities support the collection of timely data. Health assessment and risk adjustment based on clinical data make gaming somewhat more complex. Using historical data in geographic areas undergoing rapid population or healthcare delivery changes can lead to volatility in the underlying indicators for the adjustment. Once again, understanding the source and validity of the data used to build these measures is crucial.

Adequate risk adjustment tools that are used with thoughtfulness can reduce the variation between expected and actual costs for a group. However, there may still be risks that the managed care entity should not assume.

A plan can reasonably expect that some portion of enrollees will incur nonrandom high-cost or catastrophic expenses. Insofar as the risk adjustment methodology accommodates this, the plan may be minimally affected, reducing the incentives for selective enrollment. However, some researchers suggest that if high-cost cases could be identified in advance, their care could be paid for under an actual cost methodology similar to fee for service. This mixed payment method, under which plans are paid on both a capitation and fee-for-service basis for a group of enrollees, reduces further the incentive either to not enroll or to undertreat the high-cost cases. From the manager's perspective, because the risk can't be controlled, it is not assumed, and actual costs for these high-intensity services are compensated. From the enrollee or policymaker's perspective, access to the plans can be maintained, even for the potentially and predictably expensive individuals.

Current studies in risk adjustment should make us better informed about the role of diagnosis, severity of illness or other epidemiological indicators in the prediction of costs of care by individuals and groups. Simulations and demonstrations in mixed-payment systems (in which there is both capitation and actual cost reimbursement) should allow a careful examination of access and quality. Healthcare managers need to keep abreast of these developments to understand enrollees, predict expenses, and minimize negative incentives. Hopefully, the implementation and evaluation of these risk-adjustment and mixed-reimbursement methodologies will lead us to the efficiency and effectiveness expected from managed care, with ultimate improvement in the health of the population.

"PROFILING" MANAGED CARE

Propelled by the quest to understand and to improve the healthcare system, significant progress has been made toward the identification, measurement, and monitoring of clinical outcomes. Some in managed care circles, however, would say that outcomes-related research has overshadowed the importance of examining the processes behind delivering clinical care—in spite of their undeniable contribution to quality. One key component of these processes can be captured through "profiling"—describing how the physician or provider group uses appropriate clinical judgment and resources, for a particular panel of enrollees, within the managed care philosophy and structure.

One traditional avenue toward understanding the processes of healthcare focuses on using administrative data to describe provider behavior. Commonly, attempts to measure behavior in this manner have concentrated on utilization management protocols. Many of these protocols assess the appropriateness of an admission and length of inpatient stay, primarily for medical or surgical conditions, for patients with particular diagnoses and other characteristics. Algorithms such as these for determining allowable inpatient use have long been a part of medical care payment systems, and in some cases are the sole measures used to indicate level of quality of care.

With the implementation of diagnosis-related groups (DRGs), physician profiling as we knew it was used both as a resource monitoring tool and as a feedback mechanism for the provider. Hospital administrators and medical directors were encouraged to use the provider-specific DRG "profiles" as a means to illustrate to physicians if and how their admission and care patterns deviated from the norms within the hospital. DRGs, as a measure of resource use, drove payment levels, but also were the basis for defining the acceptable variations in quality care provided by physicians within the institution. The empirically based, mean levels of resource use became the norm, or gold standard, for cost and behavior.

On the positive side, such models of process review force simple scrutiny of potentially high-cost use. But what these approaches lack is the capability to identify other key components of the provider's behavior that truly affect the quality of, and accountability for, the care delivered. In managed care, in which the provider is responsible and accountable for most or all care, unaddressed issues are related to: (1) the provider's control over which patients present and with what conditions; (2) how to measure the determinants of resource use, including the relative contribution of outpatient versus inpatient services within an episode of care; (3) the validity and reliability of the data sources and measures of risk, behavior, and organizational structure; and (4) the relationship between expected and observed resource use, and the appropriate levels of any variance between the two.

In addressing these issues, clearly the attributes of both the patient and the provider must be recognized. For instance, most providers employed by or under contract with managed care organizations do not select the patients in their panels. They do not control the probability that patients will be high risk, requiring more or specialized resources. They don't control the benefit packages provided by employers to enrollees, allowing access to and coverage of certain services, affecting how frequently or how soon enrollees seek care. Providers also don't control the odds that patients will present with acute, self-limiting conditions, or conditions that, with good quality care, will resolve quickly and without serious sequelae.

What is under their control is how well they diagnose, treat, or prevent the condition, or educate and share important information with the patient (e.g., how quickly insulin therapy is started or how chest pain is treated) after patients contact the system. The key, of course, is to recognize those circumstances and conditions that are under the control of the patient, and those that are under the control of the provider. Once these are recognized, the data must measure those provider behaviors that, when implemented, result in the appropriate resolution of or improvement in the condition. For managed care, an extension of the traditional notion of physician profiling is worth examining.

One goal of profiling in managed care is to recognize the characteristics of the patients and providers that help explain the variation between what is the expected level of resource consumption and what actually occurs. Means to measure the patient mix, or case mix, or to "risk adjust" the panel of enrollees, are being developed both for capitation purposes and for quality assessment. Techniques vary in the selection of indicators to measure, the source of the data used, and the software supporting the analysis. These risk adjusters usually include demographic and clinical data, and some recognize the contribution to resource measurement of services such as outpatient radiology, prescription drugs, and home visits. Most rely on administrative data and, most commonly, on traditional claims systems. Limitations in some of these systems obviate the need for actual medical records or patient questionnaires, in combination with claims or encounter data, to gather patient compliance or functional status measures. These additional measures provide insight into processes of managed care potentially more indicative of quality treatment.

Profiling the risk status of the panel of patients for whom the physician is responsible is but one step, albeit a critical one. How the provider cares for the panel within the structure of the managed care environment is another important aspect of quality, and one for which the provider and plan is accountable. The entire condition-specific, decision-making time period and the managed care organizational structures that support those processes need identification.

Research on measuring the entire episode of care, including the assessment, treatment, and long-term ramifications, has always been complex. Merely defining the episode itself is a challenge for most conditions. Definitions of episodes based on dates of services, time between visits, or packages of procedures and diagnoses are being tested for validity. Some psychiatric disorders and, in general, chronic illnesses, with their periods of remission and exacerbation, make episode identification particularly difficult. The random turnover in enrollee populations, and turnover imposed by annual contracts, often make collection of relevant data for adequate time periods impossible. Piecing together a long episode of inpatient and outpatient care is difficult, but required, so that questions related to the quality of care delivered by the provider can be answered.

Because managed care requires attention to the health of the enrollees and not just the treatment of patients, the contribution of organizational features that affect, for instance, access to care or alternative provision of alternative services, must be factored into the profile. Measuring those organizational features that support or hinder good care processes is necessary (i.e., what role does nurse practitioner support or telephone triage play in the probability of successful care, and how does one control for or accommodate the different managed care techniques in interpreting the profile of successful or unsuccessful resource use by a provider or group?).

Profiling providers is similar to profiling plans. The techniques require recognizing the mix of patients, the standards for quality, and the aspects of selection and treatment that are under the control of the plan, provider, enrollee, and patient. After these attributes are measured, how does one determine what is significant variation from the norm or the expected? How likely are false negatives or false positives in the determination of aberrant resource use or quality-related behaviors, and what is their significance? Do ways exist to improve measurement and to reduce the error in interpretation, such as by expanding the sampling frame across several managed care groups, or by reducing it to specific provider specialties or specific markets?

The attraction of consumers, managers, and policymakers to "report cards" for plans and to "profiling" for providers must be balanced by the recognition of limitations in the art and science of medicine, the availability of quality data, and the sophistication of the research methodology and statistical analysis. Efforts at theory-driven, empirically based research on risk adjustment, organizational assessment, and resource measurement are under way. Managed care organizations and providers must insist that the "process" of care is not neglected. They must maintain their involvement in the collaborative work of developing, testing, and critiquing these methodologies to insure their appropriate and timely implementation in the managed care field.

MANAGING BEHAVIORAL HEALTH

There was a time, not too long ago, when psychotherapy and most other mental health services were considered uninsurable. The possibility of mental health service overuse because of insurance coverage was thought to overshadow the benefit that arises from spreading the risk of substantial medical expense. For years, the analysis of the tradeoffs between risk spreading and appropriate incentives favored and resulted in considerable consumer cost sharing for mental health services. The discussion seldom rose to the level of benefit expansion, let alone utilization management; rather, it tended to focus on whether the basic principles of insurability used by the industry could apply to this poorly understood field.

By the early 1980s, through the efforts of several stakeholders and researchers, economic and clinical studies established that benefits could and should be provided, from an actuarial, medical, and public policy perspective. Before long, many employers included mental health benefits as part of their indemnity packages. This coverage often was included as part of overall medical care coverage, subject to deductibles and copayment for service use, but usually was accompanied by lower annual, lifetime, or per-case levels of benefits than was traditional coverage of medical care.

Although some parties viewed the substandard levels of benefits for mental health as a disgrace, others saw this expansion of insurance coverage as supporting the holistic view of health and healthcare, with both physical and psychological components. For instance, this model of personal healthcare allowed and financed the treatment of depression by primary care physicians in their offices. For persons concerned with the chronically ill, children with behavioral needs, or the severely mentally ill, this coverage was seen as supporting a comprehensive approach to care, as well as providing a potential reduction in the financial barriers to appropriate care.

Others viewed this new model as economically induced medicalization of mental disorders, promoting a procedural focus that encouraged inappropriate admissions to inpatient units, while ambulatory, family-based, integrated care was in order. Research showed that patients with indemnity coverage had lengths of stay commensurate with the days covered in their insurance policies. Public mental health systems, including community mental health centers, saw increases in the numbers of employed patients receiving care. The criminal justice system became the de facto mental health system in many rural areas, where geographic distances precluded access to clinics or emergency rooms. It seemed that the private mental health care system, although perhaps improved for some, was inaccessible for many who required long-term, comprehensive, complex care. By the late 1980s and early 1990s, both private employers and state health systems saw cost-increase rates for inpatient mental health services that far exceeded those of traditional medical care.

By the early 1990s, as managed care made inroads into the financing and provision of medical care, alternative models for organizing, managing, and funding mental health care again gained attention.

Several approaches to managing mental health care have gathered momentum at varying rates in the public and private sectors. Case management, in which an individual organizes all care for the user, is a model that has been in existence for some time but that for many reasons has not been universally embraced. Total care/life models, in which social, family, housing, medical, and mental health care needs are addressed and managed by an entity, looked promising in effectiveness but were economically worrisome. The special attention commanded by mental health advocates and the expense of services to managed care organizations, employers, and state mental health departments have in some cases resulted in separate budget mechanisms. These mechanisms focus attention on budgetary line items for mental health recipients and services and make explicit the policy implications of budgetary decisions.

A new alternative model that has seen rapid expansion in both the private and public sectors is the mental health carve out. In behavioral health management, as this field has come to be known, a specialty organization or vendor assumes the responsibility for identifying a network of mental health providers, establishing a mechanism for accessing those providers, and providing varying levels of utilization management. Goals of increasing access and controlling cost of high-quality services generally parallel those of the managed care industry. A point-of-service arrangement is often in place, under which the user can decide, at the time services are required, whether to use the network. Economic incentives usually allow for a reduced price to the consumer when network providers are used. Types of enrollees and services under contract can differ across purchasers. Different contracts can be written for adults, children, or adolescents, or for the actively employed or retired. Services can include mental health care and substance abuse treatment, inpatient day treatment, or specialty residential care.

Carve-out models differ in the extent to which they share the risk of the expenses associated with services utilization. Many carve outs operate within an administrative services only (ASO) arrangement with the purchaser, in which the vendor is paid an administrative fee based on the number of covered lives. Recently, an increasing proportion of contracts written between private employers and carve-out companies include a shared-risk arrangement, in which a target level of use or expenditure is negotiated, and the financial burden of not adhering to the target is shared between vendor and employer.

An additional level of risk sharing is only recently coming into focus. This risk sharing relates to the relationship between the vendor and the providers in the network. Most commonly, the purchaser, such as the state or employer, contracts with the vendor and shares risk, but the vendor pays providers on a negotiated discount from the typical fee. The next wave of change in the behavioral management industry is likely to reveal an increasing number of providers sharing risk with the vendor. In addition, as seen in the general managed care market, there will be growth in the number of direct contracts between purchasers and providers, without relying on an intermediary.

The managed behavioral health industry is growing rapidly and consolidating quickly. According to industry statistics, over 60 percent of the U.S. population is enrolled in a managed behavioral health plan. The majority of states have already carved out mental health benefits from regular benefits for their Medicaid programs, or are in the process of doing so. Last year, Iglehart reported that ten firms covered between 80 and 90 percent of the managed behavioral health market. Recent statistics show that the four largest firms control 60 percent of the market. Industry newsletters recommend that vendors become providers of care and the backbones of mental health delivery for integrated delivery systems. These trends, in combination with increased risk sharing and capitation arrangements by carve-out vendors, are likely to lead to additional changes in the mental health services delivery and financing system.

Not all employers and other purchasers have accepted the inevitability of separate mental health benefit design and provision. In response to employee demand, some companies are "carving back in" their mental health benefits. It remains to be seen whether this approach is the beginning of a trend or an anomaly.

The next phase in the organization and financing of mental health care will be market-driven, will depend on the results of ongoing research, or will result from some combination of the two. Current research is analyzing the early phases of public sector managed behavioral health arrangements in Massachusetts, Utah, Colorado, and elsewhere. Relatively consistent is the finding that after a carve-out there are decreases in inpatient use and costs, via reduced admissions and lengths of stay, as well as reduced emergency department use. Although results are mixed on the outpatient side, most researchers report increases in numbers of people using outpatient mental health services, accompanied by fewer visits per user. In studies of the implementation of carve outs in the private sector, similar overall results have been reported, although it is challenging to isolate the effects of the carve out from the effects of other benefit changes faced by employees.

Research in behavioral health is known to be difficult. Because studies rely on analysis of use, cost, and quality data, consolidations among employers or mergers among vendors can slow considerably the acquisition of valid, reliable information. Because behavioral health arrangements are embodied in contracts, the product being offered can vary immensely, compromising generalizations across studies. In addition, the effects of major changes in financing and delivery, such as those seen in models like the carve-out model, are likely to manifest themselves differently over time. Longitudinal study of the observed changes in use and cost is necessary; the effects of enhanced-quality or reduced-quality mental health care may not be observable in the very near term.

Important research is under way on this first decade of behavioral health management. Use and cost studies outpace studies measuring important dimensions of quality or the effects of varying risk sharing among purchasers, vendors, and providers. Managers need to assist in understanding the contract process, in providing data, and in interpreting results. They need to examine carefully whether incentives are aligned among providers, consumers, and purchasers. Most importantly, managers need to contribute actively to the discourse on whether the current models of managed behavioral health contribute to a remedy for the fundamental flaws in the healthcare system, as we have believed managed care does.

THE CHRONICALLY ILL AND MANAGED CARE

Managed care institutions differ in their structures and strategies, but their organizational missions consistently include the improvement of community health. Despite this avowed mission, it is increasingly evident that this vital goal remains unmet for certain segments of the communities served. "Vulnerable" populations with "special needs" by definition require special attention. Patients and their families, regulators, insurers, and researchers are recognizing the importance of better serving these special groups. Those responsible for quality improvement, risk adjustment, and outcomes assessment are realizing that service to such groups is a critical component of the managed care model.

Chronically ill individuals have long fought the battles and faced the disappointments inherent in the traditional healthcare system. These challenges are well known to include barriers to entering the system, caused by inadequate insurance coverage, extensive travel times to a specialist, lengthy wait times for an appointment, or disinterest by providers. Once these barriers are overcome and the patient is in the system, inadequate treatment often results from delays, discontinuity, inaccessible specialists of choice, cultural incompetence, or the lack of psychosocial support required to cope with symptoms, treatment, and complications.

A focus on special populations benefits not only the afflicted, but also the managed care organization and the community at large. Careful efforts to serve special needs patients can motivate an organization to reexamine basic strategies and operations. The critical importance of data collection, patient education, provider cooperation, and community linkages are highlighted by an analysis of the processes and outcomes of care provided the chronically ill. This analysis presents an opportunity for the organization to evaluate carefully its incentives, communication channels, and delivery system design. Improved healthcare, educational and social system linkages, potential early warnings of disease trends, and increased empowerment, all help accomplish the broad mission of improving community health.

Because the delivery and financing of managed care often parallels the acute care, visit-based, procedural orientation of the fee-for-service sector, challenges remain. However, the organization, governance, and financial incentives of managed care organizations present the potential for innovative approaches and improved quality. The core processes and external interfaces involved in managed care provide natural opportunities throughout the institution's operations to accommodate the unique needs of disadvantaged groups. The characteristics of a group, including age, gender, types and multiplicity of conditions, and prior utilization, must be considered, from the beginning in the early stages of community health assessment and must continue to be a consideration through contract negotiation, service delivery, pricing, and outcomes evaluation. Success of the care management model depends upon the managed care organization's view of itself as a pivotal point within both the healthcare system and the entire community.

Many factors can blur managed care's focus on the health of populations. The boundaries of a chronic illness management program can be constrained by conflicting goals and markets, sources of financing, and research limitations. In reality, the purchaser of care often drives the model, and the perspectives of employers, business coalitions, and other organizations whose members are primarily working enrollees do not necessarily include all the interests of the broader community.

Research on disease management and treatment protocols is developing. Additional research is being conducted on the epidemiology of chronic illness and the measurement of outcomes in the care of the chronically ill. Studies based on individuals in treatment, as well as on community-based populations, are required for results useful to a managed care organization. For those who present for care, it is crucial to have disease management protocols in place. For an organization whose mission is to improve the health of the population, it is equally important to understand the likelihood that enrollees will become patients and the mechanisms that have the potential to slow or prevent that transition. Although a firm's market position and the community's health can both be improved by translating research findings into illness surveillance, prevention, and education efforts, the task can prove uncomfortable and time-consuming for an organization struggling to survive in competitive markets.

Care for the chronically ill requires interactions among many different service organizations with potentially disparate goals, funding sources, and political orientations. Effective mobilization and management of services involve more than adding services to a treatment plan. They require mediating the components of care such as medical treatment, education, psychosocial support, physical rehabilitation, and job training. To the extent that target markets for these service organizations differ, the risks of fragmenting the care for the individual and of segmenting the population served by the managed care organization are increased.

Both transitional and long-term designs must acknowledge market realities and the responsibility of managed care organizations for the health of their communities. Care management programs for vulnerable populations require knowing the market and understanding potential partnerships. Public health agencies, skills training centers, and traditional safety-net providers can offer valuable links to specialty care for the chronically ill. The experience of managed care organizations in establishing alliances with provider groups or hospitals could be invaluable in designing innovative relationships with nontraditional health institutions, such as elementary and secondary schools. Although seldom viewed as a new type of chronic care delivery partner, schools can provide the mechanism for managed care organizations to screen and detect chronic disease, to implement disease prevention programs, and to monitor medication regimens.

Relatively little research exists on the ideal mix, organization, or orientation of providers to satisfy effectively the needs of the chronically ill patient. We do know that the traditional model of periodic visits by a chronically ill patient to a primary care physician is ineffective without a team possessing the expertise, time, and resources to manage care. As important as the medical and social service providers is an engaged patient who is active in the planning, delivery, feedback, and evaluation of care. To affect outcomes that are functionally and clinically relevant, the interactions must be effective within the facilities, across the service providers, and among the team members, which are defined as patient, family, provider, and community.

The effectiveness of chronic care management models relies on data provided by and for the clinicians, agencies, and patients. Both management information and clinical decision support systems are essential. Ideally, these systems are composed of a registry of diseases and practice protocols or guidelines to which new cases can be added and from which symptom-based or diagnosis-oriented information can be extracted and analyzed to provide alternative pathways for care management. Data must also support management of the organization. Both the complexity of care management and the fixed-price basis of many managed care arrangements require mechanisms for data collection, monitoring, and feedback. Decisions whether to provide services internally or to contract for services from external agencies are made initially and throughout the care management process. These make-buy decisions and the transactions associated with them rely on accurate financial and clinical data, much of which are collected as part of the standard medical encounter record and accounting systems.

As already noted, chronic illness management is more than a periodic review of the diagnoses, procedures, and progress notes from the medical provider's chart. Patients, providers and managers must be able to integrate, access, respond to, and modify health and healthcare data. This capability is necessary to assess health status, to identify the appropriate provider, to select therapies, to monitor costs, and to measure results. These data are crucial to an effective infrastructure and responsive management of chronic illness.

Managed care concerns the alignment of financing, service delivery, patient care, and population health. New structures and strategies addressing the needs of the chronically ill can comfortably reside within traditional managed care models, as well as within newer organizations based on provider networks, community alliances, or hospital-centered delivery systems. The importance of serving special populations demands that the administrative and research challenges be met. The espoused missions of managed care organizations and the legitimate expectations of the public require accountability for the health and healthcare of the entire community.

MANAGED CARE AND PHYSICIAN CONTRACTING

Medical school candidates, current students, and house staff remain committed to caring for the sick and disadvantaged through the exercise of their considerable skills and talents. But during their weekly rotations into office-based practices, these providers discover what practicing physicians experience on a daily basis—the rapid change in almost every aspect of medical practice and medical practice management. Providers quickly realize that contractual arrangements negotiated with partners, plans, or employers may be hazardous to their health. Physicians must adapt constantly to new organizations and new governance structures, increased oversight, shifting employment relationships, insurance modifications, and varying payment methods. New physicians are prepared for the pace of clinical change; however, when confronted with the realities of practice management, including regulation, purchase, consolidation, and dissolution, they proceed through the classic stages of loss.

Payment systems imposed by numerous managed care arrangements create much of the risk and stress facing physicians. A 1995 Commonwealth

Fund/Harris poll found that 90 percent of physicians care for patients who are covered by managed care plans, and more than half of all physicians participate in five or more plans. The transition from fee-for-service to capitation-based payment has introduced at best an administrative nightmare, and at worst mass frustration and dangerously conflicting incentives. Compensation arrangements between physicians and health plans are of acute interest to providers, plans, and patients.

Key to achieving the financial objectives of managed care is the prospectively set, per-enrollee payment to providers, who accept the risk of furnishing all care. Several nonfinancial aspects of the supporting infrastructure are critical to successful implementation of the model: an information system that allows the capture and reporting of linked clinical and cost data; a governance structure that matches responsibility, control, and accountability; a culture of communication among clinicians, managers, and patients; and oversight by competent, respected, and integrated staff who are aligned financially and organizationally with the mission of the group. Few physician practices or managed care operations are adequately equipped to implement and manage these complex elements with the speed demanded by the current environment.

Providers' contracts based on capitation and other risk-related concepts should rely heavily on insurance principles and general notions of risk. The probability of a severely ill panel of patients exposes the provider to potential monetary loss, but the promotion of appropriate incentives demands that medical and financial risks be separately considered in designing a compensation contract. Medical practice seeks to reduce illness or disability by teaching, diagnosing, and treating patients. To achieve this overriding objective, physicians must be equipped with technology, time, and access to the expertise of other practitioners. Decision making, treatment continuity, and patient satisfaction can be impaired when practitioners risk the costs of necessary resources. Studies supported by the Commonwealth Fund reveal that, among physicians in practices with large managed care penetration, well over two-thirds report serious problems accessing inpatient care; almost half report dissatisfaction with the amount of time they can spend with their patients.

Physicians should be placed at risk only for those aspects of medical practice under their control. The compensation system can be designed to support this principle. To a significant extent, physicians manage the frequency, type, extent, and location of treatment, including the technology applied, use of pharmaceuticals, and reliance on specialty care. Except for special enrollment practices of the plans with which they associate, the geographic locations of their offices, or general marketing of their individual practices, physicians cannot control the types of patients or the severity of their presenting illnesses.

Compensation methodology can support efficient decision making, resulting in effective treatment. Options are available from an extensive menu. Physicians can be paid prospectively, retrospectively, or both. They can be paid a capitated amount, a discount from standard fees, or some combination of the two. The basis of payment can be calendar year, episode, visit, enrollee, or patient. The extent of physician responsibility and financial risk can include primary care, all outpatient care, inpatient services, prevention programs, rehabilitation, or a combination. The selection of features and their incorporation into the compensation mechanism depend on the specific situation, the goals of the negotiators, and the time and data available for analysis. The wide variety of possible formulas can lead to vastly differing incentives.

Information needed to arrive at the optimal arrangement includes patient demographics, health status, utilization histories, and provider practice patterns. Several factors bear upon the physicians' willingness to assume the risk of specialty service costs for a patient group that may include a large number of chronically ill, complex cases. These factors include the time at which such cases can be identified and possible relief mechanisms for resulting costs. If "outlier" cases can be identified in advance, for instance in the case of the chronically ill, a prospective payment can be arranged, covering the actuarially determined expected costs of care. If cases are identified during standard care, an agreement for retrospective compensation, or a means of accessing a reinsurance arrangement, can ensure that effective clinical decision making is not stifled by anticipated depletion of capitation accounts or withheld funds.

Stop-loss arrangements and retrospective cost reimbursement can be combined with capitated payment in proportion to the expected distribution of patient severity. The presence of stop-loss terms based upon per patient or per level of expenditure allows a provider at risk for all care to prescribe necessary high-cost treatment without being constrained by financial barriers. Risk adjustment methodologies permit identification of individuals and groups likely to require varying levels of resources. However, most plans cannot supply physicians with data on health status and expected use of their panels, and risk adjustment of enrollee groups is still in its infancy. In addition, researchers have noted that the potentials for selection bias and moral hazard exist despite implementation of risk-adjustment systems. Plans suffering from the effects of both phenomena seldom have in place an information system allowing rapid detection and effective adaptation.

Development of compensation contracts for physician groups, regardless of size, demands extensive communication and negotiation. The complexity of clinical decision making, constraints on health resources, and the nature of human behavior require the scrutiny of payment arrangements for their intended and unintended incentives and consequences. Contracts should be reexamined if they withhold large portions of compensation for targets or bonuses, if they impose total financial risk-bearing on small groups of physicians, or if they base payment on small patient-risk pools. Similarly, compensation arrangements should be critically reassessed if they are based solely on capitation and do not provide reinsurance or reimbursement mechanisms for unexpectedly high-cost or complex cases or retrospective review of care and expenditures.

One goal of a compensation arrangement should be to support the best aims of the managed care financial model—the efficient and effective use of limited resources. An equally important goal should be to provide the best possible medical treatment without jeopardizing the passion for caring and the compassion for people that drove individuals to practice medicine in the first place.

COLLABORATION AND QUALITY IN MANAGED CARE

The central goal of managed care is assuring the delivery of high-quality care. Health plans and medical practices dedicate significant resources toward this aim, but also toward measuring, monitoring, and improving the quality of healthcare. While some of these efforts are responses to legal and regulatory mandates, many health plans have voluntarily invested substantial amounts in researching, developing, and implementing practice guidelines, effectiveness tools, and improvement methods to assure quality.

This quest for healthcare quality is valuable but expensive. Because research on clinical outcomes and quality measurement is complex, plans require extensive expertise to understand, implement, track, and manage high-quality care and improvement methods. The team of experts must draw from numerous disciplines. Knowledge of research methods is required to translate clinical research into clinical practice; one must determine which studies are worth replicating or which techniques are worth implementing in the health plan environment. Extensive understanding of the health plan organization, its management capabilities, and its available human resources is needed to adapt behaviors, practice styles, or prescribing patterns to new guidelines or policies. Proficiency in clinical diagnosis, treatment, prevention, and public health is of paramount importance. The management information system is indispensable in the collection and analysis of data on quality; it is critical to involve, at an early stage, personnel who create, manage, and use the system. The expert staff and consultants must remember the importance of involving consumers in identifying and evaluating issues related to the delivery of services to patients, enrollees, and the community.

The costs of healthcare quality generally are borne separately by each managed care plan. This independence of action is self-imposed but understandable, considering historical relationships, competitive pressures, contractual covenants, antitrust concerns, and differing management styles. However, the importance of the quality imperative, combined with the complexity and cost of attaining it, argues for an alternate approach. Collaborative efforts, recognizing similar interests and compatible missions, and further recognizing the realities of a competitive marketplace, could offer mutually beneficial solutions to the plans, providers, purchasers, and consumers.

Under the collaborative scenario, cooperating plans would propose selected issues, practice challenges, or community needs for study, recommendation, and action. The scope of the study; the contribution of data, expertise, and resources; and the form and ownership of the product could be negotiated among the plans to suit the situation. For instance, community-based educational efforts designed to meet the preventive health needs of an area's vulnerable populations may be more comprehensive and effective if jointly funded by private plans acting together or in concert with public agencies. New clinical guidelines requiring that the general population be educated to improve treatment effectiveness may be implemented more rapidly and permeate a community more quickly if several health plans contribute to the design, funding, and educational effort. Dialogues among health plans and representatives from the juvenile justice system might accelerate the development of more appropriate crisis services, triage methods, or treatment protocols for at-risk youths in the community.

At the *plan* level, organized efforts to measure and improve particular dimensions of quality have received national attention and significant federal resources. At the *patient* level, and even though clinical effectiveness research has received increasing modest federal funding, support for translating empirically generated guidelines into evidence-based practices continues to be precarious. Shared efforts by collaborating plans can accelerate clinical responsiveness and community involvement. Educating enrollees about health behaviors or life-saving techniques may improve the health of the community while enabling plans to offer more effective services. Formulating compatible methods for collecting and analyzing person-level data may enable recognition of life-threatening trends in illness or may highlight the need for special services in a neighborhood or region.

Market pressures demand the exercise of caution in these collaborations. Health plans compete fiercely for providers, purchasers, and enrollees in a region; it would be foolish to share potentially compromising information. The participants, recognizing both the opportunities and the potential threats, must carefully select issues for which collaboration is the correct strategic response.

Already, collaborative activities are being externally imposed on health plans, at least to the extent of sharing plan data and best practices. In some areas, large purchasers and employer groups are requiring plans with whom they contract to participate in forums designed to identify data, services, and processes for quality measurement and improvement. Business groups and purchasing coalitions are imposing data collection requirements and feedback mechanisms. The economic power of these organizations, based on their ability to deliver enrollees to plans, results in significant influence over the care delivered to patients.

Managed care was originally intended to reduce incentives for waste and inappropriate care that were attributed to the fee for service system. By coordinating information, ensuring access to a provider, supporting relationships among providers, and reducing the administrative and financial burdens faced by patients, it was thought that managed care could deliver higher quality, more efficient healthcare services. Although there is evidence that managed care controls costs, at least in the short run, a growing suspicion of the financial incentives and the perceived preemption of more important patient care issues have led to alarm and outrage among the public and confusion in the industry. The resulting movement toward accountability has in many cases impeded progress toward greater quality. Measurement of outputs has clouded measurement of outcomes. The eroding level of trust voiced by consumers, regulators, and purchasers deserves a response that once again emphasizes the original mission of managed care.

Shared efforts to improve healthcare quality serve many interests. If plans collaborate on activities that are inherently important, yet challenging to identify, understand, implement, and evaluate, both the plans and the public gain. In addition, plans need opportunities to inform the public of the underlying motives for their existence. We are at or near the time when plan selection will be based on price and quality. Consumers will select plans and providers from organizations that not only meet acceptable performance scalars, but that generate a level of trust. Shared interests in the well-being of the patient and of the community must transcend separate fiscal goals. By collaborating on quality and quality improvement, managed care firms can gain control over quality issues, accelerate the translation of clinical and effectiveness research to medical practice, protect their own viability, and, most importantly, improve the quality of care and the health of their communities.

PART

II

Operations

INTRODUCTION

With the overview provided in Part I of this book, the foundation is in place for a more detailed look at the specific operations that take place in a managed care environment. Drawing on the writing of researchers, scholars, and consultants, Part II describes concrete strategies by which healthcare professionals can achieve organizational goals for financial success and improved community health.

One of the most obvious effects of managed care has been a shift in how covered individuals choose their primary care providers, access those providers, and obtain referrals through those providers. Chapter 5: "How HMOs Structure Primary Care Delivery" reports results of a study into what types of healthcare professionals act as primary care providers, how the gatekeeper model works, and what effect this model has on consumers and providers.

Chapters 7 and 8 look squarely at what a provider needs to do to effectively contract with managed care payers. "Developing Structures for Effective Managed Carc Contracting" reviews the core competencies—including those related to medical, financial, operations, and marketing management—providers need to deliver a continuum of care to a defined population and to support that effort in such a way that services are delivered efficiently and effectively. "Taking the Step toward Capitation Payment in Managed Care Contracts" explains the basic process by which risk is shared among payers, provider organizations, and physicians under capitation.

One of the most problematic functions for any provider organization today is information management. The growth of managed care has presented special challenges, especially while providers care for patients under both fee-for-service and capitation arrangement. Chapter 8: "Information Systems: Managed Care Applications" discusses how effective information management can be used to assess community health, manage financial risk, improve clinical practice patterns, and present appropriate information to stakeholders, including the public, practitioners, managers, and payers.

Another activity influenced by managed care is how providers market their services to the public, employers, and payers. Chapter 9: "Marketing and Managed Care" offers a series of succinct tips on how a provider can most effectively distribute its marketing dollars, what possible marketing strategies can be employed, and how marketing activities can be timed.

On a continual basis, payers, employers, and providers must determine not just whether managed care arrangements are financially feasible, but whether consumers are satisfied with them. This activity is especially important given that, in less than a generation, patients have had to adapt to transformations in the quality and even availability of care; in addition, more patients are even finding themselves having to cope with the administrative aspects of their own care. Chapter 10: "Using Consumer Satisfaction Surveys to Assess Quality of Care: Current Practices and Issues," discusses how surveys given to consumers of managed care products can be used to gauge the quality of service and care.

The goal of the preceding chapters—and those that follow—is to help healthcare providers succeed under managed care. However, success can be defined variously. Is success measured by increased market share? By enhanced margin? By consumer satisfaction? By improved community health? These goals are all important, but healthcare professionals are concerned that some may be pursued at the expense of others. Is it possible, for example, to control overutilization of health services while still enhancing community health? The final chapter in this section, "Can Ethical Management and Managed Care Coexist?" presents a model for resolving the ethical conflicts associated with managed care.

CHAPTER

5

How HMOs Structure Primary Care Delivery

Suzanne Felt-Lisk

Managed care's increased influence on health care delivery highlights the need to better understand how people in managed care obtain primary care and referrals. A recent literature search found that previously published research on the topic is generally dated, derived from a limited subset of plans, inattentive to important structural differences between plans, and responsive to a narrow set of related issues.[1] Here, results are presented from a detailed study of primary care staffing in 23 health maintenance organizations (HMOs). Differences among HMOs are explored: who they use as "gatekeepers," how they use nurse practitioners (NPs) and physician assistants (PAs), and their policies on how people obtain referrals to specialists. The study also explored plans' initiatives to expand or better define a scope of practice for primary care physicians. To conclude, the implications of the findings are discussed.

STUDY DESIGN

The study design consists of on-site interviews with senior health plan officials in 23 HMOs nationwide in winter and spring of 1994. The study was conducted by Mathematica Policy Research, Inc. for the federal Health Resources and Services Administration.[2] This sample of HMOs was con-

Reprinted with permission from *Managed Care Quarterly* 4 (4): 96–105.

structured using a two-stage process, in which markets of varying HMO penetration and provider supply level were selected, and then a variety of plans were selected within these markets. The final sample consists of nine group or staff model plans in eight large urban areas and one rural area, nine network or IPA model plans in the same eight large urban areas and in one small urban area, and five plans selected because they have relatively high Medicaid enrollment (25 percent or more of their total enrollment). Mixed-model plans were accommodated by selecting plans based on predominant model type and studying the staffing of each model type component.

The eight selected urban markets cover the range of the 54 largest metropolitan statistical areas in terms of their population, physician-to-population ratio, and HMO penetration rate. A greater proportion of large plans than exist nationwide was selected so as to include greater numbers of physicians and enrollees. Thus, the sample is more representative of HMOs that have enrollments greater than 50,000. It is also more representative of the distribution of enrollees in HMOs nationally.

At each HMO, the site visitors used semistructured interview protocols to interview the key personnel who make staffing decisions, usually the medical director, provider relations or network development director, and marketing representative, and often also the chief executive officer, a government programs staff person, and a regional representative if the plan was large and somewhat decentralized. Generally, one or two site visitors spent about a day on site.

The sample of HMOs was designed to represent the full range of HMOs in the nation and to facilitate an understanding of how differences in model type, high Medicaid enrollment, and market factors affect primary care staffing. However, about half the HMOs originally selected declined to participate, requiring substitution of another HMO with similar characteristics, and the sites were selected primarily through a judgmental rather than random process; thus, both the study design and the relatively small number of plans means that the results are more useful for providing insight about staffing processes than specific point estimates of prevalence.

SELECTION OF A "GATEKEEPER"

Basic to managed care is the idea that a patient accesses care through primary care providers chosen from a health plan's associated network of providers. However, the study found wide variation in the extent to which enrollees were required, versus encouraged, to select a single primary care provider to act as a gatekeeper.

New health plan enrollees generally are asked to choose a specific medical group/IPA or health center in the plan's provider network; they are then encouraged or required to select one primary care provider. As Table 5.1 shows, just over half of the group/staff model plans and a quarter of the network/IPA model plans required enrollees to select a specific primary care provider (6 of 11 plans and 3 of 12 plans, respectively). Half of the network/IPA model plans delegate the selection rules to the contracted group or IPA—typically because of the plan's payment policy, which capitates the group or IPA only, not individual providers.

The plan's decision to require rather than encourage selection of a primary care provider may be related to its proportion of Medicaid enrollees, since plans with high Medicaid enrollment appear less likely to have this requirement. The reason for this is unknown, although the pattern is consistent with what plans cite as the challenges of treating Medicaid patients. For example, the basic challenge of promoting appropriate use of primary care providers rather than emergency departments might be more easily met than expectations for compliance with more strict requirements for contacting a particular provider.

Regardless of whether a plan requires enrollees to select a provider, the plan typically allows providers other than the one selected to also provide primary care to the patient. For example, group/staff model plans accommodate enrollee "crossover"; that is, enrollees sometimes seek care at two or more different health centers in the plan, and the plan accommodates this. Network/IPA plans that contract with large medical groups mentioned

Table 5.1 Types of Plans Requiring Selection of One Primary Care Provider

	Rules for Selecting a Primary Care Provider (*n* = 23) Percentage of HMOs			
	Encouraged but Not Required to Select an Individual	**Required to Select an Individual**	**Neither Encouraged nor Required to Select an Individual**	**Plan Has No Preference/ Groups or IPAs Determine Rules**
All plans (*n* = 23)	30	39	13	17
Predominant model type				
Group/staff (*n* = 11)	36	55	9	0
Network/IPA (*n* = 12)	25	25	17	33
Medicaid enrollment				
None (*n* = 12)	25	42	8	25
1–24 percent of total enrollment (*n* = 3)	0	100	0	0
25+ percent of total enrollment (*n* = 8)	50	13	25	13

that some of the primary care providers in these groups see one anothers' patients freely (without restriction) within the same site.

TYPES OF PROVIDERS USED AS GATEKEEPERS

HMOs typically use a combination of family practitioners (FPs), general practitioners (GPs), pediatricians, and internists as gatekeepers. Obstetrician/gynecologists (OB/GYNs) and subspecialist physicians may deliver primary care but are not often used as gatekeepers. Similarly, plans generally do not offer NPs and PAs as gatekeepers.

PRIMARY CARE GATEKEEPERS FOR ADULTS

Generally, adult enrollees select a primary care provider from a list of FPs, GPs, and internists who focus most of their practice on primary care. (Plans told us some of these internists have specialist designations, but they have chosen to largely practice primary care and so the plan lists them with general internists as primary care providers.) Though these providers form the core of plans' primary care provider lists and are most often selected by enrollees for this role, most plans also allow some other providers to be selected. In a third of the network/IPA type plans, the contracted groups or IPAs have the flexibility to set their own rules on provider selection, with the result that some allow OB/GYNs and/or subspecialists to be selected as primary care physicians. In fact, a significant minority of plans (10 of 23) allow selection of OB/GYNs as gatekeepers, though the extent to which OB/GYNs actually play this role is reported to be minimal. Although not often selected as a primary care provider through which care is channeled, OB/GYNs appear to provide a substantial amount of primary care. Most plans reported that OB/GYNs provide well-woman and obstetric and gynecological care upon patient self-referral to complement care delivered by the regular primary care provider; about three fourths of plans allow at least some self-referral for OB/GYN care.

Other common policies on who acts as a gatekeeper are allowing specialists to serve as primary care providers on a case-by-case, approved basis, and allowing NPs and PAs to be selected if specifically requested by the patient although these providers are not on the publicized list of primary care providers. A few plans had a unique approach reflecting their particular philosophy or circumstances; for example, in remote rural areas served by one plan, PAs or OB/GYNs may be selected due to a lack of the types of providers the plan uses in other parts of its service area.

Plans do not frequently use subspecialists as primary care providers, though more than three fourths of the plans allow them to play this role on a rare or exceptions basis, and about a third freely allow enrollees to select these providers as gatekeepers. Many plans view subspecialists without additional primary care training as poor providers of primary care, reporting that they tend to do more specialty care than other primary care providers, to be unhappy and want to return to their specialty, and refer to others too much for conditions they, as primary care providers, should handle. The eight plans that allow subspecialists to be selected as a primary care provider on more than an exceptions basis generally reported they do so because (1) they believe this practice is cost-effective (e.g., the plan otherwise had excess specialist capacity), (2) there is a large number of subspecialists in the market area who would not be able to stay based only on the basis of demand for specialty care, or (3) they want to provide consumers with as much choice of providers as possible within their network. These plans generally reported that while subspecialists are permitted to act as primary care providers with few restrictions, they generally do not play this role often, either because they are not selected by patients or because they do not choose to act in this role.

Plans vary in the extent to which they rely on internists compared with FPs for primary care. (Plans almost never distinguished between FPs and GPs in their policies or statistics, so following their lead both groups are labeled FPs for simplicity.) In over 60 percent of the plans (14 of 23), internists greatly outnumber FPs, or vice versa—that is, the plan clearly prefers and has experience with one type of primary care provider or the other. The remaining nine plans (39 percent) have a relatively even mixture of internists and FPs. Table 5.2 shows plan differences in this mix by model type. The reasons for the fact that internists greatly outnumber FPs in some plans did not always surface in discussion, but seem likely to be related to the

Table 5.2 Differences in Mix of Internists and Family Practitioners by Model Type

	Percentage of HMOs		
Primary Care Physician Mix*	**Group/Staff (n = 11)**	**Network/IPA (n = 12)**	**All Types (n = 23)**
Internists greatly outnumber family practitioners	46	17	30
Near even mix of internists and family practitioners	27	50	39
Family practitioners greatly outnumber internists	27	33	30

*Internists were considered to greatly outnumber FPs if the number of internists providing primary care was at least 50 percent greater than the number of FPs, or the plan described itself as heavily reliant on internists relative to other primary care providers. (The two pieces of information never conflicted but we did not have both pieces for every plan.) The reverse was true for categorizing plans where FPs greatly outnumbered internists.

plan's origin, when it was closely associated with a multispecialty group, to restrictions in some areas on admitting privileges for FPs by the hospitals with which the plan contracts, and to plan-imposed restrictions on FP practice, such as not allowing FPs to see children under a certain age or not allowing them to deliver infants, which would make plans with these restrictions less desirable to FPs seeking a full range of patient types. Differences in the competitive environment of HMOs may be another reason for different use of internists versus FPs, among network/IPA model plans. None of the network/IPA model plans in areas with high HMO penetration heavily used internists relative to FPs, although internists heavily outnumbered FPs in two of four plans in low penetration areas. If this pattern is real rather than coincidental, it could reflect greater pressure to reduce costs in areas with high levels of HMO competition.

Several plans now using some FPs expressed their intent to use more of them. For example, one found it more cost-effective when moving into a new area to hire one FP rather than both an internist and pediatrician. Several plans see them as more flexible than internists given the larger range of ages they treat. However, other plans are more ambivalent about FPs and thus are not planning to use them more relative to other primary care providers. One plan found that FPs are more acceptable in the lower income areas than in other areas in its market. Another noted that while adults in its market are indifferent to seeing an internist or FP, they prefer that their children see a pediatrician.

PRIMARY CARE GATEKEEPERS FOR CHILDREN

Children in the study plans have a pediatrician or an FP as their primary care physician gatekeeper. Plans in which internists heavily outnumber FPs tend to use more pediatricians for their enrolled children, since internists do not treat children. Few plans (only three) require children to see pediatricians rather than the FPs who are available. There were not many rules or specific policies on primary care for children. The exceptions were one plan that had a specific policy requiring contracted providers to arrange with other providers to ensure 24-hour coverage for their practice, and that those who agree to provide coverage must treat patients of the same ages as those treated by the provider being covered (many pediatricians restrict their practice to children under a certain age, e.g., 15 or 18; and many internists see patients only over a certain age, e.g., 15 or 18, but the age limits vary by practice). A second plan had specific guidelines for when children must be seen by a pediatrician rather than another type of provider (e.g., sick children under age 1). Plans generally do not specify an age at which a patient must switch from a pediatrician to an internist but allow this to vary by pediatrician and internist practice.

USING NURSE PRACTITIONERS AND PHYSICIAN ASSISTANTS

Only two plans (of the 23) allow routine selection of NPs or PAs as gatekeepers; two others allow enrollees to select an NP or PA as a primary care provider if they specifically ask to or if medical group/IPA rules allow. Importantly, however, NPs and PAs provide primary care as part of a patient care team in most of the HMOs we visited. NPs, in particular, make up a large part of group/staff model plans' primary care staff, as shown in Table 5.3. Nearly two thirds of group/staff model plans use NPs extensively, and one third use PAs to some extent (more than "rarely"). (Plans were classified by frequency of use of NPs and PAs to show the major patterns of use, but the classifications are rough rather than precise. For example, plans were considered "heavy" users of NPs or PAs if they had at least one NP or PA for every five primary care physicians, or, if this figure was not available, if they considered themselves or their physicians to be heavy users of these providers. In the case of a plan that used some NPs or PAs, did not qualify as a "heavy" user, and did not specifically describe use as "rare," we classified the plan as having "some use.") Only one group/staff model plan does not use NPs, all use PAs to some extent, and much but not all of this use was for primary care. The general pattern of use for NPs and PAs was similar, though PAs were used somewhat less than NPs.

Group/staff model plans in the sample in areas with high levels of HMO penetration use NPs more heavily than other plans; all four of the group/staff model plans in areas with high HMO penetration (25 percent or more of the insured population) heavily used NPs, versus only two of the four in lower penetration areas. If the difference is real and not only a result of the markets we selected or other contributing causes related to these markets (e.g., the location of markets with high penetration), potential reasons for it could include better consumer and physician acceptance of NPs in areas with a long history of managed care, or increased pressure on plans to reduce service delivery costs in areas with heavy competition from other HMOs.

Table 5.3 Use of Nurse Practitioners by Model Type

	Group/Staff Model Plans (Percentage of HMOs)	**Network/IPA Model Plans (Percentage of HMOs)**
Heavy use	64	0
Some use	9	33
Rare use	18	59
No use	9	8

Plans reported that NPs and PAs most commonly work six areas:

1. general primary care (13 plans)
2. urgent care (7 plans)
3. specialized positions (6 plans)
4. pediatric care (6 plans)
5. OB/GYN care (5 plans)
6. telephone triage (3 plans)

Four plans expressed a desire to increase use of NPs or PAs, but were finding recruiting very difficult. For example, one plan reported having to raise NP and PA salaries twice by mid-1994 to keep up with the competition and retain its own providers. It has also begun to use market surveys on a continuing basis to gauge this trend and keep its salaries in line.

A large minority of plans (8 of 23) are very supportive of NPs and PAs, and the rest are less supportive, neutral, or negative. (The classification of plans into "very supportive" or "less supportive, neutral, or negative" was considered both in terms of their use of NPs and PAs, and in terms of any special actions or plans to enhance their role or increase their number.) Only one or two plans could be categorized as being generally negative toward these providers. As Table 5.4 shows, very supportive plans tend to be group/staff model plans and plans without Medicaid contracts. It is not surprising that group/staff model plans were found to be more supportive, given that their general structure (organized multispecialty group or medical center settings rather than individual offices) is more conducive to providing ample work for NPs or PAs. It is not clear how to interpret the finding that plans with Medicaid contracts tend to be less supportive of NPs and PAs. The box

Table 5.4 Types of Plans More and Less Supportive of Nurse Practitioners and Physician Assistants

	Very Supportive	Less Supportive, Neutral, or Negative*
All plans	35	65
Predominant model type		
Group/staff (n = 11)	64	36
Network/IPA (n = 12)	8	92
Medicaid enrollment		
None (n = 12)	50	50
1–24 percent of total enrollment (n = 3)	33	67
25+ percent of total enrollment (n = 8)	13	88

*Only one or two plans could be categorized as generally negative toward these providers.

provides examples of how and why plans are more or less supportive of NPs and PAs. The most common reason for lower levels of support is that the plan views decisions on NPs and PAs as being within the discretion of the medical group or physician.

Both plans that are generally supportive of NPs and PAs and those less supportive reported that a substantial proportion of their physicians have negative views on the usefulness or cost-effectiveness of these providers. Such views appear to be a major barrier to increasing the use of NPs and PAs.

STRUCTURING ACCESS TO REFERRALS

The primary care provider selected by enrollees generally functions as a gatekeeper, authorizing referrals for all or most specialty care according to plan rules. In less restrictive plans, any primary care provider the patient sees may perform this function, or, rarely, patients are free to make their own referral choices. Even when gatekeeping policies are generally restrictive, plans normally specify certain services that patients may access without a referral. The most common clinical areas for which plans allow self-referrals are shown in Table 5.5.

Plan policies for gatekeeping and referral vary widely, and although there are not strong patterns by model type, there is some tendency for network/IPA plans to delegate gatekeeping policies to their contracted groups/IPAs. Thirty percent (7) of the 23 plans use a strict or fairly strict gatekeeper model. That is, these plans require enrollees to select a primary care provider, then limit self-referrals requiring most care to be referred by the primary care provider. Even among these plans, however, most permit self-referral for limited OB/GYN care (6 of 7 plans). At the other extreme, 30 percent have very open policies or practices. Enrollees in these plans are able to access a wide range of primary care and specialty providers without

Table 5.5 Common Clinical Areas Where HMOs Allowed Enrollees to Self-Refer

Clinical Area	Number of HMOs (n = 23)
Limited OB/GYN	15
Mental health	7
Optometry	7
Substance abuse	5
Dermatology	2
All or nearly all care	3
No self-referrals	1

Nature of Support for NPs and PAs

Supportive Actions

- Two plans already heavily using NPs and PAs are considering expanding their use—one created a task force to review the advantages and disadvantages of more extensive use.
- One group/staff model plan was raising the status of NPs and removing their nursing duties in hopes of better retaining them.
- One plan had recognized some group physicians using NPs as nurses and influenced them to more appropriately use these providers.
- Heavy use of NPs by 7 plans and PAs by 2 plans.

Supportive Comments

- NPs and PAs are cost-effective providers.
- Consumers in the plan feel more comfortable talking to them than to physicians.
- Consumers like them (generally).
- NPs have a feel for preventive care and teaching due to their training.
- Physicians like them because it enables their practice to be more productive, thus benefiting them financially.

Other Comments

- Most network/IPA plans were neutral or offered verbal support only, because they viewed decisions on NPs and PAs as an IPA or medical group decision.
- Many of the network/IPA plans did not track NP or PA use by their contracted providers.
- Several plans reported physicians were mixed in their views on these providers:
  - —Some physicians favored using them.
  - —Others viewed them as not cost-effective, too inclined to refer patients back to them, too inclined to spend excessive time with patients, or requiring too much supervision.
- Some plans reported mixed views by consumers. One plan's consumer-based strategy was in part distinguishing itself from its competitor by not using NPs or PAs.
- One reported being cautious about contracting with groups that use PAs due to the medical director's past experience with finding they were used without appropriate supervision.
- One heavy-Medicaid plan reported that it does not view NPs and PAs as very useful for its enrollees because the Medicaid clients tend to be sicker than other populations.
- One plan cited lack of availability of hospital privileges as a factor for NPs and PAs.

getting a referral from their gatekeeper (if they chose one). Two plans in this group allow any physician within a patient's chosen health center to treat the patient without a referral, although referrals are required for any other care. Seventeen percent (4 plans) lie between these extremes. For example, they require a primary care provider to be chosen but allow nearly unrestricted access to other providers. Or they encourage but do not require selection of a primary care provider. The requirements for referrals to specialists are more strict than those of the plans described in the preceding item.

The remaining 22 percent of plans (5), all of which are network/IPA plans, either allow their contracted groups or IPAs to make these policies (4 of the 5 plans), or the rules differ depending on whether the contracted entity is a group or an IPA. If the entity is an IPA, a primary care provider must be chosen on the theory that more loosely structured entities need this rule to manage care by their providers.

The higher level of competition that plans face in areas with high HMO penetration may tend to influence them toward more open gatekeeping policies, (e.g., because of consumer preferences for more open access) although the small numbers prevent conclusions on this point. Only 1 of 7 plans (14 percent) in areas with high HMO penetration maintained strict gatekeeping policies versus 4 of 8 plans in areas with low to moderate HMO penetration.

Referrals must usually be in writing, although some plans allow referrals by phone or are equipped for electronic referrals. Face-to-face contact between a patient and a physician is not always required for a referral, for example, if the physician knows the patient and has discussed his or her problem by phone. Most plans allow patients to self-refer to specialists for at least one or two types of care, most often for a limited amount of OB/GYN care (Table 5.5).

In general, plans appear to be moving toward tighter gatekeeping arrangements and self-referral policies. Even two of the three most open plans support tighter gatekeeping arrangements in theory; their policies are open only because of major transitions. The main reasons plans gave for tighter arrangements is the perception that they enhance access to and continuity of care, and permit the plan to hold a provider accountable for a patient's care. Concerns about access and accountability are perhaps best explained by one plan as follows. Before the plan required patients to select a primary care provider, they would sometimes diagnose themselves as needing a specialist and call the specialist's office for an appointment. The administrative assistant who received the patient's request would often have to inform the patient that the physician had no appointments for many weeks, and the patient would try another specialist, perhaps in a related field, to gain access to care, perhaps with a similar lack of success. The frustrated patient would complain to the plan, but the plan had no one to hold accountable for the care of the patient. In the current system, the primary care provider can (1) ensure the patient is referred to the correct specialist, (2) facilitate access to this provider, and (3) be held accountable by the plan if he or she does not perform the first two functions.

Plans that have recently tightened their gatekeeping arrangements or are considering doing so indicated that the process takes considerable time and effort. One plan just completed an 18-month process; another reported it would probably tighten its system in the near future, but the medical director knows from experience about the difficult and controversial nature of the process.

Plans are not uniformly moving toward tighter gatekeeping. Five plans reported having recently and selectively eliminated referral requirements, for example, for optometry, after finding that primary care providers do not do any related screening or care, and thus contact with the primary care provider seemed unnecessary. Further, several plans are content with an open policy of care at the chosen health center and require referrals for care from physicians outside the center. Two predominantly group/staff model plans feel this way, and one network/IPA model plan noted that it often finds the groups that are more experienced with managed care are open about on-site referrals (these tend to be large, organized multispecialty group or health center settings). Only one plan directly challenged the concept of gatekeeping as a useful tool for managing care or containing costs. This plan believes that patients can effectively refer themselves for many conditions, and that capitating specialists should be the main mechanism for encouraging appropriate allocation of both resources and care between primary and specialty care providers.

SCOPE OF PRACTICE

Overall, plans perceive that the scope of practice of primary care physicians has not changed much in recent years. Beyond this generalization, all agree that there is not one agreed-upon set of conditions or treatments that constitute the scope of practice of primary care. Thus, the level of care received from a primary care provider may vary depending on the provider's comfort level and experience with certain procedures or conditions more than on any consensus about the scope of practice for primary care providers.

Specific primary care responsibilities may be defined under primary care capitation arrangements; that is, to the extent that physicians are capitated for primary care, they will have responsibility for a defined set of services associated with the capitation amount. (Since examining individual physician payment arrangements was beyond the scope of the study, the evidence is suggestive rather than conclusive in terms of the link between the definition of primary care and payment strategy.) However, not all primary care providers are paid on a capitated basis; in some and perhaps many cases, the medical group or IPA is capitated but chooses to pay its physicians on a discounted fee-for-service basis.

While the content of care practiced by primary care physicians does not appear to have changed substantially, or while such changes are at most limited to a few areas, there is some evidence that changes may soon occur. The study identified three main factors affecting what services are provided by primary care providers rather than specialists: (1) plan financial or other incentives to increase the range of primary care practice (six plans); (2) malpractice liability risk, which has reduced the range of primary care practice in certain areas (two plans); and (3) plan efforts to standardize what is considered primary care; in theory the efforts could either increase or decrease the range of primary care practice (three plans). In practice, it seems likely that plans are interested in standardizing the definition in order to encourage a wider range of practice for those primary care providers who tend to do less than others in their plan.

The financial or other means to increase the range of primary care practice include expanding lists of procedures considered to be primary care. For example, one plan reported adding ECG, minor acne, and allergy injections to its list; another added immunizations, ECGs, pregnancy and other routine tests, colonoscopies, and endoscopies. One plan pays a higher capitation amount to the primary care provider if the patient sees him or her rather than an OB/GYN for a routine gynecological exam. Another provides a financial incentive to primary care providers for performing instead of referring flexible sigmoidoscopies. Other plans simply noted that their compensation models (e.g., capitation to a group that includes specialty services) encourage a broadening of primary care practice.

In addition to expanding the list of procedures, another effort to increase the range of primary care involves redirecting patients with defined borderline conditions back to primary care providers. The plan making this attempt has identified low back pain, minor lacerations, and mild inflammatory bowel disease, for example, as conditions that primary care providers, rather than surgeons, should be treating. The plan is assessing referral patterns for these conditions to develop practice guidelines.

On the other hand, plans in two markets reported that malpractice liability risk has reduced the scope of practice for primary care providers. Some of those who once provided obstetrical care or care for newborns have now reportedly discontinued these services because of the real or perceived high risk of malpractice suits.

The study found three examples of plan efforts to standardize the definition of primary care. The first plan is more specifically defining what primary care providers should do by using lists of procedures because of the current need for computer software packages that could identify payable bills versus procedures included in a primary care capitation amount. The second plan is circulating among providers medical management guidelines that define what primary care providers should be doing. Providers were to comment on the guidelines. The medical director's intent is to encourage physicians to buy into the list of guidelines. The effort stemmed from his observation of wide differences among individual primary care providers in the types of patients they feel comfortable treating. The third plan is analyzing the types of conditions that are being referred from primary care providers, then convening groups of specialists and primary care providers to attempt to reach a consensus on what can be done by primary care physicians. This plan reported that additional training for some primary care providers is the natural follow-up to such an effort, and that it is organizing and will support this training.The plan reported a positive outcome from the process it used to develop this list. It perceived that the primary care and specialist physicians left the meetings with stronger working relationships and a better understanding of each other's capabilities and responsibilities.

The second and third efforts were in progress at the time of the site visit, and therefore the nature of primary care has not yet substantially changed in these plans.

IMPLICATIONS

While HMOs generally pursue a more organized primary care delivery strategy than the fee-for-service sector, their strategies vary substantially across plans. Even the plans with tight gatekeeping systems allow patients access to some services without referral (OB/GYN self-referrals were allowed on a limited basis in 15 of the 23 plans) though beyond OB/GYN plans do not agree on which services patients should directly access. Also, not all plans required selection of a single primary care gatekeeper, though all at least encouraged it. Plans truly ranged from virtually unrestricted access to the plan's full network of providers at one extreme, to plans that strictly required nearly all care decisions be channeled through the chosen primary care provider.

Contracting provider groups have a large role in structuring primary care delivery in network/IPA model plans. This is an increasingly important observation since much of the growth of managed care is occurring in this type of plan.[3,4] Contrary to the popular notion that health plans determine most aspects of delivery, many of the network/IPA type plans we visited paid medical groups or IPAs on a capitated basis, then took a hands-off attitude toward delivery. It was often the medical group or IPA that was responsible for rules regarding choice of primary care provider, and use of NPs or PAs, for example.

Also, the care a patient receives from a primary care physician appears to vary depending on the provider's level of comfort and experience with certain procedures or conditions more than on any consensus about the scope of practice for primary care physicians. There are signs that the scope of practice of primary care physicians may expand for those physicians who now practice primary care within a narrower scope than their peers. For example, 6 of the 23 HMOs reported having financial incentives or educational initiatives to expand the content of primary care. However, they described these as small steps that were not likely to result in large changes in primary care practice in the near future.

Finally, plans' views on the use of subspecialists and OB/GYNs as gatekeepers raise a cautionary note. As policy makers and providers seek opportunities to balance the number of specialists relative to primary care providers, use of specialists in primary care roles may become more common. Yet the findings suggest that plans often view the primary care skills of such providers negatively. At a minimum, initiatives to retrain specialists to practice primary care will be critical to address the perceived problems of over-referral and specialty orientation. Further, some plans were skeptical that primary care was a fitting role for many subspecialists, since the skills used in primary care differ greatly from those attracting physicians to certain specialties (e.g., radiology).

In sum, the diversity among health plans in their primary care strategies is evident from the study. However, the relative desirability of the various strategies has to do with both value judgments (e.g., about what organization or person should be held accountable for an enrollee's care) and unanswered research questions about how different strategies and incentives toward expanded primary care practice affect health care costs, outcomes, and satisfaction with care.

ACKNOWLEDGMENTS

The 23 health plans that volunteered senior management time to participate in the site visit interviews on a confidential basis are gratefully acknowledged. Marsha Gold, a Senior Fellow at Mathematica Policy Research, Inc., acted as a senior advisor to the study and provided useful comments on an earlier draft of the manuscript. Jessica Townsend, at the Office of Planning, Evaluation, and Legislation within the Health Resources and Services Administration, saw the need for this study, served as the project officer for the study, and also provided useful comments on a draft of this manuscript. Hilary Frazer, Karyen Chu, and Timothy Lake were other project team members who contributed to collecting the information for this analysis.

REFERENCES

1. Gold, M., et al. "Behind the Curve: A Critical Assessment of How Little Is Known About Arrangements Between Managed Care Plans and Physicians." *Medical Care Research and Review* 52 (3) (September 1995): 307–41.
2. Felt, S., Frazer, H., and Gold, M. "HMO Primary Care Staffing Patterns and Processes: A Cross-Site Analysis of 23 HMOs." Washington, D.C.: Mathematica Policy Research, Inc., December 23, 1994R.
3. Group Health Association of America. *1995 National Directory of HMOs*. Washington, D.C., GHAA: June 1995.
4. Group Health Association of America. *1993 National Directory of HMOs*. Washington, D.C., GHAA: June 1993.

CHAPTER

6

Taking the Step Toward Capitation Payment in Managed Care Contracts

Douglas Conrad, Robert Bonney, Michael Sachs, and Robert Smith

Of the pricing alternatives under managed care contracting, capitation represents the greatest financial risk to health care providers. Examining the issues associated with capitation contracting provides a natural transition to the structural and managerial challenges that must be met as provider organizations evolve to integrated health care systems.

THE PARADIGM SHIFT IN ECONOMIC RELATIONSHIPS

A fundamental premise is that capitation is the primary mechanism for connecting payment and risk. Capitation forces the provider organization to measure and manage costs, which accordingly requires the organization's infrastructure and clinical and managerial behaviors to develop in directions different from those developed over the past 50 years. Figure 6.1 diagrams the new economic relationships between volume, fixed and variable costs, and revenue under capitation, the quintessence of managed care.

In the economic model of fee-for-service (FFS) payments, charges for units of service represent a source of funds, whereas in a capitated environment those same charges become a source of *costs*. FFS revenues increase proportionately with volume per person. Past the break-even point,[1] profits

Reprinted from Conrad, D. et al. 1996. *Managed Care Contracting: Concepts and Applications for the Healthcare Executive.* Chicago: Health Administration Press.

Figure 6.1 Managing Cost/Quality versus Revenue: How Prepayment Changes the Challenge

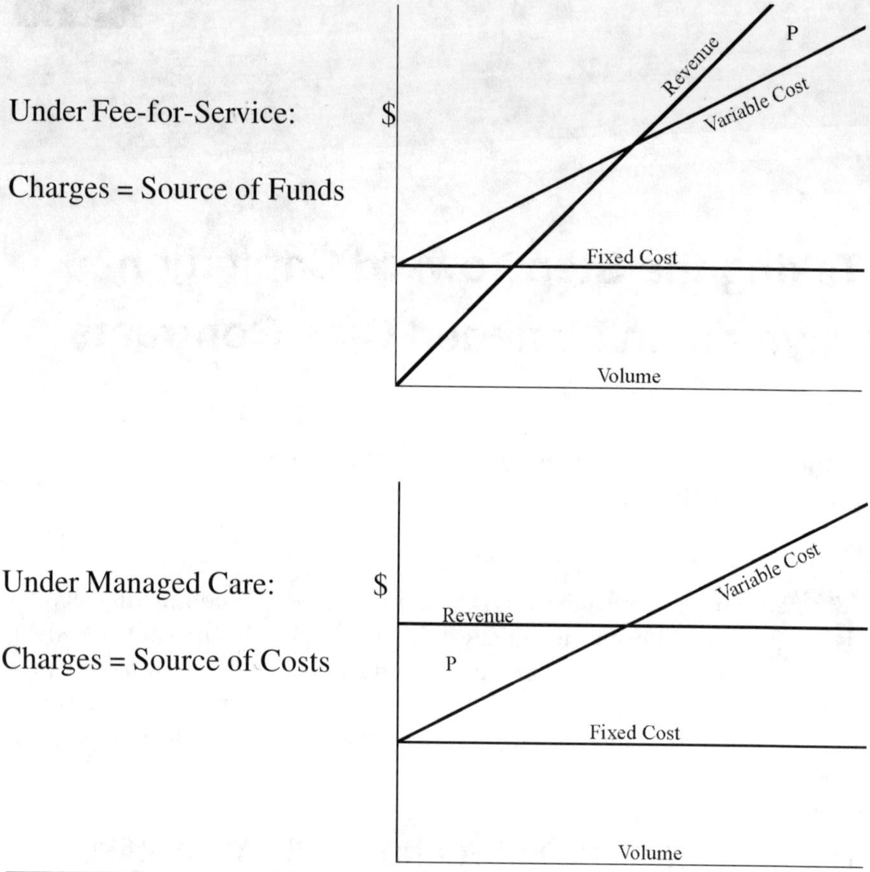

are earned and increase with higher volume. Capitation turns this logic on its head: Profits are earned at low volumes of service per person and decrease with higher volumes past the break-even point. Thus, providers approach breaking even for the other direction—by decreasing volumes.

The commonality between both regimes, FFS and capitation, is that revenues increase (given constant volume of services per person) with an increase in the number of persons served. The critical difference is that under capitation the currency of the realm for providers shifts from the volume of services per person to an emphasis on recruiting more covered lives. Of course, it is still true that under capitation that, in order to attract and retain persons to the provider's panel (or population served), the volume and quality of the service must pass the test of the marketplace.

MANAGING THE RISK POOL UNDER CAPITATION REIMBURSEMENT

Figure 6.2 highlights the elements of the risk pool under capitated arrangements and the variety of considerations that must be taken into account in managing dollars under capitation. Five elements are central to managing the risk pool: (1) defining the enrolled population; (2) measuring and controlling the internal costs of the delivery system; (3) measuring and controlling the variability in contract cases (e.g., small versus large groups selecting a given managed care product); (4) managing the contract portfolio (e.g., in terms of the benefit structure of particular managed care products and the sociodemographic and economic characteristics of the population selecting a given product); and (5) managing the utilization of health services.

The provider's risk pool can be managed partially by decisions related to the population being enrolled. For example, the population can be defined according to geographic area, demographic attributes (e.g., age, sex, family size), occupational categories, and other natural classifications. Each decision has implications that can be tied back to the revenue-cost picture in Figure 6.1. For example, the decision to enroll a geographically dispersed population will have important fixed-cost implications for the delivery system. To provide access across a wide area involves building transportation networks and leads to increased transaction and communication costs throughout the system. To amortize the fixed costs of creating and maintaining such diffuse infrastructure, the provider system needs to lock in long-term relationships with individual consumers and large organized

Figure 6.2 Sources of Risk

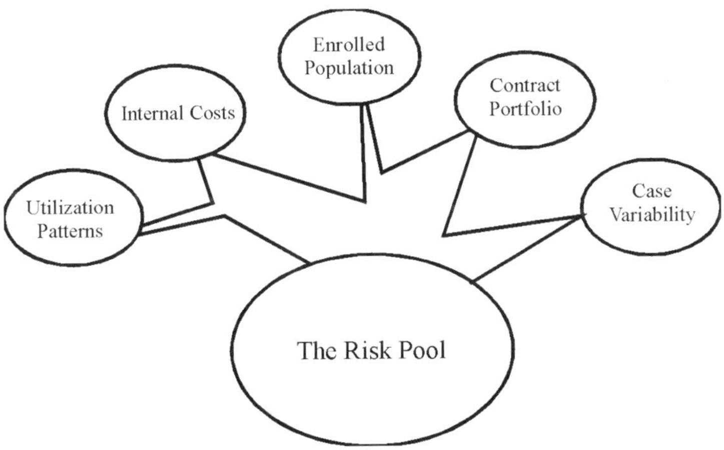

purchasers. The logic is twofold: (1) the long-term tie is necessary to recover the up-front investment costs; and (2) the long-run relationships sustain high volumes of covered lives, so that fixed costs per person are minimized by spreading them over a larger population base.

On the other hand, if the provider's dominant enrollment strategy is driven by sociodemographic or economic (e.g., age/sex or family status) factors, then the organization's fixed investments will be directed principally to defining age-related service needs and delivery system structures, such as geriatric assessment clinics and vision and rehabilitation programs for an elderly enrollment. Similarly, a focus on enrolling women and families would imply increased investment in women's health services, obstetric services, and pediatric and primary care. Thus, the focal dimensions of the enrollment strategy shape the cost structure of the managed care organization.

Internal cost control is the second key element to managing the organization's risk pool. Interestingly, the *nature* of the cost-control incentives differs under FFS and capitation regimes. First, consider variable costs per unit of service: the provider reimbursed on an FFS basis will gain more than under capitation by lowering variable costs per unit of output. This is because, under FFS reimbursement, not only is the variable-cost reduction spread over higher volumes per person, but the provider actually gains an extra increment of profitability (equal to the price) relative to capitation on each additional unit of volume supplied, as the clinician responds to the incentive of a lower variable production cost per unit.

On the other hand, reductions in per person, volume-fixed costs[2] affect profitability the same way under capitation or fee-for-service arrangements if one assumes that reductions in per person costs do not induce providers to expand the size of their enrolled population. However, if lower per person costs do create incentives to expand enrollment, the gain from lowering per person costs will depend on the relative size of the average profit per person under the two payment regimes. In a market with capitation payments that are relatively generous compared to fee-for-service equivalents, the incentives to lower these per person, volume-fixed costs will be greater under capitation than fee-for-service regimes.

The greatest difference, of course, between the cost-control incentives under capitation and fee-for-service payment systems is with respect to managing *volumes*. The capitated provider essentially loses an amount equal to the variable cost of a service times the number of persons served for every unit increase in volume per person (e.g., one additional specialty referral per enrollee). Alternatively, the FFS provider *gains* an amount equal to the contribution margin (price minus variable cost) times the number of persons served for every unit increase in volume per person). If increased volume per person encourages new enrollment of average risk (i.e., health care cost per person), this demand response will exacerbate the losses under capitation arrangements and enhance the gains under FFS systems. These differences will be heightened if the provider's increased demand comes primarily from persons who are above average in their health care costs per capita. The capitated provider would see this demand shift as adverse selection, whereas the same change in demand would be a boon to the provider paid on an FFS basis.

In summary, then, the paradigm shift in cost management experienced in the move from FFS to capitation payment is concentrated on the new incentive to reduce the volume of service per person and to control the costs of volume-fixed infrastructure associated with serving a defined population. Our analysis also shows, however, that the provider's incentive to reduce variable costs per unit of volume is actually weakened under capitation arrangements because the additional profit from unit-cost reductions is less than under FFS systems, because under FFS payment each unit of volume earns the price of that service. Because capitation payment severs this link between volume of service and price, the gain from achieving variable-cost economies is mitigated.

Contract case variability also affects the intrinsic cost of the risk pool. Different insured groups pose distinct underwriting risks to the health plan and the provider. Accepting capitation payment amounts to sharing the underwriting risk of a given population with the health plan, in which case the provider becomes the partial insurer of that group. Small groups generally include a higher proportion of individuals with greater needs for health care because the influence of each individual on the choice of the group's health plan is greater for small groups and the potential insured person knows more about his or her health status than does the insurer. Thus, higher-cost persons are less likely to pay premiums that reflect their expected health care cost to the insurer. Failure to price for this adverse selection will imply higher utilization rates. Hence, the provider accepting capitation should inquire about a number of features of the health plan's underwriting practices:

- the size of the group;
- the employer's or group sponsor's share of premium contributions;
- the proportion of the group that must enroll in a particular health plan option for the insurer to underwrite the group; and
- the claims and utilization experience of the group.

Managing the risk pool also can be likened to controlling the risk of a portfolio. The principles of diversification and the law of large numbers apply to the management of contract-portfolio risk. The provider organization should contract for as broad a cross section of health risks as possible to achieve the full benefits of diversification. The provider's portfolio should contain both sexes and a wide range of ages, income levels, industrial and occupational categories, individual and family contracts, and contract sizes. If the number of covered lives represented by a particular health plan's contract is sufficiently large—say, 1,000 or more—the provider can be reasonably assured that the group's past claims experience will provide a relatively precise estimate of the group's future average costs per capita.

However, for smaller groups, the law of large numbers is less applicable to forecasting the group's future per capita costs. In those cases, the provider needs to pay especially close attention to the health plan's rating and underwriting methodologies. Specifically, the capitation rate will impose on providers less risk of underestimating future costs if the contract groups' premiums are based on experience rates that are fully credible (100 percent experience-based, not at all determined by "manual" or community rates) and if the plan requires a relatively high premium contribution by the employer or group sponsor (e.g., the government, the union) or some other means of achieving high participation by group members. Those conditions increase the likelihood that the group constitutes a broad cross section of risks.

The rate-setting approaches used by health plans can be sorted into a hierarchy of credibility. Other things being equal, the provider is taking less risk by accepting capitation reimbursement for a group of contracts as the group's rating credibility increases. The hierarchy starts with community-rated groups, whose rates are based on the average amount for a large population (not necessarily comparable to the specific contract group). Moving up the ladder of rating credibility, community rating by class, adjusted community rating, prospective experience rating, and retrospective experience rating are plan rate-setting methodologies that progressively reduce the *actuarial risk* that the health plan is shifting to the provider by capitation payment. The logic is that the more precisely estimated are the premium rates assessed the contract group by the health plan in the first place, the less actuarial risk assumed by the provider in accepting capitation reimbursement. The same logic applies to the plan's underwriting methodologies.

THE FLOW OF FUNDS UNDER CAPITATION ARRANGEMENTS

Figures 6.3 and 6.4 illustrate the flow of funds, first, under a capitated arrangement and, second, within a multi-institutional, organized delivery system. From the standpoint of a hospital and physician group jointly

Figure 6.3 The Flow of Funds in a Capitated Environment

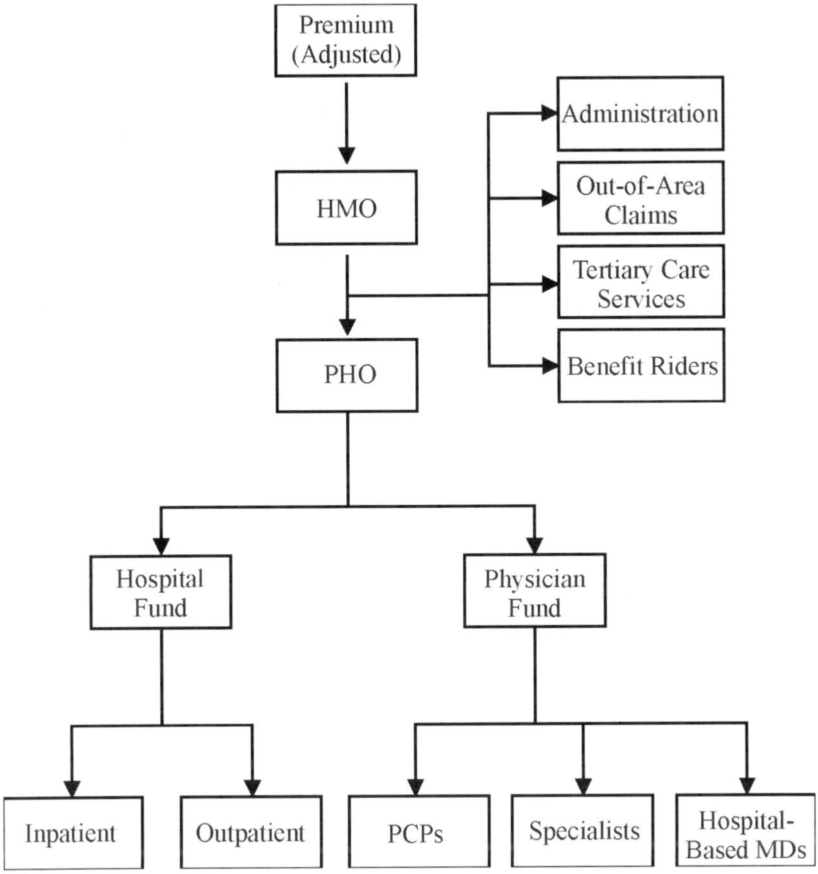

accepting capitation reimbursement, Figure 6.3 depicts how the capitation payment might be divided. At the first step, the HMO or health plan would split out the portion of the adjusted premium received from the group that will go toward the costs of administration, out-of-area claims (for which the locally contracting provider organization would not be responsible), tertiary care services that are not part of the contract (e.g., transplantation), and benefit riders for other services not included in the contract (e.g., dental, pharmacy, vision care). The remainder of the premium determines the capitation payment made to the provider organization.

In the example of Figure 6.3, the physician-hospital organization then allocates the capitation to separate funds for hospital and physician professional services. The hospital fund is then distributed to inpatient and outpatient services, respectively. The physician fund is similarly divided into

Figure 6.4 The Flow of Funds in a Multi-Institutional Organized Delivery System

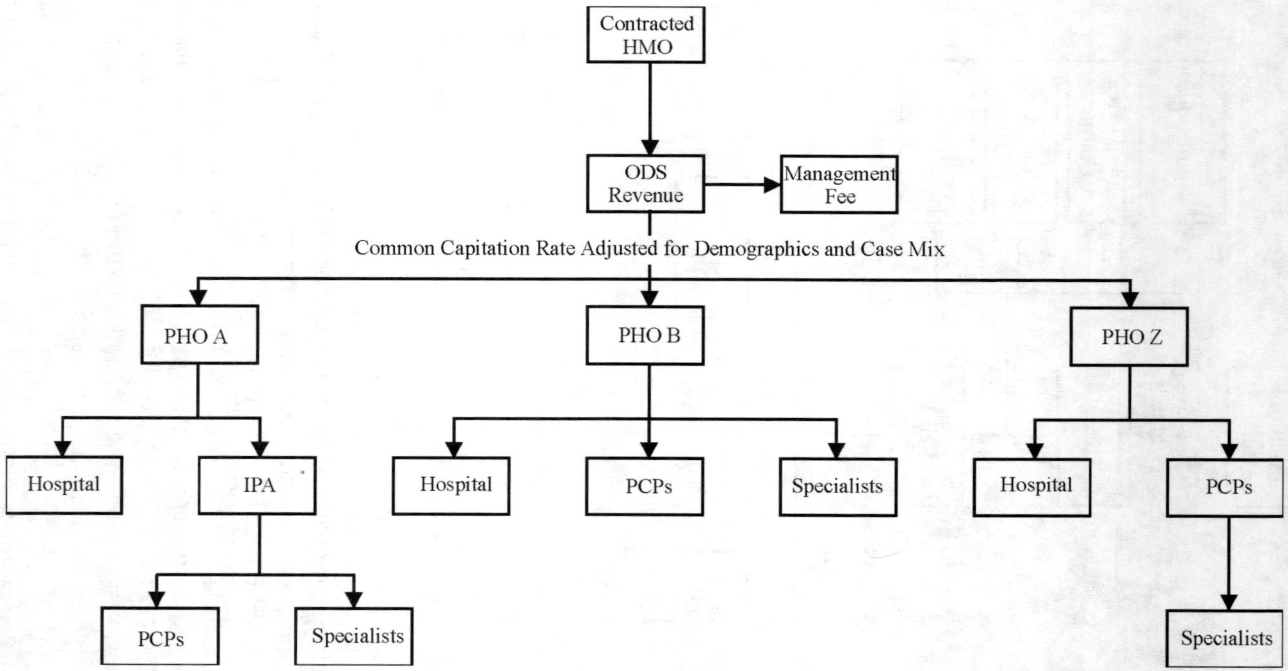

estimated allocations for primary care physicians, specialists, and hospital-based physicians (e.g., anesthesiologists, radiologists, pathologists, and emergency room physicians, often paid on salary by the hospital).

Figure 6.4 displays an analogous flow-of-funds arrangement for the situation in which the contracted provider organization is an HMO, which accepts the capitation from an independent health plan or employer group (the latter through direct contracting), then divides the capitation into organized delivery system (ODS) revenue and its management fee for administration costs. The HMO's organized delivery system, in turn, might take the form of several PHOs (A, B . . . Z in the diagram), each of which might then go at risk for its allocated share of the ODS revenue (or subcapitation).

Table 6.1, adapted from an example in the *Milliman and Robertson Health Cost Guidelines* (cited in Ward 1995), shows a typical decomposition of health plan medical costs, assuming a comprehensive benefit with $5 copayment for office visits. Ten percent to 12 percent of total medical costs has been a typical allocation for PCP services, but increasingly we are seeing the overall cost structure shifting toward PCP cost shares in the range of 15 percent as the payments for primary care rise relative to those of specialists. As the PCPs themselves enter into capitation agreements and are placed at risk for specialty referral costs, they will ask if the PHO itself is specialty-driven.

Joseph Coyne (1995), of HealthCare Data Bank, Inc., has developed recent estimates of the range of various medical cost components for a sample of seven HMOs. Those data are displayed in Table 6.2, as a complementary

Table 6.1 Typical Health Plan Allocation of Medical Costs

Cost Category	Percentage of Cost by Category	Cumulative Percentage of Cost by Category
Hospital Services		
Inpatient	28	
Outpatient	11	
Total Hospital Services		39
Physician Services		
Primary Care	12	
Specialty Care	20	
Total Physician Services		32
Other Medical Services		5
Ancillary Services		15
Prescription Drugs		9
Total Medical Costs		100

Source: Adapted from D.L. Ward. 1995. "Operational Finance and Budgeting." In *Essentials of Managed Health Care*, edited by P.R. Kongstvedt. Gaithersburg, MD: Aspen Publishers, Inc., p. 195. Used with permission of Milliman and Robertson, Inc.

Table 6.2 Range of Capitation Payment Components for Seven HMOs, 1991–1993

Medical Expense Category	Percentage of Premium Contracts	Per Member per Month Contracts
Physician Services	35–40	$35–49
Psychiatric and Other Professional Services	7–8	$7–10
Emergency Room and Out-of-Area Services	2–3	$2–4
Inpatient, Ancillary, and SNF	29–32	$29–39
Pharmacy and Other Medical Services	7–9	$8–11
Total	80–92	$81–113

Source: Joseph Coyne. HealthCare Data Bank, Inc. 1995. "The Future of Risk Sharing. Capitation and Integrated Delivery Systems." Paper delivered at the Thirty-Eighth Annual Congress on Administration of the American College of Healthcare Executives. Chicago, 9 March.

source of plan cost information comparable to the Milliman and Robertson data presented in Table 6.1.

THE ROLE OF PHYSICIANS IN DEVELOPING AND SUSTAINING CAPITATION ARRANGEMENTS

The fundamental concern driving capitated payment arrangements is the desire to control variation in practice patterns. Williamson, Goldschmidt, and Jillson (1979) documented common medical practices in three internal medicine subspecialties and found that fewer than 10 percent of the practices were based on the results of published medical research. Other studies cited by Brent James (1993) suggest that "80 to 90 percent of common medical practices have no basis in published scientific research" (p. 20).

The principal lesson from interventions designed to reduce practice variation is that the aim should be to manage health care's clinical and administrative processes, not physicians. John Wennberg's work on small-area variations in medical practice (cf. Wennberg, Barnes, and Zubkoff 1982; Wennberg et al. 1977) and the research by John Eisenberg (1986) show the power of *shared information* on the behavior of physicians. The target of this information is to isolate common-cause (systematic) variation and to reduce it via process control.

Capitation payment provides a strong incentive for such process control in the health care organization. Process control necessitates information, feedback, and intervention. As the ultimate "knowledge workers," physicians must be integrally involved in that undertaking. We suggest several axioms for maximizing the participation of physicians and securing their long-run commitment to making capitation work:

- Physicians serve a dual role in the system. They influence cost and quality in two ways: first, by deciding which preventive, diagnostic, and treatment interventions to apply for a given patient; and second, by choosing the level of resource use within each of those patient interventions (what to do and how much to do).
- Physicians do practice differently, sometimes simply due to random variation and often because of systematic differences in socialization, training, and available information. Some systematic variation is healthy—it provides benchmarks for peers to emulate in many instances (e.g., unusually low postoperative complication rates, high rates of satisfaction and functionality after rehabilitation) and responds to subtle, difficult-to-measure, underlying patient differences in case severity or treatment preferences (such as social or family reasons for increased length of stay). The goal of process control is to minimize unintended and unhelpful variability in care patterns. Direct participation by the physicians involved in the design and implementation of clinical protocols for controlling variation is crucial.
- No single approach to modifying physician behavior works by itself.

Available research (summarized in Eisenberg 1986; and Greco and Eisenberg 1992) suggests that a hierarchy of component interventions will have the most powerful effect in changing physician practice patterns. These interventions are especially salient in a capitated market, where the incentives and constraints of the environment have already captured the organization's and physicians' attention. These component interventions have a certain natural order of influence on physician behavior.

First, the organization should work with physicians through an array composed of education; soliciting their input to the design of specific medical management models and practice-pattern targets; the implementation of written guidelines, criteria, and targets for administrative and clinical performance; and then feedback on organizational, individual, and comparative performance.

We argue that these steps in securing the participation, involvement, and commitment of physicians should *precede* the application of financial incentives and risk sharing, which constitute the logical next step. Sanctions and penalties would come last and should be relatively rare unless the system is exhibiting a high degree of dysfunction.

Markers of a successful transition to capitation payment include that it:

- is responsibly introduced and expanded when reasonable;
- covers services that a majority of physicians would be expected to provide;
- includes adjustments to reflect expected demographic variations;

- derives from a clear underlying relative value scale for pricing units of service and is based on specific volume assumptions; and
- compensates primary care physicians directly for assuming the responsibility for managing the overall care of their panel and for bearing financial risk.

The financial incentives themselves should be tied to individual performance and should address factors that the physician directly and substantively controls. The incentive factors should be concrete, objective, relevant, and reliably measured. The physician's and manager's span of control is limited to a few important incentive factors, both to focus attention and to increase the likelihood that the incentives will be understood and accepted by physicians.

Many health plans contracting on a capitated basis with PCPs are setting PMPM payments at roughly 130 percent of fee-for-service equivalents, in return for assuming the gatekeeping and care-management function as well as the attendant financial risk. PCPs seem to be more inclined to accept capitated risk when they deal directly with prepaid group practice HMOs in an integrated delivery system arrangement as opposed to in their contracts with freestanding health plans relying on a network or IPA-type model. This may relate to the potentially tighter coordination of care inherent in those more closely coupled patient care systems, which reduces the incremental utilization risk being borne by the contracting PCP. *Variable capitation* rates, which adjust the payment based on the age/sex distribution of the enrolled population, are generally more acceptable to physicians. Also, provider organizations and health plans that involve their physicians directly in setting utilization targets are more likely to achieve their cost-performance goals.

Towers Perrin (1992) has developed rating factors for the medical costs of primary care and referral care in a typical HMO population. Table 6.3 shows the figures for a typical commercial population and a group of seniors age 65 and over. The data suggest an overall cost multiple (utilization factor) of 3.2 for seniors relative to a typical commercial group in HMOs.

Table 6.3 Primary Care versus Specialty Care Costs in HMO Populations: Typically Commercial and Over Age 65

	Commercial Cost	**Senior Cost Multiple**	**Senior Cost**
Primary Care	\$9.00 (23% of total)	2.1	\$19.00 (15% of total)
Referral Care	\$31.00 (77% of total)	3.5	\$109.00 (85% of total)
Total	\$40.00 (100%)	3.2	\$128.00 (100%)

Source: Towers Perrin, 1992.

Primary care accounts for less than one-fourth of the PMPM costs in both the commercial and the over-65 groups. These numbers are not applicable to every situation, of course, but should provide some useful benchmarks for provider organizations, particularly medical groups, that are taking their first steps toward capitation reimbursement.

The changing relative economic position of PCPs and specialists, together with the emerging evidence on the effects of increased managed care involvement on physician incomes, does suggest that capitated arrangements—properly crafted—will be increasingly adopted in paying PCPs. For example, the Center for Research in Ambulatory Care Health Administration based a recent study on 209 group practices and 2,116 family practice physicians and found that:

- Average family practice physician (FP) incomes rose from approximately $106,000 per year in 1991 to $112,000 in 1992.
- FPs in single-specialty groups earned $9,000 less per year than those in multispecialty groups.
- FPs who derived at least half their income from managed care (at-risk) arrangements earned about $5,000 per year more than those with no managed care.
- HMO-affiliated FPs earned approximately $116,000 per year versus $103,000 for hospital-affiliated FPs.

Another study by Cejka & Co., St. Louis, surveyed physicians in multispecialty groups. Their survey data suggested that:

- Since 1988, FPs' median compensation had increased by 25 percent, pediatricians' by 23 percent.
- The largest annual increase, 6.5 percent, occurred in 1992, by which time average annual FP incomes had reached $112,285.
- Most specialists during that period had experienced declining incomes. General surgeons' incomes were down 1 percent and plastic surgeons' 8 percent, while cardiovascular surgeons' and neurosurgeons' incomes were holding steady.

Among representative clients of McNerney Heintz, Inc., PCPs had incomes during this time span that ranged from 110 percent to 160 percent higher under capitation payment, as compared to fee-for-service arrangements.

The bottom line is that, at least at *current* payment levels, capitation can be used as a carrot to induce PCPs to enter into at-risk arrangements with HMOs, health plans, and organized delivery systems—particularly if PCPs are allowed to participate in savings derived from utilization. However, as capitation rates are squeezed down by the competitive forces playing on health plans, physicians, hospitals, and other providers, the generosity of capitation rates will be less of a factor, and plans and hospitals will increasingly have to rely on the other compensating advantages that they can offer to PCPs accepting capitation: the quality of the information they provide to clinicians on practice patterns and outcomes, the incremental volume they can deliver to the PCP, and the benefits of reduced transaction and administrative costs to the professional practice.

From the perspective of the physician-hospital organization, there are several reasons to accept capitation reimbursement. First, the capitated payment allows the provider organization to exercise autonomy in managing the fixed dollars allocated for patient care. In concert with assuming economic risk, the hospital and its physicians are all encouraged and allowed to develop their own care management protocols. With this autonomy comes the corresponding financial accountability of the PHO. Capitation enhances organizational control over the allocation of resources, the credentialing of clinicians, the development of the physician network, and the establishment of the standards of care. More important, the discipline of fixed prospective payment per capita aligns the incentives of the physicians and hospitals more fundamentally than any other reimbursement alternative. Finally, capitation payment offers the opportunity for joint financial gain to physicians and the hospital through predictable cashflow, guaranteed payment and elimination of uncollectables, and the inclusion of a management fee within the global payment.

The experience of provider organizations managing dollars within capitated arrangements suggests the following critical elements for success:

- A fundamental requisite for capitation to succeed is the presence of an experienced and qualified management and support staff. The increased economic risk and financial accountability require a quantum leap in the organization's ability to manage scarce dollars and to focus its resources and patient care processes.
- The capitation must be adequate for the level of risk assumed. The PMPM amount should be justified by detailed actuarial and utilization data on the population for which economic risk is being assumed, or a similar population.
- Medical staff leadership is crucial. Those leaders must be knowledgeable, committed, and involved in the management of the organization and the allocation of resources to patient care and administrative functions.
- The provider organization will be characterized by the excellence of its medical-management program. The use of care-management strategies (e.g., clinical pathways, guidelines, and case-management algorithms) will pervade the organization that succeeds under capitation.

- The information system's capacity to identify the physicians, encounters, and resource costs associated with the care of a specific patient and, in the aggregate, for defined populations or particular health problems, is fundamental to successful capitation. The risk-bearing provider organization must be able to provide *decision support* to clinicians engaged in real-time patient care, while also producing reports of resource use and the quality of care for regular *organizational assessment.*
- The best-performing capitated arrangements typically evolve toward capitation of selected specialists, as well as primary care physicians. The economic discipline of fixed payment aligns the incentives of the PCPs and specialists in much the same way that capitation creates a symmetry between the economic interests of the hospital and physicians.
- Well-designed mechanisms for sharing risk and reward must accompany the development of joint capitation. Typically, the reward level will match the degree of risk being assumed by the different parties and their varying ability to control specific components of risk. For example, to encourage efficiency in inpatient care, a typical arrangement might offer physicians a 50–50 share with the hospital in any surpluses in the hospital inpatient care risk pool, but a 100 percent share of the savings in the specialty care (referral) risk pool.
- Finally, the successfully capitated provider organization will be very specific in excluding from the capitation agreement those patient care services that are not under its control. Consider the example of transplantation services in the case of a small or medium-size community hospital, which may lack both reasonable contractual access to those services and the scale of covered lives to spread the economic risk associated with such high-tech tertiary care. For the same reasons, the provider organization assuming capitated risk will implement stop-loss and reinsurance provisions to protect itself against exceptionally high cost and uncontrollable cases.

DEVELOPING THE CAPITATED BUDGET

Table 6.4 displays a sample budget for a start-up PHO that is contracting for physician and outpatient services. The information is presented in the form of an income statement, with revenue, medical expense, and administrative expense separately identified. The income statement shows three plans (A, B, and C), totaling 50,702 contracted member months. The revenue sources are the capitation payment and estimated reinsurance payments, which vary by plan, and the inflow from coordination of benefits (COB)/subrogation with other payers. Incentive payments (e.g., bonuses for positive utilization and medical expense performance) and interest income were not present in

Table 6.4 Developing the Budget for a Start-Up PHO (Physician and Outpatient Services)

	Plan A	Plan B	Plan C	Total
Member Months	2,102	29,160	19,440	50,702
Revenue (PMPM)				
Capitation	$35.00	$48.00	$47.83	$47.40
Reinsurance	1.00	.89	.89	.89
COB/Sub	.28	.28	.28	.28
Incentives	.00	.00	.00	.00
Interest	.00	.00	.00	.00
Total Revenue	**$36.28**	**$49.17**	**$49.00**	**$48.57**
Expense (PMPM)				
Medical				
PCP Capitation	$9.84	$9.84	$9.84	$9.84
PCP Incentive	.98	.98	.98	.98
PCP Total	**$10.82**	**$10.82**	**$10.82**	**$10.82**
Specialist Capitation	3.06	3.06	3.06	3.06
Specialist FFS	15.57	19.44	15.57	17.79
Specialist Total	**$18.63**	**$22.50**	**$18.63**	**$20.85**
Hospital Capitation	$0.00	$6.65	$6.65	$6.37
Hospital FFS	.00	2.20	.68	1.53
Hospital Total	**$0.00**	**$8.85**	**$7.33**	**$7.90**
Total Medical	**$29.45**	**$42.17**	**$36.78**	**$39.57**
Administrative	$5.03	$5.03	$5.03	$5.03
Total Expense	**$34.48**	**$47.20**	**$41.81**	**$44.60**
Excess of Revenue over Expense	**$1.80**	**$1.97**	**$7.19**	**$3.97**

this situation for any of the three plans. The budgeted expense in this example includes:

- the PCP capitation ($9.84) and a budgeted incentive of 10 percent of that capitation ($0.98);
- a capitation for selected specialty services and estimated FFS costs for other specialists;
- the hospital capitation and a separate hospital FFS component; and
- administrative expenses budgeted for each plan or product line served by the PHO.

The specific line-item expenses are illustrative of existing arrangements in the marketplace, but the actual numbers are less important than the concepts highlighted in the example. For example, the PHO in Plan A is simply a *management support* vehicle for the PCPs and specialists to contract on a mixed capitated and FFS basis with the health plan. In Plans B and C, on the other hand, the physicians and the hospital are jointly at risk through the PHO for their share of the capitation. Administrative expense would include functions like general plan management, physician management support services, provider credentialing, member services, actuarial services, accounting and finance, and claims processing. The health plan products could be provided directly (sponsored) by the PHO itself, or the PHO might contract with an independent health plan or HMO. Certain services, such as actuarial and claims processing might be contracted out by the PHO (outsourced) or delivered in-house, depending on the managerial and information systems capacity of the provider organization.

Capitation is growing as a method of payment by HMOs. While only 6 percent of all covered lives are capitated for all professional services (InterStudy 1994, 20), a substantial percentage of HMOs are currently using capitation as a reimbursement method (pp. 35–36):

- 69.3 percent reimburse primary care physicians on a capitated basis.
- 30.2 percent pay for specialty care on a capitated basis.
- 18.0 percent pay capitation for hospital services.

The growth of capitation creates a kind of "billboard effect."[3] More than any other change in the health care environment, it announces to market players that all participants must manage within a budget of fixed health care resources. The provider organization that accepts this method of payment is therefore making an explicit statement to the marketplace that it has received that message and is ready to assume financial and clinical accountability for the health care needs of a defined population.

Understanding the *strategic* requirements of managed care contracting, particularly capitation, is necessary, but not sufficient, for success. The high-performing managed care organization must develop the *structures* to support that strategic understanding.

NOTES

1. This break-even point of volume, at which total revenues equal total costs, is reached under the FFS payment system when the following holds true: Fixed Cost = Price – Variable Cost per Unit of Volume. Thus, as long as price exceeds variable cost (i.e., there is a positive contribution margin), each additional unit of volume contributes toward covering the provider's fixed costs. If variable costs and revenues are not directly proportionate to volume (i.e., if prices vary at different levels of volume or if variable costs per unit are not constant but instead vary over different levels of volume of services), the diagram gets more complicated, but the basic point remains: higher volume equals greater profit under the typical FFS reimbursement agreement.
2. By "per person, volume-fixed" costs, we mean costs that do not vary with volume of services per person, but do vary with increases in the number of

persons the provider serves. Examples would be the cost of infrastructure, such as information systems and transportation networks, and other transaction costs in the delivery system that depend on the scale of population but not on the volume of health services per se.

3. We owe the term "billboard effect" to David Lansky, Ph.D., Director of the Center for Outcomes Research and Education, Sisters of Providence Health System, who uses it to describe the effect of capitation payment in capturing the attention of both PCPs and specialists, particularly in encouraging the more rapid adoption of care-management strategies and new hospital-physician relationships.

REFERENCES

Coyne, J. 1995. "The Future of Risk Sharing, Capitation, and Integrated Delivery Systems." Paper delivered at the Thirty-Eighth Annual Congress on Administration of the American College of Healthcare Executives, Chicago, 9 March.

Eisenberg, J.M. 1986. *Doctors' Decisions and the Cost of Medical Care.* Chicago: Health Administration Press.

Greco, P.J., and J.M. Eisenberg. 1992. "Sounding Board: Changing Physicians' Practices." *New England Journal of Medicine* 329 (12): 1271–74.

James, B.C. 1993. "Implementing Clinical Practice Guidelines Through Clinical Quality Improvement." *Frontiers of Health Services Management* 10 (Fall): 3–38.

Towers Perrin. 1992. Personal Communication with Robert Smith.

Wennberg, J.E., B.A. Barnes, and M. Zufkoff. 1982. "Professional Uncertainty and the Problem of Supplier-Induced Demand." *Social Science and Medicine* 16 (7): 811–24.

Wennberg, J.E., L. Blowers, R. Parker, and A.M. Gettelsohn. 1977. "Changes in Tonsillectomy Rates Associated with Feedback and Review." *Pediatrics* 59 (June): 821–86.

Williamson, J.W., P.G. Goldschmidt, and I.A. Jillson. 1979. Medical Practice Information Demonstration Project: Final Report. Office of the Assistant Secretary of Health, DHEW, Contract #282-77-0068GS. Baltimore, MD: Policy Research Inc.

CHAPTER

7

Developing Structures for Effective Managed Care Contracting

Douglas Conrad, Robert Bonney, Michael Sachs, and Robert Smith

This chapter discusses developing structures in managed care contracting and addresses the following questions:

- What basic functions are involved in managed care contracting?
- What are the structural components of the system within which managed care contracting takes place?
- What form of strategic architecture is best overlaid on these components to ensure successful managed care contracting?

BASIC FUNCTIONS IN MANAGED CARE CONTRACTING

Four basic functions are crucial to effective implementation of managed care contracting. As shown in Figure 7.1, they are operations management, financial management, marketing management, and medical management. Intentionally and emphatically, the diagram places medical management (based on successful physician relations) at the center of these interrelated functions.

All four of these functions require a strategic information system in order to be performed effectively and to build the strategic architecture portrayed in Figure 7.2.[1] The building blocks in that structure are the management services in operations and finance, services to support medical

Reprinted from Conrad, D., et al. 1996. *Managed Care Contracting: Concepts and Applications for the Healthcare Executive.* Chicago: Health Administration Press.

Figure 7.1 Basic Functions and Their Interrelations

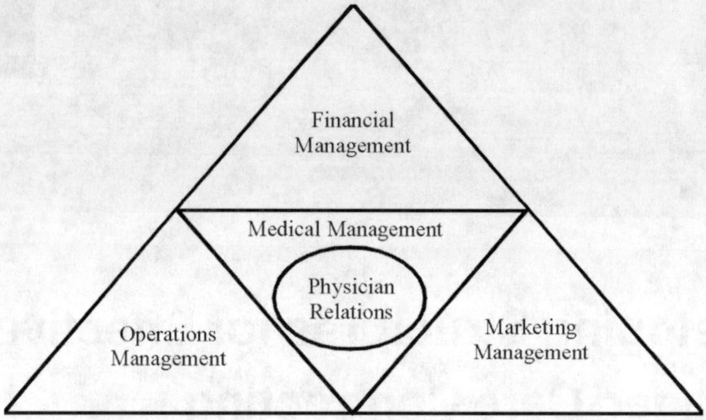

management, an organized delivery system, and health plan capacity. The provider organization (e.g., the hospital or medical group) will face a progressive series of "make-buy" decisions regarding whether to own and directly control each of those building blocks. Whether owning or contracting for those building blocks, however, the organization's success in managed care contracting will depend significantly on the strength of each component.

Thus, the provider organization that is simply contracting with health plans on a per case of DRG basis for hospital inpatient services will focus on the financial viability and strength of each of the health plans and will ensure that its own pre- and postdischarge arrangements are configured to facilitate minimum inpatient length of stay and ancillary resource utilization. The hospital's management services germane to that contracting situation would be limited to basic administration and office management. Medical management services would emphasize inpatient case management. The hospital would specialize in the inpatient-medical-services stage of production in the vertically integrated, organized delivery system. And the hospital's relationship with the health plan would be strictly at arm's length.

In contrast, the provider organization that has created an organized delivery system and is the owner or sponsor of a health plan, for example, a multispecialty group practice organizationally integrated with its own hospital (or hospital network) and health plan, must erect a much more tightly cemented strategic architecture. To wit, going from right to left in Figure 7.2. (from health plan to management services), that organization must:

- construct (or at least contract for) the capacity to function as a licensed health plan (with license or common operating agreement, capital, underwriting or rating capability, promotional and sales activity);

Figure 7.2 Developing the Regional Organized Delivery System: Building the Strategic Architecture

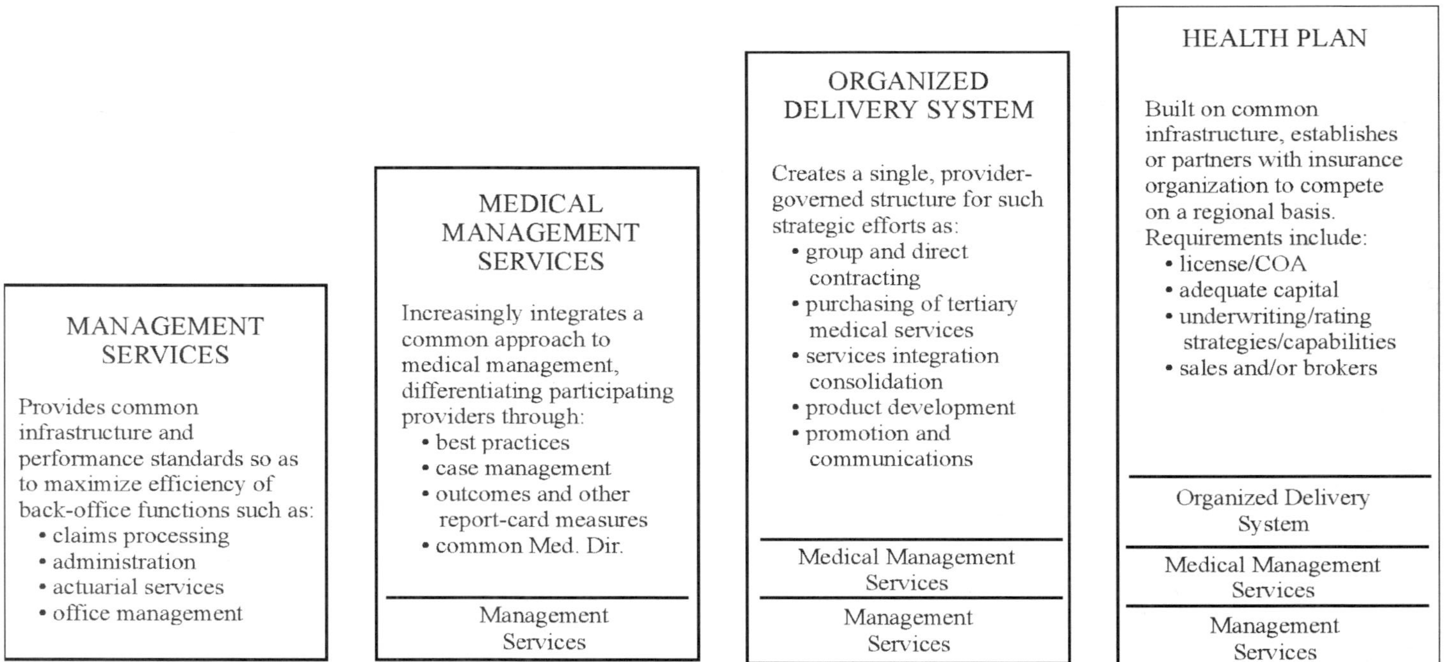

The term "strategic architecture" is from *Competing for the Future* by G. Hamel and C.K. Prahalad

- deliver an organized continuum of care to defined populations (enrollees of the health plan), with capacity for group and direct contracting, the purchase or delivery of tertiary care services, the integration and consolidation of an array of health services, new product development, promotion, and communications;
- develop a common approach to medical management that bridges different participating providers through a single medical director, best-practices standards, care management models, and a focus on outcomes and accountability; and
- provide common managerial and systems support and performance standards to increase the efficiency of administration, office management, actuarial and underwriting services, and claims-processing services.

We propose that the key structural feature that will tie these disparate pieces of the strategic architecture together into a coherent whole is the development of a *strategic information system.* This is the common link that can cement the four building blocks of managed care contracting. Provider organizations will differ in the *height* of each building block, that is, the extent to which they provide within a commonly owned and managed entity the full complement of management services, medical management services, the continuum of health care services, and their own health plan. However, whatever the results of the make-buy decisions within each of these building blocks, the hospital or medical group must fashion an *information system* and *information management processes* that will facilitate effective delivery of care and assumption of risk by the organization.

In the next section we delineate the properties of such a strategic information system, with variable shapes depending on the organization's specific strategy. Peter Drucker (1995) poses the challenge well:

> What is important is not the tools. It is the concepts behind them. They convert what were always seen as discrete techniques to be used in isolation and for separate purposes into one integrated information system. That system then makes possible business diagnosis, business strategy, and business decisions. That is a new and radically different view of the meaning and purpose of information: as a measurement on which to base future action rather than as a postmortem and a record of what has already happened.
>
> The command-and-control organization that first emerged in the 1870s might be compared to any organism held together by its shell. The corporation that is now emerging is being designed around a skeleton: *information*, both the corporation's new integrating system and its articulation.

THE STRATEGIC INFORMATION SYSTEM

In conceptualizing the information system as a strategic tool, we begin with four major premises. First, any consideration of information systems must start with a list of introductory but critical questions that define the tasks of, expectations for, and level of success of those systems. Second, four parameters of the provider organization's external and internal environment should define the content of the information system:

1. the direction and scope of change in health care delivery;
2. the evolving roles and expectations of purchasing and performance in health care;
3. the nature of the physician-hospital organization (the PHO in a generic sense, not wedded to any single structural form) as an integrated, managed care organization; and
4. the relationship of the information system to the organization's specific level of development as a regionally organized delivery system and to the level of its future commitment to becoming a more vertically integrated health care system.

Third, the operational needs of an organization bearing substantial economic risk (capitation or percentage of premium arrangements) include the majority of systems requirements of the HMO, from registration and claims adjudication to practice profiling and electronic data interfaces. Fourth, effective management of risk requires a routine set of reports that provides an overview of the performance of the organization as a whole and that provides insight into specific aspects of performance from multiple perspectives.

PRELIMINARY QUESTIONS

The first questions in designing the strategic information system to fit the organization's managed care contracting strategy relate to the organization's contracting objectives:

- What specific geographic market areas or populations (defined in terms of demographic characteristics or health conditions) does the provider wish to serve more extensively?
- What are the measurable goals associated with those market objectives (e.g., increased market share, increased panel size per PCP, recruitment of additional physicians to serve an expanded population)?

The next question in determining system design is whether the provider organization will accept risk and manage benefits. If so, another series of related questions emerges:

- How much risk is the organization willing to assume?
- What specific measures will the provider organization use to measure the utilization or financial risk of the population under its managed care contracts? If those measures are different from the

algorithms used by health plans in adjusting their payments to the provider, what "crosswalks" will the provider use in translating the risk measures from its own information system into the information systems the plans employ in setting provider payments?

- How much of the provider organization's risk will be passed along to other entities (e.g., through stop-loss or reinsurance provisions)? Will those reinsured risks be calculated on a per case or aggregate (per accounting period) basis? How will outlier provisions be handled?
- How will benefits be managed under the provider organization's managed care contracts? Will there be preadmission authorizations for hospitalization, and will referrals be limited either to a restricted list of specialists or by prior authorization from a primary care physician?

The organization aggressively seeking managed care contracts must also choose the parameters on which it wishes to compete. This point parallels our earlier observation that building and sustaining *comparative advantage* is the key to a successful long-run managed care contracting strategy. The hospital and its medical group should identify those dimensions of health services on which they mutually provide the greatest added value and where their capacities best fit the market demands of individual consumers, organized purchasers (e.g., public programs and employers), and private health plans. Certain questions of comparative advantage relative to competitors have immediate implications for the strategic information system:

- Against what specific measures will the providers attempt to compete: cost per case, per diem, or per capita; health status measures (adjusted for case mix); or indexes of the cost-effectiveness of specific procedures or treatment regimens?
- How will the value of care be defined, measured, and monitored, and to whom will that information be disseminated on a systematic basis? For example, Virginia Mason Medical Center in Seattle has developed a value equation: Value = Appropriateness 5 [(Quality of Outcomes + Service) / Cost], which expresses value as a function of the appropriateness of services delivered and the care setting plus the cost-effectiveness of the overall package of care delivered by the organization. In the context of that approach, which specific indicators would be monitored, and how would they be presented to consumers, employers, and health plans?
- What new services must be added to the organization's continuum of care in order to extract the full value of its comparative advantage, and what new demands would monitoring the cost and health outcomes of those additional services place on the information system?

Another set of preliminary questions speak to the transformation in the structure of the hospital and medical group's interactions with, and relationships to, other entities:

- between physicians;
- with physicians;
- with other provider organizations (e.g., PHOs); and
- with payers.

These relationships and interactions will govern choices concerning the types of communication software, reporting mechanisms, database management tools, and reporting capabilities need to be built into the information system.

Finally, the information system cannot be static, but must be built for change and flexibility from the very beginning. From the PHO's perspective, for example, some of the specific components and structuring of the information system will change over time as the organization's relationships with health plans, employers (and other director contracting groups), and physicians change. Perhaps the best strategy is to build one's information system incrementally and to avoid large, irreversible investments wherever possible. Having said this, the organization nonetheless must face up to certain preliminary questions in constructing a flexible and responsive system:

- What continuum of services is the hospital most likely to provide in the next five years?
- What are current purchasers' major demands for information, and how are those likely to change over the longer run, especially as the organization's mix of purchasers changes?
- What information do the physicians and care teams need right now to manage care most effectively and efficiently, and how are those needs evolving over time?

In preparing itself for the directions of change in organized community care, the provider organization must build a strategic information system that can accommodate several realities. First and foremost, the system must allow for:

- periodic rethinking of the organization's vision, strategies, and, consequently, its strategic objectives as the marketplace evolves and customer expectations change;
- redesigning of workflows (and, consequently, information requirements) around processes, rather than departments or individuals;
- reorganizing the division of labor toward more lateral, or horizontal, flows of communication and accountability, as opposed to vertical hierarchies; and
- redefinition of the organization's customers and its product and service lines.

This reengineered health care provider organization moves the focal point from the hospital-factory to a flotilla of resources, poised to move quickly in response to the waves of changes and with an emphasis on software over hardware and on targeting key data to the knowledge workers (physicians and care team) first. *Decision support* precedes, both in priority and real time, *managerial oversight* in this model for the strategic information system.

REPORTING HIERARCHY

The organization can begin the transformation to a strategic information system designed to meet the needs of state-of-the-art managed care contracting by working backward from the end-user requirements for reporting and analysis. Figure 7.3 displays a hierarchy of these information uses. This hierarchy relates to: (1) the organization's overall needs for performance measurement and reporting; (2) the informational needs of medical managers and those with budget responsibility and accountability for specific cost components (treatment-type detail) and for certain populations served (contracted-plan detail); and (3) the reports and clinical profiling demanded by individual physicians and medical groups wishing to asses their own practice patterns and those of peers.

In a properly structured information system, organizational performance reports will be produced with no more than a six-week lag, based on two sets of data: financial statement analysis and assessments of performance relative to health plan and employer criteria for performance (e.g., HEDIS). Quarterly income statement and balance sheet information should be augmented by a memorandum assessing profit and loss (P&L) experience, and the system should support ad hoc inquiries on P&L and the status of the organization's assets and liabilities. Qualitative reports should be producible on effectiveness and quality of care, access to and satisfaction with health services, and the enrollment and utilization experience of specific health plan populations. The information system should also generate financial ratios and other measures of financial viability and organizational efficiency.

As suggested in Figure 7.3, the medical expense variance reports should flow directly, or burst, from the quarterly P&L reports and from the utilization and enrollment data systems maintained by the provider organization. The key is to be able to track (with not much more that a 90-day lag) the utilization and cost performance of the organization relative to each plan contract on a quarterly basis and to isolate the unit cost and use rates by plan by medical expense component (e.g., pharmacy, primary care, inpatient, outpatient).

Also, the strategic information system should generate quarterly practice-pattern reports and profiles. These profiles are part of the core of the

Figure 7.3 Reporting and Analysis Hierarchy

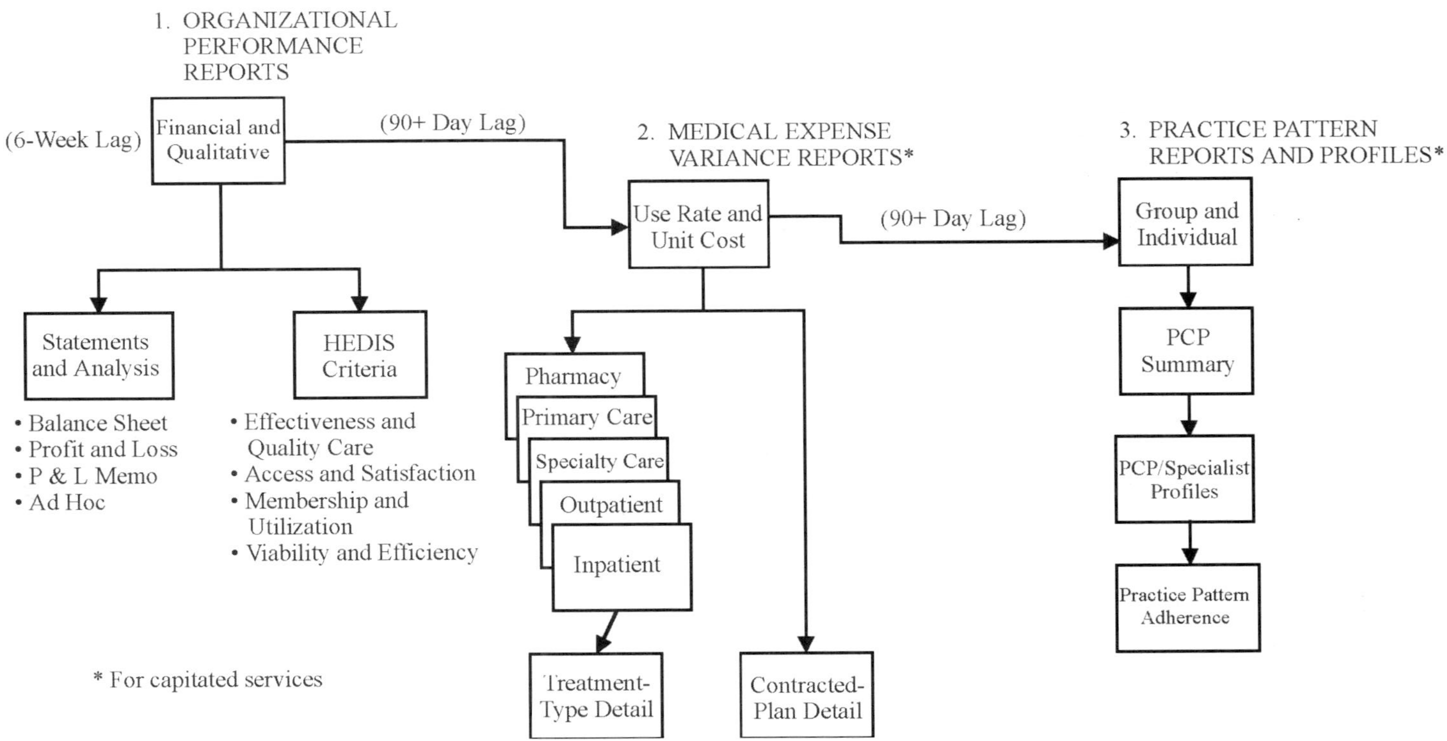

clinical assessment function for the organization and should include reports as the physician group and individual level:

- a summary of primary care physician utilization and cost per plan enrollee, for all enrollees in the individual PCP's panel, adjusted for case mix, and for specific health conditions, chosen as tracers of clinical performance by the medical group;
- PCP/specialist profiles, focusing on referral rates by PCPs in the aggregate and per tracer condition, as well as reports of average PMPM cost and utilization of PCPs and specialists; and
- adherence by both specialists and PCPs to practice-pattern expectations, based both on peer comparisons (normative) and mutually agreed criteria of quality (standards-based).

By completing its determination of the system requirements implicit in this reporting and analysis hierarchy, the organization has taken a major step in designing the strategic information system. However, of equal importance is the creation of a decision support capacity that is effective, efficient, reliable, and timely. Retrospective reports and analysis are essential for management control and oversight, but the real bread-and-butter of the information system is its ability to deliver real-time decision support to clinicians for the choices they make daily. Thus, we recommend that the provider organization build its strategic information system *in parallel*, actively engaging clinicians in both the planning of system reports and analysis and the design of prospective and real-time (concurrent) decision supports.

The principles of total quality management (TQM) offer a useful framework for orchestrating the development of a strategic information system. Figure 7.4 traces the flow of the processes that must be carried out and the communication flows required in implementing an organizationwide strategy for health system measurement and improvement. In this model strategy, the corporate data base feeds the processes of:

- creating and adopting tools for measuring performance;
- measuring the system;
- analyzing system performance and subsequently identifying areas for improvement; and
- documenting the improvements.

This strategy relies on the development of TQM knowledge among clinicians and draws on their expertise to identify methods for improving system performance. Figure 7.4 suggests that, to support full implementation of this information-based strategy, the information system itself should include publicly available information sources and on-line services as a form of resource center for each of the steps. Examples include Grateful Med of the National Library of Medicine, the clinical practice guidelines published

Figure 7.4 A Strategy for Health System Measurement and Improvement

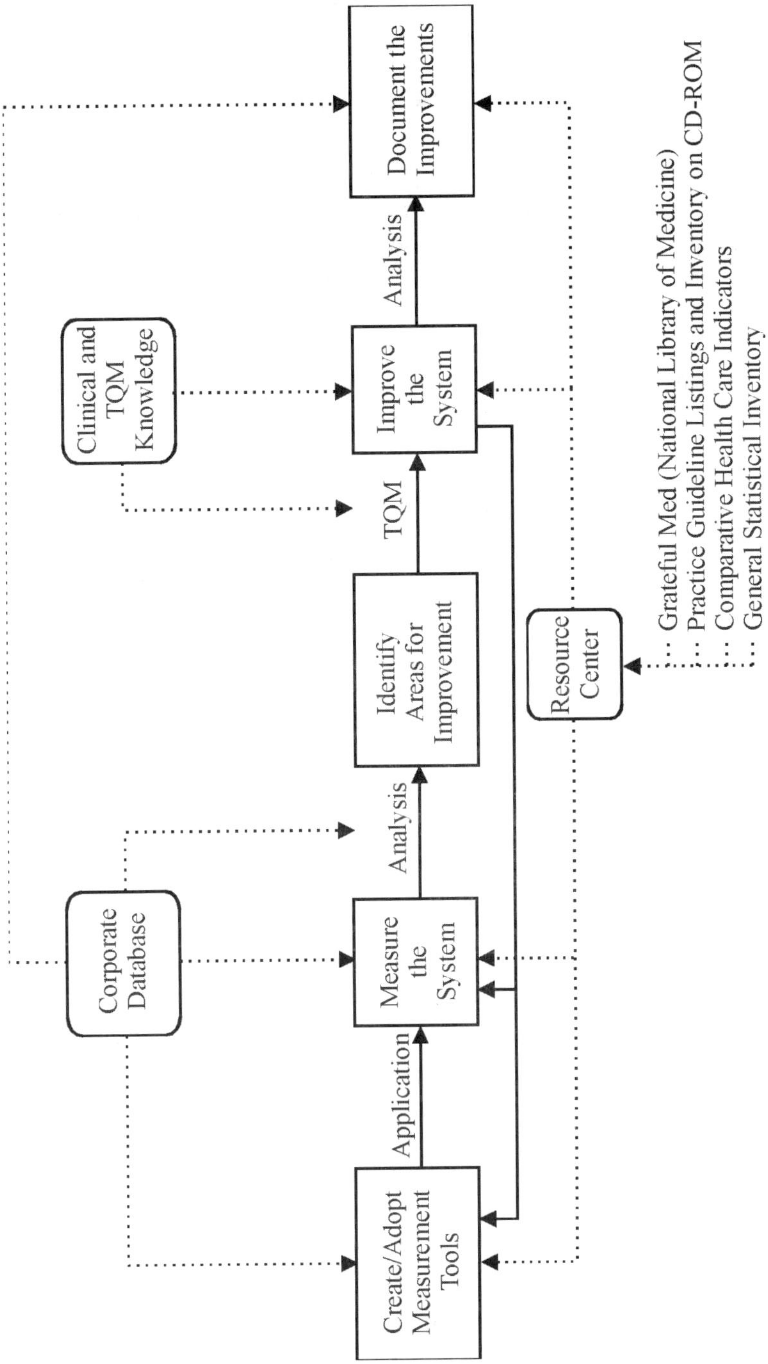

by the Agency for Health Care Policy and Research (AHCPR) and developed by professional societies and consensus panels, and the comparative health care indicators and general statistical inventory available from the National Center for Health Statistics.

According to the intramural research division of the AHCPR, 26 states now have hospital discharge abstract systems that are publicly available. These systems contain valuable information on resources used, procedures (including surgery), length of stay, and charges per hospital discharge, which can be used as benchmarks for the individual hospital's practice patterns. Together with population and demographic data on local areas (usually available from state planning, financial, and population forecasting departments), these hospital discharge data can be analyzed to produce analyses of variation in small-area practice pattern for the individual hospital's market area. Such analyses represent a very important strategic tool for the hospital and medical group in managed care contracting.

INFORMATION SYSTEM CAPABILITIES

Three levels of system capability are required for effective managed care contracting: functional, clinical, and integrative and networking.

Functional Capability

Functional capability relates to managing operations and the establishment and management of a standard database. Requisite functions include:

- membership enrollment;
- benefits management;
- utilization and medical management;
- claims processing and provider payment (including the capacity to accommodate capitation and other payment mechanisms);
- billing and accounts receivable;
- administrative support; and
- reporting (periodic, cumulative, and comparative) on both financial and qualitative performance.

The membership enrollment subsystem should incorporate a transaction history related to enrollee eligibility and the ability to track multiple unit assignments by the PHO or IPA. Benefits management requires that the information system be able to track multiple health plans, different managed care products, and various levels of benefits and coverage. Defined benefits and events must be traceable, as must benefit limitations defined by services or dollar amounts of coverage.

The utilization-review and medical-management component must be capable of triggering and monitoring the authorization or referral process (by provider, care management protocol, and benefit level). The core capacities of the medical-management subsystem must include the ability to report on utilization by plan, by provider, and by type of treatment and to isolate and compare practice patters of individual providers and care teams.

Claims processing and payment capabilities central to managed care contracting are:

- linkage of premiums or capitation charges paid to eligibility, benefits, and authorization;
- matching of claim to diagnoses, procedures, location, and service codes;
- the ability to mix capitation (multiple models) systems with fee-for-service systems;
- calculation of payments;
- routine edits to rule out duplicate claims;
- generation of explanations of benefits and payments;
- tracing multiple risk options and withhold arrangements;
- processing payments under PPO options, for preferred and nonpreferred providers, and third-party administrator (TPA) fund management; and
- claim check capabilities or interface.

Billing and accounts receivable (A/R) tracking are similarly essential in managed care contracting. A/R should be differentiated by rate structure and contract type. The system should be able to monitor and generate assigned amounts for different subscribers, as well as track copayment, coinsurance, and deductibles under different contract provisions. A well-integrated information system will also provide administrative support such as generating correspondence, tracking documents, and keeping track of coordination of benefits among secondary and primary payers.

Increasingly, as the provider organization assumes financial risk, the functional capability of its strategic information system resembles that of a health plan or insurance organization. This is inevitable, because—in accepting risk—the provider is functioning like an insurer to the defined population of the health plan and thus must have comparable information to measure and manage that risk. However, the provider organization can outsource some of its information system functions, for example, by having a third-party administrator maintain most or all of the functions outlined above. This would be an example of the provider choosing the "buy" alternative in its make-buy decisions regarding the information system.

In making its choices regarding which information system functions to own (or "make") versus buy, the provider is trading the greater control and "brand name" achievable by owning for the greater flexibility and reduced fixed costs associated with purchasing those functions in the market. Two of the system functions seem to offer relatively higher benefits to providers who own them: (1) utilization or medical management and (2) reporting. The two pose different challenges in designing an integrated functional capability for the information system.

The provider's comparative advantage would seem to rest in designing and implementing more effective protocols for *medical management*. Doctors, nurses, and interdisciplinary care teams within the organization have the most at stake in implementing effective processes of patient care, are closest to the relevant real-time information and have the greatest expertise to interpret and act on available clinical data. The efficacy of a "1-800" phone consultation approach to utilization management pales in comparison to care management algorithms developed and agreed upon by the organization's own clinical team. A corollary of this thesis is that the provider would need to play an active role in the design, and control the products, of the medical management component of its information system.

Clinical Capability

Clinical capabilities of the strategic information system are fundamentally important and are the primary distinctive competency for a provider-based information system. Health plans may distinguish themselves by efficiency and economies of scale in transactions processing and information systems integration and networking, but the heart of the provider's comparative advantage will be in its clinical efficiency and capacity. These capabilities include the ability to support medical management, quality improvement, and the enhanced assessment and management of risk. Three elements of clinical information are pivotal: (1) quality indicators linked to outcomes measures and comparisons to peer providers and organizationally derived and accepted clinical performance standards; (2) reporting of utilization rates and unit cost performance, adjusted for case mix and severity; and (3) the comparison of practice-pattern profiles with accepted protocols.

For clinicians to commit to medical management based on such reporting, they must be convinced that the data are clinically meaningful and that utilization and cost comparisons have been adjusted properly for variation in case mix and severity. There is no one consensus choice as to the preferred case-mix or case-severity classification schema, so the best approach is to work with the organization's clinical leadership to decide on an *acceptable* approach. All-payer DRGs for inpatients and MedisGroups are examples of widely used inpatient classifications, while a variety of ambulatory case-mix groupings are currently available: diagnosis clusters, ambulatory visit groups, ambulatory patient groups, ambulatory care groups, and the products of ambulatory care.

Two aspects of these case-mix systems are significant. First, it is important that comorbidities, signs, symptoms, and laboratory test and x-ray results be incorporated in the categorization to enhance the precision of the case-mix severity classification. Second, the classification of case mix and severity should reflect the *baseline* characteristics of the person at entry to care, not the procedures subsequently performed.

Integrative and Networking Capability

Integration and networking constitute the third critical capability of the strategic information system. The crux of this dimension is the ability to provide shared data between health plans, purchasers, and providers within the sphere of the provider organization's managed care contracting. Specifically, the system must have the capabilities of:

- enrollment, demographics, and benefit verification;
- claims submission;
- medical records;
- referrals;
- laboratory reports and other results reporting; and
- pharmacy.

In conclusion, the strategic information system must deliver on the promise of its functional and clinical capabilities and must create "connectivity" (integration and networking) among the various data subsystems (e.g., medical records, claims submission, pharmacy) for managed care contracting to succeed. Moreover, the information system should contribute to the organization's overall ability to sense the future evolution of its marketplace and the demands of its customers. This environmental surveillance function is one of the less appreciated sources of comparative advantage for health organizations, be they hospitals, physician groups, or health plans. Only by integrating the separate pieces of the data puzzle (utilization, cost, enrollment, demographics, and financial and qualitative performance measures) can the organization analyze not just where it has been historically but where it is headed in the future and where it must go to fulfill its strategic objectives. Thus, the system's ability to link, integrate, and distribute data throughout its network of data users and decision makers is a critical ingredient in utilizing information as an environmental sensor. The successful managed care organization's information system will enhance its ability to operate to standards of clinical and administrative performance, as valued by the customer, and to measure and improve that performance.

The organized delivery system and physician-hospital organizational relationships will all depend on and shape the strategic information system just discussed. We now proceed to consider the structural dimensions of the successful managed care organization.

STRUCTURING THE PHYSICIAN-HOSPITAL RELATIONSHIP AND THE ORGANIZED DELIVERY SYSTEM

We postulate that the first step in building a more closely structured relationship between the hospital and physicians is the integration of the physicians among themselves. Figure 7.5 depicts the array of physician-to-physician structures that facilitate the integration of physicians with each other. These arrangements range from the least integrated end of the continuum, solo practice, to single-specialty group practices (with or without walls containing the physicians in the group), to multispecialty group practices and medical foundations at the most integrated end of the continuum.

As Shortell (1993) and Conrad (1993) have argued, *clinical integration* is essential to vertical integration and to the creation of more effective and coordinated care delivery. Thus, we posit that physicians will gravitate toward physician-physician collaborative structures that offer the strongest prospects for clinical integration. Shortell, Gillies, and Anderson's (1994) work on organized delivery systems further suggests that physician-system integration is strongly associated with clinical integration. While the empirical work shows a correlation, but cannot by itself establish causality (i.e., does physician-system integration lead to greater clinical integration, or vice versa?), we suspect that integrating physicians more tightly with the

Figure 7.5 Physician-Physician Structures

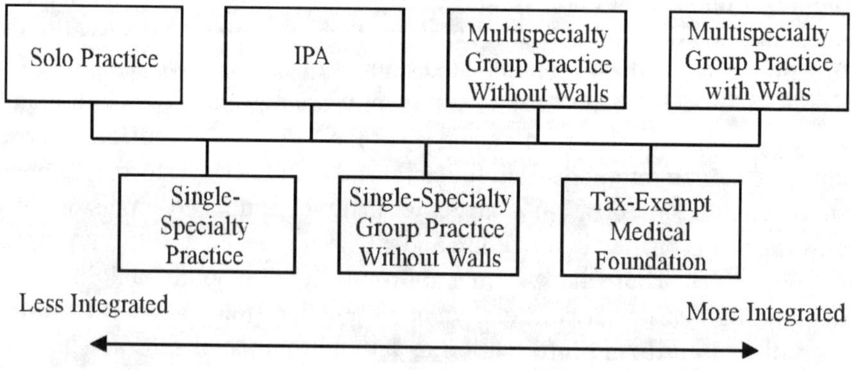

Source: Ropes and Gray, Boston, MA.

system will directly promote greater clinical integration. Given Shortell, Gillies, and Anderson's definition of physician-system integration (p. 52)—the extent to which physicians identify with the system, use it for care of their patients, and actively participate in system planning, management, and governance—it does seem likely that physician-physician structures will evolve, in the first stages, to physician-*hospital* organizations and then physician-*system* structures. The logic and centrality of clinical integration to physicians almost compels this trajectory, and at least Shortell, Gillies, and Anderson's preliminary findings support the financial advantages of such arrangements.

The physician-hospital organization is defined as a legal entity jointly controlled by a hospital and voluntarily (self-) selected members of its medical staff with authority to contract with health plans and self-insured employers. The premise behind the PHO is that both physicians and the hospital will be more successful in managed care contracting if they combine their complementary strengths and avoid unnecessary conflict with one another.

For example, the hospital offers several advantages as a partner to physicians (Shortell 1990): size, capital, technology, political influence, and organizational and managerial depth. Conversely, the deficits of the hospital as an economic partner in contracting are that it cannot move quickly, its skills and technology are not always transferable to noninpatient settings, and its culture is diffuse. The physician organization adds complementary advantages to the partnership: a professional culture with common socialization and norms, closeness to the customer (the patient), the ability to move quickly, and an entrepreneurial orientation. On the other hand, the physician organization generally lacks capital, clout, and political influence. Also, because physician organizations are relatively underdeveloped, they tend to lack systematic mechanisms for scanning their environment and for the same reason have less managerial and organizational expertise.

This listing of the advantages and disadvantages of the hospital and the physician organization as economic partners demonstrates why the PHO has arisen. For the most part, the hospital's strengths are the physician organization's weaknesses and vice versa. Thus, the potential synergies from combining the two are obvious. However, these gains from combination will only be fully realized if both parties invest resources and management effort in the partnership. Shortell (1990) cites several examples of "administrative best practices" from his study of 10 systems and an average of 13 physicians surveyed per system:

- Communication protocols are used in working with physicians. For example, specific guidelines are established for: (1) returning phone calls promptly within at least two hours; (2) indicating the number of days to solve routine problems; and (3) closing the loop on difficult issues and providing feedback to physicians.

- When a lot of changes are occurring in the hospital, five administrators each call three doctors immediately. Influential doctors that are most affected by the change are targeted.
- "Service facilitator" groups are established for each important service. These groups consist of approximately 20 people, involving physicians, nurses, and ancillary staff. They examine issues related to productivity, service integration, emerging technologies, quality, monitoring the competition, and other issues affecting the service.
- Considerable discussions are held prior to key meetings in order to anticipate problems, air differences in advance, and extend the range of potential solutions. Meetings are sometimes held before the regularly scheduled medical staff executive committee meetings as a "dry run." The operating principle is to "avoid surprises" and to prepare each other for any "bad news."
- Physicians are strongly involved in the hospital's overall strategic planning process. Physicians will typically make up at least one-third of the membership of the strategic planning committee, may chair the committee, and are heavily involved in subcommittees and retreats.
- Special emphasis is placed on involving physicians in decision making throughout the institution and encouraging them to take responsibility for solving their own problems. Hospital administration resists solving problems brought to them by the staff that should be handled by the staff and their committees.
- Physician liaison and practice enhancement programs are used to assess and respond to physicians' needs. Physicians and their office assistants are visited regularly to assess needs and satisfaction.
- Administration makes a concerted effort to compliment the medical staff leadership for taking on difficult issues and provides the staff with needed support. A culture of "expanding the overall leadership capability of the institution" is reinforced. (pp. 27–28)

Figure 7.6 characterizes physician-hospital structures that vary from less to more integrated. At one pole, the management services organization (MSO, perhaps developed as a subsidiary of the hospital "parent") is structured to deliver support services to the physician-organized independent practice association. The more arms-length the relationship between hospital and IPA, the less integrated is the structure. Similarly, the looser the network of physicians participating in the IPA, all else being equal, the weaker the integration of the overall structure. One advantage of the MSO form is that it bonds the physicians more closely to the hospital but without forcing either party to enter into an exclusive contractual relationship (Kongstvedt

Figure 7.6 Physician-Hospital Structures

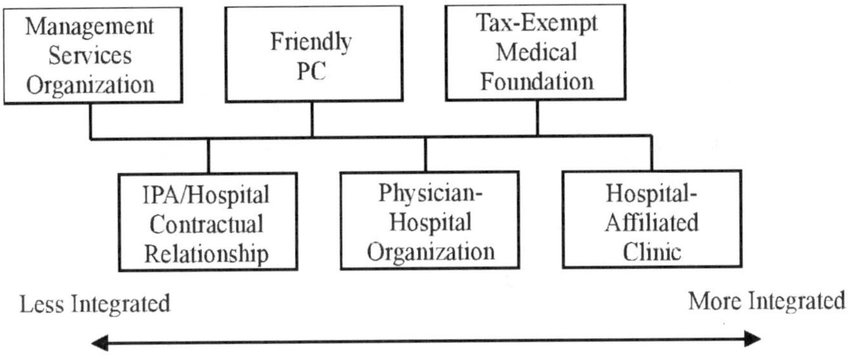

and Plocher 1995). At the same time, this advantage is a weakness in that the physicians can alter their fealties with great ease, and this structure is much less nimble in redeploying the assets of the organization to respond to changing market demand. The 501(c)(3) status of the not-for-profit hospital might also be at risk if evolution of the MSO involves purchase of physician practices and the transaction is perceived by tax authorities as leading to increment of private benefit to physicians.

Figure 7.7 displays a typical PHO structure. This reflects an intermediate level of integration between the MSO and medical foundation models. The physician-hospital organization provides a vehicle for the hospital and its physicians to contract with managed care plans. Kongstvedt and Plocher (1995) term the PHO the "first step on the evolutionary ladder in vertical integration" (p. 39). PHOs can be open or closed, depending on the extent to which PHO participation is open to all hospital medical staff. The PHO offers the advantages of a single contact point for managed care contracting, the potential to track data for both physician professional and hospital services, and a relatively reversible, low-threat means of initiating the vertical integration of facilities and physicians. However, such loosely coupled integrative arrangements have two principal disadvantages. First, to the extent that health plans have already established contracts with the hospital and most of the physicians involved, this structure is simply redundant. Second, the openness of the PHO can imply a corresponding weakness in the level of commitment of both sides to the integrating organization.

At the most integrated end of the spectrum depicted in Figure 7.6 is the tax-exempt medical foundation. In this case the hospital creates a not-for-profit foundation, purchases physician practices, and places the practices in the foundation. This approach is generally used when state law discourages the hospital either from employing physicians or from using its own funds

Figure 7.7 Physician-Hospital Organization: Typical Structure

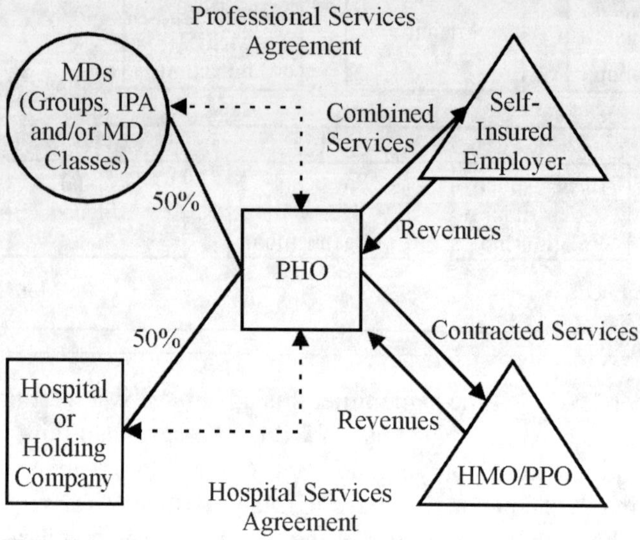

directly to purchase practices. For example, statutes often preclude the "corporate practice of medicine" or prohibit not-for-profit hospitals from owning a for-profit subsidiary. For the medical foundation to qualify for tax-exempt status, it must demonstrate that it provides substantial community benefit.

As described by Kongstvedt and Plocher (1995), the foundation does own and manage the physician practices, and the foundation becomes the sole source of revenues for the medical group. Individual physicians are members of the group, which exclusively contracts for services with the foundation. The physicians sign long-term exclusive contracts with the medical group, including noncompete clauses. While the group, foundation, and hospital are formally independent in this model (hence the avoidance of corporate practice proscriptions), effectively they are quite closely integrated. Figure 7.8 portrays one form of the medical foundation model in which the tax-exempt foundation holds all the contracts with health plans, as well as the revenues from self-pay patients.

Figure 7.9 outlines the structure adopted by the Mullikin Medical Group in California. This model illustrates a situation in which the large multispecialty medical group is at the center of the integrative structure, rather than the hospital. The Mullikin Medical Group directly contracts with the MSO partnership for management services in return for a fee. The group subcapitates the Pioneer Hospital, which acts as the operating corporation for hospital services and pays rent to the property partnerships, which hold

Figure 7.8 Medical Foundation Model: Affiliated Structure

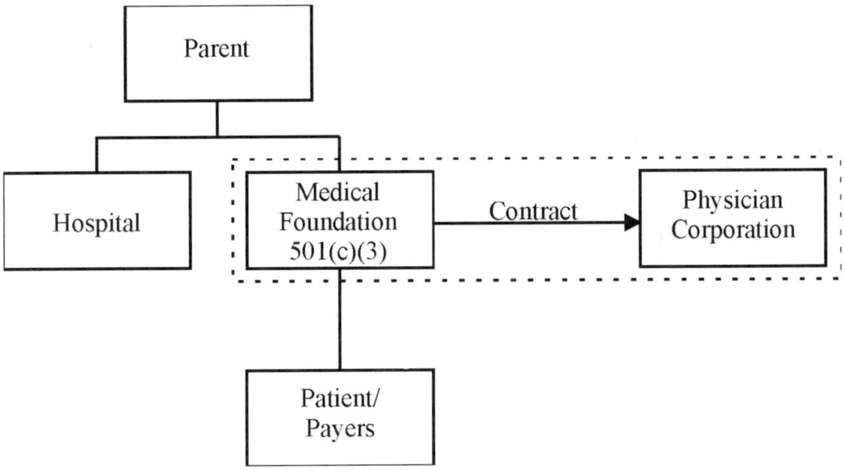

Figure 7.9 Medical Foundation Model: Mullikin Structure

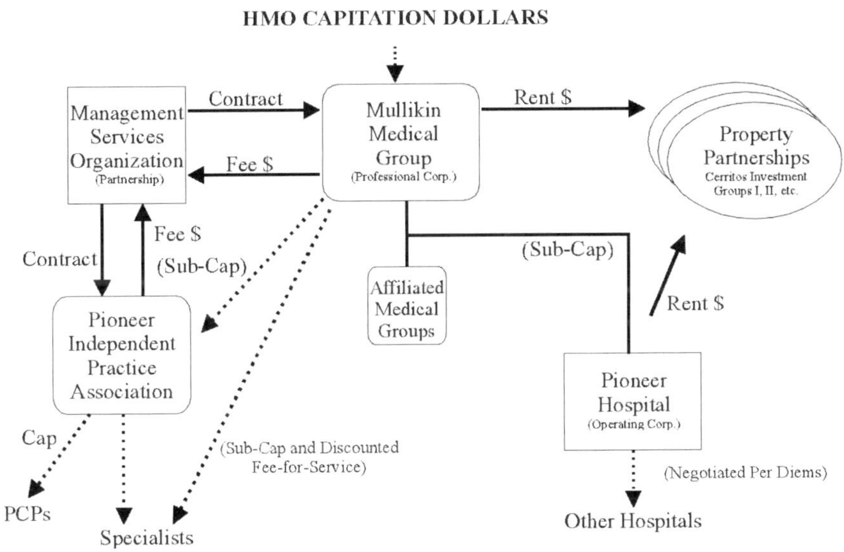

the real estate investments of the medical group. The operating corporation also writes negotiated per diems with other hospitals serving patients of the HMO. The MSO also serves the Pioneer IPA, which both capitates its own member PCPs and uses subcapitation and discounted FFS to pay specialists. The Mullikin Medical Group also enters into subcapitation and discounted FFS contracts with specialists who are not members of the Pioneer IPA. The Mullikin structure demonstrates how the large multispecialty medical group can craft an organized delivery system with extensive, full-service contracting ability, using the medical foundation as a facilitating mechanism.

NOTE

1. For a discussion of "strategic architecture," see G. Hamel and G. K. Prahalad (1994).

REFERENCES

Conrad, D.A. 1993. "Coordinating Patient Care Services in Regional Health Systems: The Challenge of Clinical Integration." *Hospital & Health Services Administration* 38 (4): 491–508

Drucker, P. 1995. "The Information Executives Truly Need." *Harvard Business Review* 73 (January–February): 54–62.

Kongstvedt, P.R., and D.W. Plocher. 1995. "Integrated Health Care Delivery Systems." In *Essentials of Managed Health Care*, edited by P.R. Kongstvedt. Gaithersburg, MD: Aspen Publishers.

Shortell, S.M. 1990. "Revisiting the Garden: Medicine and Management in the 1990s." *Frontiers of Health Services Management* (Fall): 3–32.

———. 1993. "Creating Organized Delivery Systems: The Barriers and Facilitators." *Hospital & Health Services Administration* 38 (4): 447–66.

Shortell, S.M., R.R. Gillies, and D.A. Anderson. 1994. "New World of Managed Care: Creating Organized Delivery Systems." *Health Affairs* 13 (5): 46–64.

CHAPTER

8

Information Systems: Managed Care Applications

Brian T. Malec

Managed are is an all-encompassing term describing the organizational arrangements by which health plans offer a comprehensive package of health services to members of a defined population for a set fee. The consumer/patient is given financial incentives to use physicians and facilities associated with the health plan.

CONCEPTS AND APPLICATIONS

With the advent of managed care comes a host of new requirements for the healthcare executive. Decisions must be made about capitation, community health, and the cost and effectiveness of care. Similarly, healthcare patients, who are becoming more and more savvy about the care they purchase, can use healthcare information to make more informed decisions. An information system can collect and process healthcare data to assist in cost containment and quality assurance.

After reading this chapter, readers will also be able to discuss the implications of managed care for an organization's information systems. They will be able to list the users of healthcare information in the managed care environment and the type of information they need.

Enrollees' out-of-pocket costs are usually small and entail a copayment for delivery of service or the purchase of prescriptions.

Reprinted from Austin, C. A., and Boxerman, S. B. 1998. *Information Systems for Health Services Administration.* Chicago: Health Administration Press.

According to the 1996 Annual HIMSS/Hewlett-Packard Leadership Survey, "Managed care continues to be the dominant force in health care as organizations focus on the bottom line and control of costs." (HIMSS/HP 1996) Forty-nine percent of survey respondents believe that managed care is the single most important factor driving information technology in healthcare. Fifty-seven percent believe that managed care will have a positive influence on healthcare by either lowering costs or improving outcomes (both of which are information-intensive activities). However, 41 percent felt that managed care will have negative consequences for the delivery of healthcare to consumers. Respondents believe that knowledge of managed care, along with its implications for information systems and the management of those systems, will occupy a significant portion of a health administrator's day-to-day responsibility.

This chapter will discuss the application of information systems (IS) within the managed care environment, including: (1) information needs in the managed care marketplace; (2) users of information in the managed care environment; (3) the managed care software market; and (4) a brief case study of the IS needs of a Medicaid HMO.

INFORMATION NEEDS IN THE MANAGED CARE MARKETPLACE

Managed care plans have special needs for information systems that differ from those of fee for service systems. The healthcare market has responded to managed care in four ways: (1) the change in economic incentives; (2) the emphasis on wellness and prevention; (3) the shift to capitated payment; and (4) the need to demonstrate quality of outcomes. Information requirements resulting from these market responses are discussed.

Economic Incentives. The move to a managed care environment has resulted in many new economic incentives in the healthcare delivery system. These incentives to produce services in a way that balances the cost of production with the expected outcome are a departure from the past. Changing economic incentives have, in turn, resulted in a number of changes in the way services are provided, for example:

- delivery of care in the least costly environment (inpatient vs. outpatient vs. home based);
- use of generic rather than brand-name drugs;
- use of primary care physicians, "gatekeepers," and restricted access to specialists;
- use of clinical guidelines to ensure quality and reduce costs;
- more effective use of healthcare workers (multitasking);
- development of formal quality review programs; and

- financial incentives for patients to use physicians and providers within the plan for care rather than going outside of the plan.

Information systems take on great importance in this environment. For instance, providers, consumers, and purchasers of care need information to monitor the cost, quality, and utilization of services provided by the managed care plan.

Wellness and Health Promotion. Managed care plans emphasize wellness and health promotion in order to help reduce the costs of treating illness among enrollees. Conversely, the traditional healthcare system has historically been grounded in managing the delivery of services to sick or injured persons. It emphasized diagnosis and treatment of acute and chronic illnesses. But, under managed care, providers receive fixed payment for all covered persons; therefore they have an incentive to provide services to the "well" population in addition to treating those who are sick.

Managed care plans need information systems that enable them to continuously monitor the health status of the population being served. Epidemiological data on community health status can be obtained from public health agencies at the state and local level. Careful monitoring of service utilization by enrollees can help identify conditions that could have been prevented through wellness programs (health education, periodic checkups, screening, and immunization). Information systems to support epidemiological surveillance are essential in managed care. Managed care organizations (MCOs) are combining software that can analyze population-based information, such as census data and epidemiological information, with geographical information systems to evaluate and map the covered population. (DesHarnais, Marshall, and Dulski 1994)

Capitation. Capitation is a negotiated payment to a provider on a per member per month basis to provide care over a given time period. It places providers and insurers at risk should the cost of providing services exceed the available pool of resources. The provider must stay within the capitated rate or assume all or part of the financial risk for the additional cost of treatment. "Risk pools" are established based on capitated payments from members of the health plan. If money remains in the pool at the end of a contract period, then some or all of the remaining funds are paid to those who managed the risk. Under fee-for-service payment systems, the costs of production are passed through to insurers who pay usual and customary costs. In an "at-risk" contract, the provider has an incentive to reduce the use of resources and space in high-cost facilities and to use the least costly combination of labor to provide care.

Information systems that monitor costs and utilization of services are essential under capitation. They serve as the basis for negotiating rates to be paid under capitated contracts. In addition, they provide essential information to management for service planning and cost control.

Quality of Outcomes. Purchasers of healthcare (employers and public and private insurers) and consumers of care are demanding information on the quality of services provided by their health plans. Employers and health plan members demand information about the value of treatment received or information to "evaluate the effectiveness of treatments and compare results across settings." (Kibbe 1994) This focus on quality outcomes requires providers to design and implement information systems capable of reporting patient-care specific information on the quality of services rendered. "Increasingly, information about performance and outcomes of care delivery can be thought of as a product." (Kibbe 1994, 593)

"Report cards" on the costs and quality of healthcare have been developed by individual employers, industry coalitions, some large health maintenance organizations (HMOs), and accrediting organizations.

The National Committee on Quality Assurance (NCQA) is a nonprofit, voluntary organization that accredits health maintenance organizations and other managed care plans (Web site: http://www.ncqa.org). NCQA has developed the Health Plan Employer Data and Information Set (HEDIS) for use in accreditation of health plans and as a source of information for employers and consumers in making health plan choices. HEDIS currently measures HMO performance in eight majors areas:

1. effectiveness of care;
2. access to/availability of care;
3. satisfaction with the experience of care;
4. health plan stability;
5. use of services;
6. cost of care;
7. informed healthcare choices; and
8. health plan descriptive information. (Penner 1997, 254–56)

Within these eight categories, specific HEDIS measures include such items as consumer satisfaction, member disenrollment, immunization rates for children and adolescents, physicians under capitation, and length-of-stay in hospitals. To participate in the HEDIS rating system, HMOs must agree to be reviewed by NCQA. (DesHarnais, Marshall, and Dulski 1994) At present, 87.2 percent of HMOs report either HEDIS or similar data to employers and the public. (McCormack 1997, 48) While the distribution of information is limited and the review is voluntary, the measurement does provide information that is useful for comparison.

The marketplace for quality information as a "product" is growing and new instruments will be developed to help employers, patients/consumers, and regulatory agencies make more informed decisions.

USERS OF MANAGED CARE INFORMATION

Four groups generate, consume, interpret, or modify the information present in a managed care environment: (1) purchasers who pay health plan premiums; (2) consumers of services; (3) service providers (physicians, hospitals, and other health services organizations); and (4) managed care plans (HMOs, preferred provider organizations [PPOs], and exclusive provider arrangements [EPAs] developed by integrated delivery systems). These users expect to have the information they need to make decisions in a timely, cost-effective manner and at the location where they need it. This section reviews the information needs and related decision models of each group.

Purchasers

Employers are a primary purchaser of managed care products as part of their health insurance programs for employees. In addition, the federal government is a major purchaser of HMO products for Medicare recipients, and many state governments are contracting with HMOs for the Medicaid population. These purchasers need information to help evaluate the benefit package of each managed care plan, the costs and quality of services provided, and the service utilization patterns of their employees or recipients. To do this, they need information such as:

- comparison of the costs and benefits among alternate health plans;
- demographics of the covered population;
- utilization history and claims experience of the covered population; and
- report cards on plan performance (e.g., HEDIS scores).

There is growing demand being placed on providers from individual employers, as well as business and community coalitions, for information about the quality and utilization of health services. These purchaser groups are demanding accountability. They want to know how much care was consumed, from whom, and for what. This information helps the employer develop business strategies for reducing premium costs and selecting among health plans. Some businesses also use the information to develop employee education, wellness, and health promotion activities.

Consumers

Consumers who are considering enrolling in an HMO, PPO, or other type of health plan need information to decide among the competing alternatives. Whether the employer pays the entire premium or part of it, the consumer needs information to answer questions such as:

- What alternate enrollment choices are available?
- What is the cost of each alternative?
- How does the range of benefits differ among plans (limitations, copayments, deductibles)?
- What is the quality of the provider pool?
- Where is the nearest provider located?

HEDIS reports are helpful to consumers by providing some comparative information. The marketplace is also addressing the information needs of consumers by way of the Internet and various Web sites.

Providers of Health Services

Healthcare providers need information to stay competitive in a managed care environment. Physicians and healthcare organizations with managed care contracts have information needs that differ from those of employers and consumers. Some larger health services organizations operate their own HMO or PPO plans and have information requirements similar to managed care plans as described in the next section.

Clinical and administrative information systems produce much of the information needed by individual providers to respond to the demands of managed care. In this section, the focus is on those unique information applications needed under managed care. Table 8.1 lists critical functions performed by providers in a managed care contract environment and the IS applications related to these functions.

Financial Monitoring. All healthcare organizations, whether operating under managed care or not, must have information systems that provide basic financial information. Within the managed care environment, the need for a cost-accounting system becomes critical because so much of what management has to do depends on the availability of accurate cost information. An ideal cost-accounting systems provides cost information by type of service, diagnostic category, physician and medical specialty, facility location, and managed care contract. (Hampshire and Rosborough 1996) Information generated by the cost-accounting system aids in contract negotiations, monitoring of existing contracts, and capitation rate setting.

Management of Capitated Contracts. Capitation contracts place the provider at risk and must be carefully managed. Special subsystems have been developed to help providers with electronic claims processing, enrollee profiles, treatment authorizations, and other components. Managed care has generated the need for detailed information on the quality of services provided and the populations served under capitated contracts.

Strategic Planning and Decision Making. The need for decision-support systems increases under managed care. Budgeting and forecasting

Table 8.1 Provider Functions and Associated Information Requirements

Provider Functions	**Examples of Applications**
Financial Monitoring	• Balance Sheets • Income Statements • Financial Statements • General Accounting • Cost Accounting • Premium Billing and Accounts Receivable
Management of Capitated Contracts	• Provider Profiles and Contracted Fee Schedules • Historical Data and Utilization of Services • Membership Reports by Age, Gender, Benefits Plan • Capitation Reconciliation and Verification Reports • Delivery of Services Reports: Utilization Rates, Charges per Service per Member per Month • Physician Profiling—Hospital Admission Patterns • Summaries of Hospital Admissions: Length-of-Stay, Hospital Days and Cost by Category, Physician Specialty, and Facility (Herrie and Pollock 1995)
Strategic Planning and Decision Making	• Forecasting Models • Contracting Models for Negotiation and Management • Budgeting Models • Utilization Management • Development of Clinical Pathways, Guidelines, and Other Physician Monitoring Devices • Member Demographics • Geographic Information Systems (Mapping) • Capitation Tracking and Modeling • Marketing Support (Posner 1996)
Patient/Member Services	• Health Promotion and Education • Access to Information About Services/Providers
Management of Multiple Lines of Business	• Multiple Managed Care Contracts • Government Accounts (Medicare, Medicaid, etc.) • Individual Coverage • Group Billing, Benefits Management, Eligibility • Management Service Organization (MSO)

models, development of care maps, and other management decision-support systems are essential. Providers are also using geographic information systems (GISs) to map patient and facility location data to plan for better coverage of the capitated populations that they serve. (Franzblau 1994)

Patient/Member Services. With the increased presence of managed care in most marketplaces, providers are using information systems to communicate with patients and provide information on programs and services offered including health education and promotion.

Management of Multiple Lines of Business. Providers often have contracts with multiple managed care organizations. Information systems that separate out unique aspects of each individual line of business are essential. Keeping lines of business clearly focused and separated helps the organization maximize its total profitability.

MANAGED CARE ORGANIZATIONS

Managed care organizations are businesses that must have financial and human resources, facility scheduling, and other applications that support the effective management of the organizations. However, MCOs also need specialized applications to support their core managed care functions. Because MCO services span a wide portion of the continuum of care, management software also spans a considerable range of possible applications. John McCormack (1997, 45) points out that many HMOs are finding vendors to provide satisfactory solutions to core applications such as management of enrollment, referrals and treatment authorization, and processing of claims. However, these same HMOs are then building in-house applications to meet specific needs such as tracking various market indicators to determine how the competition is doing.

Table 8.2 presents both core MCO functions and other specialized functions supported by information systems. (Kissinger and Borchardt 1996)

Financial Monitoring. Managed care organizations are similar to provider organizations in the need for basic financial information on the operations of the business functions of the health plan. MCOs use financial information to monitor existing contracts with providers, aide in new contract negotiations, and set capitation rates.

Preparation of Standard Analytical Reports and Decision Models. An example of a Standard Analytical Report necessary for effective management of an MCO is "utilization management statistics." A utilization report might contain such information as: patient encounters, claims, referrals, use of ancillary services, and trend data. This series of reports is useful for negotiating future managed care contracts; deciding capitation rates; computing physician and other provider productivity measures; and helping with outcome research. (Posner 1996) Managed care information systems also are important in tracking referral patterns, out-of-network utilization, and provider profiles. The reports and decision models listed in Table 8.2 help MCOs manage the relationship between input resources, the flow of con-

Table 8.2 Managed Care Organization Functions and Associated Information Requirements

Core Functions	Examples of Applications
Financial Monitoring	• Balance Sheets • Income Statements • Financial Statements • General Accounting • Cost Accounting • Premium Billing and Accounts Receivable • Payment Tracking for Contracts, Subcontracts
Preparation of Standard Analytical Reports and Decision Models	• Performance Statistics • Utilization Management • Provider Reporting: Inpatient and Outpatient • Referral Patterns • Inpatient and Outpatient Out-of-Network Utilization • Case-Mix Analysis • Provider Profiling • Actuarial Analysis
Management Control and Reporting	• Membership Analysis • Eligibility/Verifications Tracking • Utilization Rates by Groups, Age, Gender • Quality Indicators • Financial Reporting • Regulatory Reporting • Budgeting Models • Forecasting Models • Contract Modeling and Projections
Claims Payment and Prospective/Capitation Payment Processing	• Capitation Payments • Claims Payment, Network and Out-of-Network • Claims Adjudication • Encounter Statistics • Claims Grouping by Episodes of Care
Management of Multiple Lines of Business	• Government Accounts (Medicare, Medicaid, etc.) • Individual Coverage • Group Billing, Benefits Management, Eligibility
Marketing and Sales Support	• Enrollment and Disenrollment Trends • Geographic Distribution of Members and Providers • Contract Negotiation and Management • Rate Management/Actuarial Services • Account Management and Analysis • Forecasting Models • Provider Databases and Credentials
Profitability	• Per Member Per Month Costs and Premiums • Medical Loss Ratios

Table 8.2 Managed Care Organization Functions and Associated Information Requirements (*continued*)

Core Functions	Examples of Applications
Member/Customer Services	• Customer Service Inquiry • Internet Access to MCO • Member Health/Wellness Education and Promotion • Epidemiological Analysis
Employer Information Needs	• HEDIS Reporting • Outcomes Measurement • Employer Group Enrollment Tracking and Reporting • Utilization History and Claims Experiences of Covered Population

sumers through the system, and the standards of productivity for the organization and its providers.

Actuarial and epidemiologic information systems are essential tools for MCOs. Health plans must track trends in health status and disease incidence among their members. Some organizations do not have the internal expertise to do the necessary analysis and therefore contract with consultants to provide actuarial reports on the covered populations.

Clinical pathways, or care maps, are becoming a standard mechanism for monitoring business practices and evaluating clinical outcomes. A care map is an optimum, standardized clinical care plan designed to provide care for a typical patient for a specific procedure or condition. (Meyer and Feingold 1995) When combined with other systems, a care map can help estimate the expected cost for each episode of care for a particular procedure. (Posner 1996) For example, epidemiological analysis of the covered population might result in an estimate that 0.2 percent of that population potentially could need a particular procedure within the next year (i.e., repair of a broken leg). Based on that analysis and the application of a care map, MCOs can allocate resources for an economically efficient and clinically effective treatment.

Management Control and Reporting. In addition to standard financial reports, forecasts, and decision models, MCO managers need information on membership characteristics, utilization of services, and various quality measures.

Claims Payment and Prospective/Capitation Payment Processing. Claims payment and processing is a specialized function of a managed care organization. MCOs must have information systems that process claims and make payments to providers who are members of the health plan network as well as to out-of-network providers if authorized by point-of-service options available to members. Out-of-network claims will normally be reimbursed at a lower rate with the enrollee paying increased copayments.

Management of Multiple Lines of Business. MCOs are complex businesses that have contracts with numerous employers, governments agencies, and individual members. Information systems that monitor the performance of each individual line of business are essential.

Marketing and Sales Support. Information systems are needed to support the marketing and sales functions of MCOs. Marketing information systems will monitor trends in enrollment and disenrollment of members, the geographic distribution of covered populations, locations of providers and facilities, and general demographic characteristics of plan members and the community at large. Geographic information systems are useful tools for graphic analysis and modeling of demographic and marketshare information. (Environmental Systems Research Institute 1996)

Profitability. MCOs must monitor financial indicators that are commonplace in the insurance industry. Medical loss ratios (benefits paid divided by premiums received) are important indicators of the profitability of health plans. The smaller the benefits paid out, the larger the difference will be between expenses and revenue, resulting in a smaller "loss" ratio. The difference between revenue and expenses covers the administrative and marketing costs of the health plan and is also used to pay stockholder dividends in for-profit MCOs.

Member/Customer Services. A customer focus and service orientation is critical for success in managed care organizations. One tool is an information system used to communicate with the membership. Automated systems can provide information about hours and locations of operations, new services available, wellness programs, and healthier lifestyles. They can also answer common questions concerning benefits. Many MCOs are developing home pages on the Internet to provide information to current and prospective members.

Employer Information Needs. As discussed, the employer is an important consumer of managed care information. Through HEDIS reporting and analysis of utilization data, employers can design benefit packages that meet the needs of their employees and reduce the company's premium costs. Employers are demanding accountability from the health plans with whom they have contracts. Managed care organizations must be prepared to provide information on costs, quality, and utilization of services when requested by employers and other purchasers of care.

In summary, managed care organizations (MCOs) have all the basic needs for administrative information systems plus the special functional requirements discussed. The difference between an application of an information system in a managed care environment and other more traditional method of healthcare delivery is often a matter of degree. The special requirements of managed care plans and provider organizations who offer managed care products include information systems for the negotiation, monitoring, and management of capitated contracts; quality control; marketing and enrollment services; and customer support.

THE MANAGED CARE SOFTWARE MARKET

The vendor market for managed care software applications is volatile and expanding rapidly. Table 8.3 gives examples of the types of software products available in 1996. Because of the pace of software product changes and the volatility of the market, no company names are provided. The examples are abstracted and condensed from vendor literature, other printed sources, and various Web sites.

The vendor market has many small companies, each with specialty products. In the future it is expected that the market will consolidate with fewer and larger vendors who offer a full range of products and services. The healthcare manager can either use a strategy to select vendors carefully who will survive the test of time in the marketplace or be prepared to adapt quickly to new systems and vendors as the market changes.

Volatility in the managed care software market reflects the rapid change occurring in the healthcare delivery system. These changes create a challenging environment for management, including:

- the political and economic uncertainty of the healthcare market;
- the unstable nature and short life cycle of some vendor products;
- the high cost of conversion from older information systems; and
- the lack of management understanding and experience in using technology to enhance decision making in a managed care environment.

CASE STUDY: L.A. CARE

Across the United States, Medicaid and Medicare HMOs are being established in the hope of controlling the growth in state and federal government expenditures for populations covered by these programs. In California, the Medicaid program (called Med-Cal) has begun the process of moving all Medicaid recipients to a managed care plan. In the Los Angeles area, the state has authorized two managed care health plans for Medicaid recipients. One is a commercial for-profit health plan and the other is a local initiative nonprofit health plan. When fully operational, the local initiative plan (called L.A. Care) will cover more than 700,000 members, will have 3,000 primary care providers and 10,000 contracting physicians, and will result in 4 mil-

Table 8.3 Healthcare Software Vendors

Representative Company	Number of Installations as of 1996	Target Market for Software	Examples of Modules and/or Application
Vendor A	3	IPAs PPOs HMOs	Enrollment/Eligibility and Benefits Encounter, Referral and Claims Tracking Tracks Practice Patterns of Primary Care Physicians Claims Adjudication Account Processing (Provider Reimbursement)
Vendor B	50+	IPAs HMOs	Provider Profiles Benefit Summary and Coverage Enrollee Profiles Specialist and Hospital Treatment Authorization Capitation Payment to Providers Risk-Sharing Arrangements
Vendor C	15	Small-to-medium HMOs, PPOs, and PHOs	Enrollment and Eligibility Premium Billing Utilization Management Capitation and Fee-for-Service Reimbursement Ad Hoc Reporting
Vendor D	3	IPAs	Payor and Provider Contracts Claims Processing Central Data Repository User-Defined Reports
Vendor E	39	PHOs MSOs HMOs IPAs	Membership Eligibility Capitation and Provider Risk Management Utilization Management Reinsurance Management Check Processing Electronic Data Interchange Claims Status and Submission Authorization and Referral Processing Provider Reimbursement

lion outpatient visits and 210,000 inpatient days annually. (Massey 1997) L.A. Care is a "health plan for health plans" because the actual delivery of services will be carried out and administered through seven plan partners. The plan partners are existing MCOs that contract with L.A. Care to provide services to a specified number of Med-Cal recipients. The plan partners include Blue Cross of California, Care 1st Health Plan, Maxicare, Tower Health, United Health Plan, Kaiser Foundation Health Plan, and Los Angeles County Community Health Plan.

As a start-up organization, L.A. Care had to create an information system from the beginning. Calvin Massey, the chief information officer of L.A. Care, was charged with developing a high-level systems architecture, defining the business processes, and developing an RFP for managed care, financial, and other administrative systems. L.A. Care selected packaged software for general ledger, financial, and human resources systems. The managed care functions required a software system capable of a wide variety of activities including:

- sorting monthly tapes of current enrollees from the State of California by plan partners and doctors;
- reconciling enrollee income and payout to partners via contracts; and
- monitoring the demographic characteristics of enrollees in order to match them to the appropriate service providers.

L.A. Care chose a national vendor of managed healthcare information systems, CSC Healthcare Systems to be the principal software provider. Selected CSC applications used by L.A. Care include membership and enrollment monitoring; provider profiling; reporting on capitation, network penetration, and profitablility; and preparation of HEDIS reports.

Future plans call for a budget forecasting system capable of integrating enrollment data coordinated with the managed care system for continuous updates and management control. A geographic information system (GIS) is also planned to help manage the delivery of services by the plan partners and to support the matching of Medi-Cal recipients with service locations.

SUMMARY

Managed care organizations have emerged in the current decade as a significant market force. These organizations, and the various constituencies associated with them, will continue to demand and need a wide range of information systems. The twin forces of cost containment and quality improvement challenge MCO organizations. The economic, quality, and marketing incentives of managed care drive the end-users of information to engage in decision-making activities that require integrated and flexible information systems.

There are four distinct groups that either generate, consume, interpret, or modify the information that is needed in a managed care environment. They are (1) purchasers who pay the premium; (2) consumers of healthcare services; (3) providers of services (physicians and health services organizations); and (4) the health plan or managed care organization.

Purchasers (employers and public or private insurers) require information about utilization of services by the covered population, availability of wellness programs and incentives for healthy lifestyles, ratings of quality such as HEDIS measures, and the satisfaction of consumers with the health plans. Consumers seek information on the costs and quality of alternative health plans and the ease of access to services. Providers of health services must respond to demands from health plans for cost and quality information. Providers need a range of information products that support capitated payment systems, normal business operations, quality improvement, clinical and management decision support, provider profiles, and demographic information on the covered populations. In addition to general administrative and clinical systems, managed care plans need advanced information systems to support a variety of special needs including systems for capitation management, tracking of utilization and referral patterns, actuarial analysis of financial risk, marketing, and membership and enrollment services.

The volatile nature of the managed care software market challenges administrators to select products that will be stable for more than just a few years.

REFERENCES

DesHarnais, S., B. Marshall, and J. Dulski. 1994. "Information Management in the Age of Managed Competition." *Journal of Quality Improvement* 20 (November): 631–38.

Environmental Systems Research Institute. 1996. "Geographic Information Systems (GIS) Solutions for Healthcare," unpublished material by ESRI. Internet Homepage—http://www.esri.com [Retrieved: March 1997].

Franzblau, D. 1994. "Hospitals Using Mapping Data to Plan Network Coverage." *Health Care Strategic Management* 12 (July): 14–15.

Hampshire, D., and B. Rosborough. 1996. "The Evolution of Decision Support in Managed Care Organizations." *Topics in Health Care Financing* 20 (2): 26–37.

Healthcare Information and Management Systems Society and Hewlett-Packard Company (HIMSS/HP). 1996. *Seventh Annual Leadership Survey: Trends in Health Care Computing*. Chicago: The Society.

Herrie, G., and W. Pollock. 1995. "Multi-speciality Medical Groups: Adapting to Capitation." *Journal of Health Care Finance* 21 (3): 37–43.

Kibbe, D. 1994. "Designing Quality Into Health Care Information Systems." *Journal of Quality Improvement* 20 (November): 591–94.

Kissinger, K., and S. Borchardt, eds. 1996. *Information Technology for Integrated Health Systems, Positioning for the Future*. New York: John Wiley and Sons.

Massey, C. 1997. "Local Initiative Health Authority of Los Angeles County." Unpublished presentation at Southern California Chapter of HIMSS, May.

McCormack, J. 1997. "HMO Automation Strategies." *Health Data Management* April: 44–50.

Meyer, J. W., and M. Feingold. 1995. "Integrating Financial Modeling and Patient Care Reengineering." *Healthcare Financial Management* 49 (2): 33–40.

Penner, M. J. 1997. *Capitation in California: A Study of Physician Organizations Managing Risk.* Chicago, Health Administration Press.

Posner, B. L. 1996. "The Development of an Integrated Decision Support System for Provider Risk Contracting." Unpublished master's thesis, Health Administration Program, California State University, Northridge.

ADDITIONAL READINGS

Anonymous. 1994. "Managed Care Software: The Next Generation." *Nursing Management* 25 (March): 28–29.

Anonymous. 1997. "Managed Care Systems: New Capabilities for Growing Markets." *Health Management Technology*, April: 62–67.

Austin, C. J., and P. M. Sobczak. 1993. "Information Technology and Managed Care." *Hospital Topics* 71 (3): 33–37

Bernard, A., R. Hayward, J. Anderson, J. Rosevear, and L. McMahon. 1995. "The Integrated Management Model, Lessons for Managed Care." *Medical Care* 33 (July 1): 663–75.

Brennan, C. 1995. "Managed Care and Health Information Networks." *Journal of Health Care Finance* 21 (Summer): 1–5.

Ciotti, V., and F. Zodda. 1996. "Selecting Managed Care Information Systems." *Healthcare Financial Management* 50 (June): 35–40.

Coddington, D. C., J. Pollard. 1995. "Information Systems and Integrated Healthcare: An Essential Partnership." *Health Management Technology* 16 (July): 38–40.

Conrad, D., T. Wickizer, M. Maynard, J. Klastorin, D. Lessler, A. Ross, S. Naomi, S. Sullivan, J. Alexander, and K. Travis. 1996. "Managing Care, Incentives, and Information: An Exploratory Look Inside the 'Black Box' of Hospital Efficiency." *Health Services Research* 31 (3): 235–59.

Davidson, H. L. 1996. "Contracting for Medicaid Managed Care." *Healthcare Financial Management* 50 (11): 45.

Fox, S. J . 1996. "Medicaid Capitation and Information Management." In *The Capitation Sourcebook*. Rockville, MD: Aspen Publishers.

Hard, R. 1992. "Well-Managed Information Vital to Effective Managed Care Contracting." *Hospitals* 66 (11): 50.

Keene, R. D., and F. F. Naus. 1994. *Negotiating Managed Care Contracts*. New York: McGraw-Hill, Inc.

Masters, G. M., and S. T. Valentine. 1995. *Health Care Capitation and Risk Contracting Manual.* New York: Thompson Publishing Group.

O'Connor, K. 1995. "Information Management for Managed Care." *Medical Group Management Journal* 42 (November–December): 52–56, 75.

Ribka, J. P. 1996. "Strategic Planning for Managed Care Information Systems." *Health Management Technology* (November): 30, 34, 55.

Shortell, S., R. Gillies, and D. Anderson. 1994. "The New World of Managed Care: Creating Organized Delivery Systems." *Health Affairs* 37 (Winter): 46–64.

Welge, W. 1992. "Managed Care is Limited by Information Systems." *Topics in Health Care Financing* 19 (Winter): 23–32.

Wright, C. M. 1993. "Information Technology Boosts Managed Care's Bottom Line." *Computers in Healthcare* 14 (7): 19.

CHAPTER

9

Marketing and Managed Care

Arthur C. Sturm, Jr.

YOUR NEW SELLING SEASON IS CALLED "OPEN ENROLLMENT"

Seldom has healthcare been considered a seasonal business. But managed care may be changing that. It is creating a season that is to healthcare what Christmas is to retailers—a make-or-break period.

More and more consumers are making a critical choice once a year during "open enrollment"—that annual employee benefits frenzy when workers in large companies choose their health plan for the coming year. If you're not allocating your resources accordingly, you could be missing a big opportunity that won't repeat itself for another year.

Let's look at the numbers.

In 1995, approximately 73 percent of the employed population received its healthcare through managed care, according to "The New Dominance of Managed Care: Insurance Trends in the 1990s," a study that appears in the January/February 1997 issue of *Health Affairs*. A 1997 study by New York-based William M. Mercer Inc. indicated that only 22 percent of surveyed employers are offering just a single type of plan. Essentially that means that once a year, about 78 percent of the employed adults in this country either choose or reconfirm who will provide them with care for the coming 12 months.

Reprinted from Sturm, A. C. 1998. *The New Rules of Healthcare Marketing*. Chicago: Health Administration Press.

Your goal, of course, is to be on the plan they select. And that's why open enrollment is such a critical time. If consumers select a plan in which you participate, you've essentially made the short list. If not, you're out.

The question is, how do you deploy your tactics and resources for this seemingly critical event? A reasonable approach is to create a matrix showing spending levels against penetration levels of managed care (see Table 9.1). The higher the level of managed care, the higher the proportionate spending for open enrollment.

The figures in Table 9.1 are guidelines, mind you, and subject to broad interpretation. Allocate as your market, your organization, and your overall strategy dictate.

Not Just an Advertising Expense

Marketing expenditures for open enrollment do not necessarily translate directly into advertising. Because contracting shifts from year to year, advertising can play a valuable role in informing current users and want-to-be users about the health plans in which you participate. Unfortunately, this form of advertising is more difficult to track than programs that have a direct message-response orientation, but the logic for advertising during this period is pretty compelling if you are in a Stage III or IV market.

Other forms of marketing activity are equally important. An essential and usually overlooked group during this period are the physicians and the physicians' offices. As we all know, the most pressing question among consumers during open enrollment is, "Can I keep my physician?" We generally make the consumer do all the work to answer that question and do little to help them stay.

Focus on the Physician Office

The physician setting as a marketing strategy for open enrollment needs to be explored. The activities need not be elaborate—a simple direct mail program from physician to patients encouraging them to "make sure you choose a plan in which I participate"—can be a powerful retention tool.

Similarly, the office staff can be trained to field the avalanche of phone calls about plan participation, office hours, and other benefits during this

Table 9.1 Budget Allocations for Open Enrollment Activities

MCO Development (Penetration)	Percent Open Enrollment Marketing Expenditures
≤10%	0
11–25%	15–20
26–40%	35–40
41% or more	75–80

period. Even a simple tent card in the waiting room can alert patients to a list of participating plans or an invitation to "talk to us about your health plan coverage" can be effective.

Even physicians need to be made more aware of the opportunity that open enrollment provides. Inviting questions or helping patients understand the importance of maintaining continuity of care can help increase or retain members.

The tactics are many. The key is to make the physician and the physician's staff active partners in the enrollment process.

Cutting Through a Confused Market

Business consultant Tom Peters is widely quoted as saying "Out of chaos comes opportunity." It's advice that would seem to apply to open enrollment as well.

Portability of benefits is increasing, as well as new self-choice products such as medical savings accounts. While the intent of these innovations is to provide more coverage to more individuals, they are more likely to increase confusion among an already confused population. Is it the role of the IDN to be the educator—to guide the market through the swamp? That's a difficult business decision to answer because there is no guarantee that the individual counseled will become a member. But the opportunity to capture and retain the unaligned patient is growing.

The key is to recognize and seize the potentially huge opportunity of open enrollment. Miss the window and you'll miss the market.

YOUR MANAGED CARE CONTRACT IS NO MORE THAN A HUNTING LICENSE

The word to remember here is "pull-through."

Conventional wisdom has long held that if you get the contract, you've won the battle. But that's hardly the case. Even within a contract there is no guarantee you'll get any members. You are still competing for members who must choose one of *your* physicians and use *your* services from the other providers offered in the plan.

Thus pull-through—getting the member to select your physicians and hospitals—becomes the operative strategy. If you don't pull the member through to your IDN, the contract has no value. Look at it as a hunting license, and your return should increase.

Many of the chapters/rules in this book address how pull-through can be accomplished (customer service, etc.). But you might consider some of the less obvious ways to influence marketshare.

In the previous chapter, we talked about a pull-through strategy during open enrollment using the physician and the physician office. While that is an effort that certainly needs emphasis, it is also important to look at ongoing marketing behavior.

One area often overlooked for pull-through is the employer worksite.

The Value of the Worksite

Worksite programs for screening and prevention have been in existence for years, and among many they're thought to be no longer effective. But let's revisit and recast them to see if they might not have another life to offer.

The conclusion to an article in the December 1996 *Business and Health* titled "Can Employers See Beyond Price?" talked about a surprising absence of preventive programs in the workplace despite some overwhelming evidence of their success.

"Nearly nine out of ten respondents have never conducted on site screenings for hypertension or high cholesterol," cited the article, "and fewer than three percent offer them now; more than eight in ten haven't tried smoking cessation or weight loss programs. Only about one in 10 has an in-house gym or subsidizes participation in off site programs, despite solid evidence of the benefits of regular exercise." The findings are among larger employers (20–499 employees and 500 or more).

The historical problem, of course, is that no one wants to pay for these types of activities. Employers will admit to their value, but committing money to identify them is clearly another matter—and usually a deal killer.

Worksite programs might benefit from a little imagination. Community Hospitals Indianapolis (CHI), for example, has a refreshing program for employers that shows some creativity and results. CHI has developed three programs for employers that take health promotion beyond the world of cholesterol screenings. Each is customized to the needs of the individual, depending on that individual's interest in improving or maintaining his or her health.

By applying a little creativity to a somewhat burned-out strategy, CHI has found an attractive way to engage employers and their employees. More important, they are showing that they can indeed change behaviors.

One of the programs, called "Picture This," uses an improvisational theater group. Before the performance the actors are given some key words and issues pertaining to the organization's culture. During their improv skit, they present situations pertaining to health and to the organization. At key points, the action stops, and the actors turn to the audience and start asking questions. It's a true interactive session.

Other programs at CHI focus on helping people come to a clearer definition of "health." They consider the environment in which they are working to determine what might be considered a strength or weakness related to health. As Daniel Hodgkins, executive director of Health Promotion at CHI, says, "We look at health as a combination of body, mind, and spirit. Using this framework, we can recognize as 'healthy' even a person who is, for example, a bit overweight and smokes, but is an active positive force in the community."

CHI reports a very positive reaction to the program from local businesses, but the typical reluctance to fund them. The challenge, even to the creative mind, is to demonstrate the short-term benefits of the program.

Clinical Strategies

Not all programs need be held in the public arena. In fact, clinical approaches may prove to hold greater value to the health plan and create a pull-through of a different nature. Here are a few to consider.

Case management for high-risk members

IDNs should be able to make an outstanding argument for their ability to provide case management for high-risk members. The sheer notion of integration creates a compelling platform through which to develop a case management approach.

The key of course is to link the IDN's main clinical areas with the medical needs of the health plan members. That shouldn't be difficult. Start with one or two areas and build a portfolio of programs from there.

HEDIS compliance support programs

HEDIS (Health Plan Employer Data and Information Set) and HEDIS 3.0, plus other forms of accreditation, are fundamental to health plan survival. Without them health plans simply can't compete.

The cost of documenting and implementing many accreditation programs is high, of course, but such efforts create another opportunity for the IDN to create a better partnership with health plans.

HEDIS, for one, requires health plans to demonstrate how they are serving the preventive needs of their members in particular areas. Five of the initial areas are:

1. cholesterol screenings;
2. diabetic retinal screenings;
3. pediatric immunizations;
4. mammograms; and
5. cervical cancer screenings.

Other areas are reportedly under consideration, and we can expect them to be in the list in the near future.

Those health plans that are IPA (independent practice association) models have a particularly difficult time providing those areas of service because they have so little control over their physician members. Group models, on the other hand, are in a better position to offer the services because they can exert greater control.

An IDN might consider creating a HEDIS compliance package as part of a value-added component to its contracting. HEDIS compliance can be expensive to the plan, but it usually is part of the IDN's stable of existing services. The needs of the health plan can be best served by the IDN—*your* IDN. Sounds like an opportunity.

Disease management resource group

Among the many long-term considerations for managing the healthcare of members is the notion of "disease management." It's a somewhat self-defining term. The goal is to manage the disease and the member closely and rigorously, thus lowering exposure to costly procedures. Disease management uses a range of strategies from education to compliance to reach its desired results.

Historically, disease management was the purview of the pharmaceutical industry. But in offering the programs to health plans, the drug manufacturers found a high degree of skepticism. Plans believed that the manufacturers were creating programs that were more self-serving than beneficial to the plan.

IDNs may have the opportunity to take the higher ground and offer their clinical expertise again as a value-added service. Disease management programs can be customized to the needs of the plan and the integrated skills of the network. At whatever level disease management is eventually offered, it can serve to keep the focus on quality patient care and overall costs. Both the plan and the provider can learn from each other in what may be the beginning of a more lasting partnership.

Miami-based PhyMatrix Corporation has used this strategy so successfully that they have now spun off their disease management activities into a separate company.

The Role of the Brand

Another key element in pull-through is your brand strategy. While we know there is a sizable group of "shoppers" for healthcare, we should keep in mind that an equal number of couch potatoes are simply going to check a box based on the line of least resistance.

Differentiating your network each year before the open enrollment window opens is as important as engaging in the actual pull-through activities. Clearly positioning yourself among consumers before open enrollment is an essential "pre-sell" activity. Don't assume that during open enrollment you will have enough time for effectively getting your positioning message to cut through all the noise in the market and stick in the mind of your hoped-for enrollees. One health plan operating in California reportedly says it has reaped huge success simply because its name begins with the letter A, putting it at the head of the list. Consumers are choosing it for little more reason than that.

Open enrollment is a hunting season. Choose your weapons wisely.

CHAPTER

10

Using Consumer Satisfaction Surveys to Assess Quality of Care: Current Practices and Issues

Marsha Gold and Judith Wooldridge[1]

INTRODUCTION

Managed care plans are a substantial and growing share of the market for health insurance (Gabel et al. 1994). Because managed care integrates financing with service delivery, measuring and overseeing quality and access to health care within individual plans is very important (Kongstvedt 1993). Some of this can be done by formal assessment of clinical quality using medical records, administrative systems, or similar information. However, these sources are not well suited to measuring the perceptions of the customers of health plans, for example. For identifying consumer perspectives, surveys are a very useful tool, providing more systematic data to complement information from grievance systems and other sources of consumer feedback. Surveys are receiving increased attention (AHCPR 1995) as a component of Total Quality Management and Continuous Quality Improvement to enhance quality of care and service (James 1994, Press et al. 1992, Inguanzo 1992, Kritchevsky and Simmons 1991, Berwick 1989). Though some controversy exists about the role of consumer information in

Adapted from *Health Care Financing Review* 16 (4): 155–173.

monitoring quality (Goldfield, Pine, and Pine 1991), most researchers, policymakers, and managers agree that consumer satisfaction is an important measure of quality and hence, of system and health plan performance (Cleary and McNeil 1988, Davies and Ware 1988a, Press 1994). However, because many of these applications are operational, they are poorly documented in the published literature, a shortcoming we aim to remedy with this chapter.

FOCUS AND APPROACH

This chapter discusses the nature and use of consumer surveys as a means of generating information on satisfaction with individual health plans, including health maintenance organizations (HMOs), other managed care products such as preferred provider organizations (PPOs) and point-of-service (POS) arrangements, and traditional indemnity insurance. We summarize current knowledge about how widely surveys are used or encouraged by diverse parties such as individual managed care plans, government and voluntary oversight agencies, community and consumer groups, and public and private purchasers of care. We review the different kinds of surveys (for example, all enrollees, system users, users of particular services), survey content, and survey methods. Next, we consider outstanding issues relevant to using consumer surveys to assess plan quality and particularly to compare health plans. We end with brief conclusions on the use of surveys as a tool for assessing care and recommend three types of activities to better support such efforts.

Our approach to analyzing surveys on consumer satisfaction with healthcare plans was shaped largely by the data available to us. Information about surveys of consumer satisfaction with managed care plans is evolving rapidly, and it is not part of the formal literature. Furthermore, most surveys are intended to address operational needs rather than research objectives. As a result, this chapter relies heavily on information from the "trade press" and unpublished materials. These were obtained by reviewing materials we had, making calls to a selection of large plans known or thought to be involved in survey efforts to obtain information on their use of surveys, and referencing bibliographies and collections maintained in the Group Health Association of America (GHAA) library.

Our methods generated information on the most publicized and broad-based surveys as of mid-1994. This chapter is not intended to provide a complete inventory of surveys. In addition, it contains only limited information on the nationwide prevalence of the approaches illustrated. These are not major constraints, as the focus of the chapter is conceptual, stressing methodology, purpose, and illustrative applications rather than empirical results.

NATURE AND USES OF CONSUMER SURVEYS BY DIVERSE PARTIES

Use by Managed Care Plans for Internal Management

While consumer surveys are used more widely today by managed care plans than in the past, the more established HMOs have long used such surveys. These surveys were generally initiated to support internal plan activities related to marketing and quality assurance (Kongstvedt 1993). Although most plans developed their approaches independently, there are now several examples of collective efforts by plans similar in management or philosophy.

A recently completed national survey of managed care plans documents the widespread use of consumer surveys by managed care plans. Virtually all HMOs (over 95 percent) and about half (55 percent) of the PPOs surveyed report that they conduct consumer surveys to monitor care (Gold et al. 1995b). Survey data are used to measure enrollee satisfaction and support such functions as strategic planning and marketing; improving quality; provider profiling and payment; and responding to employer requests. The more sophisticated plans use consistent survey methods over time to monitor trends and issues requiring management attention.

Surveys of new enrollees and of disenrollees are most likely to be conducted to support strategic planning and marketing. Some plans also survey area residents not enrolled in the plan to establish external benchmarks and identify opportunities for or barriers to growth. Plans will occasionally target special groups such as smokers or pregnant women to assess their special needs and their satisfaction with services.

Surveys of consumer satisfaction with various aspects of healthcare and health insurance are important input into efforts to improve quality and retain plan members (Packer-Tursman 1994). Such surveys capture information on users and nonusers of care and therefore are valuable sources of information on barriers to access. Plans vary in whether they ask individuals to answer questions about satisfaction with services they may not have used but about which they may have an opinion. To elicit information on how users of services perceive that care, plans may survey a sample of people using specific services (most often physician visits or specific hospitalizations, but also ancillary services) on their satisfaction with that specific service encounter. The success of using surveys to support quality improvement depends both on creating a structure through which results are reviewed, changes are identified, and improvements are charted, and on a commitment by staff to these activities (Kritchevsky and Simmons 1991).

In recent years, more surveys have been conducted to assess performance of individual providers or provider groups (as opposed to the plan as a whole). These techniques have been pioneered by network and independent practitioner association (IPA) models, which because of more dispersed physician practices, have a greater desire for information that promotes socialization to the norms of care management and assists in network management. Provider-specific surveys are being used to profile physician practices and compare peer profiles, to modify payment rates or provide bonuses, and to identify outliers—on the high and low ends—for closer review and potential exclusion from the network. The Group Health Association of America (GHAA 1993) reports that in 1992, 60 of the 326 plans responding to its Annual HMO Industry Survey used consumer satisfaction measures to adjust primary care physician payments, mostly on an annual basis. Among larger plans, the use of such techniques is even more common, with survey results serving as adjusters to physician compensation and also as input to decisions on physician contract renewals (Gold et al. 1995b). The most well-known applications of surveys involve sampling panel members of each physician or provider group to assess patient satisfaction, and using the results in provider payment calculations (Morain 1992).

Plans are also using surveys of individual provider performance to develop provider report cards. U.S. Healthcare, for example, develops report cards for individual practices by surveying members' use of primary care, specialists, and hospitals. These surveys focus on specific encounters or practices. At least one Kaiser plan uses its member surveys to develop quantitative ratings of physician and nonphysician providers, which are provided to facilities and physicians. Physicians are given comments written in on the surveys as part of their performance development system.

Some managed care plans enhance their ability to use survey data by participating in consortium survey efforts, typically involving other plans affiliated in some way. For example, Blue Cross and Blue Shield Association has done annual national benchmarking of consumer satisfaction since 1989, which member plans can use to aid in interpreting their performance. United HealthCare through its Center for HealthCare Policy and Evaluation has similarly developed a system to generate a performance measure that plans can use to benchmark themselves vis-à-vis others in the system, as well as to respond to external interests. The HMO Group, which consists of thirty member prepaid group practices, supports the regular exchange of data and information used to measure, report, and improve performance. They have sponsored a consumer survey biennially since 1988, again primarily as a benchmarking tool that can be used to identify quality improvement initiatives and opportunities at the plan level. Kaiser Central (headquarters) develops member and nonmember surveys that can be used to establish benchmarks and to compare the Kaiser plans with each other.

Use by Managed Care Plans for External Purposes

Though consumer surveys had their origin in internal operations, they are increasingly being applied for external uses. In particular, purchasers are requesting information from consumer surveys to help monitor plan performance, select plans to be offered, and facilitate employee choice. In 1991, 88 percent of the HMOs in the Group Health Association of America (GHAA) Annual HMO Industry Survey reported receiving requests for consumer satisfaction information from employers (GHAA 1992). Some HMOs probably meet these requests using data already collected for internal use purposes, but sometimes plans may initiate new studies to fill in the gaps or tailor information to employer specifications.

More recently, several plans have developed plan report cards, which have an external audience including both purchasers and enrollees or potential enrollees as well as a more broad-based national audience. These report cards typically include measures from administrative data, special studies, and consumer surveys. United HealthCare, U.S. Healthcare, and Kaiser Health Plan of Northern California are producing report cards (Zablocki 1994).

The issue of consistency in data definitions and measures, both across plans and across the kinds of requests made by purchasers, has created an interest in developing standardized tools that plans can use to respond to employer requests. The most prominent current effort was recently completed under the sponsorship of the National Committee for Quality Assurance (NCQA), which is the main accrediting body for HMOs.

NCQA's effort was based on version 2.0 of the Health Plan Employer Data and Information Set (HEDIS) (NCQA 1993). HEDIS 2.0 is a standardized list of about 60 measures of quality, access and patient satisfaction, membership and utilization, and finance. It does not mandate a standardized measure of consumer satisfaction, though its appendix provides as examples both the second edition of the Group Health Association of America's Consumer Satisfaction Survey and the Employee Health Care Value Survey, which includes most of the GHAA instrument along with other batteries.

NCQA's pilot project involved 21 health plans from across the country selected for diversity of model-type, size, geographic location, and type of information system (NCQA 1995). The goal was to develop a report card based on a subset of HEDIS performance measures consistently defined across plans and audited by NCQA, with the experience serving to refine HEDIS 2.0. The pilot moved beyond HEDIS 2.0 in the area of consumer satisfaction, sponsoring a survey using the GHAA Consumer Satisfaction Survey instrument (second edition) with the intention of identifying a subset of the items that will be meaningful to consumers. While HEDIS 2.0 was developed chiefly to serve the needs of commercial insurers, NCQA (with support from HCFA and states) has a grant from the Packard Foundation to develop an adaptation suitable for measuring care received from publicly supported Medicaid enrollees in managed care.

Use by External Parties to Address Public Accountability, Oversight, and Community Assessment

The chief mechanisms for ensuring public accountability and oversight of health plans are state licensure, voluntary certification as a federally qualified HMO, and accreditation by voluntary organizations. Rarely do the regulatory entities or their agents conduct plan-based consumer surveys. However, they sometimes require or encourage plans to conduct surveys, and they verify that this and other requirements are met. These verification activities vary in nature and extent.

Accreditation programs for managed care plans have become much more established over the past few years. NCQA currently is the principal body accrediting HMOs (Gold et al. 1995b). NCQA requires that plans have mechanisms to protect and enhance membership satisfaction with plan services, including membership satisfaction surveys, studies of reasons for disenrollment, and evidence that the organization uses this information to improve the quality of its service. Relevant documentation (i.e., results of member satisfaction and disenrollment surveys) is reviewed by an NCQA team during the on-site review for accreditation. NCQA also requires, as part of a managed care organization credentialing system, a periodic performance appraisal of providers. This appraisal includes information from quality assurance activity, risk and utilization management, member complaints, and member satisfaction surveys. Current NCQA accreditation requirements do not require plans to be capable of producing HEDIS 2.0. However, we have been told that plans believe they will ultimately need to provide HEDIS 2.0 for accreditation and thus are gearing up for it as part of their accreditation activities.

As managed care grows, oversight likely will as well and with it the use of surveys. The last round of health reform deliberations emphasized oversight of managed care plans and proposals, mostly not implemented at this point, for the central collection of satisfaction data. The Clinton Administration's Health Security Act, for example, called for the AHCPR to administer a consumer survey on access, use of services, health outcomes, and patient satisfaction by plan and by state (Title V.A Section 5004). Consumer satisfaction surveys have been built into some state reform efforts as well. Two states leading the reform effort—Minnesota and Washington—

are working through public-private partnerships to find ways to disseminate information on quality of care, including information from consumer surveys. A 1994 survey of senior state officials sponsored by The Robert Wood Johnson Foundation found that fewer than ten were currently involved in developing consumer satisfaction data by health plan, and that most such efforts were at an early stage. However, 73 percent of those responding perceived that data on health system and health plan performance were very important for health reform (Gold, Burnbauer, and Chu 1995).

Some plan-based consumer surveys have been sponsored independently by consumer and community organizations, occasionally with external funding. Two examples are the plan-specific consumer satisfaction survey information on 46 plans that was included as part of a detailed report on HMOs and other managed care products in *Consumer Reports* magazine (Consumer's Union 1992), and the Central Iowa Health Survey, funded by the John A. Hartford Foundation. The latter was a pilot study for the population-provided data component of the patient-centered Community Health Management Information System (CHMIS), which forms the core of the John A. Hartford Foundation's Community Health Management Initiative launched in 1991 (Allen 1993). CHMIS is intended to develop a blended data set incorporating claims, survey, and other kinds of data from competing organizations at multiple levels, including health plans, hospitals, and doctors' offices.

Use by Purchasers in Commercial, Medicare and Medicaid Markets

Purchaser-sponsored surveys represent a relatively new trend, and sponsors are, for the most part, the largest purchasers. Some surveys are sponsored by a single purchaser, while others involve groups of purchasers. The broader the purchaser coalition, the less distinction there is between this approach and community-based approaches. Most of these surveys are sponsored by employers, while fewer have been sponsored by Medicare or Medicaid so far (though this could change).[2]

The distinguishing feature of these surveys is that they involve estimates of satisfaction specific to the purchaser's population relative to the health plan overall. Leading examples include the Bank of America/Bay Area Business Group on Health (personal communication August 1994)[3]; the Minnesota State Employees (State of Minnesota Joint Labor-Management Committee on Health Plans 1993a and 1993b); the Federal Employees Health Benefits Program (Francis 1994); and the employer consortium of Xerox, GTE, and Digital Equipment Corporation (Allen 1994). These employer-sponsored surveys represent three private employers, one state government employer, and the federal government.

In addition to corporate sponsors, management consultants and survey research firms are the other major sponsor of surveys aimed at the employer market. Potentially the largest such effort, the approach developed by the National Research Corporation (NRC) (1994), rests on a methodology that involves an ongoing panel drawing on 200,000 volunteer households. NRC also conducts customized surveys for a number of managed care plans (for example, CIGNA and Family Health Plan), and markets plan-specific results by geographic areas. Other firms such as Novalis (Ribner and Stewart 1993) and Towers Perrin (HMO Manager's Letter 1992a; 1992b; 1994) have conducted surveys on employee satisfaction with health plans, but the results are rarely plan-specific.

Externally sponsored consumer surveys are used less extensively in publicly financed programs such as Medicare and Medicaid though this is changing as managed care enrollment in these programs grows. Medicare does not routinely generate plan-based consumer information for use in monitoring managed care plans. Medicare mounts a continuing Current Beneficiary Survey. Periodic surveys that do not involve plan-specific estimates have been used in sponsored evaluations (e.g., Brown et al. 1993) and to address specific programmatic issues like disenrollment (Porrell et al. 1992). A recent HCFA initiative recommended using validated surveys to evaluate the quality of care and patient satisfaction with various aspects of the health care received by managed care plans (Delmarva Foundation for Medical Care, Inc. 1994).

Consumer surveys generating plan-specific estimates also are not common among Medicaid programs currently, though their use is growing. Because of the shared federal-state structure of Medicaid, states are more likely than the federal government to sponsor consumer surveys that are plan-specific, though federal interest in this area has expanded, particularly for demonstration projects involved in broad-based reforms. An early example of state use of surveys for the Medicaid population comes from California, which sponsored a 13-plan survey for 3 years (in the mid-1970s) to monitor prepaid health plan quality in response to highly publicized problems (Ware et al. 1981). Consumer information has been used in some national evaluations (for example, the Arizona Health Care Cost-Containment System) and will be used to support evaluations of 1115 waiver programs now being implemented. Some state Medicaid programs include consumer surveys as part of their quality monitoring activity. As of September 1992, 8 of 25 Medicaid agencies surveyed required HMOs to conduct patient satisfaction surveys; 7 conduct their own surveys, to assess recipient satisfaction (USDHHS 1992). More recent efforts include a survey of Medicaid recipients in Maryland that the state is fielding with Robert Wood

Johnson Foundation funding, as well as consumer surveys conducted by states participating in a demonstration of the Medicaid Quality Assurance Reform Initiative (Felt 1995). We know of no efforts to use plan-based estimates from these surveys to support beneficiary choice and Medicaid has no parallel to the existing Medicare Current Beneficiary Survey. However, the Physician Payment Review Commission (1994) recommended that Congress fund such a survey based on research showing its feasibility for generating state-based estimates (Gold et al. 1995a). This work also highlighted the special issues that apply to surveying low-income and Medicaid populations, including limitations of the Medicaid eligibility files as a sampling frame, biases created by families not having telephones, and eligibility turnover.

Medicare and Medicaid may become more involved in sponsoring plan-based surveys to generate consumer information. HCFA contracted in 1994 for a study in which prototypes of consumer information materials will be developed. The data-based approaches are likely to involve the use of surveys (Research Triangle Institute 1994).

SURVEY FOCUS, INSTRUMENT CONTENT, AND METHODS

Variations in Survey Focus

Surveys of consumer satisfaction with health plans vary in several ways, the most important of which are illustrated in Figure 10.1. First, surveys differ in terms of the population they are intended to represent. That population may be in a given geographic area, in a particular plan, or in the specific purchaser's share of the plan. The Novalis survey is an example of a geographically based survey that provides estimates of how satisfaction varies by type of plan, though it is not market-specific. Community-based efforts, like the Central Iowa Health Survey, and plan-based surveys provide plan-specific estimates. Most purchaser surveys focus on the employer-specific population in a plan.

Surveys differ according to whether they focus on all those eligible for the plan or on healthcare users only. Within each of the three types of populations (geographic, plan-specific, and employer-specific), we find surveys that focus on either all eligibles or users. This focus may have important implications for the results and how they are interpreted. The distinction is particularly important for surveys involving PPOs, because use in itself may be an important measure of satisfaction. Even for HMOs, surveys with the same questions may yield dissimilar estimates depending on whether all enrollees or only users respond. The two focuses persist largely because there are strong opinions, but no consensus, among survey developers about how information on satisfaction with use should be collected. It is possible that this occurs in part because developers have different goals for the survey, for example, marketing or performance evaluation and quality improvement.

Although Figure 10.1 helps to create a basic understanding of survey population and focus, it simplifies reality. First, people move from one category to another over time, so changes in satisfaction may reflect changes in population composition as much as changes in plan quality or access. In addition, moves across categories vary across plans and types of population (for example, Medicaid versus commercial enrollees), creating a potential source of bias in trend estimates. Second, the unit of analysis may not always be the person but may be a user of a particular service or provider, two "targets" common among internal surveys designed to support plan management efforts. Finally, "population" may be variously defined, Estimates may be based on a sample of all individuals in one of the three categories or only on those of a particular type (for example, only insured individuals, only commercial group enrollee). In addition, items may be framed to capture information on the household, the insurance unit, the subscriber, the respondent, or a child.

Item Content

Research studies since 1980 on consumer satisfaction and other performance measures were recently summarized by Miller and Luft (1994). Their analysis highlights the importance of item content, because the studies found that satisfaction varies for different dimensions of care.

Figure 10.1 Varying Features of Samples for Consumer Satisfaction Surveys of Managed Care Plans

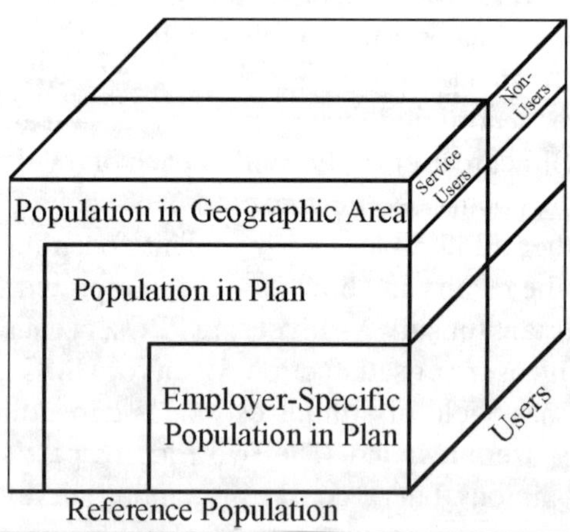

Many of today's surveys designed to develop plan-based measures of satisfaction are based on the GHAA Consumer Satisfaction Survey instrument. This instrument was based on others, beginning with satisfaction measures developed in the 1970s with grants from the National Center for Health Services Research and Development (Ware and Snyder 1975; Ware et al. 1983) that were adapted for the Health Insurance Experiment (Davies et al. 1986) and later for the Medical Outcomes Study (Marshall et al. 1993). Table 10.1 summarizes the evolution of these related satisfaction measures.

This GHAA battery has subsequently been used by the Health Institute at the New England Medical Center in the Iowa Health Survey and other projects. In addition to batteries from the GHAA Consumer Satisfaction Survey, the Iowa Survey Instrument included a modified version of the inpatient hospital quality trends (HQT) which measures satisfaction with the most recent hospitalization (if within three months) (Meterko et al. 1990) and the visit satisfaction questionnaire (VSQ), which captures satisfaction with the last physician visit (if within four months) (Rubin et al. 1993).[4] In addition to consumer satisfaction, the Iowa survey also measures health status through the SF-36 (Ware and Sherbourne 1992; Ware et al. 1993) and also included a pilot test of enrollees' ratings of management of care and coverage. The package of instruments is intended to be a reference set of batteries to be used individually or together for different purposes. This set of batteries has since been followed by the Employer Health Care Value Survey (EHCVS). The EHCVS satisfaction battery includes most items in the second edition of the GHAA Consumer Satisfaction Survey, augmented by a set of questions on the management of care and coverage (partially pilot tested in the Iowa survey). The EHCVS also includes the SF-36 and items on health risk behavior drawn from previous survey instruments.

Though GHAA's interest in sponsoring Davies and Ware to develop the Consumer Satisfaction Survey instrument was to promote consistency across surveys, most users have modified the instrument by adding and dropping items, adapting them to specific encounters or providers, and modifying the satisfaction categories. For example, the HMO Group survey instrument incorporates questions from the GHAA Consumer Satisfaction Survey but includes additional questions, for example, on prescriptions, lab tests, ease of choosing a primary care physician, and hospital care. There is also a module on out-of-plan visits. Many of these modifications reflect differences in philosophy and opinion about how certain methodological issues should be handled. The shortening of the instrument by omitting items may be intended to reduce respondent burden. It may also reflect a narrower set of purposes and individual user views on what is most valuable. While these

Table 10.1 Evolution of Consumer Satisfaction Surveys

Battery	Devel.	Items	Sources	Content	Response Scale	Major Changes from Source	Primary Use
PSQ-I	1972–75	80	Literature reviews, content review of earlier instruments, and item generation studies produced pool of 2,300 items.[1–3]	Accessibility and convenience; availability of services; continuity of care; finances; interpersonal aspects; technical quality; facilities; and general satisfaction	Strongly agree; Agree; Not sure; Disagree; Strongly disagree	NA	Multiple tests to identify dimensions of care and services; test-scaling assumptions, score reliability; response bias; and validity
PSQ-II	1972–75	68	Same as PSQ-I and results of PSQ-I studies. Items were revised to emphasize or clarify object of measurement; improve score distributions, and reduce ambiguity.[2]	Same as PSQ-I	Strongly agree; Agree; Not sure; Disagree; Strongly disagree	Shorter than PSQ-I; more focused on empirically confirmed dimensions of care	Multiple field tests to replicate methodological studies; describe healthcare attitudes of adults across practices, cities, counties, and states
PSQ-43	1971–77	43	42 PSQ-II items and "crisis in health care" item from CHAS-NORC[2,3,8–10]	Same as PSQ-I; additional item does not assess attitudes toward own medical care and services	Strongly agree; Agree; Not sure; Disagree; Strongly disagree	Shorter than PSQ-II; retains fundamental concepts	Support assessments of health care (along with other batteries) in omnibus surveys; used in this way to compare health insurance plans in the HIE; develop norms for U.S. population in CHAS-NORC survey
PSQ-III	1984–85	50	PSQ-II items; pilot tests of new items written to distinguish financial and physical access[11,12]	Interpersonal manner; communication; technical quality; financial security; time spent with physician; access to care; and general satisfaction	Strongly agree; Agree; Not sure; Disagree; Strongly disagree	New items on financial security	Medical Outcomes Study

Table 10.1 Evolution of Consumer Satisfaction Surveys (*continued*)

Battery	Devel.	Items	Sources	Content	Response Scale	Major Changes from Source	Primary Use
VSQ	1985–86	9	PSQ-III[3–15]	Physical access; telephone access; office wait; appointment wait; time spent with physician; communication; interpersonal aspects; technical quality; and overall care	Excellent; Very good; Good; Fair; Poor	Reduced in length to one item per concept; uses EVGFP response scale	Medical Outcomes Study
CHAA CSS (First Edition)	1987–88	35	Based on PSQ-III items, rewritten to be used with EVGFP response scale. (Satisfaction battery represents 1 of 3 included in entire survey; others capture prior use/experience with plan and sociodemographics.)[16]	Access; finances; technical quality; communication; choice; continuity; interpersonal care; outcomes; overall care; and general satisfaction	Excellent; Very good; Good; Fair; Poor	Uses EVGFP response scale; collapsed PSQ-III items to yield survey while retaining content; added outcomes	Made available to GHAA member plans and employers for use in producing plan-level estimates for employers
GHAA CSS (Second Edition)	1991	35 Care Svcs. 14 plan	Same care and services battery as GHAA CSS (first edition). Content of new satisfaction battery based on review of literature, individual plan surveys, and focus groups.[14]	As in GHAA CSS (first edition), but with the following additional items: services covered; information from plan; paperwork; costs of care; and overall plan	Excellent; Very good; Good; Fair; Poor	Addition of battery to yield ratings of selected managed care plan features in response to requests from plans and employers	Same as GHAA CSS (first edition)

Table 10.1 Evolution of Consumer Satisfaction Surveys (*continued*)

Source: Davies, A.: Personal communication, 1994.

Notes: PSQ is Patient Satisfaction Questionnaire. VSQ is Visit Satisfaction Questionnaire. GHAA is Group Health Association of America. CSS is Consumer Satisfaction Survey. CHAS-NORC is Center for Health Administration Studies—National Opinion Research Center. HIE is Health Insurance Experiment. EVGFP is excellent, very good, good, fair, or poor.

[1](Ware and Snyder, 1975).

[2]Ware, J. E., Snyder, M. K., and Wright, W. R.: *Development and Validation of Scales to Measure Patient Satisfaction With Health Care Services*: Volume I of a Final Report. Part A: Review of Literature, Overview of Methods, and Results Regarding Construction of Scales. Pub. No. PB-288-329. Springfield, VA. National Technical Information Service, 1976a.

[3]Ware, J. E., Snyder, M. K., and Wright, W. R.: *Development and Validation of Scales to Measure Patient Satisfaction With Health Care Services:* Volume I of a Final Report. Part B: Results Regarding Scales Constructed From the Patient Satisfaction Questionnaire and Measures of Other Health Care Perceptions. Pub. No. PB-288-330. Springfield, VA. National Technical Information Service, 1976b.

[4]Ware, J. E., Wright, W. R., Synder, M. K., and Chu, G. C.: Consumer Perceptions of Health Care Services: Implications for the Academic Medical Community. *Journal of Medical Education* 50 (9): 839–848, 1975.

[5]Doyle, B. J., and Ware, J. E.: Physician Conduct and Other Factors That Influence Patient Satisfaction. *Journal of Medical Education* 52 (10): 793–801, 1977.

[6]Ware, J. E.: Effects of Acquiescent Response Set on Patient Satisfaction Ratings. *Medical Care* 16 (4): 327–336, 1978.

[7](Ware et al., 1983).

[8]Aday, L. A., Andersen, R., and Fleming, G. V.: *Health Care in the United States: Equitable for Whom*? Beverly Hills. Sage Publications, 1980.

[9]Marquis, M. R., Davies, A. R., and Ware, J. E.: Patient Satisfaction and Change in Medical Care Provider. *Medical Care* 21 (8): 821–829, 1983.

[10]Davies, A. R., Ware, J. E., Brook, R. H., and Peterson, J.: Consumer Acceptance of Prepaid and Fee-for-Service Medical Care: Results From a Randomized Control Trial. *Health Services Research* 21 (3): 429–452, 1986.

[11]Safran, D., Tarlov, A. R., and Rogers, W.: Primary Care Performance in Fee-for-Service and Prepaid Health Care Systems: Results From the Medical Outcomes Study. *Journal of the American Medical Association* 271 (20): 1579–1586, 1994.

[12](Marshall et al., 1993).

[13]Hays, R. D., and Ware, J. E.: Methods for Measuring Patient Satisfaction With Specific Medical Encounters. *Medical Care* 26 (4): 393–402, 1988.

[14](Davies and Ware, 1991).

[15](Rubin et al., 1993).

[16](Davies and Ware, 1988b).

adaptations, particularly the omission of items, make it impossible to compare plans on the nine scales, plans can be compared on matching retained items.

Adaptations of the GHAA instrument also illustrate differences in opinion about whether individuals should be asked to rate features of care they have not used, the relative emphasis on ratings of aspects of care versus reports on actual experiences; for whom the respondent should answer (for example, self versus family); and whether satisfaction should be requested, by proxy, for children.

There are other bodies of work on consumer satisfaction or related measures of health plans. For example, the Bank of America survey instrument includes satisfaction ratings and factual reports on process and outcomes of care (for example, Does this plan offer all the health services you need? How would you categorize the attitudes of doctors, nurses, and support staff serving you under this medical plan? In the past year have you had any illness or bad reaction caused by medicine your physician prescribed?). The instrument also has items that solicit information on health behaviors that may serve as markers of adverse selection based on incidence of health risks (for example, smoking, stress). It is distinguished mainly by its emphasis on the reporting of events rather than ratings of satisfaction, though both are included. The former have intuitive appeal to some purchasers, consumers, and health plan members. Current work is under way to identify better how surveys, particularly those with consumers as the intended audience, can be better grounded in an understanding of what information consumers really use to make decisions. For example, some say that knowing which providers are affiliated with a plan is more important to consumers than satisfaction information (Winslow 1994).

Because survey instruments have evolved independently, plans vary considerably in the instruments they use (Table 10.2). However, the availability of the GHAA survey has contributed to some consistency in use of instruments among plans that have recently initiated surveys. Of the 21 survey instruments we obtained from managed care plans, 10 of them draw on the GHAA satisfaction battery in whole or part, though 3 had modified the rating system (either using the response categories "satisfied" to "dissatisfied" or inventing new rating systems, such as 1 to 10 representing "unacceptable" to "excellent"). Some of them added items, for example, covering access to specialist care in greater detail and satisfaction with the facility appearance, staff demeanor and dress, and ease of parking. The length of these instruments varied from the 47-item GHAA survey (for a first-time baseline survey of plan satisfaction) to 9 items for a survey of satisfaction with specialist care.

Table 10.2 Summary of Content of Plan-Based Consumer Surveys

Satisfaction with Aspect of Care or Service	Number of Plan-Based Surveys Included
Overall Quality and Satisfaction	21
Interpersonal Aspects	18
Communication or Information	18
Timeliness of Services	16
Intention to Recommend Organization	16
Technical Aspects	14
Time Spent with Providers	14
Access and Availability of Services	13
Intention to Use Organization Again	11
Satisfaction with Outcomes of Care	8
Choice or Continuity	8
Financial Aspects and Billing	8
Physical Environment	6

Note: Derived from 21 plan-based survey instruments collected from managed care organizations.

METHODOLOGICAL PRACTICES AND ISSUES

Frequency, Mode of Administration, and Response Rates

Of the plans for which we have information, many reported using key surveys on a continual basis or at least annually. Plans were mixed between telephone, mail, and combined approaches. The extent to which plans are using surveys appears to be growing, particularly as more aim for NCQA accreditation, as survey models become more available, and as examples of applications become more publicized. However, the range of sophistication, uses, and methods vary considerably across plans, for example, we identified instances of quota sampling rather than random sampling.

Although in-person studies of satisfaction are sometimes conducted—mostly in focus groups—the predominant modes of administering plan-based surveys are telephone, mail, and mail with telephone follow-up. Of 21 surveys for which we have information on mode, 12 were administered by mail or mixed mode, and 9 were administered by telephone.

The advantages of mail surveys are lower expense and greater anonymity. Press, Ganey, and Malone (1992) insist on the importance of anonymity in collecting objective measures of satisfaction with hospital stays, citing differences in satisfaction level between the two modes (personal communication). The disadvantage of mail surveys is that they generally yield lower response rates (often less than 50 percent, though rates increase with follow-up mailings). Plans reported mail survey response rates to single-mailing surveys ranging from 30 percent to 60 percent.

Plans use telephone surveys almost as often as mail surveys to collect information on satisfaction, and many of them use computer-assisted interviewing, which reduces cost. Telephone response rates can be higher than response rates to single-mailing surveys, achieved through repeat calls to those not answering the first time. The lowest response rate to a plan telephone survey we identified was 60 percent. We found that some of the external surveys had response rates of 70 percent or more by telephone. However, the estimates frequently involve sampling with replacement to obtain a target sample size. Hence, the response rates for telephone surveys cannot readily be compared directly with mail surveys in which such techniques are not used.

Selection of Respondents

Respondents are typically members of the plan, though they can sometimes be the spouse of a member. They are usually asked about their own health care, but in some instances they are asked to respond in a general way, which implies they are answering for the family, or they are asked to respond specifically about their children's care.

Cultural and Ethnic Diversity

We were unable to identify from the materials collected how surveys account for cultural and ethnic diversity of members. This includes non-English speakers, the possibility of low levels of literacy (particularly for mail surveys), and any cultural differences in response sets, all of which might bias the results. One plan's approach to language on a mail survey is to express each item on the same instrument in English and Spanish. This issue is important, particularly as managed care penetration grows among low income populations, some of whom speak little English.

Sample Selection

We have very little information about sampling methods for the plan-based surveys, although most plans reference random samples. Having drawn a random sample, however, some plans appear to use quota sampling to collect a specified number of responses, while others describe fielding procedures that suggest attempts to complete all of the sample initially drawn. Packer-Tursman (1994) describes the increasingly targeted sampling methods being used by Kaiser Permanente. Satisfaction data across plans that use different sampling and fielding procedures will not be comparable. In addition, the quality and utility of the data obtained by individual plans obviously depends on whether the methods minimize potential bias and provide for generalizable estimates.

Type of Measurement

Existing surveys reflect at least three kinds of differences in how measures are developed. The first involves the emphasis on ratings versus reports, that is, whether consumers are asked to rate features of care and service or to report on actual events as they experience them. Ratings are more common, but interest in reports has grown because they are viewed by some as providing both the basis for more "objective" or "normative" performance standards, and potential substitutes for or complements to other sources of direct quality measurement.

The second difference involves the form of the scale. Historically, it had been most common to ask respondents to rate their care on some form of satisfied-dissatisfied scale or agree-disagree scale. Based on research on survey design (Ware and Hays 1988), some use a four-point scale running from "excellent" to "poor," which makes it easier to compare ratings across different features of care. It is also common to add a fifth category, "very good," making this a five-point scale. While such an approach may superficially appear imbalanced, this five-point part scale discriminates better among the large majority of respondents who typically cite care as either excellent or good.

The third difference in how measures are developed involves whether the emphasis is on composite scales constructed from multiple measures or individual items. For cross-plan comparisons of complex features of care that involve several dimensions of performance, scales are likely to provide more useful measures and more stable estimates. However, individual items may be more intuitively appealing and more useful for identifying specific aspects of performance that need improvement. In practice, it is not a matter of choosing one or another as both can be readily calculated.

GENERATING COMPARABLE PLAN-BASED MEASURES

While there is considerable experience with using plan-based consumer surveys for internal management needs, the use of such data outside the plan is relatively recent. The use of survey data for cross-plan comparisons or other external purposes raises several operational issues that are otherwise nonexistent or less critical.[5] These issues are important to address if tools such as report cards are to be practical and relevant.

Developing a Sampling Frame

Health plans typically know their membership (or at least their users in the case of PPOs or indemnity products), and employers know their employees. However, lists that can be used to generate representative samples for the target population may not be available to other external survey sponsors (such as a community group). Such sponsors must therefore rely either on participating plans to voluntarily generate enrollment lists or samples or on population-based survey techniques. Plans may be hesitant to provide such lists, and they may be even precluded from participating because of confidentiality issues. Population-based sampling techniques are potentially feasible when enrollment is high in an area or can be predicted by known factors (for example, zip code). However, such techniques are generally not feasible for developing estimates for a large number of individual plans, many of which may represent only a small share of the population. This can be a particular problem in using surveys to compare health plans used by vulnerable populations like those on Medicaid, particularly since the heightened concerns for confidentiality often preclude sharing names with potential survey sponsors.

Ensuring Consistent Methods and Valid Results

There are two options for developing comparative information from consumers across health plans: collect it centrally or compile plan results individually. Central collection by a purchaser (or its agent) or other body allows for consistency in method across plans. If the central body is regarded as objective, this option is also likely to generate more credible data. Compiling individual plan reports (for example, from internal plan surveys) is less burdensome on the external entity and takes advantage of ongoing surveys. However, methods and results may not be comparable, and there may be incentives that introduce bias. A compromise is for the purchaser to provide or to agree, in conjunction with health plans, on a standardized methodology and to develop a mechanism for validating a sample of the data each plan then submits.

Developing Plan-, Purchaser-, or Purchaser Group–Specific Data

Individual purchasers (or groups of purchasers) may find plan-based data specific to their enrollees of greatest interest or value. However, only the largest employers are likely to be able to conduct surveys to collect such information. In any case, administrative costs may be high systemwide for a group-specific approach. Unfortunately, we know of little research comparing satisfaction across diverse purchasers, particularly those from a similar market segment (for example, comparing scores within commercial accounts rather than between commercial group accounts and Medicaid). Research is lacking on alternative ways of sampling or stratifying the analysis and on how these practices affect results and costs.

Market Segmentation and Risk Adjustment

Health plans serve differing market segments; hence, the characteristics of their enrollees vary. Some differences may be correlated with consumer responses to surveys, reflecting both objective differences (such as health risk or compliance) or response (for example, relative importance attributed to different characteristics or expectations). Differences of opinion exist about whether adjusting consumer responses for risk factors is appropriate, some arguing that consumer responses reflect the prevailing market and should not be adjusted. Among others who wish to compare across plans or markets, the issue is how to adjust for risk rather than whether to adjust. Unless these differences are accounted for in the measures developed from surveys, proponents of risk adjustment argue that the results may be misleading and biased in the plan comparisons they provide. For those wishing to adjust for risk, the issue can be addressed by separately reporting measures for different segments (such as group versus individual enrollees, commercial accounts versus Medicaid) or by standardizing the data to represent a standardized population across plans. However, the latter approach may not be feasible if some plans do not serve key segments of the population (in which case there are no performance data to apply to the standardized population mix). It may also imply that different standards of performance are acceptable across the population. For different purposes, it is important to present both unadjusted and adjusted data. Again, these issues are particularly germane to public purchasers.

Disenrollment Bias

The same degree of dissatisfaction may generate different disenrollment behavior across plans depending on the scope of the network. At one extreme, those dissatisfied with care under indemnity coverage retain the same health insurance but switch providers. At the other extreme, those dissatisfied under a tight network-based managed care plan with no point-of-service option may be much more likely to switch plans. Surveying only current users will overstate satisfaction and may lead to biased comparisons across plans and delivery systems with distinctly different designs.

CONCLUSIONS AND RECOMMENDATIONS

There is a growing interest in plan-based measures of consumer satisfaction with access and quality. While there is no consensus on survey content or approach, there is a growing body of work and experience that can inform future developments. The content of instruments appears to be better developed than do the methods for using them. In addition, work on rating-type approaches is more advanced than work on report-type approaches. Yet, there are enough examples to conclude that methodologically sound surveys with high response rates are achievable. The two key constraints on this effort are likely to be resources and the sophistication of users, particularly given the large number of potential sponsors and estimates desired. Current experience also suggests that item content for consumer surveys needs to be based on an understanding of the varying objectives of the surveys and that no one instrument or survey methodology can meet all needs.

Our review and analysis suggest that research and policy support can strengthen considerably the ability to develop effective plan-based surveys. Our work suggests that both increasing the availability of information on consumer satisfaction survey methods and furthering the development of these methods is important.

Existing experience with plan-based surveys is decentralized. Communication about what is being done and how is ad hoc. Proprietary interests and concerns contribute to this situation because public disclosure could limit marketing opportunities or remove competitive advantages. Yet the content of many survey instruments is readily available. In addition, there are many ongoing efforts where disclosure would not appear to create disadvantages and a little effort would make it easier for individuals and organizations to find out about those efforts. These include, for example, publicly available and current compilations of existing survey instruments and documentation of their application; and guidance to help potential users understand the strengths, weaknesses, and potential applications of alternative survey purposes, the batteries appropriate for each, and what "best practices" may exist for specific purposes.

Our review also suggests that there are several areas that need methodological study if plan-based surveys become more common. Three particularly important areas for research are:

1. **Development of methods for risk adjusting plan-based survey results.** The socio-demographic mix in managed care plans varies, often considerably. To the extent these characteristics are correlated with survey response, they may lead to biased comparisons among health plans. From a public policy perspective, such biases are of particular concern since they can create incentives diametrically opposed to desirable social responses—for example, service to the poor, the chronically ill, and those with special social or medical needs. Research is needed to assess whether risk-adjustment makes a difference to consumer responses, and, if it does, to extend current risk adjustment work from medical to social risk adjustment and to adjusters suitable to survey data. In addition, alternative forms of adjustment and correction need review.

2. **Short-form batteries for diverse needs.** Many surveys are constrained in the number of items they can include, leading users to develop various "short forms" of items from larger batteries. Often these are developed in an ad hoc manner and are not well validated. The use of diverse surveys also reduces the ability to compare across plans. A systematic study comparing the validity of existing approaches and testing alternative new "short forms" would be a valuable contribution. While such forms exist for visit and hospital services, they are much less developed for general enrollee surveys.
3. **Concordance between employer-specific, group enrollment, and plan-wide estimates of satisfaction**. Current trends will contribute to a proliferation of surveys for diverse populations. This can enhance consumer information but could add to administrative cost and burden. Yet there is little research to show how well more general measures predict sub-group responses and whether plan-wide measures are just as effective in discriminating among health plans based on performance.

A final note of caution: The healthcare system is sufficiently complex that diverse information could potentially be analyzed and distributed to consumers to help them assess access to health care provided in different health plans (see, for example, the review in Sofaer 1993). To provide it all could be expensive, could create overload, and could risk not communicating the most essential information. Moreover, consumers may not find satisfaction ratings particularly helpful.

ACKNOWLEDGMENTS

This chapter draws substantially on work originally commissioned by the Agency for Health Care Policy and Research for use at a conference on "Consumer Survey Information in a Reformed Health Care System," September 28–29, 1994, Vienna, Virginia, jointly sponsored by the Agency for Health Care Policy and Research and The Robert Wood Johnson Foundation. The full report is included in the proceedings (AHCPR 1995) from that conference. Allyson Ross Davies provided advice on sources of information, reviewed and commented on drafts of the AHCPR work, and assisted in identifying the evolution of survey content. We also benefited from the advice of Jill Bernstein, Terry Shannon, and Sandy Robinson on the staff at AHCPR. At Mathematica, Barbara Foot, Rachel Thompson, and Sabrina Perrault provided research support. Daryl Hall edited the chapter. Ann Miles, Marjorie Mitchell, and Kathleen Donaldson provided secretarial support.

NOTES

1. The authors are, respectively, Senior Fellow and Vice President with Mathematica Policy Research, Inc. This chapter is based to a considerable extent upon work commissioned by the Agency for Health Care Policy and Research under contract # 282-91-0027. The opinions are solely those of the authors.
2. This may reflect (1) a lesser extent of penetration by managed care in Medicare and (2) the fact that there are more employers than states.
3. The results were reported in *Bay Area Consumers' Checkbook* (1991), making this survey an early example of efforts to identify individual HMOs by name.
4. The VSQ is included as a model in the appendix of the second edition of the GHAA Consumer Satisfaction Survey (Davies and Ware 1991).
5. Some of the same issues arise, however, when comparing subunits within plans (for example, centers, physicians, regions).

REFERENCES

Agency for Health Care Policy and Research (AHCPR). 1995. *Conference Summary: Consumer Survey Information in a Reforming Health Care System*, AHCPR Pub. No. 95-0083. Rockville, MD: U.S. Department of Health and Human Services, Public Health Service.

Allen, H. M. 1993. "Consumer Assessment of Health and Health Care: The Central Iowa Pilot Study." Boston, MA: The Health Institute, New England Medical Center.

Allen, H., H. Darling, D. McNeill, et al. 1994. "The Employee Health Care Value Survey: Round One." Boston, MA: The Health Institute, New England Medical Center.

Bay Area Consumers' Checkbook. 1991. "Health Maintenance Organizations: Results of an Innovative Survey of Enrollees Conducted by the Bay Area Business Group on Health."

Berwick, D. M. 1989. "Continuous Improvement as an Ideal in Health Care." *New England Journal of Medicine* 320 (1): 53–56.

Brown, R. S., J. W. Bergeron, D. G. Clement, et al. 1993. "The Medicare Risk Program for HMOs—Final Summary Report on Findings from the Evaluation." Princeton, NJ: Mathematica Policy Research, Inc.

Cleary, P., and B. J. McNeil. 1988. "Patient Satisfaction as an Indicator of Quality of Care." *Inquiry* (Spring): 25–36.

Consumers Union. 1992. "Health Care in Crisis: Are HMOs the Answer?" *Consumer Reports* (August): 519–31.

Davies, A., and J. E. Ware, Jr. 1988. "Involving Consumers in Quality of Care Assessment." *Health Affairs* (Spring): 33–48.

———. 1988b. *GHAA's Consumer Satisfaction Survey and User's Manual*, 1st ed. Washington, DC: GHAA.

———. 1991. *GHAA's Consumer Satisfaction Survey and User's Manual*, 2nd ed. Washington, DC: GHAA.

Davies, A., J. E. Ware, Jr., R. H. Brook, et al. 1986. "Consumer Acceptance of Prepaid and Fee-for-Service Medical Care: Results from a Randomized Controlled Trial." *HSR: Health Services Research* 21 (3): 429–52.

Delmarva Foundation for Medical Care, Inc. 1994. "External Review Performance Measurement of Medicare HMOs/CMPs." Easton, MD: The Foundation.

Felt, S. 1995. "The First Twenty Months of the Quality Assurance Reform Initiative (QARI) Demonstration for Medicaid Managed Care: Interim Evaluation Report." Washington, DC: Mathematica Policy Research.

Francis, W., and the Center for the Study of Services. 1994. *Checkbook's Guide to 1995 Plans for Federal Employees*. Washington, DC.

Gabel, J., D. Liston, G. Jensen, and J. Marsteller. 1994. "The Health Insurance Picture in 1993: Some Rare Good News." *Health Affairs* 13 (1): 327–36.

Gold, M., L. Burnbauer, and K. Chu. 1995. "Half Empty or Half Full: The Capacity of State Data to Support Health Reform." Washington, DC: Mathematica Policy Research.

Gold, M., R. Hurley, T. Lake, T. Ensor, and R. Berenson. 1995b. *Arrangements Between Managed Care Plans and Physicians: Results from a 1994 Survey of Managed Care Plans*. Selected External Research Series Number 3, Washington, DC: Physician Payment Review Commission.

Gold, M., J. Hadley, D. Eisenhower, et al. 1995a. "Design and Feasibility of a National Medicaid Access Survey with State Specific Estimates." Washington, DC: Mathematica Policy Research.

Goldfield, N., M. Pine, and J. Pine. 1991. *Measuring and Managing Health Care Quality: Procedures, Techniques, and Protocols*. Gaithersburg, MD: Aspen Publishers.

Group Health Association of America. 1992. *HMO Industry Profile*. Washington, DC: The Association.

———. 1993. *HMO Industry Profile*. Washington, DC: The Association.

HMO Managers Letter. 1992a. "BCBSA/Gallup Survey: HMO Member Satisfaction Tops 90 Percent for 3rd Straight Year." *HMO Managers Letter* (May 26): 5.

———. 1992b. "Recent Surveys Find Managed Care's Popularity with Employers on the Rise." *HMO Managers Letter* (July 27): 5.

———. 1994. "Towers Perrin Survey Shows HMO Members as Satisfied as Members of Other Health Plans." *HMO Managers Letter* (April 4): 4.

Inguanzo, J. M. 1992. "Taking a Serious Look at Patient Expectations." *Hospitals* (September 5).

Intergovernmental Health Policy Project. 1993. "Expanding Access to Health Care: An Overview of 1992 State Legislation." IHPP.

James, V. 1994. "Quality Assurance: The Cornerstone of Managed Care." Presented at the conference, "Understanding Managed Care: An Introductory Program for New Managers in HMOs." Washington, DC: GHAA.

Kongstvedt, P. R. 1993. "Member Services and Consumer Affairs." In *The Managed Health Care Handbook*, 2nd ed., edited by P. R. Kongstvedt. Gaithersburg, MD: Aspen Publishers.

Kritchevsky, S. B., and B. P. Simmons. 1991. "Continuous Quality Improvement: Concepts and Applications for Physician Care." *Journal of the American Medical Association* 266 (13): 1817–23.

Marshall, G. N., R. D. Hays, C. D. Sherbourne, and K. B. Wells. 1993. "The Structure of Patient Satisfaction with Outpatient Medical Care." *Psychological Assessment* 5 (4): 477–83.

Meterko, M., E. C. Nelson, and H. R. Rubin. 1990. "Patient Judgments of Hospital Quality: A Taxonomy." *Medical Care* 28 (9) Supplement: S10–S14.

Miller, R. H., and H. S. Luft. 1994. "Managed Care Plan Performance Since 1980: A Literature Analysis." *Journal of the American Medical Association* 271 (19): 1512–19.

Morain, C. 1992. "HMOs Try to Measure (and Reward) 'Doctor Quality.'" *Medical Economics* 69 (7): 206–15.

National Committee for Quality Assurance. 1993. *Health Plan Employee Data and Information Set, HEDIS 2.0.* Washington, DC: NCQA.

———. 1995. *Report Care Pilot Project, Technical Report.* Washington, DC.

National Research Corporation. 1994. *Satisfaction Report Card: National Results.* Lincoln, NE: National Research Corporation.

Packer-Tursman, J. 1994. "Keeping Members." *HMO Magazine* 35 (2): 39–43.

Physician Payment Review Commission. 1994. *Annual Report to Congress.* Washington, DC: PPRC.

Pine, M., and P. R. Kongstvedt. 1993. "Quality Management." In *The Managed Care Handbook*, edited by Peter R. Kongstvedt. Gaithersburg, MD: Aspen Publishers.

Porell, F. W., C. Cocotas, P. J. Perales, et al. 1992. "Factors Associated with Disenrollment from Medicare HMOs: Findings from a Survey of Disenrollees." Waltham, MA: Brandeis University.

Press, I. 1994. "The Last Word." *Hospitals and Health Networks* (March 5).

Press, I., and M. P. Malone. 1993. "Patient Satisfaction and the Cost/Quality Equation." *Journal of Health Care Benefits* 3 (2): 40–43.

Press, I., R. Ganey, and M. Malone. 1992. "Patient Satisfaction: Where Does It Fit in the Quality Picture?" *Trustee* (April).

Research Triangle Institute. 1994. *Information Needs for Consumer Choice.* Prepared for the Health Care Financing Administration under Contract Number 55-94-0047. Research Triangle Park, NC: The Institute.

Ribner, S., and J. Stewart. 1993. *1993 Novalis National Health Care Survey: Consumer Ratings of Managed Care, A Special Report.* Albany, NY: Novalis Corporation.

Rubin, H. R., B. Gandek, W. H. Rogers, et al. 1993. "Patients' Ratings of Outpatient Visits in Different Practice Settings: Results from the Medical Outcomes Study." *Journal of the American Medical Association* 270 (7): 835–40.

Sofaer, S. 1993. "Informing and Protecting Consumers Under Managed Competition." *Health Affairs* 12 (Supplement): 76–86.

State of Minnesota Joint Labor-Management Committee on Health Plans. 1993a. "1993 Survey of Employees on Health Plans and Medical Care."

———. 1993b. *Health Plans and Medical Care: What Employees Think.*

U.S. Department of Health and Human Services, Office of the Inspector General. 1992. *A Review of HMO Quality Assurance Standards Required by Medicaid Agencies.* Washington, DC: DHHS.

Ware, J. E., Jr., B. Curbow, A. R. Davies, and B. Robbins. 1981. *Medicaid Satisfaction Surveys Research (1977–1980): A Report of the Prepaid Health Research, Evalua-*

tion, and Development Project. Sacramento, CA: California State Department of Health Services.

Ware, J. E., Jr., and R. D. Hays. 1988. "Methods for Measuring Patient Satisfaction with Specific Medical Encounters." *Medical Care* 26 (4): 393–402.

Ware, J. E., Jr., and C. D. Sherbourne. 1992. "The MOS 36-Item Short-Form Health Survey (SF-36): I. Conceptual Framework and Item Selection." *Medical Care* 30 (6): 473–83.

Ware, J. E., Jr., K. K. Snow, M. Kosinski, and B. Gaudek. 1993. *SF-36 Survey Manual and Interpretation Guide*. Boston, MA: The Health Institute, New England Medical Center.

Ware, J. E., Jr., and M. K. Snyder. 1975. "Dimensions of Patient Attitudes Regarding Doctors and Medical Care Services." *Medical Care* 13 (8): 669–82.

Ware, J. E., Jr., M. K. Snyder, W. R. Wright, and A. R. Davies. 1983. "Defining and Measuring Patient Satisfaction with Medical Care." *Evaluation and Program Planning* 6: 247–63.

Winslow, R. 1994. "Health-Care Report Cards Are Getting Low Grades from Some Focus Groups." *Wall Street Journal* May 19: B1.

Zablocki, E. 1994. "Employer Report Cards." *HMO Magazine* (March/April): 26–32.

CHAPTER

11

Can Ethical Management and Managed Care Coexist?

Leonard H. Friedman and Grant T. Savage

Oxymorons are words or phrases that have a precise dictionary meaning but may be interpreted as meaning exactly the opposite of what is intended. Some common oxymorons are "jumbo shrimp," "military intelligence," "smart bombs," and organizational "rightsizing." One final oxymoron is the derisive term "business ethics." After all, everyone knows that the only ethical principle that businesses hold to is their desire to achieve the highest level of profit regardless of cost. While ethics is a part of the curriculum or virtually every business school in the United States and articles regularly appear on ethics and social responsibility, the prevailing sentiment is that businesses exist to make money and everything else is secondary.

While many people will chuckle at these and other examples, there is no humor to be found when we move into the ethical uncertainty created when health service organizations migrate into for-profit, investor-owned status. The trends in this area are both clear and unequivocal. The number of publicly traded health care companies has grown from 33 in 1992 to 144 in 1996 with a corresponding increase in market capitalization over the same time period from $36 billion to $140 billion.[1] In 1985, California was home to 11 nonprofit and 5 small for-profit health maintenance organizations (HMOs). By 1995, there had been almost a complete reversal as evidenced by three very small nonprofit HMOs and the Kaiser-Permanente system

Reprinted from *Health Care Management Review*. 1998. 23(2): 56–62.

competing against seven large, well-organized, investor-owned HMOs.[2] For-profit, investor-owned physician management companies that manage and administer the business side of a physician's practice have grown from 3 in 1990 to 27 in 1996.[1]

The hospital industry, which has a long history with for-profit ownership, has seen Columbia/HCA move to the front as perhaps the most aggressive and opportunistic company of all. In 1996, Columbia/HCA owned or operated 343 hospitals, 136 surgical centers, and 550 home health agencies with total revenue of just under $20 billion.[3] Annual revenue growth of 19 percent since 1992 far exceeded the benchmark Standard and Poors 500 rate of 5 percent for the same time period. Put another way, the value of a $100 investment in Columbia HCA on December 31, 1990 would be worth in excess of $400 on December 31, 1995.[4]

The point of this discussion is to help frame the context under which health care organizations are now operating. While there remains a large number of community-based nonprofits with a strong mission statement underscoring their historical support of the people they serve, more and more organizations operate on the premise of giving the highest return to their shareholders. Indeed, the rapid transformation of nonprofits into for-profit systems is less than 20 years old.[5] A question that arises from this observation is whether it is antithetical for health care organizations to function under a for-profit, investor-owned model. One possible answer is that health care and profits have no historical or practical purpose being mentioned together. For example, the role of the hospital as a charitable institution in the United States is well documented.[6] Since the mid-1960s, federal and state governments have created programs to fund health insurance for the elderly, disabled, and poor in the forms of Medicare and Medicaid. As early as the 1950s, incentives were provided so that employers could help provide private health insurance for their employees as a nontaxable benefit. These programs and incentives have served to create a perception that health care is a basic right to all people and should not be treated as a commodity to be bought and sold on the open market but rather provided as a community good.

However, there is an equally compelling argument for the creation and growth of for-profit health care organizations. Physicians have historically functioned as small businesses with the intent of creating enough revenue to both cover the overhead of the business as well as pay themselves a salary or percentage of any residual funds remaining. As long as the public perceived that physicians were acting in the patients' best interests and patient satisfaction remained high, few if anyone complained about physician incomes. In the same sense, physicians owned and operated hospitals as for-profit enterprises with little if any negative feedback from their communities. In fact, around the turn of the 20th century, over one half of the nation's hospitals were run as for-profit enterprises.[5]

As interesting as the idea of physicians as business people might be, there is an even more important driver in the move toward for-profit health care. During the era of fee-for-service medicine, there were essentially no economic incentives for providers to conduct their business affairs in a cost-efficient or effective manner. All costs could be passed through to the payer or the patient with almost virtual certainty that the bill would be paid in full. Rising expenses such as salaries, new technology, additional services, or other capital improvements could easily be shifted to the payers. Costs for uncompensated care, charity, or bad debt were also passed on to the paying customers. Since insurance or the government paid the majority of the bills, these charges were transparent to the patient. The occasional voice would be raised in protest when, after examining a hospital bill, someone might notice a charge for a $5.00 aspirin tablet, but those complaints were generally pushed aside.

A second economic variable working to promote for-profit health care was the scarcity of physicians and hospitals immediately following World War II. Policies were almost immediately enacted by the federal government in order to create financial incentives for medical schools to increase the size of their entering classes. The Hill-Burton Hospital Survey and Construction Act of 1946 helped fund the construction of hundreds of new hospitals. Measures of economy and efficiency were pushed aside given the simultaneous desires to increase the nation's health care capacity, and at the same time provide employer-sponsored, tax-free health insurance.

Despite the efforts of the federal and state governments to control the rapidly rising costs of health care in the 1970s, the same economic incentives as before continued to motivate providers despite the growth of the multihospital systems that began during this time. It was not until 1983, when a real turning point was reached in the form of the Tax Equity and Fiscal Responsibility Act (TEFRA) that created the Health Care Financing Administration (HCFA) and with it, a new form of paying hospital bills for Medicare patients. Diagnosis related groups (DRGs) were the opening salvo of what has turned out to be nothing less than a total transformation of our health care delivery system. The arrival of DRGs and other methods of prospective payment including capitation, contracting, per diems, and global budgeting have effectively transferred the financial risk of health care from the payer to the provider. A countervailing argument has been made that although the government tried to control health care costs via prospective payment, it was the revolt of the employers that resulted in the burgeoning of managed care.[7] Irrespective of the source of change, the net effect is the same.

In the marketplace, this later reality has been the fundamental basis under which for-profit businesses have always operated. Risk and reward are well-known concepts in business. Successful businesses are the ones that are able to control their overhead costs yet at the same time produce a product or service of sufficient quality so that consumers will be willing to purchase what the business has to sell. The trick has always been trying to juggle cost, quality, and price in a world of other competitors and fickle consumers. Health care organizations (which produce services consumed by patients and typically purchased by employers and the government) are only recently beginning to realize what businesses have known for years. Managed care plans, capitation, and selective contracting are forcing health care providers to reduce their overhead and begin to think in terms of efficiency and effectiveness. For example, in the scenario just described, hospitals are no longer thought of as revenue centers and, instead, have become cost centers.

It should come as no surprise that, given the frame-breaking shift in health care reimbursement occurring over the past 2 decades, for-profit companies should be entering the world of hospitals and medical practice as never before. For-profits long ago discovered the tools and techniques necessary to survive and thrive in the environment currently surrounding health care organizations. While health policy experts, politicians, and consumers debate the merits and shortcomings of a market-oriented health care delivery system, the reality is that this type of system represents the here and now.[8] At the heart of this new system of for-profit health care organizations is the concept of managed care. In a managed care plan, patient care is managed in such a way as to attain the best possible medical outcome at the lowest possible cost. There is general agreement that managed care exists along a continuum of increasing cost and quality control with managed indemnity insurance plans at one end and closed panel HMOs at the other extreme.[9] At the present time, there are over 30 million persons enrolled in HMOs, the majority of which are run as for-profits.

The point of this discussion has been to demonstrate the fundamental move of health care delivery from not-for-profit to for-profit status if not actually in ownership, then at least to a change in management perspective. It is at this point that we briefly examine the principles under which for-profit businesses operate in an attempt to understand whether or not an intersection exists between business ethics and biomedical ethics.

BUSINESS ETHICS

At least four models can be used to explain the relationship between business and ethics. The first, which we will call the "principal-agent model," reasons that since executive level managers are agents of the shareholders, then the exclusive job of management is to increase shareholder wealth by increasing the present value of the organization. From this perspective, ethics is simply one more tool to increase shareholder value.[10] While managers might act in a morally proper manner to merge legal, ethical, and social concerns into business practice, any such actions are taken with the intent of adding wealth to the firm. This vision of business ethics is essentially amoral and arguably ought to be rejected.[11]

A second model advocates that managers employ a process of principled moral reasoning as a basis for making decisions. In this instance, morality is viewed as intrinsically good and should be seen as an end in itself, not just as a method for increasing shareholder wealth.[12] In a conflict between moral principles and wealth, morality should always win. However, what is lacking from this viewpoint is a definition of morality.

The third model uses a noninstrumental approach wherein ethics has a binding moral veto over the imperatives of increasing shareholder wealth and seeking profit. By definition, businesses have no special rules that override the moral obligations that managers hold as humans.[13] Students of philosophy will recognize this concept as grounded in the theories of deontological ethics in which moral rightness is not solely dependent on outcomes or results. This viewpoint was first put forth by Immanual Kant who suggests that the four principles common to the general morality of humans include not harming others, respecting authority, avoiding lying, and honoring agreements.[14] The difficulty with noninstrumental ethics in a business environment is that there is precious little, if any, moral uncertainty in the majority of decisions. In a business environment concerned with meeting the needs of customers, managers are faced with potentially high levels of moral ambiguity when customer requests conflict with these ethical absolutes. In contrast, managers of health service organizations are constantly faced with resolving difficult moral dilemmas as is witnessed in the growth of biomedical ethics committees found in most large hospital settings.

The fourth model for business ethics is expressed in a recent article by Quinn and Jones[12] who posit an agent-morality perspective. They suggest that while noninstrumental ethics are logically sound, they conflict markedly with the principal-agent model that appears to be the dominant ethical platform in U.S. businesses. The authors attempt to frame noninstrumental ethics in such a way that it becomes acceptable to businesses by arguing that moral principles are antecedent to the contract between the principal and agent and cannot be suspended by agreement between them. Only after basic moral duties have been met should shareholder wealth considerations be made a priority.[12]

BIOMEDICAL ETHICS

Persons employed as health care providers or working in health care organizations have traditionally been faced with a graver set of ethical concerns than have persons who work in other service or manufacturing industries. Four philosophical tenets serve as the basis for persons employed in managerial roles in health care facilities, including respect for others, beneficence, nonmaleficence, and justice.[15, 16]

Briefly stated, respect for others consists of respecting individual autonomy, truth telling, and maintaining confidentiality and fidelity.

Beneficence involves providing benefits to persons while at the same time balancing benefit and harm. According to the principle of beneficence, organizations (and their agents) are required to do all they can to aid patients.

Nonmaleficence is often thought to mean "first do no harm." There is an implicit balancing act between providing benefit yet at the same time doing no harm. An example of this conflict can be seen when staff are put at risk when treating trauma patients in the absence of universal precautions.

Standards of justice deal with the equitable distribution of benefits and costs among individuals, groups, and organizations.[17] Distributive justice focuses on the principle of impartiality, holding that all people should be treated the same unless there are relevant differences among them. Procedural justice focuses on the principle of fairness. This form of justice is based on the notion of a social contract between an organization and its primary stakeholders. Provision of services to medically indigent persons presents health care administrators with the clearest example of this ethical standard.

In addition to the ethical principles just described, most professional societies have a code of ethics that apply to all of their members. Examples of such codes include those written by the American College of Healthcare Executives, Medical Group Management Association, and American College of Health Care Administrators.

ETHICAL CONFLICTS IN FOR-PROFIT MANAGED CARE

Persons occupying management and administrative roles in managed care organizations are faced with the complexities of balancing their role as the agent for the shareholders of the firm with the needs of the patients and physicians. A number of conflicts are immediately apparent in this setting and can be classified according to the matrix in Figure 11.1.

The first conflict revolves around distribution of resources. Managed care organizations explicitly operate under the assumption that resources are limited to that which the insurer pays on the basis of a contractual agree-

Figure 11.1 Ethical Conflicts in Managed Care

Resources	Physicians are provided financial incentives to minimize resource consumption and see as many patients as possible in a given period of time.
Wealth	By denying access to tests and procedures, are costs controlled even though the patient will likely benefit from the test or procedure?
Equity	Recent studies suggest that the poor and elderly have worse outcomes in managed care than in traditional fee-for-service arrangements.

ment, capitation rate, or other prospective payment mechanism. Physicians are at the heart of this concern in that they are the persons with the sole responsibility of ordering tests, procedures, or hospitalizations. Variable health costs move up or down depending on what the physician orders. In most managed care, funds for referrals to specialists and hospital care reside in what is known as a "risk pool." The size of the risk pool is estimated at the start of the fiscal year and is drawn down as required. At the end of the year, any finds remaining are returned to the primary care physicians as a bonus. The chance that the risk pool will shrink is directly proportional to the tendency of physicians (who have assumed the risk) to mismanage resources. Therefore, an incentive is created that couples practice behavior with financial gain (or loss).

The second conflict centers around wealth and is at least indirectly related to the resource question. In virtually all managed care plans, there exists a mechanism whereby any costly test or hospital admission must be preapproved. In the best case scenario, this form of utilization review is conducted in order to assure the payer that the patient is receiving the most appropriate form of diagnosis or treatment for the particular disease or condition. The quest to obtain information on medical outcomes resides at the heart of this process. In most instances, managed care plans will not pay for experimental or unproved treatments. However, for many managed care plans, anecdotal reports suggest that the necessity to obtain clear approval before paying for a test or procedure has been twisted to delay or deny payment for costly medically necessary services simply as a way of holding down expenses.[18] There have also been media reports of managed care plans denying payment for bone marrow transplants for severely ill leukemia patients claiming that the treatment was experimental despite significant evidence to the contrary.[19]

The final conflict deals with the issue of equity. From the ethical standpoint of justice, patients in managed care plans with the same insurance ought to be treated equally with respect to access to services, tests, and treatments. In multiple studies comparing the medical outcomes of patients enrolled in managed care plans and traditional fee-for-service programs, no significant difference could be found. This finding supports the contention by managed care organizations that quality is not being sacrificed when costs are reduced. However, a recent study published in the *Journal of the American Medical Association*[20] reports that the elderly and poor do much worse in HMOs than in traditional insurance programs. While there has been criticism of the study,[21] serious questions are raised as to whether health services in HMOs and managed care are provided to consumers in a fair and equitable manner.

A PROPOSED MODEL FOR ETHICAL MANAGEMENT OF MANAGED CARE

Managers and administrators of organizations that provide health services based on a managed care model are by definition torn between two conflicting but equally compelling values. They include the simultaneous needs to provide an appropriate level of health services to the patients whose lives are covered by the organization, yet work to keep expenses as low as possible in order to maximize revenue and profit. From the perspective of a practicing manager, there is tremendous difficulty in achieving these goals due to control of the former by physicians and the shifting of responsibility for the latter from managed care organizations. Treatment decisions, diagnostic tests, drug therapies, and other clinical matters are exclusively in the hands of physicians who have been trained to do whatever is medically necessary for their patients—not what is most clinically and cost-effective. While administrators can and do advise physicians about the costs of their decisions as well as provide data on utilization, the clinician is the person empowered to control the resources used in patient care. The highly publicized actions of HMOs who deny certain clinical services to patient members have resulted in a public outcry against "bureaucrats," insurance executives, and other nonphysicians making medical resource decisions.

At the same time that administrators in managed care organizations find themselves unable to effectively control the resource utilization decisions of their physician providers, they are also required to act as the fiduciary agents for the owners of the firm. In that capacity, administrators are compelled to put the short-term financial interests of the owners ahead of the medical needs of patients and clinical wishes of the physicians. In the vernacular of managed care organizations, this control issue is most clearly seen by the presence of withholds whereby a certain percentage of the primary care capitation payment is withheld every month and used to pay for cost overruns in referral or institutional services.[22]

Fortunately, there is an ethical solution to this seemingly unsolvable dilemma. The key might lie in an augmented version of the agent-morality perspective. To reiterate, agent-morality theory as set forth by Quinn and Jones suggests that the moral principles of avoiding harm, respecting authority, honoring agreements, and avoiding lying have a higher priority than firm profits.[12] They suggest that because of the nature of managers as agents for the owners of the organization, they are bound to these principles, hence the term agent-morality. However, there needs to be a more persuasive element if this particular concept is to be applied to managed care in particular and health care organizations in general. Nowhere in their thesis is the concept of fairness, justice, or a level playing field mentioned. In a pure market orientation as envisioned by Adam Smith and other classical economists, while elements of the social contract and moral order were assumed, subsidization for goods or services did not exist.

The public and private subsidy of health services creates the strong perception that health care is a right of all persons as opposed to a commodity bought and sold on the open market. Social policy in the form of Medicare and Medicaid exists to ensure that the elderly, disabled, and poor receive health services. Employer-sponsored health insurance is currently treated as a tax-free benefit. In 1993–1994, President Clinton attempted to reform the United States health care system so that the 40 million plus uninsured could begin to receive a minimum level of health care benefits. As further evidence of the contention that health care is a right, federal legislation was created prohibiting the practice of patient dumping where indigent patients are turned away from hospital emergency departments. The Internal Revenue Service, in granting a 501-C-3 tax exempt status to nonprofit health care organizations, requires them to provide a high level of community benefit that is typically construed to mean charity or uncompensated care.

Given the unique status of health services, managers and administrators should take into account the moral principles of equity and fairness when they make business decisions in combination with the four principles described earlier as part of agent-morality theory. Incorporating the moral principles of equity and fairness is not just a good ethical decision but also makes good business sense for managed care organizations. One example might be providing evening and weekend appointments as well as walk-in clinics for patients who, for whatever reason, might not be able to access services during regular business hours. Another example would be low- or no-charge immunization clinics for school-aged children or the elderly. A shuttle bus sponsored by the medical group could be used to bring elderly, disabled, or otherwise isolated patients to the clinics so that they could keep their appointments. One final thought involves the provision of health promotion and health education classes and programs to all patients. In every one of these examples, there is an initial investment of capital that yields significant returns in either additional revenue or cost savings. The example of the off-hours appointment and walk-in clinic is a tremendous marketing advantage that can effectively be used to attract working families (and their associated employer-paid health insurance dollars). The immunization clinic helps reduce the likelihood that patients will experience preventable communicable diseases and the costs that the managed care plan have to absorb treating those diseases. The shuttle bus service (while initially costly) reduces the downstream expenses associated with patients missing scheduled appointments. Finally, an investment in health promotion and education in a variety of areas including prenatal classes, stop-smoking programs, stress reduction, and various support groups has been demonstrated to result in a significant reduction of long-term health costs. Even in for-profit managed care settings, it is not only possible but profitable to include equity and fairness into the calculus of difficult business decisions.

The rapid expansion of managed care as the primary health delivery mechanism in the United States has been primarily driven by for-profit and investor-owned entities. Given the importance of for-profits and the free market in this type of arrangement, business scholars have attempted to provide an ethical framework in order to counteract the principal-agent view that suggested the only role for managers was to maximize the present value of the firm. While some cynics might suggest that for-profit health care organizations operate from this principal-agent perspective, ethical standards already present for clinicians and administrators tend to require different moral standards of performance than in non-health care settings.

Notwithstanding the pervasive cynicism about the state of business ethics, multiple frameworks have been developed that attempt to guide the moral and ethical practice of business management. One of the most persuasive theories is that of an agent-morality perspective. This viewpoint posits that the values of truth telling, avoiding harm, respecting authority, and honoring agreements have a higher institutional priority than earning short-term profits. In the for-profit world of managed care, the values of social equity and fairness should be added given the unique status of health care in our society.

There is no doubt that managed care is here to stay (at least in the short run) as payers of health services attempt to control their expenses yet provide consumers with the highest and most effective quality of health care possible. The onus for control of this equation will lie in the hands of those who manage hospitals, clinics, and other provider groups that participate in managed care plans. While it may be a challenge to remember that patients must be put ahead of profits, it is both possible and desirable to optimize the health of the patient and organization simultaneously.

REFERENCES

1. The Advisory Board Committee. 1996. *The Rising Tide*. Washington, D.C.
2. Health Care Information Associates (HCIA). 1996. "Guide to the Managed Care Industry." *The Rising Tide*. Washington, D.C.
3. Columbia/HCA. 1996. *Annual Report*. Nashville, TN.
4. Columbia/HCA. 1996. *Proxy Statement*. Nashville, TN.
5. Haugland, L., and W. L. Dowling. 1993. "The Hospital." In *Introduction to Health Services* (4th ed.), edited by S. J. Williams and P. R. Torrens. Albany, NY: Delmar Publishers.
6. Friedman, L. H., and L. A., Mullins. 1998. "Acute Care Hospitals: Past, Present, and Future." In *Handbook of Health Administration*, edited by A. O. Kilpatrick and J. A. Johnson. New York: Marcel Decker.
7. Wolper, L. F. 1995. *Health Care Administration: Principles, Practices, Structure, and Delivery*. Gaithersburg, MD: Aspen Publishers.
8. Blair, J. D., M. Fottler, A. Paolino, and T. Rotarius. 1995. *Medical Group Practices Face the Uncertain Future: Challenges, Opportunities, and Strategies*. Englewood, CO: Center for Research in Ambulatory Health Care Administration.
9. Wagner, E. 1996. "Types of Managed Care Organizations." In *The Managed Health Care Handbook* (3rd ed.), edited by P. Kongstvedt. Gaithersburg, MD: Aspen Publishers.
10. Goodpaster, K. 1991. "Business Ethics and Stakeholder Analysis." *Business Ethics Quarterly* 1 (3): 53–73.
11. Carrol, A. 1991. "The Pyramid of Corporate Social Responsibility: Toward the Moral Management of Organizational Stakeholders." *Business Horizons* 34 (4): 39–48.
12. Quinn, D., and T. Jones. 1995. "An Agent-Morality View of Business Policy." *Academy of Management Review* 1 (1): 22–42.
13. Goldman, A. 1980. *The Moral Foundation of Professional Ethics*. London: Rowman and Littlefield.
14. Kant, I. 1963. *Lectures on Ethics*. New York: Harper and Row.
15. Garrett, T., H. Baillie, and R. Garrett. 1993. *Health Care Ethics: Principles and Problems*. Englewood Cliffs, NJ: Prentice Hall.
16. Rakich, J., B. Longest, and K. Darr. 1992. *Managing Health Services Organizations* (3rd ed.). Baltimore, MD: Health Professions Press.
17. Greenberg, J. 1987. "A Taxonomy of Organizational Justice Theories." *Academy of Management Review* 12 (1): 9–22.
18. Lampros, A. 1997. "PERS, HealthNet Join to Study HMO Providers." *The Sacramento Bee* 1 July: A1.
19. Larson, E. 1996. "The Soul of an HMO." *Time Magazine* 174 (22 January): 4.
20. Ware, J. E., M. Bayliss, W. Rogers, M. Kosinski, and A. Tarlov. 1996. "Differences in 4-Year Health Outcomes for Elderly and Poor, Chronically Ill Patients Treated in HMO and Fee-For-Service Systems." *Journal of the American Medical Association* 276 (2 October): 1,039–47.

21. Olmos, D. 1996. "Ill Elderly and Poor Fare Worse in HMOs, Study Says." *Los Angeles Times* 2 October: A1.

22. Kongstvedt, P. 1997. *Essentials of Managed Care* (2nd ed.). Gaithersburg, MD: Aspen Publishers.

PART

III

Effects

INTRODUCTION

What will be managed care's lasting effects? If the advent of managed care indeed represents a new age in modern healthcare delivery, it is an age that is still in its infancy. How can we begin to understand its cumulative and long-term effectiveness at this early stage, and when we must consider so many diverse factors? How can one measure its effect, for example, on cost containment? On access to and quality of care? On public health in general?

Added to the need to measure managed care's effect on areas such as quality and access is the need to understand and respond to the public's apprehension about managed care, including the perception that managed care encourages undertreatment and takes the power to make decisions about healthcare out of the hands of providers. The first chapter in this section, "The Managed Care Backlash," by Robert J. Blendon et al., draws on evidence of the public's perception of managed care to try to understand its exact nature and underpinnings.

Unfortunately, the rate of the growth of managed care does not allow for gradual measurement of long-term results. As managed care evolves and penetrates the market, competitively evolving methodologies for its measurement must arise to keep pace. The second chapter in this section, "Assessing the Effect of Increased Managed Care on Hospitals," by Charles Mowll, offers one such methodology for measuring the financial performance of hospitals, using a strategy developed by the author, the "Managed

Care Relative Financial Risk Assessment," with which hospital financial performance rates and risk assessments are compared at the state level by means of nine financial, demographic, and utilization data sources.

Whereas the financial aspects of managed care are unquestionably pertinent for healthcare provider organizations, the second chapter in this section, "Shifting the Paradigm: Monitoring Access in Medicare Managed Care," by Elizabeth R. Docteur, David C. Colby, and Marsha Gold, discusses an important aspect for patients under managed care: accessibility to care. Medicare patients constitute a significant—and growing—population, for whom managed care now presents many challenges. Systems that have been in place to monitor these patients' access to medical care are now showing their limitations and will have to be revised; meanwhile, it becomes clear that new systems must also be developed.

CHAPTER

12

Understanding the Managed Care Backlash

Robert J. Blendon, Mollyann Brodie, John M. Benson, Drew E. Altman, Larry Levitt, Tina Hoff, and Larry Hugick

Managed care has grown rapidly over the past decade, to become the dominant way Americans get their health insurance and care. During that period managed care has been credited with being one of the main factors in slowing the growth of employer health premiums. However, the nation's transition into these new types of health plans has not been free of controversy. Criticisms of managed care have led to the introduction both in Congress and in state legislatures of more than a thousand bills dealing with consumer protection in managed care, as well as the establishment of a presidential commission to examine the need for future guidelines in this rapidly growing industry.[1]

Advocates for these measures believe that they are responding to a broad public "backlash" against managed care. They point to surveys that show the public favoring some type of regulation of managed care plans. Those who oppose regulation point to other opinion surveys showing that Americans today are satisfied with their own managed care plans. Thus, opponents see no need for government regulation.

This paper seeks to explain the underlying issues that drive what has been called a backlash against managed care and the seemingly contradic-

Reprinted with permission from *Health Affairs* 17 (4): 80–94. The People-to-People Health Foundation.

tory findings between surveys showing support for regulation and those showing satisfied consumers. The focus here on public opinion relates to its likely relevance to the outcome of policy debates in areas such as these. Over the past two decades a substantial body of research has emerged showing that public opinion has a major influence on many public policy decisions.[2] In addition, studies of the 1993–1994 debate over the Clinton health care reform plan show members of Congress listing changes in public opinion as a major reason for the plan's demise.[3]

DATA AND METHODS

Sources of Data

The data presented here are derived primarily from two sources. The first is a survey designed by researchers at the Henry J. Kaiser Family Foundation and Harvard University. The interviews were conducted via telephone by Princeton Survey Research Associates (PSRA) between 22 August and 23 September 1997, with randomly selected samples of 1,204 adults nationwide and 500 adults in California.[4] The second data source consists of specific results drawn from twenty other surveys conducted nationwide between 1995 and 1997. We compiled these data from the Public Opinion Location Library (POLL) database at the Roper Center for Public Opinion Research in Storrs, Connecticut, and from the Louis Harris subscription service. These polls involved telephone interviews between 500 and 2,000 randomly selected adults.[5]

Response Rates

Response rates in the Kaiser/Harvard/PSRA survey were 49 percent for the national sample and 51 percent for California. Completion rates among contracted households were 67 percent for the national sample and 71 percent for California.

A recent methodological experiment has shown that nonresponse at the level encountered in opinion polls as they are typically conducted by reputable firms does not underestimate the views of particular segments of the American public.[6] Also, published research has shown that the techniques typically used in opinion polling have helped prominent polling firms to achieve a high level of accuracy on the outcome measure for which actual public opinion can be measured with considerable precision: vote choice in elections.[7]

How Type of Health Care Coverage Was Determined

Because many people are unsure about what kind of health insurance they have, insured respondents under age sixty-five in the national sample of the

Kaiser/Harvard/PSRA survey (778 respondents) were asked a series of four questions to establish their type of coverage. They were asked if they were required to do any of the following by their health plan: choose doctors from a list and pay more for doctors not on the list; select a primary care doctor or medical group; and/or obtain a referral before seeing a medical specialist or a doctor outside the plan. Respondents were listed as being in "heavy" managed care if they reported that their plan had all of the characteristics described above (34 percent of insured respondents under age sixty-five). Respondents were listed as being in "light" managed care if they reported that their plan had at least one but not all of the characteristics listed above (45 percent). Finally, respondents were listed as having "traditional" insurance if they reported that their plans had none of the characteristics (21 percent).[8] This distribution mirrors direct estimates of enrollment by type of plan.[9]

IS THERE EVIDENCE OF A MANAGED CARE BACKLASH?

Confirming the findings of a number of earlier studies, the Kaiser/Harvard/PSRA survey found that most insured Americans, regardless of whether they have managed care or traditional coverage, are satisfied with their own health insurance plan.[10] Two-thirds (66 percent) of adults under age sixty-five in managed care plans and three-fourths (76 percent) of adults under age sixty-five in traditional plans give their own health plan a letter grade of "B" or better.[11]

However, the same survey also confirmed earlier findings that a majority of Americans favor government regulation of managed care, even if it raises costs.[12] A slight majority (52 percent) of Americans believe that the government should protect consumers of managed care, whereas 40 percent say that such intervention is not worth the increased costs that would result. The groups most in favor of government regulation are those who describe their own health as poor, only fair, or good (the lowest three of five categories offered); those who have some college education but not a college degree; and Democrats (Table 12.1). The groups least in favor of such regulation are Republicans, those from households with an annual income of $30,000 to $49,999, those ages fifty to sixty-four, and those in self-described excellent or very good health.[13] Other surveys have raised the issue of regulating managed care without mentioning concerns about increasing the cost of benefits. These surveys find public support for such policies at 75 percent or higher.[14]

This support for regulation appears to reflect public concerns: (1) that managed care is hurting the quality of care available to patients; and (2) that this sector is nor doing as good a job for patients as other professions and institutions in health care are.

Table 12.1 Americans' Views About Government Regulation of Managed Care, 1997

Group	Percent favoring government regulation
All American adults	52
Most in favor of government regulation	
Respondents in only fair or poor health	65
Respondents in good health	58
Respondents with some college training but not a college degree	57
Democrats	57
Least in favor of government regulation	
Republicans	40
$30,000–$49,000 household income	42
Ages 50–64	46
Respondents in excellent or very good health	47

Source: Kaiser/Harvard/Princeton Survey Research Associates poll, 1997.

A plurality (45 percent) of Americans believe that during the past few years managed care has decreased the quality of health care for patients, whereas only 32 percent believe that managed care has improved quality.[15] In addition, 54 percent believe that in the future the trend toward more managed care will harm the quality of medical care that people like themselves with receive, 33 percent think that the trend will improve quality.[16]

A majority of Americans express concern that in managed care plans, people may not receive the services they need when they are very sick. Six in ten (59 percent) say that managed care plans have made it harder for people who are sick to see medical specialists; 25 percent say that managed care makes it easier. Half (51 percent) say that managed care has decreased the quality of care for people who are sick; 32 percent say that quality is increased. A majority (55 percent) of people in managed care say that they are at least "somewhat worried" that if they were sick, their health plan would be more concerned about saving money than about what is the best medical treatment; 34 percent of those with traditional health insurance feel this way.[17]

When asked about specific examples, taken from news stories, of dramatic events that might be considered statistical outliers, the public's perception is that there are fairly common occurrences. For example, two-thirds of Americans believe that a health maintenance organization (HMO) holding back on a child's cancer treatment is something that happens "often" (26 percent) or "sometimes" (40 percent); only 23 percent think that this happens "rarely." Two in five (39 percent) think that newborn babies are often sent home after just one day because of a managed care plan's policy, in spite of mothers' concerns about their children's health; another third (34 percent) think that this occurs "sometimes"; only 18 percent think that this happens "rarely."[18]

These perceptions of managed care are reflected in the ratings of the industry compared with other health care groups. Other health care groups and many other industries are viewed far more favorably than managed care plans are (Table 12.2): Solid majorities of Americans think that nurses, doctors, pharmaceutical companies, and hospitals generally do a "good job." More people do think that managed care plans do a "good job" than a "bad job" serving health care consumers, but their comparative rating is lower than any other health care group and lower even than oil companies, a traditionally unpopular industry among the public. However, for many people the jury is still out: The two surveys show that many people have no opinion about the kind of job managed care plans are doing.[19]

Four in ten (39 percent) of those in the Kaiser/Harvard/PSRA survey who think that managed care plans generally do a "bad job" serving health care consumers (21 percent of all Americans) report that the main reason

Table 12.2 Ratings of Groups or Industries on Service to Consumers, 1997 and 1998

	Ratings of groups on service to health care consumers[a]		**Ratings of industries on service to their consumers**[b]	
Group or industry	**Good**	**Bad**	**Good**	**Bad**
Nurses	83%	4%	—[c]	—[c]
Doctors	69	12	—[c]	—[c]
Computer or software companies	—[c]	—[c]	78%	7%
Telephone companies	—[c]	—[c]	76	23
Pharmaceutical or drug companies	62	20	73	23
Hospitals	61	18	73	23
Banks	—[c]	—[c]	72	26
Car manufacturers	—[c]	—[c]	69	25
Oil companies	—[c]	—[c]	64	26
Life insurance companies	—[c]	—[c]	63	24
Health insurance companies	44	32	48	47
Managed care companies	34	21	45	42
HMOs	36	25	—[c]	—[c]
Tobacco companies	—[c]	—[c]	32	60

Sources: See below.
Note: HMO is health maintenance organization.
[a] Kaiser/Harvard Princeton Survey Research Associates poll, 1997.
[b] Harris poll, 1998.
[c] Not applicable.

they feel this way is their own direct personal experience; 22 percent say that they have been mainly influenced by what they have seen or heard on television, in newspapers, or in other media. One in three (32 percent) say that the reason they feel that managed care plans do a "bad job" is what they have heard from family or friends.[20]

Public perceptions about the managed care industry are not merely the product of a rapidly changing health care marketplace, where many Americans are experiencing managed care for the first time. In California, with its long history of managed care, support for regulation and concerns about being denied care are comparable to findings nationwide (Table 12.3).[21]

ARE AMERICANS WORRIED ABOUT THEIR OWN HEALTH PLANS?

In this study we wanted to test a phenomenon observed in public opinion about other institutions: that people are distrustful of large systems but not of the individuals with whom they have contact within the system. One example can be cited from the field of medicine. Although two-thirds of

Table 12.3 Impressions of Managed Care in a State with Extensive Experience (California) and the United States, 1997

	Percent Saying	
	United States	**California**
View of government regulation		
Government needs to protect consumers from being treated unfairly and not getting the care they should from managed care plans	52%	52%
Additional government regulation isn't worth it because it would raise the cost of health insurance too much for everyone	40	35
Rating of the job managed care companies do in serving health care consumers		
Good job	34	27
Bad job	21	19
During the past few years, HMOs and other managed care plans have		
Decreased the quality of health care for people who are sick	51	46
Increased the quality of care	32	31

Source: Kaiser/Harvard/Princeton Survey Research Associates poll, 1997.

Notes: HMO is health maintenance organization. The volunteered responses "mixed," "no effect," and "don't know" are not shown.

Americans (68 percent) reported in the mid-1980s that they were increasingly losing faith in physicians, this did not affect the high level of satisfaction most people had with their most recent physician encounter (83 percent) or their positive feelings about their own physician (80 percent).[22] A frequently cited example concerns Congress: Americans generally give rather low performance ratings to Congress as a whole but express a much higher opinion of the job being done by their own representatives in Congress.[23]

If this held true in the case of managed care, we would expect the public to be anxious about the managed care industry in general but not about their own managed care health plan. However, the survey finds that people in "heavy" managed care are more worried than are those with traditional coverage when it comes to the perceived motivations of their health plans. This is true for the four measures used in the study: Americans' perceptions of how likely their plan is to pay for an emergency room visit, how likely it is to pay for most of the cost for care of a serious problem requiring a costly treatment, trust in their plan to do the right thing for their care, and worries that the plan would be more concerned about saving money than about what is the best treatment if they are sick (Table 12.4).[24]

Table 12.4 Americans' Impressions of How Their Health Plan Will Deal with Them When They Need Help, Currently Insured Persons, by Type of Plan, 1997

	All Insured	Heavy Mgd. Care[a]	Light Mgd. Care[a]	Trad. Plan[a]
Very likely that you health plan will pay for emergency room visit	64%	56%	63%	78%
Very likely that your health plan will pay for most of the cost if you had a serious problem requiring a costly treatment	55	44	54	69
Trust your health insurance plan to do the right thing for your care just about always	41	30	31	55
Very/somewhat worried that your health plan would be more concerned about saving money that about what is the best treatment for you if you are sick	47	61	51	34

Source: Kaiser/Harvard/Princeton Survey Research Associates poll, 1997.
[a] Under age sixty-five.

HOW IMPORTANT IS CONCERN ABOUT BEING ABLE TO GET CARE?

Concerns about what happens to people when they are very sick are reflected in what Americans say is most important in choosing a health plan. Although respondents rated each of seven factors on a list as very important in choosing a health plan, when they were forced to choose among them, the number-one factor was how well the health plan takes care of members who are sick (cited by 25 percent), followed closely by how much the patients have to pay (22 percent). Ranked next were whether the plan has a wide range of benefits (17 percent) and whether a person's current doctor is in the plan (15 percent). Further down the list were whether a plan offers a wide choice of doctors (8 percent) and whether one's preferred hospital is in the plan (5 percent). Lowest on the list was whether the plan had passed a review and had been accredited (3 percent).[25]

Americans' views are relatively negative about efforts by health plans to limit payment for care that doctors think a patient needs. Many say that they would have a less favorable view of a plan if patients needed to get approval from the plan before they could receive expensive medical treatment (58 percent); if the plan limited payment for certain types of health services when people are sick, to keep costs low (48 percent); and if doctors had to follow certain health plan guidelines on the types of treatments and drugs they can give to patients (44 percent).[26] In addition, 62 percent of Americans said in a previous study that they agreed that health plans should pay for medical treatment even if it costs a million dollars per life.[27]

When they learn that some health plans require doctors to follow certain guidelines in treating patients, a majority (56 percent) agree that this is a bad thing because decisions about treatment should be entirely up to the doctor; 39 percent agree that this is a good thing because all patients will benefit from proven techniques.[28]

WHO BENEFITS FROM THE COST SAVINGS OF MANAGED CARE?

Public concerns about efforts to limit payment are magnified by skepticism about who benefits from the cost savings. Many Americans are uncertain that managed care keeps health care costs down at all (Table 12.5). A majority (55 percent) believe that during the past few years HMOs and other managed care plans have not made much difference to health care costs; only 28 percent think that they have helped to keep costs down.[29] However, Americans are more optimistic about managed care's ability to contain costs in the future. A slight majority (51 percent) believes that the

Table 12.5 Americans' Views on the Cost Savings from Managed Care, 1997

	Percent responding
During the past few years HMOs and other managed care plans have[a]	
Not made much difference to health care costs	55%
Helped to keep health care costs down	28
Made costs go up (volunteered response)	5
Don't know	12
The trend toward more managed care will[b]	
Help to contain health care costs	51
Not help	42
Not sure	7
Money saved by HMOs and other managed care plans[a]	
Helps health insurance companies to earn more profits	72[c]
Allows employers to pay less for health insurance	56[c]
Makes health care more affordable for people like you	49[c]

Sources: See below.
Note: HMO is health maintenance organization.
[a] Kaiser/Harvard Princeton Survey Research Associates poll, 1997.
[b] Harris poll, 1997
[c] Percent responding "yes."

trend toward more managed care will help to contain health care costs, while 42 percent think that it will not help.[30]

In addition, majorities see the money saved by managed care plans as helping health insurance companies to earn more profits (72 percent) and allowing employers to pay less for health insurance (56 percent). Only about half (49 percent) believe that they money saved makes health care more affordable for people like themselves.[31]

WILL REPORT CARDS BE THE ANSWER?

Many experts believe that report cards on the performance of managed care plans would help to allay public anxiety about these plans by giving people information they could use to make informed choices. However, public opinion data suggest real limits to the usefulness of this approach.

The public is particularly interested in the experience of sick persons trying to gain access to the care they and their doctors think they need. In contrast, most consumer surveys today report satisfaction levels among all plan members, most of who are not very sick or burdened with the large medical bills that can be a source of contention with their plan.

In addition, surveys show that a large share of consumers do not rely on objective ratings to make decisions. Health care consumers are much more likely to rely on personal experiences or the recommendation of friends and family members (Table 12.6). If they had to choose between health plans that cost the same, more Americans would choose a plan recommended by friends and family that one rated much higher in quality by independent experts who evaluate plans. About three in four would choose a surgeon who has treated their family for a long time, even if that surgeon's ratings were not as high, rather than a surgeon whose ratings are much higher but who has not treated anyone the respondent knows personally. Similarly, most would choose a hospital they and their family had used for many years without any problems, rather than a hospital rated much higher in quality by experts.[32]

Research on decisions in other areas of consumer choice has shown a mixed picture. On the one hand, relatively few persons use consumer ratings when making important purchasing decisions. When those who had bought or leased a motor vehicle during the past ten years were asked to think back to the last time they made such a purchase, only one in three (35

Table 12.6 How Americans Choose Health Plans and Providers, 1996

	Percent responding
Suppose you had to choose between health plans that cost the same; which would you be more likely to choose?	
One strongly recommended to you by friends and family	52%
One rated much higher in quality by independent experts who evaluate plans	43
Don't know	5
Suppose you had to choose between two surgeons at a hospital; which would you be more likely to choose?	
A surgeon who has treated your family for a long time, but whose ratings aren't as high as those of other surgeons at the hospital	76
A surgeon whose ratings are much higher, but who has not had anyone you know personally as a patient	20
Don't know	4
Suppose you had to choose between two hospitals; which would you be more likely to choose?	
A hospital you and your family have used for many years without any problems	72
A hospital that is rated much higher in quality by experts	25
Don't know	3

Source: Kaiser/Agency for Health Care Policy and Research/Princeton Survey Research Associates poll, 1996.

percent) said that they turned for information to consumer magazines that test and rate products. As with health plans, the most frequently mentioned source of information was friends and family members (46 percent). In general, only one in five (20 percent) said that they go to an information source such as consumer magazines always or most of the time before making a major purchase.[33]

This tendency to rely on sources of information other than objective measures extends even to the way Americans judge the health of the economy. Asked to choose (from a list of nine possible sources) the two indicators that they think give them the best picture of how the economy is doing, only 32 percent of the public mention news reports on government unemployment and cost-of-living statistics. Nearly as many (28 percent) cite as a key indicator the amount of activity they see in stores. More than half (55 percent) rely on the personal experiences of family, friends, and coworkers.[34]

In addition, four in then insured Americans (41 percent) report that when they enrolled in their current health plan, they did not have a choice of more than one plan.[35] For this group, report cards will not be directly useful, although their employers might use them as a way of selecting the plan they offer their employees.

CONCLUSIONS

We are confronted her with two seemingly contradictory pieces of information. One suggests that Americans are satisfied with their health insurance plans, regardless of whether the plans are traditional fee-for-service or managed care. The other indicates that the public favors regulation of managed care plans, even if it raises costs. How cant his seeming inconsistency be resolved?

These two sentiments are derived from different types of inquiry: consumer ratings of health plans and public opinion questions. Consumer ratings measure the average experience of those who use a service, whereas public opinion can often be driven by rare occurrences, as well as by people's own experiences and those of their families and friends as day-to-day consumers of health care.

We believe that two important factors are influencing the public backlash against managed care. First, a significant proportion of Americans report problems with managed care plans. Based on five studies on satisfaction with nonfinancial aspects of managed care health plans, results for all enrollees combined showed less satisfaction with managed care plans than with fee-for-service plans.[36] Another study, looking at differences between managed care and fee-for-service plans for persons who are ill, found more complaints about access to specialists, tests, and waiting times by those enrolled in managed care plans.[37]

Second, we believe that the public backlash is also being driven by relatively rare events that seem threatening and dramatic but have been experiences by few consumers personally. A review of polling research in two other service-related areas—airlines and banking—shows that such events (the crash of a ValuJet plane in May 1996 and the savings and loan crisis the late 1980s) can lead to increased public support for government regulation, even though measures of consumer satisfaction remain stable or even improve.[38]

Prior research shows that an issue is more likely to emerge as part of the public's policy agenda if it involves continuing news coverage and is dramatic in nature.[39] In any given year only relatively few Americans are very ill or accumulate very large medical bills, situations that can lead to serious conflicts with their health plans. Since this is the case, we would expect people's negative impressions of managed care to come mostly from sources other than their own direct personal experiences while they were sick—including what they hear or experience through friends and family or what they see or read in the news.[40] Thus, part of Americans' interest in regulation of the managed care industry seems to derive from a concern that regardless of how well their plan performs today, care might not be available or paid for when they are very sick.

Some experts believe that providing report-card ratings of health plans will enable consumers to make the best decisions for their families and negate the need for government regulation. However, report cards will be seen as providing little protection by the large portion of the population who have no experience using this type of rating. As a result, if concerns arise about the threatening behavior of individual health plans, a share of the public is likely to support some degree of regulation rather than depending on report-card ratings as a way of avoiding the consequences of plan decisions. For example, for airline safety, although safety reports and consumer complaints are provided by airlines as a matter of public record, experience suggests that these reports have not quelled the public's desire for some level of government safety regulation. On the other hand, report cards could play a role in the decision making of employers who want to make the best choice of health plans for their employees. This in turn could have an influence on the quality of plan available in the marketplace.

Public concerns about the need for increased regulation of managed care are likely to be with us for the long term. Experience in other industries suggests that Americans have limits on how far they will allow marketplace decisions to put them at individual risk. As with airline safety and banking, public support for regulation is being driven in part by the anxiety the public feels relating to the occurrence of visible events questioning the behavior of managed care plans, as well as the problems people experience in their own lives. As a result, debate about regulation of the managed care industry is likely to be a permanent fixture on the health care agenda for years to come.

NOTES

1. "Health Care in America: Your Money or Your Life," *Economist* (7 March 1998): 23–26.
2. See for example, A.D. Monroe, "Consistency between Public Preferences and National Policy Decisions," *American Journal of Political Science* (January 1979): 3–19; A.D. Monroe, "American Party Platforms and Public Opinion," *American Journal of Political Science* (February 1983): 27–42; B.I. Page and R.Y. Shapiro, "Effects of Public Opinion on Policy," *American Political Science Review* (March 1983): 175–190; R.Y. Shapiro and L.R. Jacobs, "The Relationship between Public Opinion and Public Policy: A Review," in *Political Behavior Annual*, ed. S. Long (Boulder, Colo.: Westview, 1989), 149–179; G.C. Wright Jr., R.S. Erikson, and J.P. McIver, "Public Opinion and Policy Liberalism in the United States," *American Journal of Political Science* (November 1987): 980–1001; R.S. Erikson, G.C. Wright Jr., and J.P. McIver, "Political Parties, Public Opinion, and State Policy in the United States," *American Political Science Review* (September 1989): 729–750; B.I. Page and R.Y. Shapiro, *The Rational Public: Fifty Years of Trends in Americans' Policy Preferences* (Chicago: University of Chicago Press, 1992); L.R. Jacobs and R.Y. Shapiro, "Public Opinion and the New Social History: Some Lessons for the Study of Public Opinion and Democratic Policy-Making," *Social Science History* (Spring 1989): 1–24; and L.R. Jacobs and R.Y. Shapiro, "Debunking the Pandering Politician Myth," *Public Perspective* (April/May 1997): 3–5.
3. O. Hansen et al., "Lawmakers Views on the Failure of Health Reform: A Survey of Members of Congress and Staff." *Journal of Health Politics, Policy and Law* (Spring 1996): 137–151. On the decline in public support, see R.J. Blendon, M. Brodie, and J. Benson, "What Happened to Americans' Support for the Clinton Health Plan?" *Health Affairs* (Summer 1995): 7–23.
4. Henry J. Kaiser Family Foundation/Harvard University/Princeton Survey Research Associates poll (Storrs, Conn.: Roper Center for Public Opinion Research, 22 August 1997).
5. When interpreting these findings, one should recognize that all surveys are subject to sampling error. Results may differ from what would be obtained if the whole population of adults had been interviewed. The size of this error varies with the number surveyed and the magnitude of difference in the responses to each question. Most national public opinion surveys have sample sizes of about 1,200 persons, in which the results will, with a 95 percent degree of confidence, have a statistical precision of ±3 percent of what would be obtained if the entire population has been interviewed. The sampling error for 500 respondents is ±5 percent; for 2,000 respondents, 3± percent.

   Possible sources of nonsampling error include nonresponse bias, as well as question wording and ordering effects. Nonresponse in telephone surveys produces some known biases in survey-derived estimates because participation tends to vary for different subgroups of the population. To compensate for these known biases, the sample data are typically weighted in analysis, as they are in the August 1997 Kaiser/Harvard/PSRA survey, using parameters from the most recent available census data. Other techniques, including random-digit dialing, replicate subsamples, callbacks staggered over times of day and days of the week, refusal conversions, and systematic respondent selection within households, are used to ensure that the sample is representative.

6. In this nonresponse experiment, two surveys were conducted simultaneously asking exactly the same eighty-five questions on a wide range of political and policy issues. The standard survey, using typical polling techniques and interviewing over 1,000 adults over a five-day period, achieved a 42 percent response rate. The second survey, using a more rigorous methodology over an eight-week period to interview 1,000 adults, achieved a 71 percent response rate. The two surveys produced very similar results. Of the eighty-five questions, only five showed statistically significant differences between the two surveys. The differences were sharpest on questions concerning racial issues. Pew Research Center for the People and the Press, *Study of Survey Nonresponse* (Washington: Pew Research Center for the People and the Press, 1998).
7. F. Newport, "The Pre-Election Polls Performed Well in '96," *Public Perspective* (December/January 1997): 50–51.
8. Kaiser/Harvard/PSRA poll, 22 August 1997.
9. KPMG Peat Marwick, *Health Benefits in 1997* (Arlington, VA: KMPG Peat Marwick, 1997).
10. ABC News poll (Storrs, Conn.: Roper Center for Public Opinion Research, 24 August 1997); K. Donelan et al., "All Payer, Single Payer, Managed Care, No Payer: Patients' Perspectives in Three Nations," *Health Affairs* (Summer 1996): 254–265; K. Davis et al., "Choice Matters: Enrollees' Views of Their Health Plans," *Health Affairs* (Summer 1995): 99–112; *Los Angeles Times* poll (Storrs, Conn.: Roper Center for Public Opinion Research, 17 June 1995): Minnesota Health Data Institute/Maritz Marketing Research, *You and Your Health Plan: 1995 Statewide Survey of Minnesota Consumers* (Minneapolis: Minnesota Health Data Institute, 1995); Coalition for Medicare Choice, *American Attitudes toward Managed Care: A Review* (Washington: Coalition for Medicare Choice, 1995); and "Regardless of Health Status, HMO and FFS Patients Report Similar Levels of Satisfaction," *GHAA News* (26 July 1995): 1–3.
11. Kaiser/Harvard/PSRA poll, 22 August 1997.
12. R.J. Blendon et al., "Voters and Health Care in the 1996 Election," *Journal of the American Medical Association* (16 April 1997): 1256–1257.
13. Kaiser/Harvard/PSRA poll, 22 August 1997.
14. Princeton Survey Research Associates/Pew Research Center for the People and the Press poll (Storrs, Conn.: Roper Center for Public Opinion Research, 19 February 1998); Wirthlin Worldwide/Patient Access to Responsible Care Alliance poll (Washington: Patient Access to Responsible Care Alliance, 2

October 1997); and Henry J. Kaiser Family Foundation/Harvard University/Princeton Survey Research Associates poll (Storrs, Conn.: Roper Center for Public Opinion Research, 12 December 1997).

15. Kaiser/Harvard/PSRA poll, 22 August 1997.
16. Harris poll (New York: Louis Harris and Associates, 20 August 1997).
17. Kaiser/Harvard/PSRA poll, 22 August 1997.
18. Ibid.
19. Ibid.; and Harris poll (New York: Louis Harris and Associates, 25 March 1998).
20. Kaiser/Harvard/PSRA poll, 22 August 1997.
21. Ibid.
22. R.J. Blendon, "The Public's View of the Future of Health Care," *Journal of the American Medical Association* (24 June 1988): 3592.
23. K.D. Patterson and D.B. Magleby, "The Polls—Poll Trends: Public Support for Congress," *Public Opinion Quarterly* (Winter 1992): 539–551.
24. Kaiser/Harvard/PSRA poll, 22 August 1997.
25. Ibid.
26. Ibid.
27. R.J. Blendon et al., "Who Has the Best Health Care System? A Second Look," *Health Affairs* (Winter 1995): 220–230.
28. The question read as follows: "As you may know, some health plans require their doctors to follow certain guidelines in treating patients. Some people think this is a good thing because all patients will benefit from proven techniques. Others think it is a bad thing because decisions about treatment should be entirely up to the doctor. Which comes closer to your view?" Henry J. Kaiser Family Foundation/Agency for Health Care Policy and Research/Princeton Survey Research Associates poll (Storrs, Conn.: Roper Center for Public Opinion Research, 26 July 1996).
29. Kaiser/Harvard/PSRA poll, 22 August 1997.
30. Harris poll, 20 August 1997.
31. Kaiser/Harvard/PSRA poll, 22 August 1997.
32. Kaiser/AHCPR/PSRA poll, 1996.
33. Ibid.
34. R.J. Blendon et al., "Bridging the Gap between the Public's and Economists' Views of the Economy," *Journal of Economic Perspectives* (Summer 1997): 115.
35. Kaiser/Harvard/PSRA poll, 22 August 1997.
36. R.H. Miller and H.S. Luft, "Does Managed Care Lead to a Better or Worse Quality of Care?" *Health Affairs* (September/October 1997): 7–25.
37. Donelan et al., "All Payer."
38. For public opinion of regulation of airlines, see Gallup poll (Storrs, Conn.: Roper Center for Public Opinion Research, 24 August 1987); and CBS News poll (Storrs, Conn.: Roper Center for Public Opinion Research, 21 July 1996). For consumer complaints, see U.S. Bureau of the Census, *Statistical*

Abstract of the United States, 1997 (Washington: U.S. Bureau of the Census, 1997), Table 1054. For public opinion on regulation of banks, see *Roper Report* 87-7 (Storrs, Conn.: Roper Center for Public Opinion Research, 18 July 1987); and *Los Angeles Times* poll (Storrs, Conn.: Roper Center for Public Opinion Research, 6 April 1991). For consumer ratings of banks, see Gallup/American Society for Quality Control polls (Storrs, Conn.: Roper Center for Public Opinion Research, 1985, 1988, 1991).

39. A. Downs, "Up and Down with Ecology: The Issue-Attention Cycle," *Public Interest* (Fall 1972): 38–50. E.M. Rogers and J.W. Dearing, "Agenda-Setting Research: Where Has It Been, Where Is It Going?" in *Media Power in Politics*, ed. D.A. Graber (Washington, CQ Press, 1994), 77–95; and B.J. Nelson, "The Agenda-Setting Function of the Media: Child Abuse," in *Media Power in Politics*, 96–109.
40. M. Brodie, L.A. Brady, and D.E. Altman, "Media Coverage of Managed Care: Is There a Negative Bias?" *Health Affairs* (January/February 1998): 9–25.

CHAPTER

13

Assessing the Effect of Increased Managed Care on Hospitals

Charles A. Mowll

Federal and state initiatives to use managed care organizations (MCOs), specifically HMOs, to reduce the increase in healthcare expenditures have been very successful. MCOs have lowered hospital admission rates and patient lengths-of-stay by directing patients to lower-cost healthcare delivery alternatives. Several studies suggest that hospital utilization rates have been retarded by the effects of increased managed care. Studies also indicate that hospitals in areas of high managed-care market penetration have experienced diminished fiscal solvency and financial performance. Using a new methodology and different data sources, this article will attempt to confirm the results of earlier studies that have indicated that managed care has negatively affected hospitals' levels of profitability and liquidity. The results of this study will discuss the effect of HMOs and increased managed care on the utilization of hospital services and on hospital financial performance.

RESEARCH METHODS

I. Assessing a Hospital's Potential Financial Vulnerability to the Effect of Increasing Managed-Care Market Penetration

As managed care and negotiated payment arrangements between hospitals and various payors and purchasers of hospital services become more preva-

**Reprinted from *Journal of Healthcare Management* 43 (1): 68–80.
Chicago: Health Administration Press.**

lent, hospitals must be able to assess the potential financial effect of increased managed-care market penetration. Hospitals in states currently experiencing a significantly higher degree of managed care demonstrate dramatically different financial and utilization trends than hospitals in other states.

This study uses a Managed Care Relative Financial Risk Assessment (MCRFRA) methodology developed by the author to assess the relative financial risk of the effects of increased managed-care market penetration on hospitals. The process analyzes the hospital's comparative indicators of financial and utilization performance. This analysis and assessment methodology uses aggregate hospital data at the state level since several of the indicators included in the MCRFRA are population-based indices that cannot be accurately compared at the individual hospital level. The population base at the hospital-specific level is both smaller and harder to define geographically. Nine financial, demographic, and utilization measures form the basis of the risk assessment and include comparative data for admission rates, average length of stay, patient days, inpatient worker-hours per discharge, and indicators of Medicare and managed care enrollment for the state in which the hospital is located. The MCRFRA risk assessment methodology provides a quantitative predictive model that can predict the potential financial vulnerability of a hospital to the effects of increased managed care market penetration based on the hospital's state location.

The MCRFRA methodology compares hospitals within each state to a Composite Index of the top five states with the highest managed care market penetration (see Table 13.1).

Table 13.1 HMO Market Penetration by State, Five Highest and Five Lowest States

Rank	**State**	**Penetration (%)**
1	Massachusetts	42.1
2	California	38.4
3	Minnesota	35.7
4	Oregon	34.9
5	Colorado	34.7
46	North Dakota	2.4
47	Montana	2.1
48	Mississippi	1.0
49	Wyoming	0.0
50	Alaska	0.0

Source: 1995 Managed Care Digest, HMO-PPO Edition, Hoechst, Marion, Roussel, Inc.

According to the 1995 *Managed Care Digest*, in 1994, the states with the highest percentage of managed care market penetration were Massachusetts, California, Minnesota, Oregon, and Colorado. These states are referred to as high managed care states (HMCS).

States with the lowest percentage of managed care market penetration are referred to as low managed care states (LMCS); in 1994 they were North Dakota, Montana, Mississippi, Wyoming, and Alaska.

The HMCS Composite Index represents the average of the individual indicators for a particular measure, for example, average length of stay. An overall risk rate of 100 indicates that hospitals located in the comparison state are perfectly aligned with the financial and utilization performance of hospitals represented by the HMCS Composite Index. In this state of equilibrium, the hospital is maintaining an admission rate, occupancy, patient days, and average length of stays characteristic of hospitals in the HMCS composite group. A relative risk rate below 100 indicates that a hospital is vulnerable to the potential negative financial effect of increased managed care. The lower the rate, the greater the potential financial risk. This risk results from maintaining higher admission rates, occupancy percentages, and patient days that are unsustainable in an HMO-dominant market. The sources of the indicator data used in the risk assessment methodology are presented in Table 13.2.

Relative risk assessment

Nine financial and utilization indicators have been selected to assess a hospital's potential financial vulnerability or relative risk of experiencing a negative effect from increasing managed care activity. For example, the indicator "Total Patient Days per 1,000 Population" can provide an indication of a hospital's vulnerability to increased managed care utilization controls, per-diem payment arrangements, or capitation. Hospitals with significantly higher patient days than the HMCS average risk losing revenue resulting from the increased managed care cost controls that focus on patient-day reduction. Similarly, a hospital with higher admissions per 1,000 population than hospitals in HMCSs are at risk from the effects of increased managed care market penetration. HMOs and other MCOs control their costs of providing health maintenance and other health services by using more disease prevention, health promotion, and other nonacute care services. This conscientious avoidance of inpatient hospitalization and bent for lower-cost outpatient care by HMOs results in lower admission rates per 1,000 population for hospitals experiencing the effects of an increasing managed care market.

MCRFRA methodology in this study is composed of nine measures of hospital financial performance and utilization activity. These measures or

Table 13.2 Data Sources—Relative Risk Assessment

Index	Numerator	Source	Denominator	Source
Admissions per 1,000 population	Total 1994 inpatient admissions	1995 AHA Hospital STATS	1994 state population divided by 1,000	1995 Statistical Abstract of the United States
Average length of stay	Total 1994 inpatient days	The 1995 Almanac	Total 1994 admissions	The 1995 Almanac
Patient days per 1,000 population	Total 1994 inpatient days	1995 AHA Hospital STATS	1994 state population divided by 1,000	1995 Statistical Abstract of the United States
Surgical operations per 1,000 population	Total 1994 surgical operations	1995 AHA Hospital STATS	1994 state population divided by 1,000	1995 Statistical Abstract of the United States
Percentage of non-HMO population	1994 population not non-HMO enrollee	1995 *Managed Care Digest*	1994 total state population	1995 *Managed Care Digest*
Inpatient man-hours per discharge	1994 inpatient man-hours	The 1995 Almanac	Total 1994 discharges	The 1995 Almanac
Percentage on non-Medicare discharges	1994 non-medicare discharges	The 1995 Almanac	Total 1994 discharges	The 1995 Almanac
Inpatient revenue percentage	1994 inpatient revenue	The 1995 Almanac	Total 1994 Revenue	The 1995 Almanac
Occupancy percentage	Total 1994 inpatient days	The 1995 Almanac	Total available beds times 365 days	The 1995 Almanac

Sources: AHA Hospital STATS, Statistical Abstract, *Managed Care Digest*, Almanac

indicators are defined in Table 13.2. The HMCS Composite Index and associated risk for each indicator are described in Table 13.3. The associated risk described in Table 13.3 is payment system sensitive. Per diem, per case, discounted fee-for-service, and capitation payment systems provide differing incentives and provider motivations. A more thorough analysis of the effect of managed care on hospitals—an analysis beyond the scope of this study—should consider payment-scheme prevalence as an important variable in the analysis. Table 13.4 displays the actual values for each indicator for the HMCSs and for the comparison state, New Jersey. The indicator values for the five HMCSs are totaled and averaged to derive the Composite Index for each indicator.

Table 13.3 Relative Financial Risk Indicators

Indicator	HCMS Composite Index	Associated Risk
Admissions/1,000 population	112	Lower occupancy and reduced revenue resulting from HMO preference for outpatient services
Average length of stay	4.6 days	Reduced revenue under per-diem of FFS payment arrangements; increased efficiency and per-case profit margin under per case or capitated payments
Patient days/1,000 population	918 days	Reduced revenue under per-diem or FFS payments arrangements; increased efficiency and profit margin under per-case payments or capitation
Surgical operations/ 1,000 population	87	Reduced revenue resulting from movement of cases to ambulatory sites
% of non-HMO population	63%	Reduced revenue resulting from shift away from charge-paying patients to negotiated payment arrangements
Inpatient man-hours/discharge	141 hours	Reduced profit margins resulting from inefficiency and higher expenses associated with staffing
% of non-medicare discharges	61%	Greater reliance on negotiated payment arrangements for non-Medicare payors results in less predictable volume and revenue
Inpatient revenue percentage	60%	Reduced inpatient revenue resulting from movement to lower-cost outpatient services.
Occupancy percentage	45%	Reduced inpatient revenue as a result of lower HMO hospitalization rates

Table 13.4 Managed Care Relative Financial Risk Assessment (MCRFRA)

Index	CA	CO	MA	MN	OR	Composite Index (E)	NJ (O)	RFR *E/O* × 100	US
Admission/1,000	103	104	138	114	99	112	141	79	127
Average length of stay	4.5	4.4	5.8	4.4	3.8	4.6	6.7	69	5.3
Patients days/ 1,000 population	721	779	1231	1181	676	918	1271	72	1,046
Surgical operations/ 1,000 population	68	82	108	91	87	87	82	106	92
% non-HMO population	62%	65%	58%	64%	65%	63%	77%	82	79%
Occupancy %	48%	48%	61%	30%	37%	45%	69%	65	48%
Inpatient man-hours/ discharge	144	169	129	137	129	141	170	83	151
% non-Medicare	67%	68%	59%	50%	60%	61%	77%	79	58%
Inpatient revenue %	67%	63%	60%	57%	54%	60%	77%	78	62
Overall Risk Ratio (100 = No Risk)									

Patient days, admission rates, occupancy, and average length-of-stay indicators are interrelated. They do, though, provide individually different signals regarding the potential financial vulnerability of a hospital located in an area of increasing managed-care market penetration. Depending on the payment method employed by the MCO, variances in these indicators will have different revenue implications. For example, a reduction in patient days as a result of increasing levels of managed care under a per-diem payment scheme will have significant negative revenue consequences for the hospital. However, capitation payment arrangements provide an incentive to the hospital for reducing patient days since the hospital usually receives a prepaid per-member per-month payment regardless of the utilization of inpatient hospital services.

HMCS composite index

The actual performance measures for each of the nine relative financial risk (RFR) indexes are displayed in Table 13.4. The HMCS Composite Index is reflected as the average of the individual state measures for each of the nine indexes. In developing the relative risk rate for hospitals in a particular state, the HMCS Composite Index becomes the numerator (E = expected value) in the calculus. The performance measure for each indicator for the comparison state is also reflected and represents the denominator (O = observed value) in the calculus. The RFR represents the relationship between the comparison state's measures and those of the HMCS Composite Index.

An overall RFR rate can be determined by simply adding the individual relative risk factors for each of the nine indexes. Again, an RFR rate of 100 would indicate that hospitals represented by the comparison state measures perfectly align with the financial and utilization performance of the comparative control group of hospitals in HMCS. An RFR rate below 100 indicates a level of potential financial risk for hospitals with similar measures; a rate of 70 is worse than a rate of 80 and so on.

As demonstrated in Table 13.4, an RFR rate for hospitals in a particular state can be developed by comparing the observed financial and utilization performance of hospitals in the comparison state to that of hospitals represented by the HMCS Composite Index. The RFR rate for New Jersey hospitals, for example, is 79, a number significantly below the equalization risk rate of 100. This low RFR rate signals a relatively high degree of financial risk associated with a potential increase in managed care market penetration. The potential financial risk for hospitals in New Jersey, which is indicated by their RFR rate of 79, emanates from the absence of managed care utilization controls and restrictive payment schemes in the past. New Jersey's significantly higher admission rates, average length of stay, and patient days reflect the state's long history of predominant per-case and fee-for-service payments to hospitals supported in part by a state rate-setting system until 1992. Higher occupancy rates and inpatient revenue sources also indicate that New Jersey hospitals have not been subjected to the same managed care utilization controls, financial pressures and service constraints that hospitals in high managed care states have experienced.

II. Comparison of HMCS and LMCS Financial Performance

Hospitals in high managed care states (HMCS), represented by the five highest managed care market penetration states, generally report higher profitability than hospitals located in the five lowest managed care states (LMCS). Hospitals represented by the LMCS composite generally reflect better liquidity and capital structure performance than the high managed care composite group of states. Regarding overall financial performance, hospitals represented by the high managed care state composite indices are more financially viable than hospitals represented by the LMCS composite indices (reflected by their higher Financial Flexibility Index). A comparative analysis of the nine key financial ratios or indicators for both the HMCS and LMCS groups which were used to reach this conclusion are displayed in Table 13.5. The analysis includes a comparison of three liquidity ratios or indicators, three profitability indicators, two capital structure ratios, and one overall measure of hospital financial performance, the Financial Flexibility Index developed by William Cleverley, Ph.D., at Ohio State University.

Table 13.5 Comparative Financial Analysis—HMCSs and LMCSs

Financial Ratio	HMCS	LMCS	New Jersey	United States
Total margin	3.8%	3.3%	2.7%	3.2%
Operating margin	2.8%	1.6%	2.5%	2.7%
Return on investment	9.9	9.0	8.7	8.9
Current ratio	1.72	2.79	1.58	1.79
Days cash on hand	86	67	96	98
Average payment period	63	49	70	62
Long-term debt to equity	.61	.34	.88	.74
Debt service coverage	3.6	5.0	2.4	3.1
Financial flexibility index	2.69	1.78	1.61	2.00

Sources: The *1995 Almanac of Hospital Financial & Operating Indicators*
Note: The Financial Flexibility Index is a composite of seven financial ratios that measure a firm's ability to control funds flow and is intended to provide a measure of the overall financial health of a firm.

RESULTS

Comparative Profitability

The three indicators of hospital profitability used for this study are total margin, operating margin, and return on investment. The total margin reflects profits from both operations and non-operations. In 1994, both the HMCS and LMCS groups out-all other hospitals in the United States. Nationally, hospitals, reported an average total margin of 3.2 percent in 1994 while HMCS hospital total margins averaged 3.8 percent and LMCS hospitals averaged 3.3 percent. The operating margin ratio represents the proportion of revenue realized in income from operations. In 1994, the HMCS composite group slightly out-performed all hospitals in generating a 2.8 percent operating margin compared to the U.S. average of 2.7 percent. LMCS hospital profitability (1.6 percent), as measured by the operating margin, was significantly below the national average in 1994. Similarly, hospitals in the HMCS group reported a higher return on investment (9.9) than did LMCS hospitals (9.0) or hospitals nationally (8.9). Analysis of hospital performance data from 1990 through 1994 confirms the indication that hospitals in HMCSs experience greater profitability than hospitals in LMCSs. The HMCS group reported the same total margin performance (3.7 percent average per year) as did the LMCS group during the same period. Return on investment performance was similar during this five-year period with the HMCS group (9.5 ROI) slightly out-performing the LMCS group (9.1 ROI). However, HMCS hospitals posted a significantly higher operating margin (2.3 percent) than did hospitals in the LMCS group (.9 percent) between 1990 and 1994. While the data included in this analysis indicates that there is not a positive relationship between increased managed care and diminished hospital financial performance, specific state hospital financial performance data does seem to indicate that a direct correlation exists between increased managed care market penetration and diminished profitability. As portrayed in Table 13.6, Colorado and Massachusetts hospital experience, for example, demonstrates that as the level of managed care market penetration increases, profitability, as defined by total margin, decreases.

Comparative Liquidity

Hospitals in low managed care states enjoy significantly higher liquidity as measured by the current ratio and the average payment period. The LMCS group reports a collectively higher current ratio, the relationship of current assets to current liabilities, of 2.79 compared to the HMCS group ratio of 1.72. Similarly, hospitals represented by the LMCS composite experience a much faster average payment period of 49 days compared to either the HMCS

Table 13.6 Relationship Between Hospital Profitability and Increased Managed Care

Colorado			Massachusetts		
Year	**Total Margin**	**% HMO**	**Year**	**Total Margin**	**% HMO**
1991	7.0%	22.5%	1991	2.3%	30.6%
1992	6.1%	26.6%	1992	2.5%	35.4%
1993	5.1%	28.7%	1993	1.7%	38.9%
1994	4.1%	34.7%	1994	1.5%	42.1%

group (63 days) or the national average of 62 days. However, HMCS hospitals report a higher level of days cash on hand (86 days), nearly 20 days higher than the LMCS group (67 days), but still below the national average of 98 days. This disparity between the HMCS and LMCS composite data for the days cash on hand indicator is misleading, however, since a high outlier in the HMCS group (Colorado with 108 days of cash on hand) and a low outlier in the LMCS group (Alaska with only 31 days of cash on hand) skew the result. Removing these two states from the analysis of days cash on hand reduces the difference to only four days with the HMCS group reporting 80 days of cash on hand and the LMCS group with 76 days of cash.

Comparative Debt and Debt Service

The comparative analysis of the 1994 data indicates that hospitals in high managed care states are nearly twice as indebted (.61 long-term debt to equity ratio) as hospitals in the low managed care group (.34 long-term debt to equity ratio). Regarding the hospitals' ability to pay both the principle and interest associated with long-term indebtedness, the debt service coverage ratio indicates that hospitals in the LMCS group maintain a much stronger debt service capacity (5.0) than do hospitals in the HMCS group (3.6). Both groups, however, are above the national average debt service coverage ratio of 3.1.

Comparative Overall Financial Viability

As measured by the Financial Flexibility Index (FFI) described in Table 13.6, hospitals represented by the HMCS are in better overall financial health than hospitals in the LMCS group of states. HMCS hospitals report an FFI of 2.69 while the FFI for hospitals in the low managed care group is 1.78. An FFI of 2.00 or above is desirable; in fact, the national average was 2.00 in 1994.

CONCLUSIONS

As demonstrated by the Managed Care Relative Financial Risk Assessment model, which was developed by the author as a method of assessing the potential financial vulnerability of a hospital to the effects of increased managed care market penetration, a hospital's potential risk associated with greater HMO market influence can be predicted. By examining the key hospital financial and utilization indicators most influenced by HMOs, we might identify trends characteristic of hospitals in high managed care areas that can be applied to other states, and to other hospitals, to estimate the financial ramifications of an increasing managed care market. This study confirms that the utilization of acute care hospital services in HMCSs has been suppressed compared to the utilization of hospital services nationally. Specifically, admission rates (112 admissions per 1,000 population), patient days (918 patient days per 1,000 population), and occupancy (45 percent) experienced by hospitals in HMCSs are all significantly lower than the national averages of 127 admissions/1,000, 1,046 days/1,000, and 48 percent occupancy. As the percentage of managed care market penetration increases in a particular area, hospitals can predict the financial effect of the change by utilizing the indicators of relative financial risk contained in the model presented in Table 16.4.

This study was not able to confirm the study's original assertion that increased managed care activity negatively influences the financial solvency of hospitals subject to the change in managed care market presence. While hospitals in LMCSs do seem to maintain better financial liquidity as measured by the Current Ratio and the Average Payment Period, hospitals in HMCSs demonstrate better cash positions and higher profitability. The operating margin, the most common measure of hospital profitability, for the HMCS group (2.8 percent) was significantly higher in 1994 than the average margin for the LMCS group (1.6 percent). This higher profitability of hospitals in HMCSs in 1994 was not an aberration in the data; hospitals in HMCSs also significantly out-performed hospitals in the low managed care group regarding profitability, for the five-year period 1990 through 1994. While HMCS hospitals were generally more profitable in 1994, they were also twice as indebted as hospitals in the LMCS group. The LMCSs also posted a stronger debt service capacity than did hospitals in the high managed care group of states. Overall, the financial health and viability of hospitals in the HMCSs is superior to the overall financial condition of hospitals in the LMCSs identified in this study. The Financial Flexibility Index, developed by Ohio State University, was the indicator upon which this conclusion was reached.

The author recognizes that other confounding factors may very well have influenced the results of this study, such as the average age of the state's population, socioeconomic differences among the states being compared, the absence or presence of healthy lifestyle habits among the populations being compared, how urban or rural the states area, the influences of state certificate-of-need laws, and the level of state regulatory oversight of healthcare delivery. However, for the purposes of analyzing both the potential and realized financial effect of increased managed care on hospitals, it is assumed that because the states in this study were selected exclusively based on their degree of managed care market penetration, the potential confounders may randomly occur in the study group of states; therefore, our conclusions are both valid and reliable.

While data from Colorado and Massachusetts indicates that hospital profitability diminishes as the level of managed care market penetration increases, the overall study results indicate that hospitals in HMCSs demonstrate a better cash position and higher profitability than hospitals in LMCSs. Hospitals in HMCSs are, however, more heavily indebted in relation to equity and have a weaker debt service coverage capacity. Moreover, the overall financial health and viability of hospitals in HMCSs is superior to that of hospitals in LMCSs.

REFERENCES

1995 Managed Care Digest, HMO-PPO Edition. 1995. Kansas City, Missouri: Hoechst, Marion, Roussel, Inc., p. l6.

American Hospital Association. 1996. *Hospital STATS, 1995–1996 Edition*. Chicago: American Hospital Association.

U.S. Department of Commerce. *Statistical Abstract of the United States, 1995*. Washington, DC: September 1995, p.28.

CHAPTER

14

Shifting the Paradigm: Monitoring Access in Medicare Managed Care

Elizabeth R. Docteur, David C. Colby, and Marsha Gold

INTRODUCTION

Managed care currently plays a small but growing role in the Medicare program. At the end of 1995, 10.7 percent of Medicare beneficiaries were enrolled in managed care plans (Physician Payment Review Commission, 1996). Enrollment is heavily concentrated in plans that are paid under a risk contract to deliver services in exchange for a fixed payment per enrollee.[1] Enrollment in those plans has increased more than 30 percent since 1994, and the proportion of beneficiaries who obtain medical care through capitated plans is expected to continue to increase. Such expectations are fostered both by the increasing proportion of enrollees with managed care experience and by growth in private health plan participation in the risk program. In addition, increased beneficiary enrollment would be anticipated under policy proposals to expand the range of health care delivery alternatives available under Medicare.[2] Proposals to do so have been endorsed recently by both the Administration and by Congress.

The growth of managed care presents a number of challenges for Medicare policy, not the least of which is how to continue to fulfill the program's responsibility to ensure beneficiaries' access to care. In this article, we consider the implications of Medicare managed care growth for efforts to monitor

Reprinted with permission from *Health Care Financing Review* 17 (4): 5–21.

beneficiaries' access. Systems currently used for monitoring access need to be revised, and data and measures suitable for monitoring will need to be developed. Ultimately, under a Medicare program that offers a wide array of health care financing and delivery options, monitoring efforts will need to be unbiased for the mode of health care delivery.

APPROACH TO MONITORING ACCESS

Ongoing monitoring efforts provide information on Medicare beneficiaries' ability to obtain medical care. Annual reports on beneficiaries' access are produced by both HCFA and PPRC. These monitoring efforts were mandated by Congress to track the impact of the Medicare fee schedule (MFS) and to provide information for updating the conversion factor under the process for setting Volume Performance Standards (Health Care Financing Administration, 1995b; Physician Payment Review Commission, 1995). Therefore, by design, these efforts have focused on access in FFS Medicare.

Policy interest and the availability of beneficiary-level Medicare data have supported numerous studies using a variety of methods for analyzing beneficiaries' access to care in the traditional Medicare program. In this section, we describe the dominant theoretical approach to evaluating access that has guided past studies, and the measures and data that have been used in both one-time studies and ongoing efforts to monitor access.

Conceptual Framework

Aday, Andersen, and colleagues established the conceptual framework for most subsequent analyses of access to care (Andersen and Aday, 1978; Aday and Andersen, 1981). In these researchers' view, access is a function of three categories of variables: (1) predisposing factors, such as personal resources, education, race, and age; (2) enabling factors, such as the availability of providers in a community, and individual's insurance coverage, and existence of a regular source of care; and (3) finally, an individual's need for health care, as indicated by health status and symptoms.

Using this framework, the effects of these variables on access to care can be observed through measurement of health care services utilization. Studies of access have lent support to this framework by demonstrating variation in the use of services that could be explained by differences in health status, sociodemographic factors, and characteristics of the health care market.

Although most studies of access focus on utilization as a measure of realized access, some studies have taken a different approach. For some researchers, access is a relatively narrow concept. For example, some equate access with having a usual source of care (e.g., Berki and Ashcraft, 1979). Others take a more expansive view of access as a multidimensional concept. Penchansky and Thomas (1981), for instance, describe the dimensions of access as availability, accessibility, accommodation, affordability, and acceptability.[3]

Because these definitions and frameworks were developed in the context of a system in which health care financing and delivery were largely separate systems, a distinction between the concepts of access and quality could be made. Palmer, Clark, and Lawthers (1994) describe the relationship between access and quality, noting that the former concept has traditionally been defined as entry into the health care system. Quality, by contrast, has been considered to be more driven by an individual's experience within the system. This distinction is blurred, however, where financing and delivery systems are merged.

More recently, the Aday-Andersen access definition and framework were modified and adapted by the Institute of Medicine (IOM) (Millman, 1993). The IOM model expands upon Aday and Andersen's earlier work by linking use of services to outcomes. The IOM definition of access (adopted in this article) entails "the timely use of personal health services to achieve the best possible outcomes" (Millman, 1993). The revised framework (Figure 14.1) helps to make the important distinction between factors that are patient-related and those more associated with the health system. Evalua-

Figure 14.1 Institute of Medicine Framework for Access

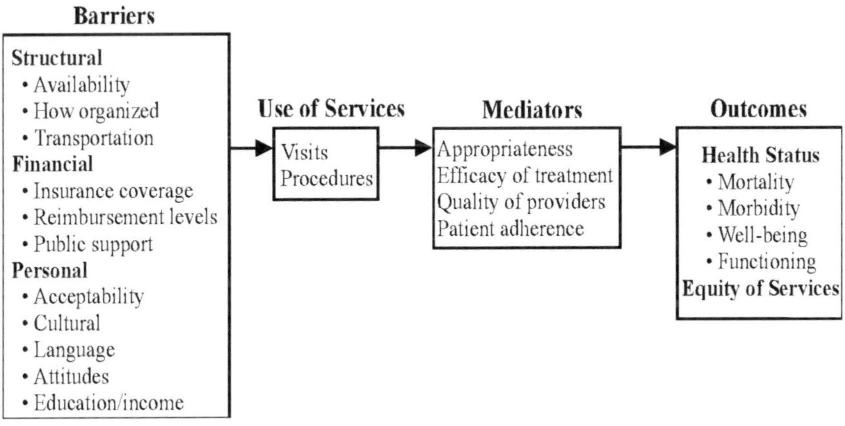

Adapted with permission by the authors from a figure in Millman, M., ed. *Access to Health Care in America*. Washington, DC: National Academy Press, 1993, courtesy of National Academy Press.

tion of access under this model involves both health-status outcomes and the equity of access across groups.

Viewed this way, the distinction between access as system entry and quality as processes and outcomes of care is less distinct, with a unified framework showing their interrelationship. This integration, as we discuss later, is a very important building block for conceptualizing access in an environment where cost containment is of growing concern.

Measures

Various measures have been used to monitor access in the traditional FFS Medicare program. The choice of measures has been driven by the populations studied, the access barriers, and the available data.

Population-Based Utilization Rates

Utilization rates are among the most widely used measures of access to care. Many studies implicitly assume and some explicitly state that higher utilization indicates better access. Other studies compare utilization rates for a specific service with established standards for use of that service. Either of these types of studies may entail contrasting the utilization of subgroups of beneficiaries or tracking trends in utilization over time.

Many different types of services have been assessed in studies of Medicare beneficiaries' access to care. Access to preventive services, for example, has been monitored by determining the proportion of beneficiaries receiving influenza immunizations (Health Care Financing Administration, 1995a). It is more difficult to analyze access to some other preventive or diagnostic services. For instance, diagnostic data are needed to make valid interpretations of utilization rates for Pap smears (Physician Payment Review Commission, 1994).

Beyond preventive care, other types of utilization have been studied in evaluations of access. Broad indicators of hospital use, such as length of stay and hospital charges, have been used in some studies, while other studies have focused on utilization of surgical and procedural services. Escarce and his colleagues, for instance, documented differences in utilization of such services by race (Escarce et al., 1993). As part of its monitoring efforts, PPRC (1995) analyzed a recent decline in cataract lens replacement surgery, noting that this decline could be explained in part by depletion of the pool of Medicare beneficiaries eligible for the procedure. The shortcoming of most of these use-based measures—particularly the more aggregate ones—rests in the absence of information about the efficaciousness of the care addressed by the measures.

Measures of Appropriate Care

Measures of appropriate care go beyond utilization measures in that they compare information about the process of care that is provided or not provided to established medical standards. Application of these measures is constrained by limitations in the ability both to identify those patients in need of specific care and also to determine what care is appropriate to a given need.

It is possible, for instance, to identify the proportion of Medicare patients who fail to receive expected followup care. Researchers in one study that exemplifies this approach looked at nine medical diagnosis groups that required hospitalization and evaluated the probability, by race, of beneficiaries' receiving appropriate followup care after hospital discharge (Moy and Hogan, 1993).

Some such measures are now included in efforts to monitor beneficiaries' access (Physician Payment Review Commission, 1995). A set of 47 clinically based indicators of access to care was developed by RAND under a PPRC contract. By drawing on demographic and clinical information available in claims and enrollment databases, these indicators can be used to determine the rates at which appropriate care is provided.

Health Outcomes

Morbidity and mortality rates are commonly used outcomes indicators. But given that the consequences of inadequate or poor quality care may take years to become evident, these are not particularly useful measures for policy purposes. More timely measures of the outcomes of care can be created by identifying health conditions that could have been prevented had appropriate care been received as the need arose. These condition-specific outcomes measures may also provide better information regarding a specific health care delivery environment because they are more likely to be sensitive to care received in the short term. By contrast, the more global outcomes generally tend to be more heavily influenced by factors such as personal history and behavior, socioeconomic factors, and other factors operating independently of current health care delivery arrangements.

Sentinel health events, also known as ambulatory-care-sensitive conditions, are an extension of the public health practice of measuring standard morbidity and mortality rates. These events are defined as diseases, disabilities, and deaths that can be prevented, treated, or controlled with access to appropriate primary care. Such events serve as indicators of potential unmet need. For example, research studies using sentinel events have examined avoidable hospital conditions as indicators of poor access to primary care (Weissman, Gatsonis, and Epstein, 1992; Bindman et al., 1995).

Some outcomes measures that can be used for monitoring access in the Medicare program have been identified. For example, the set of clinically based measures developed by RAND for PPRC included a few measures of avoidable adverse outcomes. Among these were rates of nonelective hospital admissions for specific conditions, emergency department visits related to certain diagnoses, and readmissions following an initial hospitalization (Physician Payment Review Commission, 1995).

Provider Participation Measures

Because provider availability is thought to be an enabling factor in determining access, the extent of provider participation in the Medicare program has been used as an access measure in ongoing monitoring efforts.[4] Specific indicators that have been used include the ratio of physicians to beneficiaries, the number of physicians newly serving and ceasing to serve beneficiaries, and the concentration of patients among physicians serving beneficiaries (Physician Payment Review Commission, 1995).

Other Access Indicators

Other types of access indicators have also been used. Measures of the extent to which beneficiaries have trouble obtaining or delay seeking medical care, and the extent to which they have a particular physician or office as a usual source of care are considered direct measures of access. Measures of barriers to care, such as language or transportation problems, aid the ability to interpret these findings. Indirect access measures include beneficiary satisfaction with various aspects of their care and their ability to obtain care. Finally, descriptive measures on supplemental insurance coverage, out-of-pocket costs for health care, waiting times for appointments, sites of care, and distance traveled to care all provide information that can be used to assess beneficiaries' access. All of these measures serve as fairly gross indicators; however, they may be sensitive to important changes in access for particular groups.

Data

In monitoring Medicare beneficiaries' access, the various types of measures already discussed can be developed predominately from three routinely generated sources of data: claims, beneficiary surveys, and enrollment files. These data have served as a foundation for measuring access to care across a number of dimensions. Other data have been generated to supplement ongoing monitoring efforts, and these have been analyzed to provide insight on access questions.

Claims

In the traditional Medicare FFS program, claims that are submitted by providers for payment supply information on services, beneficiaries, and providers. Claims data have been used to track patterns of utilization in specific areas, to develop clinically based indicators of access, and to measure the extent of provider participation in the Medicare program.

Medicare has a standardized claims reporting system. Before the mid-1980s, each of 56 Medicare carriers had its own data system and coding conventions. Since then, Medicare has gradually developed a national system, first with the Part B Medicare Annual Data (BMAD) system, and now with the National Claims History File (NCHF). Since 1985, HCFA has required the use of Current Procedural Terminology codes for most physician services and has standardized the use of specialty, type of service, place of service, and modifier codes. With implementation of the MFS, the final standardization of Medicare data was achieved by eliminating most local procedure codes and by nationalizing payment policies. Data for other provider sectors are also available through the NCHF.

In addition to standardizing data elements, Medicare claims data are available in a relatively timely fashion. Under the NCHF, claims can be monitored on a flow basis, if desired.

BENEFICIARY SURVEY DATA

Self-reported beneficiary data on access is routinely generated through the Medicare Current Beneficiary Survey (MCBS), a continuous survey of longitudinal design. The MCBS is a survey of about 12,000 beneficiaries sponsored by HCFA's Office of the Actuary. The MCBS was constructed to be representative of the Medicare population as a whole. The oldest-old and disabled beneficiaries under 65 years of age were oversampled to support analyses of these populations. To maintain the longitudinal panel, additional beneficiaries are added to replace those no longer in the sample because of death, emigration, or refusal to participate (Adler, 1994).

The survey and its supplements contain information on access, utilization of services, expenditures, health insurance coverage, health status, and physical functioning as well as demographic data. The access supplement survey is conducted yearly. It provides information on beneficiary satisfaction and perceived barriers to care as well as direct measures of access, such as waiting times for appointments and out-of-pocket costs.

Enrollment Data

A third source of data for monitoring access is enrollment records. From enrollment data, a denominator file has been developed that includes information on beneficiary eligibility, location of residence, and limited sociodemographic characteristics. This file makes it possible to compare utilization and outcomes rates across some subgroups of Medicare beneficiaries.

Monitoring Access of Vulnerable Populations

Monitoring efforts that focused on the impact of the MFS have tracked access for groups that were thought to be at risk for problems in obtaining care because population averages could cloak access problems for these groups. In general, the vulnerable populations chosen for targeted monitoring efforts were ones that had lower incomes and that had experienced discrimination. Subgroups that have been selected for targeted monitoring efforts include black beneficiaries, beneficiaries without supplemental insurance, and beneficiaries living in poverty areas (Health Care Financing Administration, 1995b; Physician Payment Review Commission, 1995).

Analyzing access of vulnerable populations serves a secondary purpose in that these groups might be expected to be among the first to experience any declines in access caused by MFS implementation. Such targeted monitoring efforts thus may provide an early warning to policymakers when access problems arise. Although ongoing monitoring efforts have not shown reductions in access for these groups, analyses have confirmed that these vulnerable populations continue to have poorer access than other beneficiaries. PPRC found that black beneficiaries and those who live in urban Health Professional Shortage Areas or urban poverty areas use fewer physician services and have poorer health outcomes (Physician Payment Review Commission, 1996). In addition, beneficiaries with low incomes, without supplemental insurance, or with functional disabilities that cause them to require assistance disproportionately report difficulty in obtaining medical care.

A limitation of currently used definitions of vulnerable subpopulations is that these definitions focus on broad characteristics that can be readily measured from available data. Others have defined vulnerability using clinically based or socially based criteria. For example, although her work was not specifically focused on the Medicare program, Aday (1993) theorized that those at risk for poor physical, psychological, or social health are those who have limited resources in terms of social status, social capital, and human capital. Her list of vulnerable populations includes those who are chronically ill, disabled, mentally ill, and homeless, among others. The issue of better defining vulnerable subpopulations will be a particularly important one as access-monitoring approaches are modified to reflect the evolution of the Medicare program.

NEW PARADIGM FOR CONCEPTUALIZING ACCESS

As alluded to in the previous discussions, the existing approaches for assessing access were developed in the context of an FFS system. These approaches may not adequately reflect the processes that influence care in the managed care environment. To respond to recent and ongoing changes in the Medicare program, reevaluation of the system used for monitoring beneficiary access to care is now required.

This reassessment will need to account for the growth of managed care, the growing emphasis on cost-effective delivery, and the wider range in health care delivery options likely to be made available in the Medicare program. First, the traditional access-monitoring approach must be modified to reflect features that are relevant to beneficiaries who use managed care arrangements. This will entail changes in the conceptual framework and along with it, changes in both the measures and the data used for measurement. Second, the traditional access-monitoring approach will need to be strengthened to better address growing concerns regarding efficiency and equity; this will entail more emphasis on the care provided to complement current emphasis on system entry, and will also require more refined techniques for identifying populations at risk. Third, there is a need for better risk adjusters in both cross-sectional and longitudinal analyses of access in the Medicare program.

Adapting the Framework

Existing frameworks for conceptualizing access generally fail to account for the fact that managed care plans are organized systems with both financing and delivery responsibilities. To revise the framework to represent the access issues that arise in managed care, it is necessary to account for the ways in which both of these responsibilities interact to affect access.

Obtaining access to care is a two-stage process in a managed care system. Individuals first select among the health plans available to them, with structural, financial, and personal characteristics influencing plan selection. People then seek care within the structure established by their plan. This structure may include unique care-delivery processes and rules for seeking care that, along with other factors not related to the specific health plan, may influence access for plan enrollees.

Given these differences, we have made preliminary modifications to the IOM conceptual framework in order to incorporate the influence of managed care on access (Figure 14.2).[5] Structural, financial, and personal variables labeled "barriers to access" in the IOM model are expanded and relabeled to account for the fact that they both determine plan selection and

Figure 14.2 Revised Framework for Access Accounting for Managed Care Systems

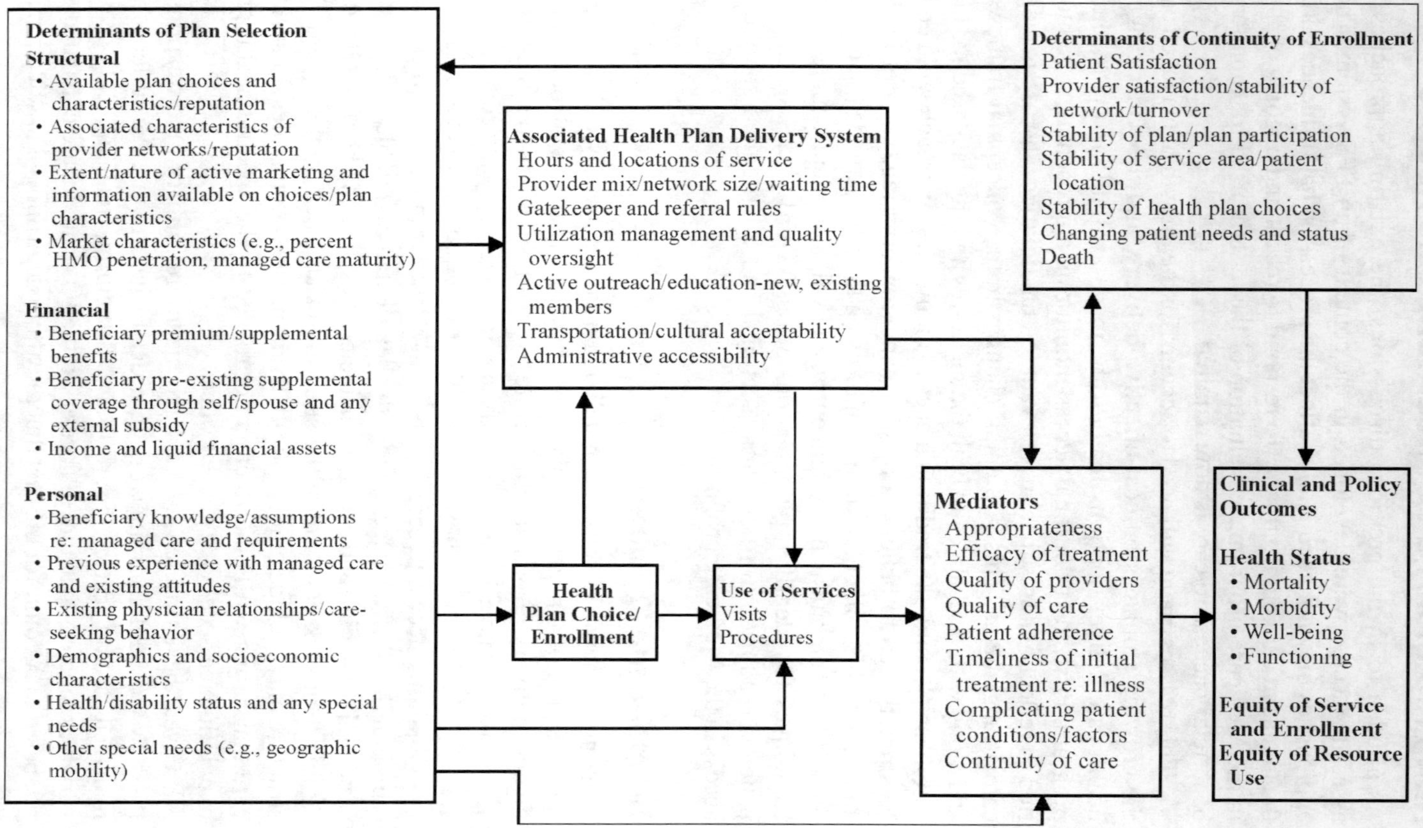

Source: (Gold, 1995). Unpublished working paper. Washington, D.C. Mathematica Policy Research, Inc. 1995.

influence care received, and that they can have both positive and negative effects on access. The revisions also reflect the Medicare program's specific characteristics (e.g., supplemental coverage, needs associated with an elderly and disabled population).

The revised framework shows that a beneficiary's health plan selection situates him or her in a specific delivery system with its own attributes and procedures. These, as well as the more traditional financial and personal variables, influence the use of services. Mediating processes between use and outcomes are broadened from the IOM framework to include other mediators such as timeliness of initial treatment. The framework shows more directly that these processes are influenced not just by the use of services but also by features of the plan. Outcomes are generally similar to the original model, but issues of equity are expanded to include enrollment.

The framework also explicitly accounts for disenrollment and the reasons it occurs. This is useful in differentiating types of disenrollment behavior, particularly when disenrollment can be voluntary or involuntarily and can occur at the end of any month. The framework assumes that mediating processes determine beneficiary satisfaction, which influences continued enrollment. Provider turnover influences this, as studies have shown that patient behavior is heavily influenced by a desire to retain provider relationships. In addition, any changes in the choices available influence whether enrollees stay in the plan. Disenrollment may also result from changes in patient needs and health status. Such disenrollment, from a policy perspective, may be desirable, neutral, or problematic, depending on the circumstances and the effects of disenrollment on access to care.

In contrast to voluntary disenrollment, involuntary disenrollment is presumed to occur when plans drop out of the program or change their service areas, or when beneficiaries move or die. In either case, beneficiaries who disenroll may return to traditional Medicare or join another Medicare managed care plan. As with voluntary disenrollment, involuntary disenrollment may affect access to care, particularly insofar as continuity of care is disrupted or the ability to obtain supplemental insurance is constrained.

Access Measures for Managed Care

Revisions in the conceptual framework for access will need to be supported by the development of new measures for monitoring access in the Medicare managed care program. Some traditional measures of access are not applicable, and those that are applicable may be insufficient to provide a complete picture of access to care in a more complex health care financing and delivery system. Therefore, additional measures are needed to assess the influence of various managed care plan processes and characteristics on access.

Traditional Measures of Access

Certain types of measures used in access monitoring in the traditional FFS Medicare program become obsolete in the managed care environment. Most importantly, many measures of service utilization, which have figured prominently in traditional access-monitoring efforts, appear to be of limited value in managed care monitoring. Because service use is expected to be lower in a system where care is effectively managed, comparing levels of utilization in the traditional Medicare program and the risk program would not provide much insight into differences in access. Similarly, monitoring aggregate trends in utilization and the use of specific services in the risk program is not likely to yield valuable information.

On the other hand, several types of traditional access measures are applicable to Medicare beneficiaries in both the FFS and the managed care programs. Measures of satisfaction with care and with the ability to obtain care, for example, can provide information for evaluating the access of all beneficiaries. Similarly, measures of the extent to which care is delayed or not obtained when believed to be needed and the rates at which beneficiaries experience trouble obtaining care are also universally relevant, as are measures of perceived barriers to care. Information on beneficiaries' waiting times for appointments and distance traveled to obtain care remains a consideration in assessing managed care access.

As noted previously, both the shift to managed care and the related emphasis on cost-effectiveness increase the value of focusing on measures of access that reflect quality and outcomes of care as well as system entry. Under the traditional framework, the major barriers to access were viewed as stemming from financial and structural (e.g., provider supply and participation) factors that limited system entry. Thus, access and quality were considered relatively independently.

With philosophies and cost constraints changing, the emphasis in access monitoring needs to be shifted to reflect the broader range of factors that determine access under a managed care model. Measures of access also will need to be more closely linked and broadened to include measures that take into account efficacy and cost-effectiveness of care as measured through process of care and outcomes indicators. Balancing these two perspectives—ease of obtaining care and quality of care—is not easy and may be among the more controversial elements of a refined access-monitoring system. This may be true particularly in the transition from the current conceptualization of access, which may be biased toward the features of the FFA environment in which it was conceived.

The use of clinically based measures of access appears particularly promising as a way to monitor access in all types of health care financing and delivery models in which information on service use and enrollment demographics is available. These types of measures can be used to determine whether appropriate care is provided and when avoidable outcomes occur. These indicators have been tested in the traditional Medicare program using claims data and could be applied to Medicare managed care access monitoring if encounter data were to be developed.[6]

New Access Measures

Access measures that account for relevant aspects of the Medicare managed care program and the participating plans will be needed to supplement applicable measures used in traditional FFS access monitoring. Many types of access measures reflect beneficiaries' experiences and perceptions. Use of these measures will require development of beneficiary survey data. Other measures draw on administrative data to provide objective assessments of access to care.

A new area in which access measures are needed is beneficiaries' understanding of managed care. Because a direct determinant of managed care enrollees' access to care is their ability to comply with the processes established by the plan, measures of ability to do so could provide important information on determinants of access. Measures in this category could include those to assess beneficiaries' understanding of their plans' primary-care gatekeeper arrangements and restrictions on use of non-network providers, and of their rights to appeal plan decisions not to provide or pay for a medical service. One challenge in developing such measures is to account for ways in which managed care plans might legitimately differ, such as in the offering of a point-of-service option that covers beneficiary use of non-network providers under some circumstances. As the types of health plans available to beneficiaries expand, these measures might become more difficult to interpret.

Process-of-care measures are also needed for understanding access in managed care systems. Because the processes developed by a managed care plan for the provision of health care will directly determine beneficiaries' access, measures of these processes and their perceived effects can be used in evaluating access. Processes of interest include those for selecting a primary-care provider, making an appointment, obtaining a referral to a specialist, and obtaining care when travelling outside of a plan's service area. The new-enrollee orientation process and the process for appealing a plan decision could also affect access. Finally, managed care plans may develop activities to promote access, such as new-enrollee risk assessment, case management, or distribution of materials promoting preventive care. Specific measures to address these processes include the extent to which they are perceived to facilitate or impede a beneficiary's ability to obtain care and the nature of any problems experienced. These types of measures may be very useful from a policy perspective in that the access problems they are designed to identify could be addressed through targeted interventions.

Another type of beneficiary-oriented measure used in access measurement is the satisfaction measure. Traditionally used measures of satisfaction will need to be supplemented for evaluating access in Medicare managed care. Beyond issues of satisfaction with care and with the ability to obtain care, measures of a beneficiary's satisfaction with the health plan and its features can also serve to assess access indirectly. For example, measures of beneficiary satisfaction with choice of primary-care providers and specialists could provide useful information, as could measures of satisfaction with the value of the benefits received, given the premium charged. These types of measures may be particularly useful in identifying the source of any access problems indicated by other measures.

In addition to these beneficiary-oriented access measures, some types of measures may be used to characterize the managed care plans participating in the Medicare program. In terms of access to providers, traditional provider participation rates may need to be replaced with measures of the geographical proximity of the provider panel, their willingness to take on new Medicare patients, and provider turnover rates.[7] New access measures may need to be created to reflect the plan's role in influencing access. For example, measures of plans' telephone arrangements, such as average time waiting on the telephone to make an appointment, and the rates at which enrollees terminate their telephone calls to their plans because of delays in plan response could be calculated. Other measures could also be developed to assess a health plan's capacity to ensure access for enrollees. Research on plan characteristics or practices that influence access to care for enrollees in general or for vulnerable groups in particular may provide the insight needed to develop such measures.

As shown in our revised conceptual framework, the opportunity for Medicare beneficiaries to change health care financing and delivery modes presents a new type of access consideration. A number of measures will be needed to capture the effects of managed care enrollment, disenrollment, and plan-switching on access to care. First, the rates at which each type of change occurs within groups of beneficiaries and over time are of interest, as such rates could provide an indication of changes in access to care. Distinction between voluntary and involuntary disenrollments must be made and information on the reasons underlying beneficiaries' decisions to change their enrollment status will be needed.[8] In addition, analysts will need to examine the effects of changing enrollment on access. For example, measures of changes in usual source of care or primary-care provider that are associated with the change in enrollment status could be important, as could measures of disenrolling beneficiaries' ability to obtain supplemental insurance coverage.

Data for Monitoring Purposes

Data for monitoring access in Medicare managed care are currently limited. Most notable is the lack of systematic, national-level data on managed care enrollees' use of services and their satisfaction with the ability to obtain care through their plans. As previously discussed, claims data and beneficiary survey data have served as the foundation for most efforts to monitor access; therefore, their lack in the Medicare managed care program has implications for the current ability to monitor the access of these enrollees. Other types of data are available that pertain exclusively to Medicare managed care enrollees, however, that could serve in an access-monitoring system geared toward these beneficiaries.

Utilization Data

The Medicare program does not now collect information on the use of services by enrollees in the risk-contracting plans. Unlike FFS providers under the traditional Medicare program, the risk-contracting plans are paid a fixed amount regardless of service use by their enrollees. Therefore, any information on utilization, costs of care, and patient case mix is developed by the plans only as in-house management tools or in response to purchasers' demands for information about costs and performance. Plans vary not only in whether they develop such data but also in the completeness and accuracy of their data-collection efforts.

Previous attempts at collecting such encounter data have been disappointing. Of 27 health maintenance organizations and competitive medical plans that participated in a Medicare risk-contracting demonstration lasting from 1980 to 1985, only two could provide even partial encounter data for ambulatory services (Langwell and Hadley, 1990). Eight years after the creation of the Arizona Health Care Cost Containment System, only one-half of the managed care organizations could satisfy HCFA's standards for encounter data (McCall et al., 1993).

Data on Medicare managed care enrollees' utilization may be available in the future, however. Through various demonstration projects, HCFA will be testing plans' ability to provide encounter data to support program monitoring efforts.

Survey Data

Survey data that document enrollees' access-related experiences and satisfaction with their managed care plans are also now limited. Although some Medicare managed care enrollee survey data are available, these are not ideal for use in measuring the access to care of these beneficiaries. The MCBS, for example, includes only a small number of Medicare managed care enrollees in its sample, which limits the ability to analyze access issues by subgroups of enrolled population.[9] More importantly, the items used in the MCBS were not developed specifically for evaluating the access of beneficiaries in managed care settings. Although some traditional survey measures of access can be used for beneficiaries across all delivery models, other items are less meaningful for beneficiaries enrolled in managed care plans. In response to changes in the Medicare program, HCFA at present plans to supplement the MCBS sample and questionnaire beginning with the fall 1996 round. These changes are designed to facilitate comparisons of Medicare FFS and managed care enrollees.

To test the feasibility of using a beneficiary survey for monitoring access in the Medicare managed care program, PPRC has contracted with MPR to develop and field a survey of Medicare risk-contract plan enrollees and disenrollees. Four groups were distinguished for survey sampling and questionnaire design purposes: new enrollees, continuous enrollees, disenrollees (who returned to FFS Medicare), and plan switchers (who disenrolled from one risk plan and joined another). The project entails both the examination of sampling issues and the development and testing of measures that reflect the influence of Medicare managed care on beneficiary access. Insight gained in these areas may inform future efforts to supplement or revise the MCBS.

Other Data for Access Monitoring

A system for monitoring access will need to rely on data from a variety of sources in order to obtain a multidimensional perspective. Additional types of data that are not applicable to the traditional Medicare FFS program are available or could be developed.

Information on the characteristics and processes of the private health plans that serve Medicare beneficiaries could be used in an access monitoring system. Data on health plan premiums, enrollment size, service area, and benefits are now available. Descriptive information on the comparison of plan networks could also be analyzed and monitored over time, although analyses would be complicated by factors such as group contracting arrangements. Such information could be supplemented by plan-level survey data on activities, practices, or characteristics that may influence enrollees' access to care.

Administrative data on plan enrollment and disenrollment could be used as a component of an access-monitoring system. Available information about enrollees and disenrollees includes demographic variables, Medicaid status, and Medicare managed care plan history. These data permit monitoring of trends in rates of enrollment and disenrollment by subgroups of the beneficiary population and by subgroups of the Medicare managed care plan population. The value of using plan-level beneficiary survey data for evaluating access to care has been demonstrated in a study by the Office of Inspector General of the U.S. Department of Health and Human Services (1995).

Data on beneficiary appeals of plan decisions might also serve as a component of a Medicare managed care access monitoring approach.[10] Changes in the rates of appeals or the types of appeals filed by beneficiaries could indicate changes in access to care generally or for specific services.

Vulnerable Groups

As is true in traditional monitoring, identification of vulnerable groups for targeted monitoring efforts will continue to be important. Certain groups of beneficiaries may, on average, be more susceptible to difficulties obtaining access to care in the managed care environment.

Some of the same groups that have been identified as vulnerable in FFS Medicare may also be at risk for access problems in Medicare managed care. As already discussed, these groups include black beneficiaries and those who live in urban Health Professional Shortage Areas or urban poverty areas. Beneficiaries in these groups could continue to be at risk to the extent that the underlying reasons for their vulnerability are unaffected by the managed care delivery system; for example, where access problems stem from a lack of transportation. On the other hand, access for beneficiaries in these vulnerable groups may in some cases be improved. This would be true, for instance, where vulnerability stemmed from financial barriers to access that could be reduced in managed care plans, depending on the premium and cost-sharing arrangements.

In addition to the groups already identified, two general categories of beneficiaries may be particularly at risk for access problems under managed care delivery systems. The first group is those who may not receive adequate care from health plans responding inappropriately to cost-containment incentives. Beneficiaries with a chronic medical condition who need resource-intensive care on an ongoing basis could be included in this category, as could beneficiaries with certain medical conditions that require specialized care. The second group is those who have difficulty navigating systems of care, whether because of medical, psychological, economic, sociological, or other factors. Beneficiaries who already have difficulties obtaining care under the FFS system may find that managed care systems pose additional challenges.

Because beneficiaries in the groups that may be particularly vulnerable under managed care may be difficult to identify in advance, proxies for beneficiaries in these categories will need to be identified for targeted monitoring efforts. For example, the study of access in Medicare risk-contracting plans being conducted by MPR for PPRC will analyze the access to care of disabled beneficiaries and those over age 85 as proxy categories for beneficiaries in these vulnerable groups.

ISSUES FOR MONITORING ACCESS

Beyond the fundamental question of how best to monitor access for beneficiaries in managed care plans, the growth in managed care enrollment raises a number of additional issues that will need to be addressed in designing a monitoring approach.

Implications for Traditional Access Monitoring

The increasing availability and use of managed care arrangements in the Medicare program must be taken into account in traditional program-monitoring approaches. The majority of beneficiaries obtain their health care through Medicare's traditional FFS program and are expected to continue to do so for the near future. But the fact that most beneficiaries have the option to use other arrangements and that an increasing number choose to do so has implications for the ability to interpret the traditional measures and trends in utilization now used in monitoring access.

Beneficiaries' selection among alternative health plans may result in differences in the demographic and health-status characteristics of the underlying enrollment populations. These differences are likely to be reflected in any access-measurement efforts unless adequate adjustments that reflect underlying population differences can be made. Identification of appropriate risk adjusters will be important for interpreting trends in access as the pool of enrolled beneficiaries changes over time. Development of adjusters for outcomes and other types of measures is still at an early stage, however, and specific adjusters are not widely agreed upon. (For a discussion of the methodological issues, see Iezzoni [1994].) It is likely that the importance of making adjustments to measures will vary for different measures, assuming that some types are more sensitive to underlying characteristics of the population.

Implications of Expanding Plan Options

Policy proposals to expand the range of health-plan options that are available to Medicare beneficiaries also would have implications for access-monitoring approaches. Medicare restructuring proposals developed by Congress and by the Administration would open up the Medicare program to a wider variety of health plans. The Seven-Year Balanced Budget Reconciliation Act (passed by Congress in November 1995 and vetoed by the President), for example, would have expanded options under Medicare to include medical savings accounts, provider-sponsored organizations, preferred provider organizations, and so-called unrestricted FFS health plans, which would place no constraints on utilization or provider choice. These options could range widely in terms of benefits provided (beyond the basic Medicare benefits package), cost-sharing arrangements, lock-in requirements, provide incentives, and care-management strategies. Wide variation would be expected both across plan types and within categories of plans.

Monitoring access to care under a restructured program would be challenged by limitations in both measures and data. Increased diversity in health-plan options would mean that only those access measures that are unbiased for health care delivery models would be useful for monitoring at the program level. For example, measure of the extent to which beneficiaries fail to obtain or delay obtaining necessary medical care could continue to serve as an indicator of access problems. Access measures dependent on the delivery model or plan characteristics, such as those designed to assess the effects of cost-sharing arrangements, out-of-network restrictions, or the specialist referral process, on the other hand, would not be universally applicable or interpretable at the program level. Such indicators might instead be used selectively at the level of plan-specific monitoring.

The availability of data that are of uniform type and quality will greatly determine the ability to undertake access-monitoring efforts. Under a Medicare program restructured to provide a wider variety of health-plan options to beneficiaries, baseline access-monitoring efforts may need to rely primarily on beneficiary survey data in the absence of uniform information on service utilization. As more beneficiaries use alternatives to traditional FFS Medicare, the question of whether the program's ability to protect beneficiaries' access to appropriate care is compromised by the absence of these data will need to be resolved.

CONCLUSION

Our examination of the issues to be addressed in devising an access-monitoring system for Medicare managed care has shown that significant challenges remain to be addressed. Further work will be needed to identify access measures, data, and groups for targeted monitoring efforts.

Even as steps are taken toward developing the framework and methods for monitoring access in Medicare managed care, the program continues its evolution and rapid growth. Because of the need to use measures unbiased for health care delivery mode in programwide monitoring, identifying the source of access problems and potential policy solutions could become increasingly difficult in a program of diverse plan options. As diversification occurs, more analytic work will be needed to develop access measures that are universally relevant, and increased efforts to ensure the comparability of data will be necessary.

NOTES

1. At the end of 1995, 8.8 percent of beneficiaries were enrolled in a Medicare managed care plan under a risk contract, and 1.9 percent were enrolled in a plan paid on a reasonable-cost basis.
2. For example, the Congressional Budget Office (O'Neill, 1995) projects that under the Medicare Preservation Act passed in November 1995, 17.5 percent of beneficiaries would use alternative delivery systems by 1998, and 25.3 percent would do so by 2002.
3. Many of these empirical studies had normative underpinnings to their approaches. For a discussion of normative approaches to access, see the President's Commission for the Study of Ethical Problems in Medicine and Biomedical and Behavioral Research (1983).
4. In the context of Medicare access monitoring, provider participation describes the number or portion of providers actually serving Medicare beneficiaries, not merely the number who sign participating provider agreements.
5. This framework was originally developed by Gold (1995).
6. Indicators of this type have been used in the Medicare managed care program in several studies using data collected for research purposes. Examples of such studies include Retchin and Brown (1990) and Riley et al. (1994).
7. The most recent version (2.5) of the Health Plan Employer Data and Information Set (National Committee for Quality Assurance, 1995), commonly known as HEDIS, includes the number and percent of primary-care physicians accepting new patients among its measures of access and satisfaction.
8. For example, some beneficiaries may change their health plan to retain their usual source of care in cases where their primary-care physician leaves a plan.
9. The tenth round of the MCBS, administered in 1994, contained approximately 860 managed care enrollees.
10. These data are collected and have been analyzed by HCFA's contractor, Network Design Group, Inc. (Richardson, Phillips, and Conley, 1993).

REFERENCES

Aday, L.: *At Risk in America: The Health and Health Care Needs of Vulnerable Populations in the United States*. San Francisco. Jossey-Bass Publishers, 1993.

Aday, L., and Andersen, R.: Equity of Access to Medical Care: A Conceptual and Empirical Overview. *Medical Care* 19 (12): 4–27, Supplement 1981.

Adler, G.: A Profile of the Medicare Current Beneficiary Survey. *Health Care Financing Review* 15 (4): 153–63, Summer 1994.

Anderson, R., and Aday, L.: Access to Medical Care in the U.S.: Realized and Potential. *Medical Care* 16 (7): 533–46, July 1978.

Berki, S. E., and Ashcraft, M. L.: On the Analysis of Ambulatory Utilization: An Investigation of the Roles of Need, Access and Price as Predictors of Illness and Preventive Services. *Medical Care* 17 (12): 1163–81, December 1979.

Bindman, A. B., Grumbach, K., Osmond, D., et al.: Preventable Hospitalizations and Access to Health Care. *Journal of the American Medical Association* 274 (4): 305–11, July 26, 1995.

Escarce, J. J., Epstein, K. R., Colby, D. C., and Schwartz, J. S.: Racial Differences in the Use of Medical Procedures and Diagnostic Tests by Elderly Medicare Enrollees. *American Journal of Public Health* 83 (7): 948–54, July 1993.

Gold, M.: Unpublished working paper. Washington, DC. Mathematica Policy Research, Inc., 1995.

Health Care Financing Administration: *1994 Influenza Immunizations Paid for by Medicare*. Washington. U.S. Government Printing Office, 1995a.

Health Care Financing Administration: *Monitoring the Impact of Medicare Physician Payment Reform on Utilization and Access*. Washington. U.S. Government Printing Office, 1995b.

Iezzoni, L., ed.: *Risk Adjustment for Measuring Health Outcomes*. Ann Arbor, MI. Health Administration Press, 1994.

Langwell, K. M., and Hadley, J. P.: Insights from the Medicare HMO Demonstrations. *Health Affairs* 9 (1): 75–84, Spring 1990.

McCall, N., Korb, J., Cran, M., et al.: *Evaluation of Arizona's Health Care Cost Containment System Demonstration—Third Implementation and Operation Report*. San Francisco. Laguna Research Associates, 1993.

Millman, M., ed.: *Access to Health Care in America*. Washington, DC. National Academy Press, 1993.

Moy, E., and Hogan, C.: Access to Needed Follow-Up Services: Variations Among Different Medicare Populations. *Archives of Internal Medicine* 153: 1815–23, August 9, 1993.

National Committee for Quality Assurance: *HEDIS 2.5: Updated Specifications for HEDIS 2.0*. Washington, DC. January 1995.

O'Neill, J.: Letter to the Committee on Ways and Means, U.S. House of Representatives. Washington, DC. Congressional Budget Office, November 22, 1995.

Palmer, R., Clark, L., and Lawthers, A.: *DEMPAQ: A Project to Develop and Evaluate Methods to Promote Ambulatory Care Quality: Final Report*. Easton, MD. Delmarva Foundation for Medical Care, Inc., 1994.

Penchansky, R., and Thomas, J. W.: The Concept of Access: Definition and Relationship to Consumer Satisfaction. *Medical Care* 19 (2): 127–40, February 1981.

Physician Payment Review Commission: *Annual Report to Congress 1996*. Washington, DC. 1996.

Physician Payment Review Commission: *Monitoring Access of Medicare Beneficiaries*. Report No. 94-2. Washington, DC. 1994.

Physician Payment Review Commission: *Monitoring Access of Medicare Beneficiaries*. Report No. 95-1. Washington, DC. 1995.

President's Commission for the Study of Ethical Problems in Medicine and Biomedical and Behavioral Research: *Securing Access to Health Care*. Washington. U.S. Government Printing Office, 1983.

Retchin, S. M., and Brown, B.: Management of Colorectal Cancer in Medicare Health Maintenance Organizations. *Journal of General Internal Medicine* 5 (2): 110–14, March/April 1990.

Richardson, D., Phillips, J., and Conley, D.: *A Study of Coverage Denial Disputes Between Medicare Beneficiaries and HMOs*. Pittsford, NY. Network Design Group, Inc., September 1993.

Riley, G. F., Potosky, A. L., Libitz, J. D., and Brown, M. L.: Stage of Cancer at Diagnosis for Medicare HMO and Fee-for-Service Enrollees. *American Journal of Public Health* 84 (10): 1598–1604, October 1994.

U.S. Department of Health and Human Services: *Medicare Risk HMO Performance Indicators*. Office of Inspector General. Washington. U.S. Government Printing Office, October 1995.

Weissman, J. S., Gatsonis, C., and Epstein, A. M.: Rates of Avoidable Hospitalization by Insurance Status in Massachusetts and Maryland. *Journal of the American Medical Association* 268 (17): 2388–94, November 4, 1992.

PART

IV

Future Models

INTRODUCTION

The rapid growth of managed care has led to some eager crystal-ball gazing as providers, payers, and others attempt to position themselves for future success. In Part IV, this book presents three versions of what the future of managed care might have to offer.

Russell C. Coile, Jr., in "The Sixth Stage of Managed Care," uses the most innovative and successful contemporary healthcare organizations as a basis for ten models that payers, providers, and suppliers might employ as payment rates and hospital occupancy rates continue to decline. Among the models are consumer-sponsored health plans, provider-payer mergers, and public-provider partnerships.

In "Managed Care: The Next Generation," Michael Sachs presents a thorough argument for a consumer-driven healthcare future in which survival is determined by focusing on factors most important to consumers.

Combining empirical research and interviews, James C. Robinson traces the transformation of managed care organization to date and uses that information to envision the future system. Robinson's chapter, "The Future of Managed Care Organization," proposes that successful managed care in the future will move away from local, single-product offerings and toward national, full-service endeavors.

The only unchangeable factor in healthcare today is change. Healthcare professionals of all types in organizations of all types must have a solid foundation of knowledge about the structure and function of the healthcare system, must employ the most effective strategies for the current market, and must keep their eyes on the horizon and plan for a future that is difficult to envision. While doing all this, healthcare professionals must also keep their sights firmly on their core mission: to improve health. This situation brings to mind the ancient Chinese curse, "May you live in interesting times." The editors hope that the information in this book helps healthcare professionals be better equipped to cope with such interesting times, because they are not likely to get any less interesting anytime soon.

CHAPTER

15

The Sixth Stage of Managed Care: New Models for the Post-Reform Era

Russell C. Coile, Jr.

A wave of mergers and alliances is transforming the nation's trillion-dollar health care system. Without waiting for the outcome of the Congressional health debate, providers of medical care—including hospitals, physician groups, and nursing homes—are joining to form bigger networks.

Milt Freudenheim (1994, p. A1)

After the healthcare system has been transformed by the five stages of managed care's rise to market dominance, after healthcare has been restructured into capitated networks, and after most Americans belong to an HMO, what comes next? Already, the innovators and leading-edge healthcare systems are looking for new trends and models.

There will, of course, be a sixth stage in the redevelopment of U.S. healthcare organizations. This chapter will speculate on what the next few years will bring.

Reprinted from Coile, R. C. 1997. *The Five Stages of Managed Care.* Chicago: Health Administration Press.

TRANSFORMATION OF THE U.S. HEALTH SYSTEM IS AHEAD OF SCHEDULE

U.S. healthcare providers, payers, and purchasers are not waiting for Washington, D.C., to enact sweeping health reform. The transformation of the country's health system is already ahead of schedule. HMO growth is accelerating, and capitation is spreading rapidly. Consolidation and networking among healthcare providers are rampant. The development of regional healthcare networks parallels the mergers among health insurers, HMOs, and industry suppliers. Most hospitals are joining networks (Freudenheim 1994). In 1994, the SMG Marketing Group of Chicago began to track integrated healthcare networks. By January 1995, SMG had identified a total of 291, involving almost 20 percent of U.S. hospitals (Henderson 1995). A year later, the number of networks soared to 504 (Henderson 1996). Many networks also own HMOs.

All parties are positioning themselves for the post-reform era when there will be 30 million to 40 million newly insured consumers. This could lead to a surge of demand—$50 to $100 billion in new healthcare expenditures. But that will not happen overnight. Health reform will be evolutionary, not revolutionary, phased in over years of progressive efforts to cover the uninsured, probably not until the federal budget deficit is back in balance, not likely before the year 2002. National health costs could balloon as occurred after passage of Medicare and Medicaid in the 1960s, if the uninsured are suddenly given comprehensive health coverage with few controls on spending.

Tough marketplace contracting will reduce prices for services, and capitated providers will impose a new discipline on service demand. Large employers have been winning HMO rate rollbacks. Capitated medical groups and systems are lowering hospital use rates to unprecedented lows.

As employers and insurers dig in against rising expenditures, doctors are feeling the effect of market reforms, with pay cuts of 10 to15 percent and more. The president of the Los Angeles County Medical Association says that in southern California, "Specialists like cardiologists, endocrinologists and neurologists are hurting, and very close to driving taxi cabs" (Greenberg 1994, p. B1). This is a national trend. Median pay for cardiologists dropped from $499,401 in 1992 to $446,990 in 1993, while radiologists went from $271,723 to $257,414, according to the the countryn Medical Association (Greenberg 1994).

TEN NEW MODELS FOR THE SIXTH STAGE OF MANAGED CARE

What healthcare needs are new strategies and structures for reforming U.S. delivery system. Advanced models are emerging from across the nation, especially in markets with high levels of HMO and managed care penetration. Ten models may provide templates for reenvisioning tomorrow's systems.

Model 1. Consumer-Owned HMO

It is surprising there are not more consumer-owned health plans. The "mutual association" was a common form of early life insurance company, in which the policyholders owned the company and reinvested their dividends in it to increase growth. In the consumer-owned HMO model, thousands of consumers make up the investors who capitalize and manage their own health plan. A consumer-owned plan would put a high priority on customer service and on promoting the health of enrollees—the owners.

The most prominent consumer-sponsored health plan in the United States is the Group Health Cooperative of Puget Sound. This nonprofit HMO has enrolled more than 500,000 consumers in the Seattle area and is expanding across the Northwest. Consumers dominate its governance. Physicians are salaried, and most services are provided in facilities owned by Group Health. Its modern ambulatory clinics are strategically located to serve Group Health members. Group Health is a disciplined HMO with low costs and competitive premiums. Prescription drug costs are reported to be 28 percent lower than for a typical medical group (Group Health Cooperative 1993). Its market appeal has been based on benefit packages that are more comprehensive than those of competitors, and a reputation that it was run "for consumers." For example, Group Health offers premium rebates of up to 15 percent for consumers who practice healthy behaviors in seven risk areas, such as using seatbelts, exercising, and not smoking.

To strengthen its market position as one of the three dominant health systems in the Seattle area, Group Health negotiated a major strategic alliance with the Virginia Mason Clinic and Hospital, another staff-model organization. This should be a win-win partnership that brings Virginia Mason's clinical prestige and tertiary capacity together with Group Health's consumer base of a half-million covered lives. Group Health and Kaiser/Oregon announced plans to move into a closer market relationship, potentially creating a powerhouse nonprofit HMO in the Northwest.

Model 2. Statewide Network

A major market opportunity is emerging for providers to create statewide networks of hospitals and physicians. Hospitals in California, Oklahoma, and Texas are moving rapidly to do this. Some networks will be multistate. In the Washington, D.C., region, providers are organizing to serve two states and the District. Greater Southeast and the Medlantic HealthCare Group are pursuing integrated delivery strategies for a region that will stretch more than 150 miles across Virginia to Maryland's Chesapeake Bay (Sandrick 1994).

In California, health systems are creating a statewide organization designed to pursue managed care contracting with large purchasers. Called the California Health Network, the partners include Sharp HealthCare in San Diego, Adventist Health System/West and Loma Linda University Medical Center in the Los Angeles market, California Healthcare Systems in San Francisco, and Sutter Health of Sacramento. The network will combine some 24 hospitals, 15,000 physicians, and 1.2 million managed care enrollees (Lafuente 1994).

The prime market opportunity for many statewide networks is Medicaid capitation contracts. Dozens of states are actively moving toward putting contracts out to bid for hundreds of thousands of Medicaid recipients. This is a big market. On a national basis, there are more than 30 million Medicaid recipients. Those numbers could eventually grow if national health reform enfranchises the country's uninsured and Congress gives state governments the responsibility for getting them a health plan. This could mean that 15 to 20 percent of a state's population may be contracted out by state Medicaid agencies in the next several years.

California, Michigan, and Tennessee have already initiated Medicaid contracting, and more states will do so. By 1996, 13 states had received federal approvals to experiment with Medicaid reform. Some two dozen states have joined the Reforming States Group, which has been brainstorming solutions to their own problems (*New York Times* 1994).

Model 3. Brand Name Chain

Sears, Kmart. HealthSouth. Tenet Healthcare. The concept of a brand name works in every other sector of the economy. Why not healthcare? Brand-name healthcare systems exist in every region of the country. Most are regional, like Sentara (Norfolk/Tidewater, Virginia), InterMountain (Rocky Mountain stages), Partners and the CareGroup in New England, and Catholic Healthcare West (West Coast). A few are national. Among nonprofit health systems, Denver-based CHI (Catholic Health Initiatives) currently manages dozens of hospitals in six regions across the United States. CHI's facilities range from large urban medical centers with more than 400 beds to rural facilities with fewer than 50 beds.

Columbia HCA began an aggressive branding and marketing campaign in the mid-1990s, featuring CEO Richard Scott. But the chain's national advertising program was quickly cancelled when Columbia fell under federal investigation. Columbia's current management has "unbranded" the local facilities, many of which have returned to their pre-acquisition identity (Lutz and Gee 1998). Another national healthcare chain, Birmingham, Alabama-based HealthSouth, has been more successful in its national brand management. HealthSouth is the largest operator of inpatient rehabilitation hospitals in the United States, and operates hundreds of outpatient rehab units and ambulatory surgery centers. A Columbia competitor, Santa Barbara, California-based Tenet Healthcare has built a new brand name and a new identity after merging several large multi-hospital companies. Tenet has successfully grown a reputation in the management of academic medical centers as well as smaller facilities. In building its brand, Tenet has clustered its acquisitions in selected market regions (e.g., Louisiana) where it can be one of the three top health systems.

Brand-name healthcare organizations are now concentrating their focus on clinical niches. Lavish clinical "centers of excellence" are the next battlegrounds for market share and brand competition. Women's services, cancer, and heart surgery are only a few of the clinical services where regional and national chains are establishing brand identity (Myerson 1997). Nashville-based MedCath has opened several heart-only hospitals in the Southwest, and is expanding nationally into California, Ohio, and other markets. Other for-profit chains are adopting the approach, such as Pennsylvania-based Universal Health Services, which opened the McAllen Heart Hospital, with a revolving lighted red heart on the hospital's roof. The McAllen hospital also opened a new Women's Pavilion, featuring family-centered childbirth in deluxe labor/delivery/recovery rooms that the patient occupies during the entire birthing experiencing. Another well-appointed chain, the Salick Cancer Centers, with nine facilities across the United States, has been purchased by a leading pharmaceutical firm.

Model 4. Provider-Payer Merger

True integration in healthcare requires a combination of financing and delivery. Staff-model HMOs like Kaiser and Group Health of Puget Sound can operate with as little as 5 to 8 percent administrative costs. The challenge for America's hospitals and HMOs is to find a common ground, merging to achieve real efficiencies in management while providing one-stop shopping for purchasers.

Insurer-provider mergers will make increasing sense in market-driven system, and the forces promoting integration will increase at each stage of managed care's market penetration. Key factors accelerating the integration of payers and providers include:

- price wars between HMOs and managed care plans;
- employer demands for reduced HMO administrative costs;

- HMOs' and insurers' need to cut patient care costs;
- employer coalitions' leverage to get HMO price cuts;
- purchasers' demand for data on provider quality;
- providers' surplus capacity needs for committed HMO volume; and
- capitation teaching providers how to manage costs.

In the long run, providers and HMOs will discover that it less costly to cooperate than to compete. As employers demand lower costs and proof of quality, HMOs can reduce their costs by delegating to providers responsibility for managing patient care costs and quality. Why should HMOs and providers duplicate functions such as network management, provider credentialing, utilization management, and quality assurance? HMOs and insurers will learn that they are competing on the performance underlying provider networks. Staff-model HMOs with employed physicians have significantly lower administrative costs, in the range of 5 to 8 percent.

It may be easier for providers to start their own HMOs than to engage in the extensive due-diligence and organizational restructuring of a full merger with a managed care plan. InterStudy lists some 130 provider-sponsored HMOs in its national directory; they manage more than 10 percent of all HMO lives across the United States (Hamer 1996). Four successful models of provider-sponsored HMOs include:

Presbyterian Health Plan (Albuquerque, New Mexico). Presbyterian's current HMO is its second. The first was closed after physician dissatisfaction about HMO payments. The second HMO has 80,000 enrollees, and the system contracts for another 50,000 capitated lives.

First Option (New Jersey). Owned fifty-fifty by a network of 50 hospitals and 9,400 physicians, First Option is a true provider partnership. The hospitals contributed their employees to jump-start initial enrollment and turned a profit in only 14 months. The plan covers 225,000 members and is competing hard with Aetna/U.S. Healthcare and Blue Cross for statewide marketshare.

General Health System (Baton Rouge, Louisiana). This health system's HMO, Gulf South Health Plans, has captured 32 percent of the market, with 60,000 full-risk lives and 150,000 enrollees. The HMO's growth has not been without tensions, as Gulf South has had to cut physician reimbursement to keep rates competitive.

Secure Care (Des Moines, Iowa). Mercy Medical Center launched its HMO cooperatively with its 320-physician medical staff and quickly grew to 10,000 enrollees through 50 contracts. In the long-term, Mercy hopes to link its HMO into a statewide model in collaboration with other physician-hospital organizations (Rovner 1996).

Model 5. Public-Private Partnership

Many of the nation's largest hospitals are publicly owned teaching medical centers. A new model of public-private partnership may give these government-owned hub hospitals a distributed network of for-profit hospitals. Columbia/HCA is offering a merger proposition to Arizona's Maricopa County that would bring the national chain into a business partnership with the county's public hospital. Struggling with a $60.6 million debt burden, Maricopa County could use a partner with deep pockets and management expertise. A potential deal could unite the public hospital with Columbia/HCA's two for-profit community hospitals in Phoenix.

As for-profit chains run out of other investor-owned facilities to acquire, they are turning to purchasing nonprofit hospitals. For example, Columbia/HCA purchased the Samaritan Health System and San Diego–based Sharp Healthcare, which could give the big chain the position of market leader in the influential California market (Olmos 1995).

Model 6. Information Network

Hospitals and health plans may organize networks linked by the information highway. InterMountain HealthCare utilizes an extensive regional information system to link its two dozen facilities across five Western states. Well over $100 million has been invested in its award-winning community health information network (CHIN). Lutheran General's CEO Stephen Ummel believes no integrated delivery system can function with an information system framework (Bergman 1994). Detroit's Henry Ford System uses telemedicine linkages to bring speciality care to remote areas.

Integrated networks will compete on their performance. That means data, translated into useful information and available across a region or statewide delivery network. The survivors in the managed care marketplace will be the providers and HMOs that use data to create a sustained competitive advantage. CHINs will provide the architecture and linkages for:

- managing patients in real time, with data instantly available on costs and quality;
- reducing length of stay and expenses per case by closely following computerized clinical pathways and "care maps";
- eliminating high-cost variations in patterns of care by individual physicians; and
- public reporting of costs, clinical outcomes, and patient satisfaction to major employers.

Developing network CHINs won't be easy. A recent panel of experts identified a number of issues facing America's healthcare information network pioneers:

- integrating diverse platforms of hardware and software across a network;
- making clinical information systems universally available, easily accessible, and relevant to clinicians;
- handling security, privacy, and confidentiality concerns;
- maneuvering through multiple-vendor issues;
- strengthening the role of the chief information officer;
- potentially huge investments to create the information system architecture; and
- applying managed care protocols across a decentralized provider network. (Bergman 1994)

Employers are demanding comparative data from HMOs and providers. Sophisticated companies and business coalitions are requiring their HMOs and insurers to report data using HEDIS. The system is quickly becoming the industry standard for healthcare data (Miller 1995b). HMOs must report data on use of preventive care, member satisfaction, healthcare costs and utilization rates, and the financial stability of the health plan.

Strong leadership will be needed to bring the CHINs together. New partnerships will link hospitals, universities, vendors, and governments to capitalize on expertise and maximize investments in research and development. Chief information officers must work closely with health system CEOs to put the necessary information environment in place to link these diverse settings and services.

National health information networks are coming. Health-OnLine is the first national on-line information service targeted for the health industry. Denver-based Kaiser Associates, a consulting firm, joined with Healthcare Forum in San Francisco to pioneer an electronic communications and information network (Lutz 1994). Health-OnLine has reached 350 users, and has signed up the Catholic Health Association to link its 600-hospital membership.

Model 7. Virtual System

The "virtual" integrated delivery system relies on contractual linkages and business cooperation to create an integrated health system. Like the virtual company, this model owns no assets. It is a strategic alliance between health plans and providers, who align their organizations to share capitation and market management. The virtual system is the opposite of an asset-merged model. One example is the linkage between the Legacy Health System in Portland and Blue Cross/Blue Shield of Oregon. The two organizations share interlocking boards and have launched a joint managed care product with three large physician groups to compete against staff-model Kaiser and the Sisters of Providence.

Futurist Jeff Goldsmith recommends taking an alternative path to integration (Goldsmith 1994). The virtual system is based on market-specific affiliations between providers and established health insurers or HMOs. The partnership is built on shared values and vision. The principal assets are information systems and cash, not bricks and mortar. These systems can use sophisticated mechanisms for evaluating practice patterns, selecting preferred providers, and experimenting with incentives such as capitation.

Providers need to learn from network-model HMOs like PacifiCare of Fountain Valley, California, Humana of Louisville, Kentucky, and United HealthCare of Minneapolis, Minnesota, which do not own hospitals or employ physicians. These companies enter into multiyear arrangements with selected physician groups, hospitals, and health systems. Using contracts instead of capital, the health plans can move rapidly into a market, establish a provider network, and market to local employers trading upon the reputation and capacity of the providers.

The secret to successful vertical integration efforts is a true partnership. In Albuquerque, New Mexico, the St. Joseph Health System has a five-year strategic alliance with FHP, a California-based HMO. The FHP agreement uses St. Joseph facilities and doctors on an exclusive basis. A senior administrator from FHP now manages St. Joseph's hospitals. FHP is now more than 25 percent of St. Joseph's business, and growing. Creating a strategic alliance with St. Joseph has given local credibility to the out-of-state FHP plan. Both FHP and St. Joseph believe their strategic alliance is essential to compete with other local integrated systems, including the Lovelace Clinic, a staff-model clinic owned by Cigna, and Presbyterian, a statewide hub-and-spoke model with its own HMO.

Model 8. Physician Clinic

Physician-sponsored group practice "clinics," which integrate doctors, hospitals, and health plans, represent a sustainable model for tomorrow's health system. The nation's largest medical clinics are rapidly positioning themselves as integrated healthcare systems with a financing mechanism. James Unland of the Health Capital Group in Chicago believes physician-led networks will have an inside edge in future competition: "Physician-directed managed care organizations will become increasingly prevalent. . . . Physicians, particularly primary care physicians, will govern resource utilization in the future" (Unland 1994). He predicts that 70 percent of physicians will practice in groups of 10 or more by the year 2000.

The most successful clinics in the future will own an HMO. Larger clinics will own their hospitals, although enlightened physicians will view hospitals as a costly expense center to be used as a last resort. In Danville, Pennsylvania, the Geisinger Foundation operates a multispeciality group practice, a hospital, satellite ambulatory facilities, and a 160,000-member HMO. Geisinger's expansion under its nonprofit umbrella have been frustrated by opposition from the Internal Revenue Service, which has challenged Geisinger's bid to obtain 501(c)(3) status for its HMO (Burda 1994b).

Brand-name medical groups will put their labels on HMO products. Prestigious medical groups may lend their brand-name status to HMOs in return for a share in an HMO venture with insurers. Partnerships and joint ventures offer a low-risk way for big medical groups to get into managed care, with little or no capital contribution by the doctors. In Arizona, the Mayo Clinic announced a managed care partnership with national insurer John Alden Life Insurance (Miller 1995c). The partnership of Mayo Healthcare Network with John Alden in Phoenix will jointly market a new insurance product, with Mayo's 150 Scottsdale-based physicians as the provider network.

Model 9. Wellness Plan

The HMO concept is just now beginning to fulfill the implicit promise of "health maintenance." In California, the giant Kaiser health plan is now aggressively identifying high-risk enrollees for targeted health promotion. As capitation gains market acceptance, more provider networks and health plans will increase their health promotion investments. Aetna's Philip Nathanson predicts that, on a long-term basis, promoting health will lead to improved financial performance: "We know, for instance, that every dollar we spend on pediatric immunizations saves $3 in costs down the road" (McManis 1994).

Progressive health systems are investing in community health. In New York's South Bronx, the huge 1,700-unit Melrose Commons housing project is being renovated to include health centers for the resident's impoverished population. New York's Department of Health and Hospitals is now renovating its network of 25 community health clinics like the Charles R. Drew Center, a satellite center of the Queens Hospital Center.

Health education is receiving a boost in New Albany, Ohio, from the U.S. Health Corp. The town is the site of a growing model community that will promote health awareness and lifelong learning. With assistance from U.S. Health Corp., a "healthy living" curriculum will be a model for education in grades 1 through 12. Students will keep journals and computer databases of their health status. A 2,000-square-foot Wellness Center is being constructed, adjacent to a senior center, to include health education, day care, health fairs, counseling, and examination and treatment facilities. Physicians from Riverside Methodist will provide backup services.

Model 10. Mega-Network

Network organizers are thinking big, bigger, and biggest. In Kansas City, Health Midwest merged with Menorah to create a 10-hospital system with 1,800 beds (Scott 1994). Two more facilities are expected to join the system. Today, most of the region's hospitals belong to systems or networks. Mid-America Health First operates 8 hospitals, and 5 hospitals have aligned with the 464-bed University of Kansas Medical Center in the Jayhawk Alliance, a hub-and-spoke model. The pot is bubbling in this market. Columbia/HCA has acquired two hospitals in the region, and Kaiser is planning to expand its HMO enrollment there through an alliance with one of the three mega-networks.

In Arizona, a linkage between Samaritan Health System and HealthPartners of Southern Arizona would create Integra Health System, the state's largest nonprofit health system (Lutz 1996). The deal could be expanded to include Mercy Healthcare of Phoenix, forming a system with nearly 3,000 beds. Next, Samaritan is weighing the potential advantages of a strategic alliance with a for-profit partner, such as Columbia/HCA, Tenet Healthcare or OrNda. Nashville-based OrNda is the largest for-profit chain in Arizona, with six facilities, five located in Phoenix.

Another mega-network is shaping in Dallas. Texas providers always think big. This time three of the largest nonprofit systems in the region are forming strategic business relationships, aligning Baylor Health Care System, Presbyterian Healthcare System, and Methodist Hospitals of Dallas. Mega-networks may dominate smaller markets, too. Roper Hospital and Bon Secours–St. Francis Xavier, in Charleston, South Carolina, discussed a merger, ultimately uncompleted, that would have combined 41 percent of the region's hospital beds in a three-facility organization (Burda 1994a). The construction of a mega-network must overcome local rivalries, including a bitter certificate-of-need battle over which hospital would build in a growing suburban sector.

Physician organizations—not hospitals—may be the building blocks for mega-networks. The Florida Independent Physicians Association, a statewide physician contracting network with 5,000 doctors in 11 regional organizations, covers all 65 counties in Florida (Miller 1995a). Now the sprawling medical network is creating a sixty-forty joint venture with the Coastal Healthcare Group of Durham, North Carolina. Coastal Healthcare owns HMOs and manages physician groups, combining the two businesses in such ventures as Doctors Health Plan, an IPA-model HMO launched in early 1995 to cover 27 counties of North Carolina.

The deals keep coming in diverse markets across the country, as the level of managed care penetration rises. In Cleveland, a Stage 3 market with eight HMOs, the Cleveland Clinic and eight other local healthcare organizations formed the Cleveland Health Network. To cover the northeastern Ohio market, Cleveland-area providers are aligning their market strategy for joint managed care contracting. They will compete with the Meridia Health System/Blue Cross venture, which anchors a 21-hospital regional network organized by the Blues (Bader 1996).

THE MOST INTEGRATED HEALTHCARE MARKET IN AMERICA

Anyone wanting a glimpse of a post-reform market should watch Minneapolis–St. Paul. If all U.S. hospitals were located in the Twin Cities, utilization would be 20 percent lower, saving the country an estimated $12 billion annually, according to Baltimore-based HCIA, a market research firm (Melville 1994). According to the researchers, 20 percent of hospital days would be rated "clinically unwarranted" if the Minneapolis–St. Paul Market were used as the standard.

Market-driven health reform started in Minnesota. This progressive state enacted health reform in 1992, with a target date of July 1994 for implementation, since extended to 1997. The plan for MinnesotaCare would pool Medicaid patients and the uninsured, and contract for care with local provider-insurer organizations called integrated service networks. ISNs replace HMOs and insurance plans, providing comprehensive care packages defined by the state. A mandate requires all employers to contract with ISNs for their employees. Fee-for-service will be an option, but hospital and physician prices will be regulated by the state. All hospitals and physicians must belong to at least one ISN. Consumers would have a choice of networks.

Legislative support for such a radical plan is waning now, but the result has been to encourage rapid integration among Minnesota providers and insurers and HMOs. There seem to be at least monthly mergers among hospitals, doctors, and insurers and HMOs in the Twin Cities. Developments include:

HealthPartners, the largest staff-model HMO in Minneapolis–St. Paul, formerly "rented" beds from several health systems. Now the HMO has added two hospitals to its base of 500 employed physicians, one facility on each side of the metropolitan area. St. Paul–Ramsey, the former public hospital in downtown St. Paul, has affiliated with the HealthPartners system, bringing with it a 200-physician clinic. The Park Nicollet Medical Clinic and Methodist Hospital in the west metropolitan area signed a ten-year agreement with HealthPartners. HealthPartners has been contracting with the Large

Employer Initiative; it won the bid in 1992 to provide comprehensive healthcare to 150,000 enrollees from the biggest companies in the Twin Cities, but that contract expored in 1996.

Blue Cross/Blue Shield of Minnesota is building a provider network through acquisitions and exclusive contracts. In 1994, Blue Cross completed the acquisition of the Aspen Medical Group, a 100-physician group practice with an excellent record in managed care. More physician practices are likely to be acquired. To provide hospital services, Blue Cross is contracting with the University of Minnesota hospital, allaying fears that the university might be excluded from integrated service network participation.

HealthSpan, a multihospital organization created in 1992 by the merger of the HealthOne and LifeSpan systems, is moving to reposition itself as an ISN serving the entire Twin Cities metropolitan region. HealthSpan is acquiring physicians and groups to solidify its physician base and has merged with Medica, the second-largest HMO in the area. Medica is a subsidiary of United HealthCare, one of the nation's largest HMOs. The new company, Allina, has coexecutives to oversee its managed care and delivery network divisions.

HealthEast, a system that once boasted nine acute hospitals in St. Paul, is moving strategically to create a fully integrated model that brings together the "above-the-line" insurer-HMO functions of marketing and finance with the "below-the-line" provider-delivered activities of patient care, quality assurance, and utilization management. HealthEast conducted an intensive "Constitutional Convention" planning process with key physicians and trustees. The result is a multitrack model with options for physician affiliation and ownership, potentially including a new for-profit holding company with equity shared by physicians. HealthEast is committed to a physician-friendly strategy of fifty-fifty sharing of governance and capital investment with doctors. The new model is driving reductions in hospitals and beds. In 1994, HealthEast cut back to three facilities. The system announced the closure of Divine Redeemer Hospital, converting the facility to long-term care, and adding an ambulatory care center. In mid-1996, HealthEast announced plans to close Midway Hospital and open a small, 70-bed facility in the suburbs for better geographic distribution.

Fairview Health System, with six hospitals in the west metropolitan area of Minneapolis and suburbs has been building a primary care network through acquisitions and affiliations with doctors across its local market. Fairview CEO Rick Norling comes from California and has strong managed care experience. Fairview created a closed-panel physician-hospital organization that demanded exclusivity. Fairview doctors joining the PHO were prohibited from also affiliating with the physician network of Fairview rival HealthSpan. Fairview has been in discussions to strengthen its future with an alliance with Blue Cross and has negotiated a merger with the university that will stabilize the future of the medical school.

HealthEast and *Fairview* with *North Memorial*, the last independent hospital in the Twin Cities, together held the small employer coalition contract for three years to serve 200,000 enrollees of small and midsized employers. Prudential was the insurance partner but decided to exit the competitive Twin Cities market at the end of the contract. That opened the door to Medica, the regions's second-largest HMO and newly merged with HealthSpan to form Allina, to win a five-year contract with the Minnesota Employers Association. Medica won another employer contract by offering Minnesota state employees a whopping 25 percent price reduction (Sardinha 1995). Now each has organized a local care system to participate in the direct contracting program with the large-employer coalition, beginning January 1997.

Rural Minnesota may also be a bellwether market for managed care trends in nonmetropolitan areas. Minnesota's Blue Cross/Blue Shield plan is moving rapidly to dominate out-of-state markets, with a series of provider partnerships around the state (Cochrane 1993). In Southwestern Minnesota, the plan negotiated an arrangement with Affiliated Medical Center, a large rural group practice. A profile of Blue Cross data showed the doctors to have good cost profiles and lengths of hospital stay. Although the group had little managed care experience, it agreed to cover 14 counties in southwestern Minnesota. Blue Cross will provide the information system and administrative support to the physicians. The Dakota Clinic, a 160-physician group in Fargo, North Dakota, will cover the northwest portion of Minnesota. The Minnesota Blues plan is positioning itself for certification as a statewide ISN.

STAGE 6 MEANS HOSPITALS SHOULD PREPARE FOR 0.8 BEDS PER 1,000

As the nation moves through Stage 3 and higher up the scale of healthcare transformation, many hospital boards and medical staffs still struggle with the effects of managed care and locally driven reform. The central purpose of tomorrow's healthcare organizations is to provide comprehensive health services to an enrolled population. Keeping hospital beds full is based on the old paradigm of fee-for-service reimbursement. Keeping enrollees healthy and out of the hospital is the new paradigm, which will propel the business, clinical, social, and moral mission of the healthcare organization in the future. Richard McCann, chair of the board of the Northeast Ohio Community Health Plan, advises: "The goal is not to fill the hospitals; it's to gain managed care business" (Bader 1996, 19).

From 1950 through 1980, the widely applied planning formula was "4 beds per 1,000." Government programs like Hill-Burton subsidized hospital construction across the country, using such bed-based formulas to grant millions of dollars in loans and guarantees, which led in time to the current surpluses of hospital beds. Compare that formula today with the performance of Mullikin Medical Centers of Long Beach, California, which manages more than 300,000 HMO enrollees with an effective bed demand of 0.8 to 1.0 beds per 1,000. Most healthcare markets in the United States are substantially overbedded, with between 3.0 and 4.0 beds per 1,000 population. The California Healthcare Association's environmental forecast for 2000 to 2005 assumes that hospital bed demand could fall to as low as 0.6 to 0.8 beds per 1,000 in the twenty-first century (Coile and Menkin 1996).

There is evidence that the declining demand for inpatient care could bottom out at some level. HCIA, a healthcare research company, found that hospital stays rose slightly in 1995, to 5.1 average days, up from 5.0 days in 1994 (Anders 1996). HCIA analysts speculated that so many lower-intensity cases had been switched to ambulatory settings, that higher-acuity patients were driving up stays. Even with a stabilizing of length of stay, however, the problem of excess hospital capacity remains extreme. A downsizing of the hospital system is the inevitable next step in the transformation to a managed care marketplace.

LESSONS FROM OTHER INDUSTRIES FOR A VIEW OF THE FUTURE

Hospitals and physicians seldom look to other industries for inspiration in developing new models. This insulated attitude could be a mistake. For example, the U.S. industry's experience with reengineering the corporation has lessons for hospitals. Futurists Ian Morrison and Greg Schmid, the authors of *Future Tense*, caution that adopting the reengineering approach in the health industry could be shortsighted. In other industries, downsizing has undermined consumer confidence and worker loyalty. Companies that leveraged core competencies by contracting out key functions weakened their ability to develop new products and services (Morrison and Schmid 1994).

Morrison and Schmid do criticize healthcare's "fractured" system of paying for care on an episodic basis. They predict that new organizations such as the Friendly Hills Health Care Network in southern California, with 200 primary care physicians and specialists and its own hospital, will be the integrating force that reinvents healthcare delivery. The Friendly Hills network is one of the most efficient capitation managers in the West, with utilization rates barely one-third of national averages. Recently acquired by Caremark, since merged with MedPartners/Mullikin of Birmingham, Alabama, the Friendly Hills network will now have the backing of a well-capitalized for-profit company for growth and expansion.

Stanford University Hospital has engaged in a four-year reengineering program. In the process, Stanford looked at similarities between healthcare and airlines and banking (Sherer 1994). Stanford was searching for lessons from the experiences of these sectors. The airlines, for example, have been seeking solutions to the problems of overcapacity and variable demand. What can hospitals learn from Southwest Airlines' strategy of eliminating seat assignments and turning around their planes in less than 20 minutes at the gate? Business has a substantial experience in strategic alliances—the network strategy.

LOOKING FORWARD: THE PAST IS HISTORY. THE FUTURE IS NOW.

The era of a "kinder, gentler world," in healthcare is over. Now! Hospital administrators and physicians who believe they can pursue "transitional strategies" of maximizing revenues are doomed to failure. Halfway measures that hope to protect a freestanding, fee-for-service, go-it-alone world will not work in an integrated marketplace. Organizations that persist in clinging to the past are about to become history themselves, replaced with a new wave of healthcare and physician executives who will welcome capitation, and who will close hospitals without tears or a backward glance.

The new world of capitation and reform awaits:

- Healthcare delivery will be converted from a "retail" market to "wholesale" transactions for hundreds of thousands of enrollees.
- Price wars between HMOs, insurers, and self-insured provider networks will shake-out smaller health insurers.
- Competition will drive the prices of health plans down to 3 to 5 percent annual increases.
- Providers will contract with a few, very large healthcare purchasers.
- Many health plans will acquire their own primary care physicians and use them as gatekeepers to hospital and specialty services.
- Hospitals and doctors will join one of three or four regional provider networks on an exclusive basis.
- Academic medical centers will become "niche" providers of a limited range of high-tech services.

- Demand for hospital beds will shrink by 15 to 25 percent in the next three to five years.
- Most—95 percent—of the 650,000 active physicians in the United States will join group practices or managed care networks within five years.

This is not the beginning of the end. It is the start of *twenty-first century healthcare*, a whole new era in providing community-based healthcare with a formula that emphasizes capitation, clinical protocols, ambulatory care, noninvasive surgery, and substantial reliance on nonhospital alternative settings such as subacute and home care. Healthcare can learn a lesson from other U.S. companies seeking to reinvent themselves: (1) create vision and leadership; (2) put customer needs first; and (3) move quickly to implement new strategies. Every day spent in waiting to confirm trends before taking a new direction is going to be very costly.

STRATEGIES FOR PROVIDERS, HMOS, AND SUPPLIERS

All major players in the healthcare market—providers, HMOs, and suppliers—should heed this advice:

Consolidation

Everywhere, it seems, there are announcements of the formation of networks, joint ventures, and regional and statewide integrated delivery networks. This game of musical chairs may not have enough seats for all participants. Those who consolidate now can make their market and assure their future.

Timing

The time is *now* for America's hospitals, physicians, health systems, and healthcare suppliers to combine to form new and innovative delivery systems. The players must not fall victim to the "paralysis of analysis," deferring choices while others make the first moves. The best partnerships will be the combinations of "strong plus strong" organizations that recognize their mutual need and the advantages of alignment.

Bias for Action

This is the ground floor of twenty-first century healthcare. Providers, HMOs, and suppliers: wait no longer. The window of opportunity is closing, and the time for change is dawning. the American sixth stage of U.S. healthcare market evolution will be here by the millennium.

SOURCES

Anders, G. "Hospitals' Push to Shorten Patient Stays May Have Hit Its Limit, Study Suggests." *Wall Street Journal*, 2 May 1996, p. B6.

Bader, B. 1996. "The 'Grand Experiment': The Meridia Health System/Blue Cross Venture." *Health System Leader* 3 (1): 19–27.

Bergman, R. 1994. "Health Care in a Wired World." *Hospitals & Health Networks* 68 (16): 28–36.

Burda, D. 1994a. "Former Charleston, S.C. Rivals Open Dialogue on Affiliation." *Modern Healthcare* 24 (32): 62–64.

———. 1994b. "Geisinger Ruling May Mean Fewer Tax Exemptions." *Modern Healthcare* 24 (32): 40, 58.

Cochrane, J. 1993. "The Ultimate Model for Integrated Healthcare?" *Integrated Healthcare Report* 2 (10): 8–11.

Coile, R., and H. L. Menkin. 1996. *A View of the Future: Competition, Capitation, Consolidation and Cooperation*. Sacramento, CA: California Healthcare Association.

Freudenheim, M. "Health Industry Is Changing Itself Ahead of Reform," *New York Times*, 27 June 1994, pp. A1, C4.

Goldsmith, J. C. 1994. "The Illusive Logic of Integration." *Healthcare Forum Journal* 37 (5): 26–31.

Greenberg, D. S. "Health Reform Is Happening Anyway." *Baltimore Sun*, 23 October 1994, p. B1.

Group Health Cooperative. 1993. "HMO Employer Data and Information: A Special Report Measuring Utilization, Quality and Value at Group Health Cooperative." Seattle, WA. September; cited in *Capitation I: The New the American Medicine*. 1994. Washington, DC: The Governance Committee, Advisory Board.

Hamer, R. 1996. "HMO Industry Report." *InterStudy Competitive Edge* 6 (1): 1–136.

Henderson, J. A. 1995. "Life After Reform: Health Providers and Suppliers Readjust in 1995." *SMG Market Letter* 9 (1): 1–8.

———. 1996. "Aligned Missions of MCOs and IHNs Spark Alliances." *SMG Market Letter* 10 (5): 1–2.

Lafuente, D. 1994. "California Health Network Recruits Three New Systems." *Modern Healthcare* 24 (21): 8.

Lumsdon, K., and M. Haglund. 1994. "For-Profits: The Right Medicine for Some Markets?" *Hospitals & Health Networks* 68 (12): 34–42.

Lutz, S. 1994. "Groups Form Desktop Health Networks." *Modern Healthcare* 24 (32): 66-70.

———. 1996. "Arizona Mega-System Weighs Partners." *Modern Healthcare* 26 (29): 10.

Lutz, S., and E. P. Gee. 1995. *The For-Profit Healthcare Revolution: The Growing Impact of Investor-Owned Health Systems in America*. Chicago: Irwin Professional Publishing.

———. 1998. Columbia/HCA: Healthcare on Overdrive. New York: McGraw Hill.

McManis, G. 1994. "The New Delivery and Financing Realities." *Hospitals & Health Networks* 68 (16): 38–42.

Melville, B. 1994. "Copying Minneapolis–St. Paul Hospitals Could Save $12B a Year." *Health Care Competition Week* 11 (2): 1–2.

Miller, J. 1995a. "Coastal's North Carolina HMO Starts Up and Florida IPA Joint Venture Is Launched." *Integrated Healthcare Report* 4 (1): 15.

———. 1995b. "Integrated Healthcare Information Systems." *Integrated Healthcare Report* 4 (1): 1–11.

———. 1995c. "May Enters into Arizona Joint Venture with John Alden." *Integrated Healthcare Report* 3 (1): 15.

Morrison, I., and G. Schmid. 1994. *Future Tense: The Business Realities of the Next Ten Years.* New York: William Morrow and Co.

Myerson, A. R. 1997. "The Battle for Hearts and Tonsils: Hospitals Specialize to Enhance Profits." New York Times. Oct. 7, pp. C1, C4.

New York Times. "State Officials Strive to Bring the Health Care Debate Home." 25 September 1994, p. 13.

Olmos, D. R. "Appetite for Expansion: The Changing Healthcare Industry." *Los Angeles Times,* 21 February 1995, pp. D1, D3.

Rovner, J. 1996. "Should Providers Run Their Own HMOs?" *Health System Leader* 3 (1): 4–11.

Sandrick, K. 1994. "Washington, DC: The Capital's a Company Town, But the Company's Not Quite There Yet." *Hospitals & Health Networks* 68 (12): 60–64.

Sardinha, C. 1995. "Price Cuts Help Medica Win Market Share and Improve Risk Selection." *Managed Care Outlook* 8 (2): 1–2.

Scott, L. 1994. "Affiliation Boom, Battle for County Hit K.C." *Modern Healthcare* 24 (32): 138–44.

Sherer, J. 1994. "Strategy by Analogy." *Hospitals & Health Networks* 68 (12): 58–59.

Unland, J. J. 1994. "Hospital-Physician Relationships in the Managed Care Environment." *Journal of Medical Practice Management* 10 (1): 6–10.

CHAPTER

16

Managed Care: The Next Generation

Michael A. Sachs

INTRODUCTION

The future is now. Those searching for the healthcare delivery model of tomorrow need look no further than the innovative Twin Cities' Buyers Health Care Action Group or the Community Health Purchasing Corporation of Iowa. Under these models, the *consumers* directly choose a system of care to meet their needs.

Today's economic model of managed care—the HMO—will mature into the organizer of care with no medical management responsibility. Its counterpart, the medical care delivery model, will evolve into the primary care deliverer with total medical management responsibility. In both cases, consumer preferences have cast the mold that will shape each model and its modified mission.

Managed care as we know it will evolve into a mechanism for providing access to care systems that will self-organize around distinct competencies, geographies, or patient groups. The historic role of managed care, buying on behalf of employees in an attempt to control costs, will be replaced by a competitive market model where *focused care* systems will compete against each other for increasingly sophisticated purchasers or consumers.

Managed care advocates will contend that the focused care model won't work, because no one will be managing medical care or monitoring the use

Reprinted from *Frontiers of Health Services Management* 14 (1): 3–26.
Chicago: Health Administration Press.

of services. To the contrary, focused care systems, reacting to market pressure, will provide the least costly care to meet the needs of customer groups.

Given recent research showing that HMOs do not deliver on the wellness promise (HMO patient health status is not affected more positively than the health status of people covered by other types of insurance) and the high cost of their operations, it is clear that this managed care model is out of line with today's market realities.

MANAGED CARE DEFINED

A discussion of managed care logically begins with a common definition. However, the definition of managed care suffers from a severe case of "source effect," where the source point of view skews the meaning. Here are a few examples of differently shaded managed care definitions:

> ". . . systems or techniques generally used by third-party payers expressly to provide what they consider an appropriate mix of medical and social services at the lowest cost to payers and patients."
>
> —American Medical Association

> ". . . systems that integrate the financing and delivery of appropriate healthcare services to covered individuals. . . "
>
> —Health Insurance Association of America

> ". . . a variety of interventions of health-care delivery and financing intended to eliminate unnecessary and inappropriate care and to reduce cost."
>
> —Congressional Budget Office

> ". . . an organized system of medical care that integrates financing and delivery of appropriate health care and organizes care around the consumer, that provides seamless continuity of health care services."
>
> —American Managed Care and Review Association

Whichever definition you accept, there are two common threads woven throughout: appropriate healthcare and cost containment. The underlying reason for these recurring themes can be traced to the genesis of health insurance itself: the desire of employers to provide employees with a tax-advantaged benefit—healthcare. It is in the employer's best interest to have healthy employees and to achieve that health for the lowest reasonable cost. The employer must find a cost that does not compromise the quality of care and, in turn, employee satisfaction with the benefit.

THE MANAGED CARE CONTINUUM

How did managed care come into being? What prompted corporations and consumers to seek alternative means of coverage and care? For the answer, we must turn back the pages of history.

Prepaid medical care took root in 1938, when Dr. Sidney Garfield formed the first prepaid medical group to care for Kaiser Steel shipyard workers. The agreement was simple: Take care of our employees, and we'll pay you a flat amount in advance. The prepay proposal was designed to shift the emphasis from treating sickness to promoting wellness.

An outgrowth of this wellness perspective was the introduction of a multiphasic screening process, a battery of tests for enrollees designed for early detection of illness. The protocol covered an extensive blood panel, respiratory assessment, and epidemiology work up.

Serendipitously, Kaiser physicians noted a remarkable side benefit to the medical group approach. Working in such close proximity, doctors found they exchanged information more readily about treatment protocols and approaches and that this information exchange was reducing the cost of healthcare delivery. This phenomena still holds true for multispecialty group practices, which consistently record lower utilization rates.

During World War II, the concept of health insurance first developed. Instead of providing employees with benefits such as meals or cars, employers sought an alternative that was tax deductible to the firm and tax free to the recipient. The answer: health insurance.

Under the private pay system, patients paid for medical care with after-tax dollars. Under the employee benefit system, health insurance costs are paid by the company, on behalf of the employee, with pre-tax dollars. To this day, healthcare insurance remains the only benefit of such magnitude that enjoys tax-free status.

Through time, health insurance began to evolve, adapting to the demands of employers and their representatives. One of the most dramatic developments was the emergence of "first dollar coverage" in the 1970s. A perquisite first proposed by the auto workers' union, "first dollar coverage" theory posits that worker health expenses should be covered from the first expense, or the "first dollar," with no deductible and no coinsurance.

This was a creative response to the restrictive wage and price controls imposed during the Nixon administration. In lieu of raising wages, employers would wrap themselves in the cloak of benevolence, granting an allegedly equivalent—albeit less costly—benefit instead.

As a result of this paternalistic system, the end user of healthcare became disaffected. Rarely seeing a bill for physician, diagnostic, or treatment services, consumers moved further away from the source, and utilization skyrocketed. Further contributing to the escalation was the pay-for-service arrangement that provided incentives for physicians to conduct expensive tests and adopt costly technologies even if for marginal clinical benefit.

Other factors escalating healthcare expenditures included an aging population that required more care; an aversion to nontraditional, lower-cost therapies; high-tech breakthroughs with demonstrable diagnostic and treatment benefits such as renal dialysis, open heart surgery, magnetic resonance imaging, and CT scans; and a seemingly endless flow of funds from Medicare, Medicaid, and private insurers.

In 1973, the federal government passed the Health Maintenance Organization Act, which mandated that any company with 25 or more employees must offer a health maintenance option to employees. Initially, the HMOs were more expensive than traditional insurance, with the exception of union plans, because they covered more services because of federal statute and as a result were costlier.

CHANGE IS AFOOT

In 1982, alarmed by rampant healthcare inflation, the federal government made a bold move to curtail medical spending in the Medicare program. It converted from a cost-plus payment system to a flat payment-per-admission program.

While federal programs were attempting to decelerate payments, the engine of cost/payment was still in high gear. Hospitals responded to the public sector's limits by off-loading costs to private sector sources in the form of rate increases. As a result, a type of cross-subsidy developed, with corporate America essentially underwriting the perceived federal underpayments.

Around 1988, big business was fed up with big premiums and double-digit increases. Foreign competition in virtually every sector of the economy had forced belt-tightening to an anorexic level, and one of the last bastions of free spending—health insurance—was now fair game. Managed care providers were waiting in the wings.

Managed care companies successfully negotiated payments with physicians, hospitals, and associated providers, reducing the public/private payment gap. By the early 1990s, hospitals had begun to reduce absolute operating costs to the point that Medicare and Medicaid once again became the better payor.

According to a study by Foster Higgins (1996), the first reduction in healthcare costs to employers in decades was realized in 1994, when the average cost per employee dropped by 1.1 percent.

CLASH OF THE TITANS

Achieving this modest cost reduction came at the expense of tremendous emotional angst, when entrenched institutions and professions were forced to abandon legacy philosophies and balance cost of care with quality of care. Traditional healthcare systems operated under a mandate of "if you build it, they will come," leading to an oversupply of hospitals, beds, medical specialists, and expensive equipment.

To the managed care contingent, the solution was obvious. The total cost of care was a function of two factors: the units of care purchased and the price per unit. Managed care began its drive toward efficiency by focusing first on the price per unit, then shifting attention to volume considerations.

ECONOMIC MODEL CHARACTERISTICS

In response to employer demands for a solution to ever-increasing healthcare costs, economic model plans emerged to fulfill a broad charter:

- educate patients about wellness and cost issues;
- monitor quality of care through physician profiling and outcomes tracking;
- control units of care through medical management;
- reduce costs by leveraging the power of their large insured pool to negotiate optimal rates; and
- minimize employer costs and administrative paperwork.

Many economic model plans are for-profit enterprises, with an implicit overriding directive to maximize their return to shareholders. Participating physicians act as gatekeepers, providing care according to plan protocols, with incentives to minimize unnecessary testing and specialist referrals. Primary care physicians are either plan employees or contracted providers paid on a fee-for-service or a capitated basis.

Examples of this model include United Healthcare, Aetna–U.S. Healthcare, and Oxford Health Plan.

Critics of the economically driven care model hold the belief that good care and good profits are mutually exclusive objectives, and, when in conflict, quality of care suffers. Others contend that, in a free-market system, the exercise of consumer choice will resolve this dilemma. In "The Soul of an HMO," (1996) *Time* magazine stated:

> No one disputes that managed care has at last put the brakes on medical spending, or that it has proved an effective vehicle for rationing health care. . . . At issue, rather, are the costs of the process itself—the effort and delay inherent in acquiring care and the extent to which considerations other than mere health are brought to bear by corporate managers. . . .

As Table 16.1 indicates, the perception of managed care companies as efficient operators diverges from the reality of operating statistics, most notably, the medical-loss and administrative cost ratios. Economic model

Table 16.1 Medical-Loss and Administrative Cost Ratios

Measure	Kaiser FY 1996	Aetna–U.S. Healthcare (1st Quarter 1997)	United Healthcare FY 1996	Humana FY 1996	PacifiCare FY 1996	Foundation Health (1st Quarter 1997)	Oxford Health Plan FY 1996
Enrollment (Millions)	7.5	10.8	5.0	4.8	4.0	3.2	1.7
Medical-loss Ratio	96.5%	82.6%	84.6%	84.2%	83.5%	82.8%	80.1%
Administrative Cost Ratio	3.0%	11.8%	11.9%	14.1%	12.4%	13.2%	15.7%
Operating Revenue		$2,409	$9,899	$6,687	$4,637	$1,861	$3,033
Medical Costs		$1,973	$7,180	$5,625	$3,873	$1,176	$2,421
Premium Revenue		$2,388	$8,490	$6,677	$4,637	$1,420	$3,022
S G & A		$284	$2,165	$940	$575	$425	$477

Source: Company Reports, Sachs Group Analysis

plans, founded on the principle of improved operating efficiencies, can in fact prove more costly to administer than medical care delivery models.

Weighing in for the medical care delivery model side is the California Kaiser network, which, in keeping with its mission of promoting enrollee wellness, applies fully 96.5 percent of funds to patient care, with a miserly 3.0 percent directed toward administrative overhead. Compared with economically driven managed care groups, Kaiser assigns anywhere from 11.9 percent to 16.4 percent more of each dollar to direct patient care.

The commensurate administrative cost ratio comparison is even more dramatic: Kaiser is the only plan even in single digits. All economically driven managed care groups spend at least three-and-a-half times that amount, from Aetna–U.S. Healthcare on the low end with an 11.8 percent administrative cost ratio, to Oxford Health Plan on the high end, with 15.7 percent of each dollar covering administrative expenses.

MEDICAL CARE DELIVERY MODEL CHARACTERISTICS

The sibling to the economic model is the medical care delivery model. As its name implies, the management directive for the medical care delivery model falls squarely in the court of quality care first. Physicians and providers band together for contracting purposes and, like all HMOs, hire a medical director. In addition, the HMO handles payor contract negotiations and administrative, utilization, and outcome review functions. The prepaid nature of this plan focuses attention on participant wellness.

Medical care delivery model imperatives include:

- educating patients about wellness;
- encouraging prophylactic treatment and predictive testing;
- controlling units of care by migrating best practices;
- reducing employer costs through improved patient health; and
- maximizing employee satisfaction with healthcare services.

Examples of this model include the Permanente Medical Group, Group Health of Puget Sound, and Health Alliance Plan of Detroit.

THE PLAYING FIELD EXPANDS

One of the unique features of both models is the number of players who actively participate in the system. There are patients, providers, purchasers, payors, regulators, and media, all jockeying for position and attempting to contribute to the managed care agenda.

The action takes place on a very broad playing field. In the past two decades, managed care programs have had a significant impact on the American economy and way of health. By 1996, healthcare represented 14 percent of the nation's gross domestic product. At last count, there were 630 HMOs in 1996 serving a combined user base of more than 59 million enrollees (Cochrane 1997).

Approximately 160 million Americans receive coverage from their employers, and 120 million are in a managed care setting. Fully three out of four physicians in the United States have at least one managed care contract. Healthcare has matured into a major industry, with an emphasis on business (Schear 1995). Like any good business, it continuously recalibrates products and services in response to consumer preferences.

EMPOWERED CONSUMERS EMERGE

Consumers are beginning to flex their market muscle, acting on their collective knowledge of managed care acquired through experience.[1] In general, consumers opt for lower deductibles and fixed copayments when choosing an HMO over a traditional indemnity offering or preferred provider organization (PPO) product. They accept the trade-off between open access to care for the lower cost-sharing approach of HMOs.

Table 16.2 traces the different factors driving HMO selection versus traditional insurance and PPO products across three managed care product life cycle stages.

The Market Evolution Model, originally developed by the University Health System Consortium, describes market consolidation as managed care participation increases. Stage 1 markets are fragmented traditional markets with little HMO activity.

Stage 2 market characteristics include a loose, fragmented market with a growing managed care presence. Consumers at this managed care life cycle stage select an HMO over traditional indemnity offerings and PPO products for economic reasons, such as cost sharing and premiums, and convenience reasons, such as geographic access.

Table 16.2 Why Consumers Choose HMOs over Other Producers

Health Coverage	Stage 2	Stage 3	Stage 4
Traditional Products	1. Cost sharing 2. Network access	1. Cost Sharing 2. Network access	1. Cost Sharing 2. Network access 3. Plan benefits/services
PPO Products	1. Premiums/ network access 2. Cost sharing	1. Cost sharing 2. Network access 3. Plan benefits/ services 4. Premiums	1. Cost sharing 2. Network access

Source: Sachs/Scarborough HealthPlus™, 1996, Satisfaction Predictor Index.

Stage 3 market characteristics include the beginnings of plan consolidation, tightening utilization, increased competition between plans, and the beginning signs of market maturity. Consumers at this managed care life cycle stage select an HMO over traditional indemnity offerings again for cost and convenience reasons, but, as consumers begin to acquire system operations knowledge, plan benefits and services join the list of driving selection factors.

Stage 4 market characteristics include a tight market with fewer players, a high degree of competition and continued strict utilization control. Consumers at this point select an HMO over traditional indemnity offerings and PPO products for cost and geographic access reasons.

In terms of emphasis, consumers place equal weight on cost-sharing at every stage, underscoring their value consciousness. As plan competition intensifies, consumers become less loyal and more savvy, assigning greater importance to provider location and brand identity. Finally, as markets mature and HMO product points of difference diminish, coverage is viewed as a commodity. Thus, premiums and benefits reach parity, and cost-sharing dominates the mix of decision criteria.

WHAT INFLUENCES CONSUMER HMO CHOICE?

For another perspective on consumer selection, Figure 16.1 indicates the relative position for the top 20 individual selection influencers at the Stage 2 managed care product life cycle. Indexed component importance is indicated by factor position on the vertical axis; the horizontal axis reflects the percentage of people selecting based on the specific component.

In Stage 2, the most important selection factors are the location of hospitals and doctor's offices, whether there are deductibles, the cost of premiums, who is their doctor, simplicity of paperwork, and prescription coverage. Least important are experience with the plan and plan reputation.

In Stage 3 markets, indicated in Figure 16.2, the most notable change from Stage 2 markets is that fewer respondents rated the variable "MD in plan" as being more important. Among families with children, pediatric coverage stood out as the single most important factor.

Choice components moving into the upper left quadrant —more important × less people—of Stage 3 markets include "Customer service," "Clear benefit description," "MD reputations," and "Panel of MDs available." As consumers acquire more experience with and information about managed care alternatives, they also become more discriminating in the selection process. Typical demands focus on improved process issues and medical care.

Figure 16.1 HMO Selection Factors—Stage 2 Markets

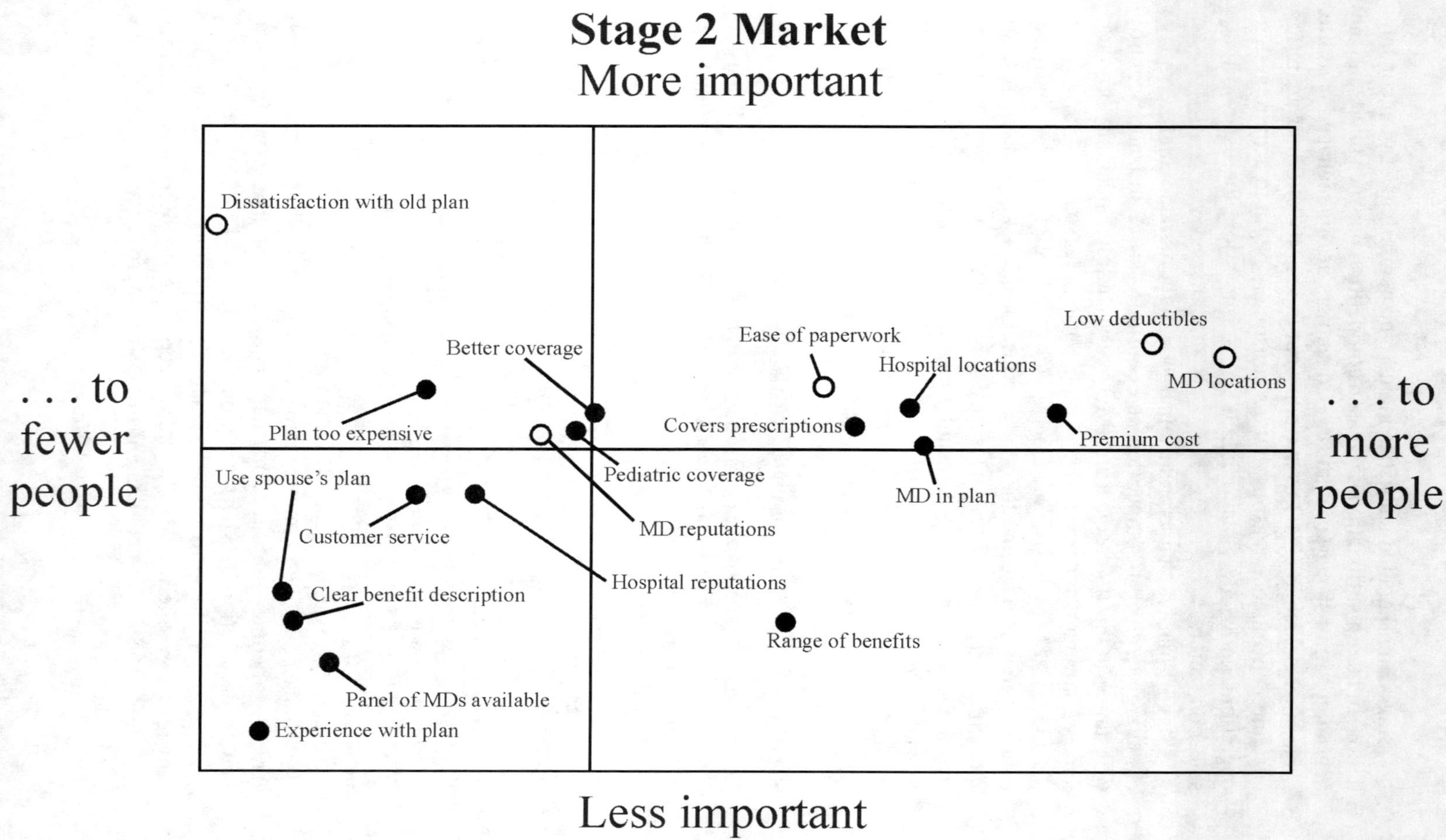

Source: Sachs/Scarborough HealthPlus™, 1996, Stage 2 market; includes members of commercial HMOs who selected among plan types.

Figure 16.2 HMO Selection Factors—Stage 3 Markets

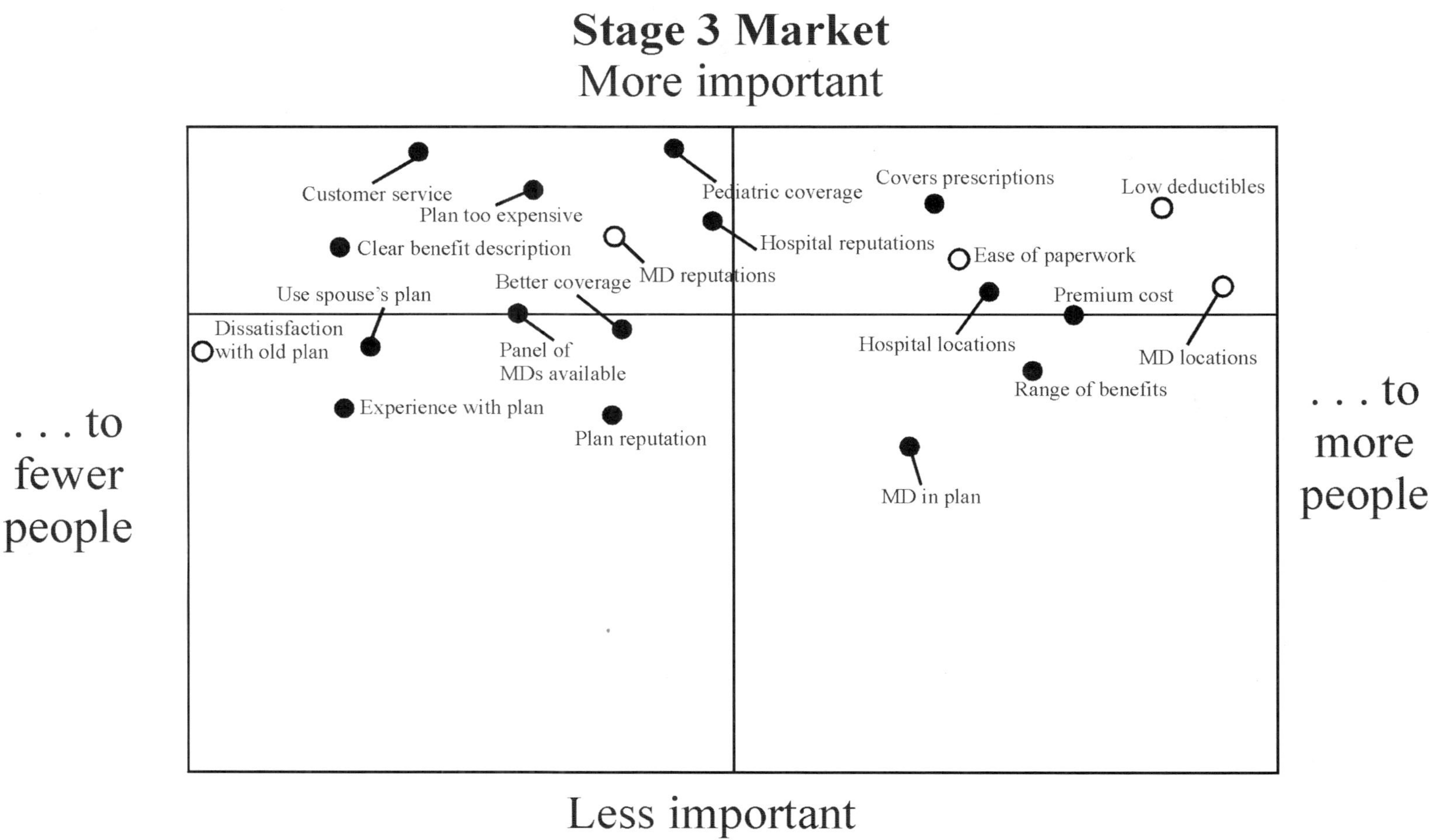

Source: Sachs/Scarborough HealthPlus™, 1996, Stage 3 market; includes members of commercial HMOs who selected among plan types.

In Stage 4 markets, analyzed in Figure 16.3, it becomes abundantly clear that consumers willingly relinquish ties to a single physician, if the institutional brand delivers on its care promise. The array of choice components occupying the upper right hand quadrant—more important × more people—suggests that consumers want it all, and, by Stage 4, believe they can get it.

The desired package includes a plan with a low premium and low deductibles, simple paperwork, convenient delivery locations, and comprehensive benefits including outstanding pediatric services and prescription coverage. It is the three Cs in action—cost, convenience, and coverage.

THE CONSUMER LEARNING CURVE

Consumer packaged goods manufacturers operate on the "smart consumer" principle. Their assumption is that consumers learn from experience and share those experiences with friends. Their conclusion is that the route to loyal, repeat business is paved with solid product values backed by responsive customer service. Anything less, and word of mouth will bury them.

The same theory applies to the managed care marketplace. To illustrate, we begin with a review of HMO penetration by market stage. Figure 16.4 shows the progression from Stage 2 through Stage 4 markets with respective penetration numbers.

Stage 2 markets—with a 36.2 percent market penetration—concentrate on increasing marketshare by acquiring indemnity lives. Stage 3 markets exhibit the first signs of consolidation, as plans become more competitive, utilization tightens, and sophisticated, dominant HMOs emerge. Market penetration increases to 41.9 percent. Stage 4 markets represent free-market arenas characterized by intense competition. A handful of HMO plans dominate the market and mete out care within a tightly managed structure.

At the same time, as the HMO marketplace has moved along the product life cycle continuum, consumers have traveled a parallel path along the managed care learning curve. Over time, consumers in Stage 4 markets register increased satisfaction with the administrative aspects of managed care such as quality of member services, quick claims handling, information available about plan eligibility and care costs, and the time spent on paperwork.

Now, for the bad news, which tolls the first death knell for managed care plans as we know them today: Experienced Stage 4 consumers indicate increasing levels of dissatisfaction with the medical side of managed care, as shown in Figures 16.5 and 16.6. Complaints include emergency care, outcome satisfaction, physician quality, and treatment thoroughness.

Supporting that point and continuing the general dissatisfaction trend, Stage 4 consumers report high levels of dissatisfaction with network efficiency, which encompassed problems with delays in receiving care, prob-

Figure 16.3 HMO Selection Factors—Stage 4 Markets

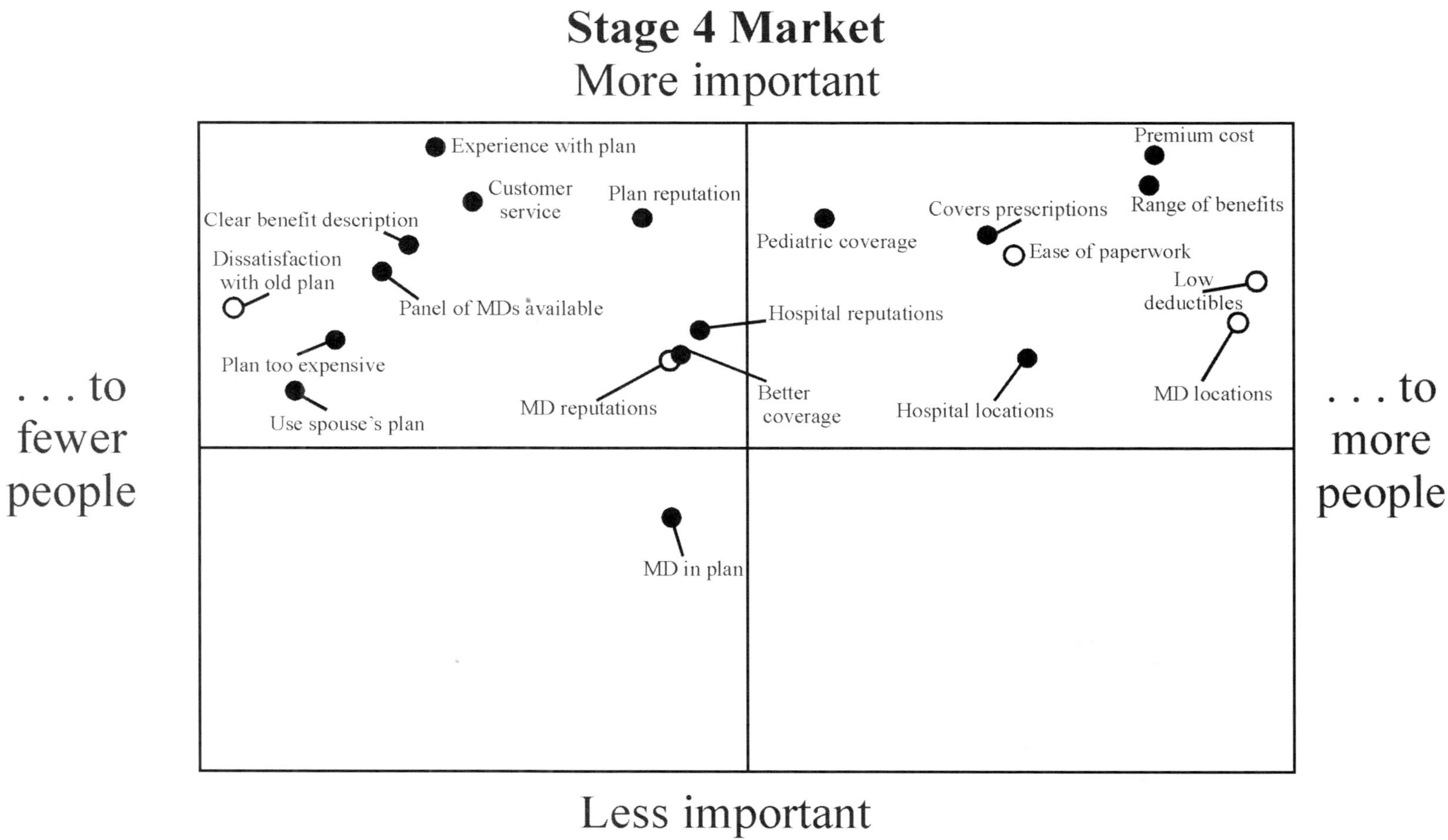

Source: Sachs/Scarborough HealthPlus™, 1996, Stage 4 market; includes members of commercial HMOs who selected among plan types.

Figure 16.4 HMO Penetration by Market Stage

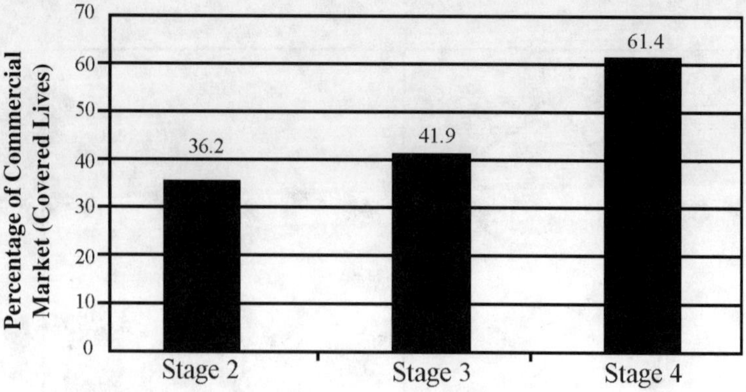

Source: Sachs/Scarborough HealthPlus™ and University Health System Consortium.

Figure 16.5 Satisfaction with Plan Services Increases as Markets Mature

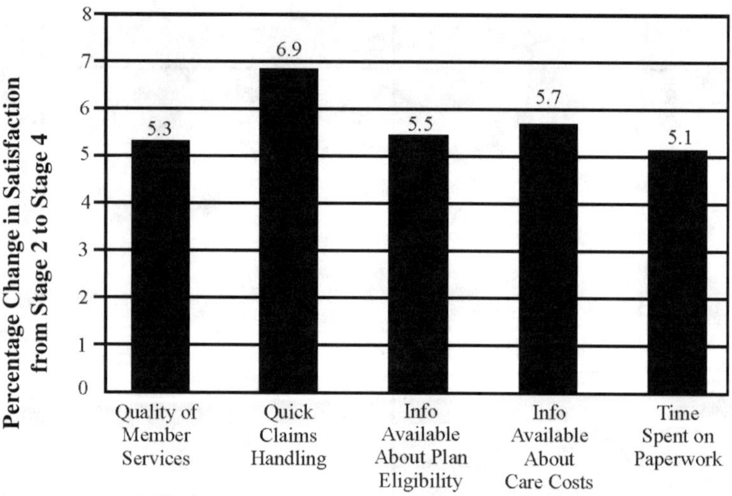

Note: This analysis is of under-65 HMO consumers only.
Source: Sachs/Scarborough HealthPlus™, 1996, Multimarket

lems receiving the necessary care once approved, and problems obtaining a specialist referral—as shown in Figure 16.7. Although specific vocabulary may differ, consumers in mature markets understand that care is being rationed in a sense, and they are becoming incensed about the waits and the roadblocks.

It comes as no surprise, then, that the likelihood of renewing coverage received abysmal scores (–2) in Stage 4 markets (see Figure 16.8).

Figure 16.6 Satisfaction with Medical Care Decreases as Markets Mature

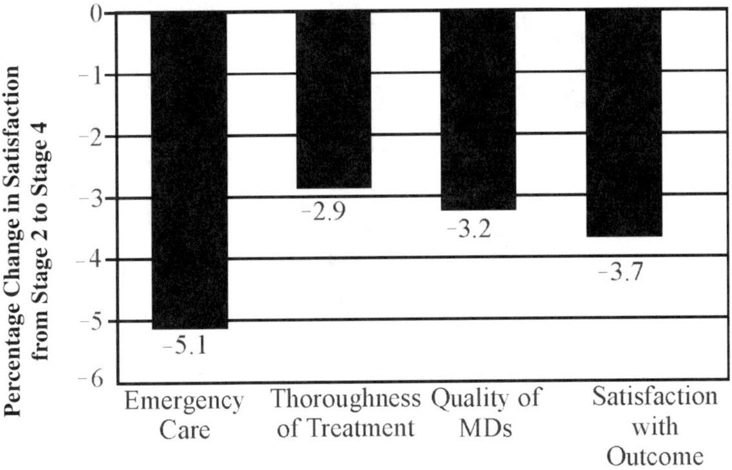

Note: This analysis is of under-65 HMO consumers only.
Source: Sachs/Scarborough HealthPlus™, 1996, Multimarket.

Figure 16.7 Medical Management Issues in Maturing Markets

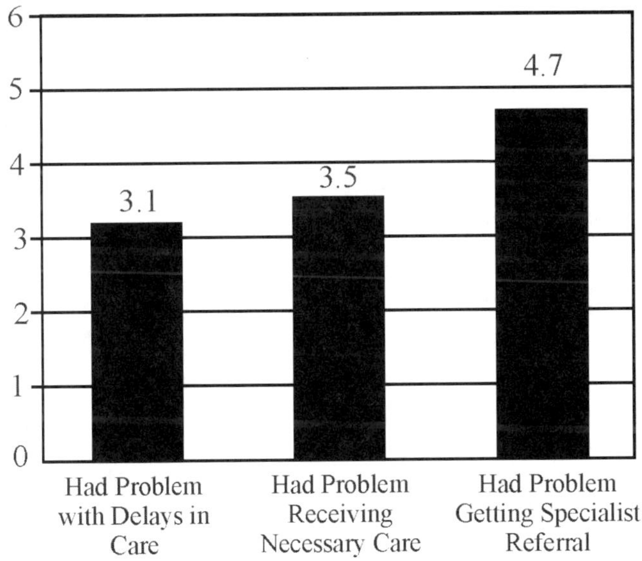

Note: This analysis is of under-65 HMO consumers only.
Source: Sachs/Scarborough HealthPlus™, 1996, Multimarket.

Figure 16.8 Loyalty and Satisfaction

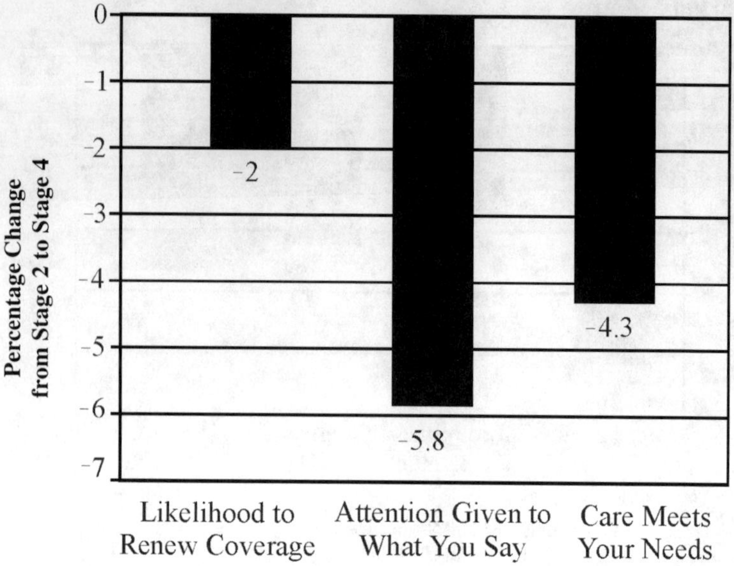

Note: This analysis is of under-65 HMO consumers only.
Source: Sachs/Scarborough HealthPlus™, 1996, Multimarket

Consumers believe that managed care personnel do not pay close attention to what plan members have to say, and that their care needs are not being fully met. In keeping with classic consumer behavior, they begin to seek redress elsewhere. When dissatisfied, consumers will vote with their feet and move to another alternative—in this case, focused delivery systems.

CAN'T GET NO SATISFACTION

Customer satisfaction: The scope is broad, the topic complex. The *Harvard Business Review* places enough store in it to assemble a special "Customer Loyalty Collection" of articles in response to reader demand. Seminal work by Jones and Sasser (1995) encourages marketers to throw out the bromide that groups "somewhat satisfied" and "very satisfied" customers together. Their work suggests that only totally satisfied customers remain loyal, and in the case of companies like Xerox, total satisfaction increased purchase likelihood by a factor of 6 over the next 18 months. Applying the same quantitative principles to a study of hospitals, Jones and Sasser discovered that loyalty is even more closely linked to total satisfaction. Despite the system constraints associated with managed care, consumers will wait until they can change, and then snap the curve.

Table 16.3 Change in Satisfaction Drivers as Markets Mature

Satisfaction Dimension	Importance for Overall Plan Satisfaction	Importance as Markets Mature	Performance Trend	Controlled by
Plan Benefits/Services	1st	Same	Better	Plan
Premium/Cost Sharing	2nd	Same	Better	Plan with employer influence
Network Access (i.e., Freedom)	3rd	Less important for POS and PPO	Worse	Plan
		Success Here Will Distinguish Future Market Leaders		
Medical Management Implications (i.e., constraints)	3rd	More important especially for PPO, somewhat for HMO	Worse	Physician alone under medical care delivery mode Physician with plan influence under economic mode
Medical Care Process/Outcomes (i.e., perceived quality)	3rd	More important for POS and HMO	Worse	Physician
Physician Access/ Administration	Not important	Same	Worse	Physician

Source: Sachs/Scarborough HealthPlus™, 1996, Satisfaction Predictor Index.

What factors contribute to consumer satisfaction? What will it take to improve enrollee renewal rates? Do satisfaction drivers change over time like selection influencers?

Satisfaction Drivers

Donabedian (1980) defines medical quality in terms of structure, process, and outcome. This paradigm can be applied to HMO satisfaction. The structural elements (see Table 16.3) include benefits/services, premium/cost sharing, and network access. Current market leaders excel in these dimensions, designing plans and networks that consistently meet or exceed consumer expectations.

Future market leaders will distinguish themselves in the process and outcome measures comprising medical management implications and medical care process/outcomes.

Plan Benefits/Services

Member satisfaction with services and benefits retains the number-one position as a critical element influencing enrollee satisfaction regardless of the market stage. When joining an HMO, consumers expect comprehensive benefits. While this is primary to satisfying members, customer service issues also are significant drivers of satisfaction. These issues range from ease of obtaining information to quick, courteous claims handling.

Cost/Premiums

Premium payments and cost sharing occupy the second-place slot on the satisfaction index. Although consumers make HMO enrollment decisions on financial grounds, once in a plan, consumers expect "first rate," not bargain, service. Plans must continue to deliver value—and consumers equate value with service.

Network Access

Immature network development earns a vote as yet another obstacle to satisfaction in early market stages. Research suggests that consumers are satisfied only if they have choice. This includes choice of doctors, hospitals, and locations. With exposure, consumers are learning to work the system and adjust to the constraints of an HMO environment. Concurrently, the system itself continues to evolve and develop to address more consumer needs and to run more efficiently, solving many access issues.

Medical Management

Moving from traditional indemnity plans to the HMO format with its emphasis on primary care and tight control over specialist utilization, consumers immediately recognize that access has been limited—and they don't like it. When they encounter delays caused by plan approvals or, more basically, problems getting specialty referrals for care they believe is warranted, satisfaction drops precipitously.

Medical Care Process/Outcomes

Consumers are unable to measure quality by HEDIS standards, but they have distinct opinions about their medical care. Consumers expect to be heard, to be treated comprehensively, and to obtain positive outcomes. Having embraced the HMO wellness premise and promise of improved overall healthcare, consumers are becoming disenchanted with managed care medical treatment.

Physician Access/Administration

Health plans set standards to enable members to get appointments quickly—both when well and when sick. Although performance is declining, this is not a strong determiner of member satisfaction.

Medical care process and outcomes, and medical management, become increasingly important as markets mature. These visceral consumer issues fall into categories where HMOs exert the least influence and control. As consumers' expectations rise, performance on these key measures declines. To remain viable, HMOs need to come to grips with the issue of medical care delivery and management.

On the subject of HMOs and medical care, the data show no difference between the mean scores for point of service, traditional indemnity, health maintenance organization, and preferred provider organization products with respect to consumers' self-reported perception of health improvement. All plans had the same mean of 2.79. This flies in the face of HMO claims, but corroborates the Stage 4 selection and retention trends discussed previously.

FOCUSED CARE OPENS ACCESS

Fortunately for consumers, and unfortunately for the proponents of the managed care economic model, relief is in sight. In an environment where there is an improved flow of consumer information, an accrued consumer experience base on managed care systems, an increasing emphasis on the institutional brand, and an ever-growing awareness that access is everything in healthcare, an HMO alternative has emerged. It is the focused care delivery system. Combining the benefits of provider empowerment associated with open access systems, and the benefits of provider ownership associated with point-of-service products, focused care delivery systems represent the next generation of consumer-driven healthcare systems.

To draw an analogy, compare managed care to the travel business. Today, HMOs function like a travel agent. They get a topline idea of consumer preferences and assemble two or three alternatives. Tomorrow, focused care delivery systems will function like travel packagers. They will maintain a Web site with virtually limitless options at different price points, and the consumer can select the best match based on their variable spending threshold and "destination" preferences.

Further developing the travel analogy, economic model plans as packagers will be responsible for putting the matrix of options together, as well as the marketing and sales functions. All medical management activities, including the lucrative risk premium spread, will reside with the medical professionals. Responsibility and authority for medical care now reside with the same party under the focused care system.

FREE-MARKET ECONOMICS RULE

If, as Milton Friedman and other monetarists believe, "free markets clear," then by extension, that argument would hold true for healthcare costs and consumption. A market-acceptable cost of care would be achieved if consumers both understood the differences in cost between providers (e.g., a local community hospital and a major market, teaching medical center) and if their personal cost of care fluctuated with provider costs. Under this scenario, there are direct economic consequences associated with utilization and provider choice.

Herzlinger (1997) asserts that the reason market efficiencies have been lacking to date can be traced to the fact that

> There is no consumer in most of the health care system. Instead, a third party, a government or an insurance company, pays for the services. As a result, the users do not know the costs of the services they use, and the payers do not know how the users feel about them.

THE BUYERS HEALTH CARE ACTION GROUP— A CASE IN POINT

How can a healthcare system bridge this knowledge chasm? The best example extant today is the Buyers Health Care Action Group (BHCAG) in Minneapolis, Minnesota. Twenty-six large, self-funded employers banded together to develop a new, consumer-driven healthcare purchasing model. Their goals were to improve care quality, increase provider competition, increase consumer knowledge and responsibility, and enhance system efficiency. Ann Robinow, BHCAG's executive director, care systems and finance, believes the approach "fosters increased provider autonomy and accountability, while empowering consumers with information to choose care systems based on their own values."

The results are impressive. To date, 90 to 95 percent of Twin Cities primary care physicians participate in BHCAG, virtually doubling the number of available delivery sites. In 1997, the plan calls for a 9 percent reduction against expected claims. Factors considered vital to BHCAG success include consumer information access, care system accountability, risk-adjusted payments, and provider incentives aligned with performance.

BHCAG contracts with distinct care systems, charging them with responsibility for providing a full continuum of care. All operate under a single charter, with a single administrator and a standard benefit set. Comparative quality, service, and cost information is made available to consumers.

Employees bypass the insurer and select one of 15 systems directly. Each employee receives a fixed voucher, and his or her monthly contribution is governed by a variable fee schedule payment model with a risk adjuster.

THE IOWA EXPERIENCE

Frustrated with a lack of integration at the provider level, major employers in Des Moines, Iowa, opted to take action. They formed the Iowa Community Health Purchasing Corporation, a coalition comprising 25 firms and covering 40,000 lives.

Employees select from three competing care systems that vie for their business, each requiring a significantly smaller out-of-pocket contribution than the predecessor indemnity plans. The competing integrated systems offer divergent combinations of clinics, primary care physicians, hospital affiliations, and specialist associates (Health Care Advisory Board 1996).

The monetarists were right. Both the BHCAG and Iowa Community Health Purchasing Corporation experiences bear out the impressive impact of information and choice in free markets.

THE COUNTDOWN BEGINS

Managed care plans that plan to still be operating in the 21st century would do well to develop their packaging competencies and move away from medical management as a primary revenue source. Factors that matter most to consumers—such as overall care quality and access issues—are the very criteria over which HMOs exert the least influence and control. Our advice to HMOs: Give it up. Manage to your strengths in marketing and sales.

Looking forward, healthcare providers will need to sharpen their pencils, develop an administrative infrastructure to minimize costs, and gear up for open market competition. Our advice to focused healthcare systems: Get ready. Be prepared to deal with a knowledgeable consumer who is armed with benchmarking data and HMO experience and who demands full value for his or her premium dollar. Let the next generation of managed care begin!

NOTE

1. Sachs/Scarborough HealthPlus™ local market consumer research is conducted in 33 markets. The survey includes the names of specific health plans and hospitals, covering topics such as satisfaction with health plans, reasons for selecting health plans, incidence of chronic conditions, utilization of hospital services, reasons for choosing and changing primary care physicians, and prescription drug information.

ACKNOWLEDGMENT

Assistance for this article was provided by Peggy Brink and Chip Perkins, both of the Sachs Group.

REFERENCES

Cochrane, J. D. 1997. "Health Care Megatrends 1997." *Integrated Healthcare Report* (December–January): 1–40.

Donabedian, A. 1980. *Explorations in Quality Assessment and Monitoring, Volume I: The Definition of Quality and Approaches to its Assessment*. Chicago: Health Administration Press.

Foster Higgins National Survey of Employer-Sponsored Health Plans, 1996. 1996. New York: A. Foster Higgins & Co. Inc.

"The Soul of An HMO." 1996. *Time*. (January 22) 147 (4). *www.acponline.org*.

Health Care Advisory Board. 1996. *Retail Care Systems: Executive Briefing for Employers and Providers*. Washington, DC: The Advisory Board Company.

Herzlinger, R. 1997. *Market-Driven Health Care*. Reading, MA: Addison-Wesley.

Jones, T. O., and W. E. Sasser, Jr. 1995. "Why Satisfied Customers Defect." *Harvard Business Review* Customer Loyalty Collection (Product 49518) Reprint 95606: 1–13.

Juster, I. A. "The Virtual Medical Community." *www.medconnect.com*.

Schear, S. 1995. "Your Money and Your Life. America's Managed Care Revolution." *Public Broadcasting System* (September 6). *www.wnet.com*.

CHAPTER

17

The Future of Managed Care Organization

James C. Robinson

We are observing simultaneously the eclipse and expansion of the managed care organization. Health maintenance organizations (HMOs) and other insurers are hollowing out, yielding one function after another to purchasers and providers and thereby evoking questions about their future role and share of the premium dollar. Large employers and purchasing alliances are retaining insurance risk and specifying benefit packages; large provider organizations are accepting global capitation and responsibility for utilization management. Pundits daily announce the dawn of direct contracting and the squeezing out of the insurance middleman. Yet health plans everywhere are in rapid expansion, diversifying into new networks, benefit designs, distribution channels, and geographic markets. Every year brings mergers and acquisitions involving millions of enrollees and billions of dollars. Health insurance hardly seems to be an industry in decline.

This paper analyzes the transformation of managed care's central organization: the multiproduct, multimarket health plan. It examines vertical disintegration: the shift from ownership to contractual linkages between

---

This paper was prepared for a policy roundtable on the future of the multiproduct health plan, sponsored by the California HealthCare Foundation and *Health Affairs*, in Oakland, California, in October 1998.

**Reprinted with permission from *Health Affairs* 18 (2): 7–24.
The People-to-People Health Foundation.**

plans and provider organizations, and horizontal integration: the consolidation of erstwhile indemnity carriers, Blue Cross plans, HMOs, and specialty plans. Diversification into new managed care products, methods of marketing, and geographic regions is driving health plans toward national, full-service corporations and away from local organizations linked to particular providers and selling to particular consumer niches. The rapid growth in health care firm size results primarily from the need to achieve minimum efficient scale in each product, channel, and market and secondarily from attempts to achieve dominance in each sector.

The demand and supply sides of the medical marketplace are fragmented, heterogeneous, and in a state of continual change. Purchasers differ widely in their preferences and willingness to pay for particular benefits and networks. Providers differ widely in their ability to bear capitation risk, managed utilization, and document quality. The diversity and complexity of health care create an enduring role for the multiproduct health plan, one that will not be displaced by corporate purchasing alliances or provider-based HMOs. Public policymakers and industry analysts often assume that there exists somewhere a truly efficient form of physician and hospital organization, an optimal benefit package, an evidence-based set of clinical protocols, and one best method of marketing and enrollment. But even a cursory examination of the medical marketplace quickly reveals that no one size fits all and that consumers do not agree on what they want, purchasers on what they are willing to pay for, and providers on what they are willing to deliver. The future of the health plan lies at the often conflict-ridden interface between consumers, purchasers, and providers, in the development, pricing, and distribution of managed care products that reconcile preferences with pocketbooks throughout the health care system.

VERTICAL DISINTEGRATION

Health plans assume an intermediate position on the chain of production and distribution, squeezed between physicians, hospitals, and other providers on one side and corporate benefits managers, governmental agencies, and consumers on the other. The boundaries of these industry segments have fluctuated continuously, with private purchasers establishing self-insured plans, public purchasers offering direct-service benefits, providers launching insurance products, insurers acquiring providers, and everyone dabbling with great enthusiasm and little success in the others' business. The most important efforts at downstream integration of purchasers into health plan functions have been the proliferation of self-insured corporate programs operating under federal Employee Retirement Income Security Act (ERISA) protection, the standardization of benefits and performance criteria by public and private purchasing alliances, and the extension of self-insurance into network management by large purchasers in the Minneapolis market.[1] The most important efforts at upstream integration of provider organizations into health plan functions have resulted from the acceptance of global capitalization and the delegation of responsibility for credentialing, utilization management, and quality oversight.[2] Many provider organizations have developed insurance products, most of which have performed poorly but some of which have become market leaders. The rage of the moment is provider-sponsored organizations (PSOs), which will contract directly with Medicare. The public policy debate over direct contracting has been intense but has shed less light than heat. Each initiative needs to be evaluated soberly and with attention to general economic principles of vertical integration.

Downstream Integration by Purchasers

The unwillingness of the American polity to directly assure universal coverage has spawned innumerable state efforts to subsidize care of the poor by imposing premium taxes, regulations, and benefit mandates on commercial health plans. ERISA exempts from state control corporate health benefit programs that self-insure, thereby giving them a significant incentive to integrate downstream into insurance risk bearing. Once confined to the largest private corporations, the religion of self-insurance has converted many midsize firms and public employee benefit programs. Large purchasers move further into the roles conventionally played by health plans as they specify the details of their benefit packages, often standardizing designs across their multiple contracting plans and sometimes across multiple purchasers. The Pacific Business Group on Health (PBGH), for example, negotiates rates with twelve HMOs for twenty-one companies, and 400,000 beneficiaries using a standard package of benefits. The California Public Employees Retirement System (CalPERS), with one million beneficiaries, negotiates rates for a standard benefit package with eleven insured HMOs and maintains two self-insured PPO plans. The Buyers Health Care Action Group (BHCAG) has developed a uniform benefit package and self-insured PPO product for 132,000 enrollees in Minneapolis, using a health plan to perform back-office functions based on negotiated fees.

The appropriation of insurance functions from health plans receives inordinate attention, since the corporate purchaser appears to be the only Godzilla big enough to grapple with the King Kong of managed care. In reality, large purchasers are wary of entering what they recognize to be a complex and risk business. Self-insurance was relatively easy in the indemnity context, especially when reinsurance for high-cost cases was available from commercial carriers without compromising the ERISA exemption. However, managed care requires developing networks of primary care, specialty, inpatient, outpatient, pharmacy, and ancillary services over a wide geographic region under continual excoriation from consumers and regulators. The federal Medicare and state Medicaid programs are seeking to exit from their fee-for-service (FFS) plans, outsourcing responsibility wherever possible to private managed care organizations. The prototype public program of the future appears to be the Federal Employees Health Benefits Program (FEHBP), which owns no health plans but contracts with private plans offering indemnity, HMO, PPO, and point-of-service (POS) products.[3] Some large employers are turning to commercial carriers to manage their self-insured products using the networks, contracted provider rates, utilization-management systems, and quality-oversight tools developed for the fully insured products. Many would be willing to go back to buying insured products if the states would desist from punishing with special taxes those employers that cover their employees in order to reward with special subsidies those employers that do not. The business mantra now is to focus on core markets and competencies. Manufacturers, banks, and software corporations should not be distracted into managing health care any more than health plans should be distracted into manufacturing drugs, underwriting consumer credit, or designing their computer networks.

Upstream Integration by Providers

In the early years of managed care many HMOs were sponsored by hospital systems and multispecialty medical groups as a way of marketing their services on a prepaid basis. Many of these early efforts failed, but some of the largest and most successful of contemporary carriers (including PacifiCare, Humana, and United) date their origins to upstream integration efforts by providers (as do, in a more distant sense, Blue Cross/Blue Shield plans). However, the most significant movement of health care providers into the roles once played by health plans has come with the recent rapid spread of capitation contracting and delegation of utilization management. Large provider organizations have begun to contract with health plans on a capitated basis for primary, specialty, and, increasingly, hospital and pharmacy services. The range of capitated services has broadened as providers have consolidated into integrated delivery systems and physician practice management (PPM) firms better able to absorb insurance risk.[4] Global capitation shifts the responsibility for network development and contracting, as the capitated provider organization takes on the chore of subcontracting with nursing homes, rehabilitation facilities, home health agencies, and out-of-area providers. A logical concomitant of capitation payment has been the delegation to provider organizations of responsibility for utilization management, including primary care referrals to specialists, hospital admission and length-of-stay, and authorization for high-cost procedures.[5] Medical groups are increasingly accountable for measurable aspects of quality, including patient satisfaction and provision of preventive services. The PBGH, for example, now is measuring performance and cooperating on quality improvement programs at the level of the medical group and hospital system, in addition to its traditional efforts at the level of the health plan.[6] The National Committee for Quality Assurance (NCQA) is exploring credentialing and other quality oversight and the provider level.[7]

The appropriation of managed care functions from health plans has spurred some physician and hospital organizations to contemplate full upstream integration. Some provider systems, such as Kaiser Permanente in California and Intermountain in Utah, have gained regionally dominant positions by developing licensed HMOs and marketing directly to employers and public programs. Most provider-sponsored HMOs, however, have fared poorly when faced with direct competition from national health plans unless they have let go of their original provider linkages. Insurers have fared no better when they have tried to integrate in the other direction by acquiring hospitals and medical groups to establish staff-model HMOs. Almost all of the national plans that plunged into vertical integration during the heyday of managed competition have since divested their staff models. Nevertheless, the ideal of vertical integration between providers and plans remains vibrant, at least in hospital circles. Some large delivery systems are now gearing up to contract directly with Medicare as capitated PSOs.

HORIZONTAL INTEGRATION

As they abjure ownership linkages with provider systems, health plans are not becoming merely vendors of back-office reinsurance and administrative services. On the contrary, they are expanding rapidly in both scale and scope, adding new functions, offering new services, attracting new clients, and penetrating new markets. Organizational enrollments and revenues are pyramiding as leading health plans merge with and acquire their rivals. The fundamental feature of the managed care marketplace is not its size, however, but its heterogeneity. Consumers differ in their preferences for breadth of physician and hospital panels, self-referral to specialty care, stringency of utilization review, and performance on quality indicators. Employers and governmental programs differ in the generosity of their premium contributions and their willingness to obtain lower premiums in exchange for higher deductibles, more significant consumer copayments, and thinner benefit coverage. The dynamics of marketing and enrollment differ dramatically across market segments, including individuals and small groups, midsize firms and large corporate accounts, public employee benefit programs, Medicare+Choice, and Medicaid managed care. States and metropolitan areas differ in demographics and economics, in provider organizations and consolidation, and in regulatory rules and purchasers' sophistication. This diversity in demand is generating a commensurate diversity in supply. Four dimensions of health plan diversification are to be emphasized: provider networks, benefit products, distribution channels, and geographic markets.

Network Diversification

Until just a few years ago most health plans offered a single network structure, either any willing provider (indemnity) or closed panel (HMO). Those plan designs have mutated considerably, and each has borrowed liberally from the other. FFS plans now sell managed indemnity coverage, combining an open provider network with requirements for utilization review, or PPO insurance, supplementing a contracted network with limited out-of-network coverage. PPO products contract on a discounted FFS basis with individual physicians and impose top-down utilization review. They capitate no services and delegate no responsibilities to integrated delivery systems or PPM firms. PPOs offer choice but not efficiency; a broad network but little coordination; not gatekeeping but high deductibles. HMOs have responded to consumers' demand for choice by broadening their networks, adding POS coverage for nonnetwork services, and facilitating access within the network by reducing primary care gatekeeping and prior authorization for procedures. They differ fundamentally from PPOs, however, in relying heavily on independent hospital systems and physician networks to manage the actual delivery of care. Capitation contracting is spreading from primary to specialty, hospital, and pharmacy services and is accompanied by delegation of responsibility for utilization and quality management.[8] HMOs offer efficiency and coordination but run counter to the current trend toward consumerism, self-referral, and self care.

PPOs and HMOs hold salient positions on a much broader spectrum of network designs, each with a different panel breadth, stringency of utilization management, and provider payment method. Unmanaged indemnity coverage, medical savings accounts (MSAs), exclusive provider organizations (EPOs), POS plans, partially insured products, and other hybrid arrangements attract particular customer segments. Separately structured subnetworks are proliferating underneath the health plans, including centers of excellence for tertiary care, capitated disease management panels, specialty PPM firms, carved-out mental health programs, complementary medicine providers, retail and wholesale pharmacy networks, ambulatory surgery chains, inpatient and outpatient rehabilitation centers, nursing homes and subacute care facilities, home health agencies, and durable medical equipment vendors.

Health plans can either focus on a single major network or develop of broad portfolio of network offerings. The dominant strategy is full diversification of services: the exploitation of scope economics in the design, marketing, and management of multiple networks. Many corporate functions necessary for the development of one network can be extended at low cost to others. Management information systems and actuarial capabilities required for an FFS, claims-driven product such as PPO or managed indemnity coverage can be applied to HMO products where it is important to evaluate capitation rates and document utilization profiles. Volume discounts with hospitals can be negotiated based on enrollment in all networks, allowing plans with large PPO enrollment to obtain attractive rates for their commercial POS or Medicare HMO products. In-house sales representatives and outside broker networks can cross-sell multiple networks to the same client base. Small and mid-size firms are particularly attracted to dual- and triple-option arrangements in which a health plan offers a PPO, an HMO, and perhaps a third network, allowing choice to employees without imposing high administrative costs on the employer. Health plans are playing the role assigned to purchasing alliances in the theory of managed competition. Rather than using a purchasing alliance to structure employee choice among multiple health plans, employers increasingly are contracting with a single health plan to structure employee choice among multiple provider networks.

Benefit Diversification

Historically, health insurance offered two benefit structures, which balanced in different ways the desire for financial coverage in case of illness and the need for controls on cost inflation. Indemnity carriers, Blue Cross plans, and FFS Medicare relied heavily on deductibles, coinsurance, exclusions of preventive services, annual limits on hospital days, and maximum lifetime payment. HMOs offered comprehensive benefits without deductibles, coinsurance, and maximums but with modest copayments at the time of service. Recent years have witnessed partial convergence, as indemnity plans cover more preventive services and HMOs experiment with higher copayments for emergency room and hospital use. The dominant trend, however, has been toward the proliferation of benefit designs to accommodate the differences among consumers in preferences and ability to pay.

Health plans now design multiple benefit packages for off-the-shelf sale in the individual and small-group market and are willing to tailor benefits to suit large corporate purchasers, public employee programs, and public programs. Indemnity, managed indemnity, MSA, and PPO products now come with deductibles that range from zero up to $10,000 or more; with coinsurance rates that vary by provider, setting, and service; and with copayment rates that vary based on whether the service received prior authorization or was deemed an emergency. Cost-sharing provisions increasingly are tiered according to whether the service was received from a provider in the HMO network, in the wraparound PPO network, from a nonnetwork provider with POS prior authorization, from an out-of-area provider, or from a provider with which the plan has no contractual relationship. Benefit packages are increasingly differentiated, with mixes of full coverage, partial coverage, or exclusion for prescription drugs, mental health services, durable medical equipment, outpatient rehabilitation, and home health services. Some designs are covering nontraditional services such as long-term care, acupuncture, therapeutic massage, and holistic medicine.

The market demand for benefit diversity favors health plans with administrative capabilities in actuarial estimation, benefit pricing, and cross-marketing. It disadvantages plans that remain attached to a uniform benefit design and a community-rated pricing structure. Firms need to balance the attractions of a broad product portfolio against the need to communicate easily with sales agents, independent brokers, individual consumers, small proprietors, and corporate benefit managers. It is possible for a plan to offer too many benefit designs, but the more common tendency is to offer too few.

Channel Diversification

Health plans traditionally focused on a few salient distribution channels. HMOs often served large public and private employers; commercial carriers favored the multistate corporations; Blue Cross plans dominated the individual, small-group, and midsize market; and Medicare and Medicaid operated their own FFS plans. Different strategies and structures reach these different customer populations. Marketing to Medicare beneficiaries and self-employed persons requires an in-house team adept at one-on-one outreach and "kitchen-table" sales. Independent brokers hold the keys to the small- and midsize-group market. Large corporate purchasers rely on consultants and human resources departments to impose detailed benefit and performance specifications. Large public employers and purchasing alliances favor nonexclusive contracting with multiple health plans. State Medicaid agencies try to stretch inadequate budgets by offering large but bottom-dollar contracts to plans. Self-insured employers, the Civilian Health and Medical Program of the Uniformed Services (CHAMPUS), state programs for uninsured children, and other enrollee groups present new marketing challenges.

Despite the differences among customer niches, health plans have discovered that they cannot afford to ignore most distribution channels. A core investment in the creation of brand-name identity is useful for every niche, as is the development of in-house capabilities to analyze the marketing needs of particular segments and coordinate outreach across segments. Some differences in distribution remain important across plans, particularly with respect to their interest in or antipathy toward low-margin Medicaid business. But once they have a full portfolio of managed care products, health plans want to be able to market through a full range of distribution channels. Channel diversification is key to achieving the enrollment volumes necessary to obtain low prices from providers as well as for spreading the overhead costs of product development and regulatory compliance.

Geographic Market Diversification

The commercial indemnity carriers traditionally were national in breadth but shallow in local market depth; Blue Cross plans held large local shares but did not cross state lines; HMOs were concentrated in particular metropolitan areas. Now leading health plans are combining local market penetration with geographic diversification. New market entry offers enormous potential rewards for well-managed health plans. Corporate overhead expenses can be diluted, and core competencies deployed over ever-larger enrollee populations, only by expansion beyond familiar markets. Purchasing power for pharmaceutical products, computer systems, and other supplies via national contracts can be enhanced by enrollment growth without regard to its geographic locale. Wall Street looks favorably at firms whose risks are diversified across markets with different business climates and across states with different regulatory climates. Multimarket and multistate networks are useful for selling managed care products to national corporate purchasers and to the increasingly mobile business and leisure traveler. A strong presence in localities with distinct business cultures and clinical practice patterns affords the health plan the possibility to identify, internalize, and disseminate best practices. The ability to enter and exit local markets expeditiously is important as purchasing alliances and provider cartels organize to shut windows of profitability.

Regional markets reveal different mixes of national and local players, but the rapid pace of mergers and acquisitions is bringing the same names to the major metropolitan markets. The consolidation of commercial carriers is nearly complete, with only CIGNA and Aetna showing staying power for the long run. Traditional HMOs, many now converted to investor ownership, are represented on the national scene by United, PacifiCare, Kaiser, Humana, and Foundation Health Systems. The heritage of the Blue Cross plans lies with WellPoint, Anthem, and a variety of regionally strong plans that could become national players if they overcome regulatory barriers to expansion.

THE ECONOMICS OF ORGANIZATION

It is important to emphasize, in this era of mind-boggling mergers and acquisitions, that larger scale and broader scope do not by themselves confer competitive advantages on managed care organizations.[9] Recent years have witnessed the dramatic decline of many formerly dominant health plans, particularly indemnity carriers and Blue Cross affiliates. Most of the multiline insurers have narrowed their product portfolios, exiting health care or divesting their nonhealth activities. Metropolitan, New York Life, Travelers, Massachusetts Mutual, John Hancock, and Lincoln are now of only historical interest from a health insurance perspective, and even Prudential is seeking to refocus on financial services. Similarly, vertical integration often confers disadvantages rather than advantages, a lesson apparently learned by CIGNA, Aetna, FHP, Foundation Health, Prudential, Humana, PacifiCare, PCA, and Blues plans in New Jersey and Massachusetts. Some of the most venerable staff- and group-model HMOs, including HIP, Harvard Pilgrim, and even Kaiser in some states, are moving toward nonexclusive relationships with their physician groups. In seeking to understand the fluctuating boundaries of the health plan, it is important to maintain a balanced view of both the economies and the diseconomies of scale and scope.

Economies of scale explain the comparative advantages that accrue from size itself, as distinct from intellectual property, market dominance, or scope of activities. Textbook examples accrue in manufacturing and transportation industries with large physical assets, the costs of which need to be spread over a large volume of production. In service industries such as managed care, fixed costs include core administrative functions and expensive computer systems. Additional size advantages derive from volume discounting with suppliers. Finally, many firms experience increasing returns to investments in marketing and brand-name recognition. Juxtaposed to these economies of scale are the disadvantages of large size, most of which can be conceptualized as forms of bureaucratization. Three dimension stand out. First, large firms often suffer from the attenuation and distortion of incentives for individual participants, including managers and employers, compared with smaller firms and particularly with owner-managed entities.[10] Second, large firms are subject to internal influence politics, as individual groups and subunits struggle for control of and access to the organizational surplus; these struggles typically increase with the internal heterogeneity of the firm.[11] Finally, large and diversified economic organizations are required to develop internal "transfer prices" that dictate how resources are allocated between subunits; transfer prices are subject to internal manipulation and are notoriously less efficient than external market prices are in indicating true resource cost.[12]

Economies of scope explain the advantages of diversified over focused firms, after taking account of scale effects. Textbook examples highlight physical or intellectual assets than can be used for multiple products without being fully exhausted by any one.[13] Joint physical assets include chemical facilities that can produce paints, dyes, and solvents or metal stamping facilities that can produce many shapes of cars and trucks. Joint assets in distribution include relationships with clients that permit the cross-selling of multiple products and brand-name recognition that confers a marketing advantage on one product because of consumer trust in another. Intellectual assets such as special know-how in a particular line of business explain diversification by customer segment or geographic locale, as when hotel corporations maintain multiple chains of facilities (such as economy, resort, and business) across many geographic areas. Diseconomies of scope explain why most firms are focused on a particular set of products, customer segments, and geographic markets, with only a few being able to sustain a conglomerate organizational form. Multiproduct and -market diversification exposes the firm to loss of scale economies in each of its particular operations, including economies in production, supplier contracting, and marketing. It leads to a loss of focus and to overload on senior management, who cannot keep abreast of rapidly changing consumer preferences and production technologies in their far-flung operations. Excess diversification can undermine brand names by spreading them across too many products of uncertain vintage, confusing the firm's image in the mind of the consumer, and encouraging competition among its products rather than with products of other firms. The boundaries of the health plan can usefully by illuminated with reference to these economies and diseconomies.

The Economics of Vertical Disintegration

Two sets of problems afflict vertically integrated organizations and explain why systems incorporating both insurance and delivery are to be found more frequently in health policy proposals than in the managed care marketplace. Vertical integration between production and distribution sacrifices the economies of scale available to firms that serve upstream suppliers and downstream distributors. With the exception of some highly concentrated markets, no health plan has enough enrollment to support a broad exclusive network. Staff-model HMOs failed to convince consumers to limit their choices to a narrow range of employed physicians and have broadened their networks. Conversely, few hospital systems can fill their beds solely with patients from their in-house insurance plan; most are forced to take patients from independent plans as well. Vertical integration does not help the health plan to spread its core overhead expenses over a broader base of operations, since it adds new administrative functions and costs as rapidly as it adds to the base of operations. The administrative, information, and clinical competencies required for an organization that actually delivers health care are quite distinct from those of an organization that develops, markets, and monitors contractual networks.

The second set of difficulties stem from the attenuation of physician incentives and aggravation of internal bureaucratic politics afflicting health plans that employ rather than contract with physicians. Physicians and other providers simply work less hard when they are employed by large insurance corporations than when self-employed or part of a physician partnership. Vertically integrated insurers often created staff clinics that were larger and more elaborate than the offices of the private-practice physicians with whom they competed. Private-practice physicians understand that they are paying personally for the extra examining rooms, nurse assistant, and continuing medical education course, while staff-model HMO physicians believe that the corporate parent bears these costs. Vertically integrated systems also suffer from the politics of transfer pricing, with the hospital and clinic divisions wanting rates to be based on their average costs while the insurance division wants rates to be based on marginal costs. In the context of excess hospital and specialty capacity, marginal costs fall well below average costs. The most successful group-model HMOs, such as Kaiser Permanente, have attenuated these problems by contracting exclusively with quasi-independent physician organizations. But most health plans have found their staff clinics to experience higher costs and lower productivity than their contracted networks experience. Incentive attenuation and influence costs also explain the failure of partial integration. Some health plans structured themselves around a core of wholly owned clinics and then extended their reach through contractual means, only to find that their clinics were the costliest rather than the most effiicient component of their networks.

The enthusiasm in health policy circles for organizational unification of insurance and delivery is so fervent that it is useful to note that the broader economic literature on markets and organizations views vertical integration as the exception to the rule, as the governance mechanism of the last resort.[14] Life-cycle theories of vertical integration emphasize that integration by producers upstream into distribution or downstream into supply has occurred primarily in the early phases of industry development when independent distributors and suppliers are not available.[15] Independent distributors and suppliers emerge as efficient alternatives to the internally owned units, which are divested or restructured as joint ventures or franchises. Transaction cost and principal-agent theories emphasize that vertical integration is efficient in mature markets only where specialized equipment, skills, or geographic locations reduce the number of available contract partners.[16] Absent these special circumstances, contractual relationships can provide adequate coordination without sacrificing scale economies and individual incentives. These conditions held in most health care markets prior to the 1980s, since health plans interested in creating capitating HMO products could not find independent medical groups and needed to build their own. Conversely, medical groups and hospital systems interested in prepayment often found it easier to launch their own HMO than to work with local insurers who remained wedded to FFS practices. In the 1990s, however, many markets have multiple managed care plans and multiple provider organizations, and vertical ownership relationships are disintegrating.

The Economics of Horizontal Integration

Two forms of scale economy are important for understanding the diversification of health plans into multiple networks, benefit products, distribution channels, and geographic markets. First and most obviously, health plans need to spread product development and pricing, finance, utilization and quality management, and computer information systems over large numbers of enrollees to hold down the administrative expense per enrollee. High patient volumes also are important for obtaining significant discounts or attractive capitation from physicians, provider organizations, pharmaceutical manufacturers, and other suppliers. Diversification into multiple benefit products and distribution channels is central to the pursuit of these scale economies, since they bring in new volume without adding significantly to the costs of managing care. Diversification into multiple provider networks brings in greater volume but also increases overhead costs and raises the minimum efficient scale for provider contracting. The competencies required to manage a hands-on PPO product are very different, for example, from those needed for a capitated and delegated HMO product. A large volume of enrollment passing through the capitated independent practice association (IPA) and medical-group networks may not help the health plan in its fee policies with individual providers in the PPO network, although common rates covering all networks can often be negotiated for hospitals, nursing homes, and ancillary providers. These factors explain why so few health plans have successfully maintained multiple market-leading networks. Most plans have a leading network design—either PPO, HMO, or POS—and then offer other options to fussy purchasers. True network diversification will be an increasingly important comparative advantage in coming years, however, given the irreducible variation in consumers' and purchasers' preferences. WellPoint, United, CIGNA, and Aetna are well positioned in this regard, whereas Kaiser, PacifiCare, Oxford, Foundation Health Systems, and many Blue Cross plans remain largely nondiversified.

Economies of scale do not explain the dramatic mergers and acquisitions that are creating nationally diversified health plans. Geographic expansion does not help health plans to cover any but their most general forms of administrative expense and adds nothing to plans' bargaining power with suppliers in particular markets. This explains why carriers that once held shallow positions in many localities have been replaced by firms that expand only into markets where they can achieve significant penetration. The scale economies achieved from inputs from national sources, such as drugs and computer systems, are not significant enough to justify new geographic expansion unless substantial local market share can be achieved. Expansion needs to follow upon rather than precede the reduction in core cost structure if it is not to court disaster, as was proven in the transportation and communication industries after deregulation and in the PPM industry more recently.[17]

Scale economies in marketing and brand-name recognition to date have been limited, with many managed care plans using different distribution networks and brand names for different products and in different regions. WellPoint, for example, uses the same name for all networks, products, and channels but different names in different states (Blue Cross of California, Unicare elsewhere).[18] PacifiCare uses one name for its commercial products and another for its Medicare product. Plans built from many mergers and acquisitions, such as Foundation Health Systems, struggle along with many different brand names (for example, HealthNet, QualMed, and Physicians Health Services). In coming years, however, common branding across networks, products, distribution channels, and geographic markets will become ever more important as plans compete on quality and service as well as on price.

Economies of scope in marketing and distribution are the key determinants of health plan diversification into multiple provider networks and benefit packages, while contributing little to diversification by distribution channel and geographic market. The ability to combine HMO, PPO, and hybrid networks into one package at one price is extremely valuable in the small- and midsize group market, where employers shun the administrative complexity and adverse selection risks of contracting with multiple plans. The ability to cross-sell medical, dental, and life insurance and other services is important for large corporate accounts, which typically offer richer benefits packages but want to simplify their administrative responsibilities.

The ability to design and price multiple benefit packages is essential for all segments of the commercial market, since employers vary widely in the generosity of their premium contributions and benefit coverage. Ironically, scope economies explain little of the decision to diversify into multiple distribution channels, since the mechanism for reaching individuals (direct advertising and brokers), small groups (brokers), corporate accounts (consultants), Medicare beneficiaries (direct advertising and physicians), and Medicaid (safety-net providers and community organizations) are quite distinct. Scope economies in distribution are a secondary aspect of geographic expansion, although broad network coverage is important for multistate employers and Medicare "snowbirds." For example, plans with heavy enrollment in the New York region, such as HIP and Oxford, have sought to follow their vacationing and retiring members to Florida.

The fundamental feature of health care is the heterogeneity of both consumers' preferences and providers' capabilities. Consumers differ in the ability and willingness to pay for broad provider networks, thick benefit packages, and direct access to specialty care. Purchasers differ in their size and bargaining leverage, interest in tailoring benefits versus buying designs off the shelf, generosity in premium contributions, and understanding of a quality accreditation. Physician organizations and hospital systems differ in their ability to take on the insurance risk of capitation and the utilization management responsibilities of delegation. Some provider systems seek to coordinate the full range of services, while others focus on particular clinical conditions, specialties, technologies, or facilities.

The continual flux in demand and supply creates an enduring role for the multiproduct health plan as the nexus of contracts that links, coordinates, and gives incentives to the many buyers and sellers of health care. Niche analysis has become a core competency as health plans strive to understand an accommodate each market segment. Health plans have little to fear from the rhetoric of cutting out the middleman. Neither the individual consumer armed with an MSA nor the corporate purchaser armed with a self-insured benefit program can achieve provider rates and utilization efficiencies comparable to those offered by large health plans. The heterogeneity among providers similarly creates an enduring role for health plan networks that cover every ZIP code and are uniformly credentialed, contracted, and accredited. Health plans have little to fear that medical groups and physician/hospital systems will integrate into insurance and marketing, once the regulatory demands for financial solvency and the marketplace demands for network access are understood. Joint ventures between particular plans and provider organizations certainly are to be expected, as are long-term relationships between particular plans and purchasers, but the diversified health plan will always participate in more networks, products, and markets than even the largest provider or purchaser. Health care is a local business. But managed care—the development, pricing, and marketing of multiple provider networks and benefit designs through multiple distribution channels in multiple geographic regions—is a national business.

NOTES

1. J. Maxwell et al., "Managed Competition in Practice: 'Value Purchasing' by Fourteen Employers," *Health Affairs* (May/June 1998): 216–226; J. Christianson et al., "Managed Care in the Twin Cities: What Can We Learn?" *Health Affairs* (Summer 1995): 114–130; and J.C. Robinson, "Health Care Purchasing and Market Changes in California," *Health Affairs* (Winter 1995): 117–130.
2. See, for example, M.R. Gold et al., "A National Survey of the Arrangements Managed Care Plans Make with Physicians," *New England Journal of Medicine* 333 no. 23 (1995): 1678–1683; S.M. Shortell, R.R. Gillies, and D.A. Anderson, "The New World of Managed Care: Creating Organized Delivery Systems," *Health Affairs* (Winter 1994): 46–64; and J.C. Robinson and L.P. Casalino, "Growth of Medical Groups Paid through Capitation in California," *New England Journal of Medicine* 333, no. 25 (1995): 1684–1687.
3. S.M. Butler and R.E. Moffit, "The FEHBP as a Model for a New Medicare Program," *Health Affairs* (Winter 1995): 47–61.
4. Shortell et al., "The New World of Managed Care;" J.C. Robinson, "Consolidation of Medical Groups into Physician Practice Management Organizations," *Journal of the American Medical Association* 279, no. 2 (1998): 144–149; and J.C. Robinson, "Financial Capital and Intellectual Capital in Physician Practice Management," *Health Affairs* (July/August 1998): 53–74.
5. E.A. Kerr et al., "Managed Care and Capitation in California: How Do Physicians at Financial Risk Control Their Own Utilization?" *Annals of Internal Medicine* 123, no. 7 (1995): 500–504. E.A. Kerr et al., "Quality Assurance in Capitated Groups: Where Is the Emphasis?" *Journal of the American Medical Association* 275, no. 15 (1996): 1236–1239; and Robinson and Casolino, "Growth of Medical Groups Paid through Capitation in California."
6. Details and data are available at www.healthscope.org.
7. For information on the provider credentialing program, see www.ncqa.org.
8. Some HMOs continue to contract with individual physicians on a fee-for-service basis and retain utilization review in house, rather than contracting with physician organizations on a capitation basis and delegating utilization management.
9. Power theories, according to which firms with significant economic and political assets cannot be displaced even if they lack production efficiency and sensitivity to consumers' preferences, do offer high explanatory power in contexts where competition has been eliminated or severely restricted by

regulation. In such contexts, political connections and perceived institutional legitimacy play predominant roles in ensuring organization success.

10. M.C. Jensen and W.H. Meckling, "Theory of the Firm: Managerial Behavior, Agency Costs, and Ownership Structure," *Journal of Financial Economics* 3, no. 7 (1976): 305–360; and E.F. Fama and M.C. Jensen, "Agency Problems and Residual Claims," *Journal of Law and Economics* (June 1983): 327–349.
11. P.R. Milgrom, "Employment Contracts, Influence Activities, and Efficient Organizational Design," *Journal of Political Economy* 96, no. 1 (1988): 42–60; and H. Hansmann, *The Ownership of Enterprise* (Cambridge, Mass.: Harvard University Press, 1996).
12. R. Eccles, *The Transfer Pricing Problem: A Theory for Practice* (Lexington, Mass.: Lexington Books, 1985); and J. Rotenberg, "A Theory of Inefficient Intrafirm Transactions," *American Economic Review* 81, no. 1 (1991): 191–201.
13. J.C. Panzar and R.D. Willig, "Economies of Scope," *American Economic Review* 71, no. 2 (1981): 268–272; D.J. Teece, "Economies of Scope and the Scope of the Enterprise," *Journal of Economic Behavior and Organization* 1, no. 3 (1980): 223–247; and A.D. Chandler, *Scale and Scope: The Dynamics of Industrial Capitalism* (Cambridge, Mass.: Harvard University Press, 1990).
14. O.E. Williamson, *The Economic Institutions of Capitalism* (New York: Free Press, 1985); and M.K. Perry, "Vertical Integration: Determinants and Effects," in *Handbook of Industrial Organization*, vol. 1, ed. R. Schmalensee and R.D. Willig (New York: North Holland, 1989).
15. G.J. Stigler, "The Division of Labor Is Limited by the Extent of the Market," *Journal of Political Economy* 59, no. 3 (1951): 185–193; and A.D. Chandler, *The Visible Hand: The Managerial Revolution in American Business* (Cambridge, Mass.: Harvard University Press, 1977).
16. B. Klein, R.G. Crawford, and A.A. Alchian, "Vertical Integration, Appropriable Rents, and the Competitive Contracting Process," *Journal of Law and Economics* (October 1978): 297–326; and Williamson, *The Economic Institutions of Capitalism.*
17. R. Victor, *Contrived Competition* (Cambridge, Mass.: Harvard University Press, 1994).
18. If the acquisition of BlueCross BlueShield of Georgia is consummated, as planned, WellPoint will use the name BlueCross BlueShield rather than UniCare in Georgia.